Textual Transvestism:

(Re)Visions of Heloise

(17th-18th-Centuries)

FAUX TITRE

398

Etudes de langue et littérature françaises
publiées sous la direction de

Keith Busby, †M.J. Freeman,
Sjef Houppermans et Paul Pelckmans

Textual Transvestism:
(Re)Visions of Heloise
(17th-18th-Centuries)

Nancy M. Arenberg

Rodopi

AMSTERDAM - NEW YORK, NY 2015

Permission to reprint previously published material has been granted by Rainer Zaiser, the editor of *Papers on French Seventeenth-Century Literature*/Biblio 17, for the article "Veiling the Erotic: (Re) Writing Heloise's Epistles," 24.47 (1997): 487-495 and for the book chapter "Recollections of Passion: Bussy Rabutin's Free Translation of Heloise and Abelard's Love Letters," ACTA, Eds. Wolfgang Leiner & David Wetsel, Tübingen & Seattle: Biblio 17, 2002. Permission granted by Vittorio Frigerio, the associate editor of DFS, to reprint the article "Colardeau's Pastoral (Re) Invention of Heloise," *Dalhousie French Studies* 39 (1997): 69-75.

The paper on which this book is printed meets the requirements of 'ISO 9706: 1994, Information and documentation - Paper for documents - Requirements for permanence'.

Le papier sur lequel le présent ouvrage est imprimé remplit les prescriptions de 'ISO 9706: 1994, Information et documentation - Papier pour documents - Prescriptions pour la permanence'.

ISBN: 978-90-420-3905-6
E-Book ISBN: 978-94-012-1187-1

Printed in The Netherlands

ACKNOWLEDGMENTS

I would like to extend my gratitude to my friend and former director at the University of Arizona, Lise Leibacher. From the time I was pursuing my doctorate at the University of Arizona, she has provided me with extensive knowledge of French seventeenth-century literature, especially in the area of sexual discourse. I shall never forget our stimulating conversations about women writers, sexual politics and culture in the seventeenth century. As my own career as a scholar took shape, these interests contributed to the pursuit of research in my field of specialization, the French epistolary genre with emphasis on questions of gender and literary transvestism.

I also wish to express my appreciation for the advice, guidance and support of my friend and colleague in Russian at the University of Arkansas, Janet Tucker. Janet's vast experience as an author has contributed greatly in showing me the path to the completion of this daunting project. I am also grateful for the technical expertise of our computer specialist, Roger Henry, who assisted me with format support. Furthermore, I appreciate greatly our wonderful staff at the University of Arkansas, especially the library staff or our ILL department. Since many of my texts are rare, they have gone out of their way to assist me in obtaining many difficult materials.

This book is dedicated to my parents and grandmother who have supported me with love throughout the course of my academic career.

CONTENTS

INTRODUCTION
Writing Love: The Origins of the Letter Novel in France 11

1.
Abelard's *Historia Calamitatum* 27

2.
The Genesis of the Love Letter 53

3.
Grenaille's Eloize as "La Magdalene Française" 99

4.
Bussy Rabutin's Letters 135

5.
Fictional Transformation of the Lovers 183

6.
Dom Gervaise's Repentant Translation of Heloise and Abelard 205

7.
The Hysterical and Pastoral Heloise 223

8.
Julie or the Devout Heloise 271

9.
Learned Heloise Regained 307

EPILOGUE
The Revival of Heloise in Popular Culture 333

BIBLIOGRAPHY 353

INDEX 385

INTRODUCTION

Writing Love: The Origins of the Letter Novel in France

The epistolary genre is an intriguing area in French literature where the focus is on complex systems of communications constructed between writer and receiver. The love letter is not a recent genre; the roots of the epistolary novel can be traced to the rich cultures of ancient Greek and Roman civilizations.[1] Clearly, however, the most influential historical precursor to the modern love letter was Ovid's *Heroides*, a work that contained twenty-one missives, written in verse, by famous mythological or real characters such as Sappho, Phaedra, Dido, Hermione or Penelope. Ovid also included exchanges between lovers in the final six epistles that concluded his text. The *Heroides* are especially relevant here because of thematic aspects that will be re-exploited later in the seventeenth century. Specifically, the heroines are all abandoned women, bereft of their lovers or husbands, whose tears spill onto the letter, which, in turn, eternalizes the pathos of their loss. Ovid's proclivity in analyzing the emotions of these famous heroines and heroes anticipates the birth of the epistolary genre much later in Europe, and Bernard Bray, Charles Kany or Laurent Versini have

[1] See Charles Kany's introduction in *The Beginnings of the Epistolary Novel in France, Italy and Spain* (Berkeley, Berkeley, UP, 1937): 1-10.

established him as the fundamental source of the genre of the love letter in France.[2]

After Ovid, the next stage of literary activity in the epistolary genre occurred in the twelfth and thirteenth centuries. During the Middle Ages, there was a preponderance of sonnet correspondence in verse form. The theme of desire was remarkably illustrated in the tradition of courtly love, but expressed in poetic form structured by stanzas. As to the love letter, no real interest was generated until the middle of the sixteenth century, a time of significant development in the history of the epistle. Humanist writers looked to Italy for their inspiration; they interpolated mood and even political tones into their missives. Letter manuals enjoyed great popularity with Etienne Du Tronchet and Etienne Pasquier as the main innovators of the genre who advocated humanist ideology and urged people to practice the art of penning epistles in order to create a portrait of their true selves. In addition, Du Tronchet also created missives as letter models for aspiring writers; yet, he was not the only one to propose an instructive format.[3] The Renaissance was a period during which some women were also composing epistles. Hélisenne de Crenne published her *Epîstres familières et invectives* in 1539. The recipient of her letters were mainly friends and other women who were seeking advice in matters of love, but the second part of the letters was written in the form of a dialogue between herself and her husband, and concerned a variety of personal topics.[4] The most salient feature

[2] Bernard Bray, Charles Kany and Laurent Versini offer the most comprehensive literary histories of the epistolary genre. See Bray's *L'Art de la lettre amoureuse. Des Manuels aux romans* (1500-1700). (Paris: Mouton, 1967). Also, Kany's *The Beginnings of the Epistolary Novel in France, Italy and Spain* (Berkeley, Berkeley, UP, 1937). In addition, Versini's *Le Roman épistolaire* (Paris: PUF, 1979).

[3] See Alain Viala's article, "La Genèse des formes épistolaires en français: et leurs sources latines et curopéennes," *Revue de Littérature Comparée* 55.2 (1981): 174-5.

[4] See Janet Gurkin Altman's article, "The Letter Book as a Literary Institution 1539-1789: Toward a Cultural History of Published Correspondences in France," *Yale French Studies* 71 (1986): 42.

of this text is De Crenne's defense of women and their silence; she demanded the right to express her voice through her literary production. Yet, she mirrored other male epistolary writers of her day as her letters also depicted a self representation, and tended to convey a moral message directed to other women. Aside from this portrayal of a woman's life in the Renaissance, there were a variety of letter manuals that came out, and they became increasingly important in the seventeenth century.

At the dawn of the Classical Age, the letter continued to attract attention and gain in popularity among readers. Letter manuals continued to flourish, but the focus was shifting away from the private domain to the public sphere, and this change, in turn, demanded a modification in letter manuals to better meet the needs of a new and different society as social conventions became more dependent on the correct forms of address to thank people, express condolences, compliment others, etc. Socialization revolved around the public perception and portrayal of the self, which redefined the conception of space. Epistolary space was in fact drifting toward the salons and court, the more visible domains of an aristocratic society. For ambitious social climbers who aspired to improve their stature at the court, these public places required that they consult manuals in order to skillfully perform the proper etiquette of the times. Letter manuals provided aristocrats with a myriad of "how to" information ranging from fashionable dress to proper diction, appropriate topics of discussion and advice as to how to flatter others in public.[5] Puget de la Serre wrote one of the most successful epistolary manuals in 1623 entitled *Le Secrétaire de la cour, ou la manière d'écrire selon le temps*.[6] In addition to these etiquette texts, interest in the genre was expanding as letters were commonly exchanged and read in the salons. The social

[5] See Viala's article, mainly pages 170-183. This discussion of letter manuels is quite useful in providing background on the humanist tradition of the epistolary genre.

[6] Viala 175.

importance and public emphasis placed on the letter gradually resulted in a redefinition of the missive. The letter was evolving into a subtle and refined art in a confidential, codified system of communications that mirrored the demeanor and social habits of the aristocrats. In the salons, a flurry of activity accompanied the popularity of the epistle. For the first time, women began to play an important, active role in intellectual circles. Madeleine de Scudéry's salon or Saturday afternoon gatherings enabled women to establish their own place where they could exchange correspondence, read, edit, discuss and collaborate on how to improve their epistolary skills.[7] Women later known as "précieuses" began to experiment with letters in prose form inspired by popular works of the day in which missives were inserted, such as Honoré d'Urfé's pastoral novel, *L'Astrée*, and later in heroic novels like Scudéry's *Le Grand Cyrus*. Scudéry enhanced the narrative of her heroic novel by interweaving love letters directly into the structure of the adventures. The reader was able to follow the plot by tracing the sequence of events through the letters, and the epistles tended to strengthen the lyrical expression of love, or bring the genre one step closer to achieving the status as an independent narrative form, which would come before the end of the century. Scudéry was a key contributor to the development of letter writing for epistolary writers and even wrote her own sentimental "how to" guides, which were intended to help women learn how to compose love letters to their lovers. Madame de Sévigné, who also frequented some of the salons, was an influential innovator as well, and she would play a very important role in the evolution

---

[7] See Joan DeJean's *Fictions of Sappho 1546-1937* (Chicago, University of Chicago Press, 1989). As a part of the background for her study of the Sapphic tradition in French literature, DeJean provides details on the evolution of letter manuals in the seventeenth century. Moreover, she includes invaluable information about Scudery's representation of Sappho as the heroine of her feminine fiction. 1-115.

of private correspondence, another significant area of the epistolary genre that would peak in the eighteenth century.

As the letter became more popular, it was moving in the direction of establishing itself as an independent narrative form. By the 1660s, a new form was emerging, but prior to this more advanced stage of development of the genre, it is useful to consider the main tenets that directly influenced the evolution of the letter novel. Bernard Bray proposes three principal sources of the French epistolary novel in the seventeenth century. He returns to Ovid as the most influential writer. Firstly, Ovid's *Heroides* were becoming more accessible to the seventeenth-century reader because of an abundance of French translations. Also, Ovid's text contained some of the thematic elements judged necessary for successful, but wrenching love stories told in letters. The second influence is precisely the importance of Abelard and Heloise's correspondence, the focus of this study.[8] Although the original text was medieval, it only became very popular in the seventeenth century, probably, as Kany and Charlotte Charrier propose, due to the first French translation published in 1687 by Bussy-Rabutin, which will be discussed in depth in the third chapter of my study. Bray's third influence is Isabella Andréini, a little-known Italian writer whose contribution is worthy of mention because her epistles were published in a French anthology of women's love letters. In fact, both Andréini's and Heloise's missives are included in a translation by François de Grenaille's entitled *Nouveau recueil de lettres de dames tant anciennes que modernes*, a text that came out in 1642. As Kany pointed out, the French epistolary novel is thus grounded in Ovid's image of the abandoned woman; the

[8] All references to Charlotte Charrier point to her monumental historical thesis on the prolific variety of translations, versions and imitations of Heloise's love correspondence. See Charrier's *Héloïse dans l'histoire et dans la légende* (Genève: Slatkine Reprints, 1977). Charrier's work is the most inclusive text on the subject of the medieval lovers and serves as a fundamental, historical source for many of the key versions to be studied in this project.

theme of the absent lover is enhanced by the violent language of passion exemplified by the turbulence and disorder inherent in Heloise's correspondence, and beneath this emotionally charged language of passion lies the sentimental lyricism of the solitary writer portrayed by innovators such as Andréini.[9] Out of this tradition, the production of the French love letter was launched.

In 1669, Guilleragues's *Lettres portugaises* received an enthusiastic response from the public. The topos of love emerged as a major narrative force in the letter novel combined with the emotional, personal experience of the "writer," Mariane, a Portuguese nun who was supposedly abandoned by her French lover. The solitary woman in love wrote within the walls of her cloister expressing her desire through a tragic, Racinien-like rhetoric of unrequited but nevertheless burning passion. The publication of this text established the letter as an effective form of articulating desire, and set off a bustle of activity to expand the creation of sentimental novels composed in letter form. In fact, the thematic ingredients of separation, anguish, desire and isolation combined to engender other fictional epistolary works in the seventeenth century. The term "portugaise" was coined, and thus represented a new literary genre of love letters based on the emotions of the writer.[10] As the popularity of the text spread abroad to England, translations began to appear in bookstores to entice the British reading public. Back in France, other letter texts followed in the wake of the popularity of *Lettres portugaises*.[11] Edme Boursault's *Lettres de Babet* came out in 1668. While this novel modified the tone as the story of love's

[9] See Bray 14-18.
[10] See Kany, p. 116. He maintains that the term became generic and was used to characterize passionate love correspondence. Solange Guénoun also comments on Madame de Sévigné's invention of the term "portugaise" in her article, "Séparation, séduction, épistolarité: le geste épistolaire," *Les Visages de l'amour au XVIIe siècle* (Toulouse: Service des Publications, L'Université de Toulouse, 1984): 210.
[11] Kany 116-126.

predicaments unfolded in a lighthearted and frivolous ambiance, in spite of burlesque elements, Boursault continued to explore human emotions. Later in 1689, Madame Ferrand wrote *Lettres de Cléante et Bélise,* also a lyrical, introspective novel, and Boursault's *Treize lettres amoureuses d'une dame à un chevalier,* published in 1697, may be used to conclude the selection of the most significant love letter novels written in the seventeenth century.[12] As Kany observes above, Boursault's text reveals that the style of his letters was most likely inspired by Guillerague's *Lettres portugaises.* The popularity of the recurring trope of the abandoned woman in love indicates a strong influence on the historical development of the epistolary genre as the "portugaise" type of sentimental fiction would continue to develop more fully in the eighteenth century. Interestingly, Bussy Rabutin was particularly taken by the term "portugaise" coined by his cousin, Madame de Sévigné, and he decided to try his hand at translating another nun's tragic love story, also told in letters. In his private correspondence, he often sent fragments of his translation of Heloise's and Abelard's love letters to his cousin, and thus, to go back to one of Bray's key tenets of the historical development of the epistolary novel, not only did Bussy rekindle interest in the medieval lovers, but as we will see, he established himself as one of the most important innovators in the genesis of the legend that disseminated around the couple. This study will demonstrate that even though Bussy's version was not the very first translation of the medieval couple's love letters, it was one of the most popular and successful, and was, in fact, imitated and repeatedly plagiarized by seventeenth and eighteenth-century translators, which, in turn, reaffirms the importance of the seventeenth century as a period

[12] Kany also points to similarities between the *Lettres portugaises* and the *Lettres de Babet,* mainly as expansions of feminine emotions. However, he reads Boursault's epistolary romance as more frivolous in its thematic portrayal of love.

that clearly influenced the development of the epistolary genre as we know it today.

In discussing Heloise's and Abelard's love letters, a chronological method is useful, but recent publications of new translations in the seventeenth and eighteenth-centuries will deviate slightly from a pure sequential approach. However, a chronological study will be carried out as much as possible in order to explore why it is important to study what happens to a woman's love discourse as it fell into the hands of male imitators throughout the centuries. Critics such as Nancy Miller and Joan DeJean have extensively analyzed this practice of fragmentation in the context of the problematic and ambiguous nature of letters supposedly penned by abandoned women, but in fact written by men. As a structural model, DeJean's *Fictions of Sappho 1546-1937* will be used since she refers to the end of the seventeenth century as the "modern creation" of Sappho, based on Ovid's *Heroides*. Curiously, Heloise's correspondence recalls Sappho's. Heloise was known to have been a poet, but her texts no longer exist; she, too, can be seen as a woman whose discourse was fragmented, molded and (re)invented throughout the centuries, especially by men. My study will show that the revisions of Heloise's persona over two hundred years may be indicative of, and have helped construct, ideological changes in expectation concerning the role of women.

The medieval text will be the first text considered here and, for logical reasons, Abelard's *Historia Calamitatum* will be used as an introduction since it is typically placed directly before the lovers' epistolary correspondence. As a long, autobiographical narrative of Abelard's misfortunes addressed by him to an anonymous recipient, it provides the reader with a detailed and useful summary of the biographical events of the lovers' lives.

The first chapter will then deal with the medieval couple's love letters, and as a primary source I will use Paul Zumthor's modern 1979 French translation of the Latin text. Special emphasis will be placed on evidence that points to Abelard's appropriation of Heloise's voice, and on the intriguing question of the possible falsification and fragmentation of Heloise's letters by Abelard as a means of constructing a discourse of complete devotion and submission to him. Interestingly, this form of female impersonation and transvestism, or to put it in Miller's terms, "pseudo-feminocentrism," was another way of infringing on women's literary productions, and thus relegating them to the margins as writers.[13] Miller defines this concept as a technique in which a male writer borrows a female persona and disguises his own, and it was commonly practiced in epistolary fiction from the end of the seventeenth century on. This perspective will be considered a seminal aspect of the course of the study and will be used as a point of critical departure for looking at other subsequent "translations" that appeared in the eighteenth and nineteenth centuries.

After briefly considering the very first translation of Heloise and Abelard's love letters, a text written by Jean de Meun around 1290, but which remained in manuscript form until the twentieth century (it was re-edited in 1991) the most outstanding and innovative seventeenth-century translations will be considered with the partial translation of Heloise's letters that appeared in Grenaille's *Nouveau recueil de lettres des dames tant anciennes que modernes*. Interestingly, although, as noted above, this anthology of real women's love letters includes one of Bray's key epistolary influences of the seventeenth century, love letters by Isabella Andréini, Grenaille's rendition of Heloise's letters remained virtually unknown to Abelard and Heloise scholars, and Charrier erroneously refers to Bussy as the first translator. However, not only did Grenaille's version, even as a partial translation, precede Bussy's by about forty years,

[13] See Miller's article, "I's in Drag: The Sex of Recollection," *The Eighteenth Century* 22 (1981): 48-53. Here, she provides a complete discussion and explanation of the term "pseudo-feminocentrism."

but he took great liberties in reworking the text in order to (re)invent Heloise as "La Magdalene Française," a self-sacrificing, Christian prototype for other women to emulate. Grenaille's translation will be the focus of the third chapter. The fourth chapter will proceed chronologically with the next seventeenth-century version, a text written by Jacques Alluis in 1675. Although Alluis' *Les Amours d'Abailard et d'Héloïse* is relatively unknown, it is noteworthy not only as it marked the emergence in activity of other fictionalized accounts of the lovers' misfortunes, but it is also of particular interest as it did not preserve the original epistolary form, and thus resulted in an abridged, short story that contained many invented, scandalous aspects. Alluis' version is worth looking into as he rewrites Heloise as a "précieuse," and thus anticipates what other male writers would later develop at the end of the century. Since Alluis' text is not an epistolary production, I will only briefly focus on the revision of Abelard and Heloise's personas to serve as an introduction to the seminal translation of the seventeenth-century, Bussy's free translation of Heloise and Abelard's love correspondence, a text which restored epistolary dialogue between the couple, but also transformed the medieval, estranged Heloise's into that of a "vraie précieuse" deeply in love with Abelard, the man. As we shall see, Bussy's translation is characterized by a courtly, conversational aspect in which the couple is pursuing a more sublimated discourse of desire, one that can be talked about in the presence of others because it is gallant and polite instead of explicitly carnal as in the medieval text. Once again, the shifting, editing and alteration of the original love letters will be analyzed through a critical lens as a means of studying what happens to the "original" personas of the medieval lovers' as they continued to be (re)written and (re)invented by these various translators. But most of all, Bussy's contribution to the development of the legend will be the focus of this chapter as his text was well received by his readers, and launched a bustle of activity, really a cult, that reached across the channel into England as other eighteenth-century imitators would subsequently try their hands at translating the lovers' correspondence.

The fifth chapter will look precisely at some of the most popular eighteenth-century imitations based on Bussy's revision of the medieval couple. However, the recent publication of a new edition has made it possible to include a discussion of some of the articles in Pierre Bayle's *Dictionnaire historique et critique* published in 1697. Selected essays on Heloise and Abelard will be analyzed as they initially embellished Alluis's scandalous narrative, yet also represented Heloise as a suffering heroine, and thus anticipated the sentimental revision of her portrayal that other imitators would enhance in their later versions.[14] Moreover, Bayle's fascination with Abelard's castration and other historical details pertaining to the couple's tragedy will be studied, as Bayle ultimately contributes to the fictional legend surrounding the couple, thus contradicting his goal to produce a "truthful" reading of their lives. The sixth chapter will consider Dom Gervaise's 1723 translation of the correspondence, a text which has recently become more accessible to scholars. The inclusion of Dom Gervaise's version is of interest because he tackles some key Enlightenment ideas pertaining to the intriguing subjects of castration and eunuchs. Thus he can be read, to some extent, in dialogue with Bayle.[15] Like Bayle, Gervaise wanted to produce a faithful account of the couple's misfortunes in reaction to the flurry of fictional versions that deviated radically from the medieval text. The latter part of this chapter will focus on an analysis of the en-

[14] The articles to be considered in the Pierre Bayle chapter focus on Abelard, Heloise, Foulques and Combabus.

[15] It is interesting to read Dom Gervaise and Pierre Bayle together because the two state their commitment to 'supposedly' restore a more faithful representation of Heloise and Abelard. However, they do not remain sincere in their objective.

gravings found in Gervaise's rare 1796 edition of the couple's correspondence, highlighting some of the most famous scenes associated with Abelard's and Heloise's tragedy. These exciting new texts widen the scope of the study of the medieval lovers' misfortunes and solidify the growing interest in their legendary story during the eighteenth century.

To compensate for the slight deviation in the chronology, the seventh chapter will group the poetic imitations to explore the international popularity of the couple's story. The dissemination of the cult in England will be mainly considered, since the most significant translation was Alexander Pope's poem "Eloisa to Abelard," a text that enjoyed such success that it was translated more than twenty-five times in prose and in verse in several languages.[16] As I will propose, Pope's main contribution was the reformulation of the narrative in abridged verse form, and the revision of Eloisa as a mad heroine whose passion for her lover virtually drove her over the edge into a state of hysteria. Pope's (re)invention of Heloise is also noteworthy since he was the first author to integrate pre-romantic, Gothic imagery into the setting of his poem. Interestingly, the two eighteenth-century imitators that I will consider both deleted Abelard from their poetic renditions, but these in turn, also showed increased authorial liberties in the borrowing of Heloise's persona and literary production throughout the course of the eighteenth century. Pierre Colardeau's "Lettre d'Héloïse," a translation based on Pope's letter that brought this author recognition and fame among the French public between 1758 and 1772 will be considered in the latter part of this chapter. Although Colardeau's poem retained many of Pope's pre-romantic elements, his version differs as he does not depict Heloise as a mad woman. He tones down her delirium and paints an aesthetic, erotic revision of her by exploring her sensual reverie. Heloise's amorous contemplation is captured through Co-

[16] Charrier 445.

lardeau's original use of a visual, still-life portrait that enhances his revision of her as a transgressive mistress.

The eighth chapter will shift back to prose with a discussion of Jean-Jacques Rousseau's bestselling novel, *Julie ou la Nouvelle Héloïse,* published in 1761. Although the novel was only loosely based on fragments of Heloise's and Abelard's story, Rousseau's Julie resembles Heloise in her struggle to reconcile desire with virtue. Once again, the male author takes great liberty in his revision of Heloise as he deliberately veils her desire, recasting Julie as a moral embodiment of perfection. The success of this epistolary novel fueled the dissemination of the legend, as the couple's tragedy reached the height of its popularity in the eighteenth century.[17]

The ninth chapter will briefly consider two versions written by women, Louise de Keralio's in the late eighteenth century, and a nineteenth-century version composed by " Marc de Montifaud."[18] These renditions are of interest since they go back to the Middle Ages to portray a more faithful representation of Heloise as a remarkable intellectual. By the late eighteenth century, Heloise's persona had been betrayed by male imitators; she was clearly transformed by men; she was reduced to being a pawn in the "Querelle des femmes." But Keralio's translation, included in an anthology that she published in 1786, *Collection des meilleurs ouvrages françois composés par des femmes,* was intended to pay homage to women writers. Her translation was perhaps influenced by Bussy's in that she restores reciprocal epistolary exchange between the lovers, but, more importantly, she reconstructs Heloise's medieval, rational persona for the first time after a very lengthy absence. Although Keralio's version is also virtually unknown, her contribution is notable as she canonized a very different Heloise and seemingly attempt-

---

[17] Charrier 473-485.

[18] These two versions by Louise de Keralio and Marc de Montifaud are especially interesting because they are virtually unknown, but are included in Charrier's book.

ed to write a revision of literary history that had historically included men's works and excluded women's claims to their own productions. "Marc de Montifaud's prose translation, entitled *L'Abbesse du paraclet: histoire galante d'Héloïse et d'Abélard*, published around 1880, will then be analyzed. Although it is not written in epistolary form, the text is of interest as Montifaud intervenes in the narrative as a critic, and endeavors to portray the "vraie" nature of the lovers in her own words. In addition, Montifaud's well-known opposition to the Church is blatant, which, in turn, paradoxically influences her restoration of the original story: she reconstructed the original, erotic passion, she removed the veils that male translators had inserted into their texts to curb Heloise's shocking, unbridled desire. For the first time since the Middle Ages, the body surfaced quite visibly in this text to tell a story charged with sensuality and passion. Interestingly Montifaud's recovery of the erotic narrative is strongly analog to the medieval text. Not only do Heloise and Abelard speak the same amorous language, as in parts of Keralio's translation, but they also totally leave aside questions of faith as their passion is placed at the nexus of the text. It is also necessary to read Montifaud's and the preceding versions through a critical lens in order to explore the question of the importance of altering Heloise's literary persona.

The concluding chapter will offer a brief look of the portrayal of the couple in popular culture, mainly in Francophone literature and in the cinema. Thus, my study will show that Heloise's discourse was invested, fragmented and reconstructed by Abelard, Grenaille, Bussy, and numerous eighteenth-century male imitators. In addition, DeJean's *Tender Geographies* will be useful as it provides substantial evidence that many texts written by women were invaded, altered and even ignored. DeJean's work is also invaluable as it serves as a model to chart the evolution of the transforming images of Heloise's voice and persona throughout the course of the seventeenth and eighteenth centuries. The unveiling of diverse representations of Heloise will reveal shifting perceptions related to women's roles in the society. The focus will also be directed to current critical, and multi-representational perspectives that offer insight into the process of fragmentation as Heloise's literary production became the property of translators over and over again, and continues to be so in contemporary literary genres of the present time.

1.

Abelard's *Historia Calamitatum*

Abelard's and Heloise's love correspondence dating from the late twelfth century constitutes one of the earliest epistolary texts in French literature. However, the first Latin manuscript was not published until 1616 in France. In fact, Barbara Newman's article on Heloise points out that the letters remained relatively unknown until the middle of the thirteenth century.[1] The couple's love story unfolds in the *Historia Calamitatum*, which is an autobiographical epistle by Abelard describing in great detail the trials and tribulations of his career. This opening text is important to analyze as a preface to the overall love correspondence because the reader is introduced to the characters, and the predominant themes that will reappear in the main body of the letters. For instance, Abelard's victimization within the political structure of the Church, his manipulative nature of Heloise's will, and a veiled, but passionate desire that eventually tore the lovers apart. According to the *Historia*, the couple's love story ended abruptly after they exchanged marriage vows and then retreated to separate cloisters. This descriptive account leading up to their inevitable isolation is highly significant as a preface to the epistolary text, grounded on

[1] See Barbara Newman's article, "Authority, Authenticity and the Repression of Heloise," *Journal of Medieval and Renaissance Studies* 22.3 (1992): 133. She notes that the letters remained unknown until Jean de Meun translated them into French around 1280.

this fundamental sense of distance and loss. For the study of the medieval text, Zumthor's 1979 translation will be analyzed. This version is considered to be a faithful and reliable rendition of the original text in Latin.

Abelard's *Historia Calamitatum* consists of the initial letter of consolation directly preceding the epistolary correspondence to his wife and sister in God, Heloise. The text was written about 1132 when Abelard was 53 years old and was residing at the monastery of St. Gildas de Rhuys. The famous scholar was approaching the end of his career as a theologian and philosopher, and thus elected to share his own story. At St. Gildas, he feared for his safety and had already survived several attempts on his life. This opening letter addressed to an anonymous friend is particularly noteworthy as it is one of the earliest autobiographical texts known to exist in the history of French literature. It is however intriguing that the role of the receiver is relatively insignificant as Abelard chooses the literary guise of consoling a friend, but proceeds to recount his own tale of misfortunes in order to minimize the plight of his friend's adversities. In essence, he indulges in a form of self-consolation. The style of the text reveals some fundamental autobiographical characteristics underlying the "consolatio" epistle based on Seneca's model. According to Chris Ferguson, Seneca's was the "archetype" for the letter of consolation followed throughout the Middle Ages.[2] In this type of missive, the writer was supposed to compare his/her adversities to the receiver's tribulations so as to console the recipient. Abelard's text adheres to the epistolary guidelines governing the letter of consolation, but the *Historia* is also of a confessional nature as the author seeks to justify the fact that he sees himself as a victim of several philosophers and theologians who set out to ruin his career in the

[2] Chris Ferguson studies the autobioigraphical genre in the medieval period in his article, "Autobiography as Therapy: Guibert de Nogent, Peter Abelard, and the Making of Medieval Autobiography," *Journal of Medieval and Renaissance Studies* 13 (1983): 188.

church. As a precursor to St. Augustine's and Rousseau's styles, Abelard retraces the events of his adversities by structuring his story in a chronological and retrospective fashion. However, the reader suspects the author of employing a technique of selecting what he wishes to discuss while omitting other vignettes that would conflict with his ultimate goal: the portrayal of himself as a victim of persecution. Abelard endeavors to plead his case to the public in the form of an open apology so that his audience will find him innocent of all unjust condemnation for his theological and pedagogical approaches to the teaching of Scriptures. Throughout his career, Abelard was a very controversial figure challenging prominent religious scholars on interpretations of Scriptures, and this political tension exploded in the burning of his debatable book on the Trinity at the Council of Soissons in 1121. The destruction of Abelard's work on the Trinity is representative of many of the introspective episodes woven into the narrative, which is also representative of the autobiographical genre, and, as Mary McLaughlin suggests, it attempts to restore a feeling of "re-integration" inside the author's self.[3] She emphasizes the cathartic nature of the purging of Abelard's adversities in order to continue on with his life and perhaps restore his reputation at the end of his career. McLaughlin is an advocate of the theory that Abelard, in his desire to set the record straight, really intended the document to circulate within the public sphere. Whether or not this was his intention is impossible to say. But Abelard's technique of selective editing, or omitting personal details surrounding his marriage, reveals a secretive style interlaced within the body of the text, and thus leaves a lot of space for Heloise's response in the love correspondence that follows this letter. For every incident that he describes, there is another mysterious layer somewhere in the shadows under the text, and it contains other in-

[3] Mary McLaughlin, "Abelard as Autobiographer: The Motives and Meaning of his "Story of Calamities," *Speculum* 42.3 (1967): 469-487.

tentions, not disclosed to the public. In any event, what he does choose to divulge consists of a listing of his misfortunes that he shares with a wider readership. Despite the focus on the individual, it is nevertheless important not to confuse a twelfth-century text with later autobiographies.

Evelyn Vitz's study of the *Historia* reaffirms the rapport with Jean-Jacques Rousseau's *Confessions,* but she is careful to warn the reader not to look for a higher understanding of Abelard as an individual.[4] Abelard does not engage in an overt search for the self.[5] On the contrary, Vitz suggests that Abelard wants his audience to draw their own conclusions from the account of his adversities. In fact, there is an encounter between the private and the public spheres. Abelard chooses the epistolary form because it allows him to tell the intimate story of his victimization by his enemies. Furthermore, the *Historia* sheds light on another inherent aspect of Abelard's textual strategy. The privacy of the epistolary confession enables the writer to fully explore his own suffering, and self-motivating interests. Later in the love correspondence, Abelard will continue to assert his selfish tendencies, which is demonstrated by his technique of ignoring Heloise's more personal epistles directly addressed to him, her husband. This structural characteristic is introduced in the *Historia* as Abelard devotes a very small amount of space to the story of their love affair and subsequent marriage. He deliberately filters out Heloise's love discourse, and in doing so seeks to silence his wife's poetic expression of their passion. In this way, the narrative depicts him as a clever manipulator who finds a strategy that allows him to maintain the focus on himself.

---

[4] Evelyn Vitz looks at the construction of the self that Abelard portrays in the *Historia*. See her article, "Type et individu dans "l'autobiographie" médievale: étude d'Historia Calamitatum," *Poétique* 24 (1975) : 435.
[5] Vitz 444-5.

The Early Events in Abelard's Rise to Fame

The text opens with background information regarding Abelard's education and formation as a young scholar. He was born in Le Pallet in the region of Brittany near Nantes. From a young age, he wanted to study philosophy and later traveled to Paris to study with William of Champeaux. Abelard soon began to refute Champeaux's arguments on the theory of universals and then set out to establish his own school at Melun. The school was eventually relocated to Corbeil, but plans were abruptly curtailed when Abelard fell ill and was forced to go back to his childhood home. After regaining his health a few years later, he was able to fulfill his intellectual aspirations and resume his academic pursuits in Paris. The text demonstrates his success through detailed descriptions of his rise to fame as a talented orator and teacher. But Abelard desired to continue to develop his expertise in other areas of study under the tutelage of the most famous scholars of the time. After he mastered a substantial knowledge of philosophy, he proceeded to study theology with his former master's teacher, Anselm of Laon, who was the foremost authority of the day. Abelard soon began to give lectures on the Scriptures, which, according to the text, marked the beginning of his recognition as a charismatic lecturer. His notoriety spread well beyond Paris, and, at the same time, so did his increasing number of opponents. As Abelard's reputation grew, Anselm became jealous and retaliated by criticizing and later persecuting him for his interpretations of the Scriptures. But this incident only added to Abelard's popularity with his students who gathered in throngs to attend his lectures in Paris. He was famous as a philosopher and theologian who appealed to many aspiring scholars. This stage of his successful career culminates in the movement towards the second structural division of the *Historia*: his scandalous affair with Heloise.

Heloise as Abelard's Object of Desire

Abelard continued to enjoy great success in his intellectual endeavors, and the text indicates that he began to grow bored. Throughout this detailed account of his illustrious career, it is curious that there are no passages pertaining to his social life, at least not until he decided to expand upon his personal relationships. Specifically, he was intent on meeting a woman in order to experience sexual pleasures. During his rise to fame, he had never cultivated any real interest in women until he became rather arrogant as a result of his powerful status in the academic world. In Paris, Abelard became intrigued by an innocent, youthful woman who was one of the canon's nieces. Heloise was renowned for an intellectual ability which was very rare for a woman in the twelfth century. As a scholar, she was well versed in Greek, Latin, and Hebrew, and she possessed a sophisticated literary background. Smitten by the combination of her beauty and intelligence, Abelard devised a scheme to seduce her to satisfy his desire, never once doubting his success:

> Je la voyais ainsi parée de tous les charmes qui attirent les amants. Je pensai qu'il me serait aisé d'engager avec elle une liaison. Je ne doutais pas du succès: je brillais par la réputation, la jeunesse et la beauté: il n'était pas de femme auprès de qui mon amour eût à craindre de refus. Héloïse, j'en étais persuadé, prêterait d'autant moins de résistance qu'elle avait une solide instruction et désirait l'élargir encore.[6]

Eager to set his seduction plot into action, Abelard convinced Heloise's uncle Fulbert, to take him in as a lodger, and subsequently gained access to Heloise. Shortly after, he was hired by Fulbert as her tutor. By allowing Abelard into the house, Fulbert virtually delivered his niece over into the philosopher's clutches and even insisted that he beat her into submission if she didn't work hard enough. Abelard describes Ful-

---

[6] All of the quotations from the *Historia Calamitatum* are taken from Paul Zumthor's translation of *Abélard et Héloïse Correspondance* (Paris: 10/18, 1979).

bert's generosity as "confier ainsi une tendre brebis à un loup affamé!" (*Historia* 56). In essence, he was given every possible opportunity to seduce Heloise in Fulbert's house, and he refers to Fulbert's free rein in the text as "donner toute licence à mes désirs, et me fournir l'occasion, même contre mon gré" (*Historia* 56). The most striking aspect of this account of his plot to seduce and manipulate the fragile will of Heloise is the fact that the reader has no idea of her personal reaction to this arrangement concerning the private lessons in her home. Under Fulbert's roof, Abelard's lessons strayed far from academics in pursuit of charting new and forbidden territory, the delights of the flesh:

> Sous prétexte d'étudier, nous nous livrions entiers à l'amour. Les leçons nous ménageaient ces tête-à-tête secrets que l'amour souhaite. Les livres restaient ouverts, mais l'amour plus que notre lecture faisait l'objet de nos dialogues; nous échangions plus de baisers que de propositions savantes. Mes mains revenaient plus souvent à son sein qu'à nos livres. L'amour plus souvent se cherchait dans nos yeux l'un de l'autre, que l'attention ne les dirigeait sur le texte. (*Historia* 56)

The closed space of the study room increases the erotic charge of the passage above. The disposition of oppressive space plays a recurring role in the memories of the physical encounters between the lovers (as shown in Heloise's sensual reverie in her second epistle of this same edition noted above). Abelard adds that he would beat Heloise so as to avoid arousing Fulbert's suspicions concerning the subject matter of their lessons. Had Fulbert known what they were doing, it would have been scandalous for Heloise. At the time, she was only about seventeen and Abelard was in his thirties. The captivating allure of the dialectic of master and subservient student plays a significant role because Abelard exhibited total control of the delicate situation, and yet the narrative never indicates that Heloise resisted his advances. She is never depicted as unwilling. On the contrary, many of the scholars of the original text including

Etienne Gilson, Charlotte Charrier, J.T. Muckle and Peter Dronke agree that she was hopelessly in love with her teacher, and cherished their lessons as much as he did.[7] However, it is worth noting that Abelard does not include any descriptions of her feelings or reactions to their illicit, amorous encounters in his version of his misfortunes. Their torrid affair continued, and they abandoned themselves freely to their desire until Fulbert eventually discovered them in bed, and Heloise later became pregnant. To spare Heloise the wrath of her uncle, Abelard had her carried off, disguised as a nun, to his own family's home in Brittany where she had their son, Astrolabe. During their separation, Abelard reached a resolution to their predicament. In the text, he openly admits that he seduced Heloise as he concludes: "j'épouserais celle que j'avais séduite" (*Historia* 60). He decided to marry her secretly, so as to avoid irreparable damage to his reputation, because the matrimonial state, if publicly known, could possibly destroy his career in the Church. He set out for Brittany to make Heloise his wife, but was unprepared for her supposedly negative reaction to his marriage proposal. According to him, Heloise believed that marriage would only tarnish Abelard's stature as a famous and highly respected theologian and philosopher; she did everything in her power to refute the idea of the marriage as she subscribed to the notion that philosophers were not to be burdened by such mundane tasks as a family and a wife. In the Middle Ages, people thought that philosophers were supposed to be solitary beings, completely devoted to their studies.[8] Their elevated intellectual status was considered to be incompatible with the social institu-

---

[7] Many scholars concur with this opinion. Charlotte Charrier and J.T. Muckle provide very detailed summaries regarding Heloise's position on love. See Muckle's article, "The Personal Letters between Heloise and Abelard," *Mediaeval Studies* 15 (1953): 47-94. Also, Charrier's *Héloïse dans l'histoire et dans la légende* (Genève: Slatkine Reprints, 1977).

[8] See James Burge's recent biography for a discussion about marriage, mainly from Heloise's perspective. *Heloise & Abelard: A New Biography* (New York: HarperCollins, 2003): 125-131.

tion of the family. Heloise's famous diatribe against matrimony is described in Abelard's text:

> Elle préférait, quant à elle, le titre de maîtresse à celui d'épouse, et le trouvait plus honorable pour moi: elle me serait attachée par la seule tendresse, non par la force du lien nuptial. (*Historia* 66)

The passage indicates that Heloise prefers to be recognized as Abelard's mistress, thus placing passion over marital duty. She is reaffirming the excessive nature of her love, which transcends and transgresses the restricting bounds of the nuptial tie. The noun "force" or constriction reinforces her opposition to the dreaded imprisoning idea of marriage. The reader must however question Abelard's motivation in including this episode in his autobiographical epistle. The fact that he clearly controls the narrative may suggest that the recollection of this incident flatters his self-importance all the more. In other words, Heloise exteriorizes her desire for him, and offers to sacrifice her own happiness just to avoid hampering his professional ambitions in the Church. This self-serving aspect will become more developed throughout the course of the correspondence.

After this turbulent discussion, Abelard and Heloise returned to Paris where Heloise was forced, against her wishes, to marry Abelard secretly. Immediately following the ceremony, they separated and Abelard had her sent to a convent at Argenteuil; ironically this was the cloister where she had grown up, prior to living with her uncle in Paris. At Argenteuil, Abelard once again imposed his will on her without her permission. "Je lui fis faire et revêtir des vêtements conformes, le voile excepté, à la profession monastique" (*Historia* 68). But their problems were far from over. Fulbert was infuriated that Abelard would attempt to convert his young niece, and he sought revenge one night by having Abelard castrated while he slept peacefully: "ils m'amputèrent des parties du corps avec lesquelles j'avais commis le délit dont ils se plaignaient" (*Historia* 68).

Abelard suffered a great sense of shame for sinning against God. He decided to seek refuge and withdrew to the abbey at St. Denis. The castration episode represents one of the most striking events in the *Historia* as the consequences of the mutilation create multiple implications for both lovers.

The Textual Significance of Castration

After suffering such great loss, Abelard sought refuge in the darkness of the cloister walls that were shielding him from the scathing tongues of public gossip. Before his decision to retreat to the monastery, he had already arranged for Heloise to reside at Argenteuil. Their physical separation at the time of the castration warrants closer attention because it anticipates the severing of the sexual implications of the nuptial tie. In fact, Abelard's mutilation recalls some aspects of Plato's myth, which is illuminating in tracing the sources of love and sexual difference. In Plato's "Symposium," Aristophanes elaborates on the origins of man's desire. In the beginning, man was comprised of a dual form. Kari Weil's text provides background on this point:

> Aristophanes posits that sexual difference both results from and precedes desire. His well known story begins with a depictions of "man's" original nature, which was dual, consisting of two bodies united into one spherically shaped being. These bodies could already be classified as one of three sexes: two men together, two women, or a union of man and woman called "androgynous"-thus indicating that sexual difference existed absolutely, from the beginning.[9]

Weil expounds on the evolution of love by following Aristophanes' account. Specifically, love evolved from the fall from the unifying state of wholeness into the state of division. Eventual-

[9] Kari Weil, *Androgyny and the Denial of Difference* (Charlottesville & London: Virginia UP, 1992): 17.

ly, Zeus decided to cut the spherical shape, containing the two bodies united into one, into a fragmented form. At this stage, love and desire are born because the newly, separated halves will now search endlessly for their other, harmonious half. As Weil opines, "the reason is that human nature was originally one and we were a whole, and pursuit of the whole is called love" (18).

Aristophanes' androgyne then searches to return to the idealized state of wholeness in order to fill the void caused by the split. This idea applies to the termination of Abelard and Heloise's marital bond. In essence, the couple is cast into the "void" as a result of the radical severing of their physical relationship. Furthermore, the loss of the partner reveals that both Abelard and Heloise demonstrate androgynous traits, but in a dissimilar way. For instance, after their retreat into separate cloisters, Heloise 's half of the mutilated whole represents the part of the "androgynous" couple that chooses to pen letters, as an attempt to restore the lost sense of unity attributed to the absence of her husband's physical presence. To apply Weil's above passage to the narrative, Heloise's half of the whole searches endlessly for that unattainable completeness. As for the other side of the couple, Aristophane's theory is also evident with regards to Abelard's predicament. In the aftermath of the castration, Abelard becomes an "androgyne" of a different kind as a result of the loss of the missing body part. Mark Amsler 's article on the *Historia* confirms this notion: the "semantic field of castration is mapped out primarily in male/female terms (46)."[10] Abelard's mutilation causes him to continually drift back and forth tracing a bipolar movement, exhibiting both female/male characteristics. The female side is characterized by the numerous references to eunuchism that he brings up within the body of the correspondence. Abelard ex-

[10] Mark Amsler, "Genre and Code in Abelard's *Historia Calamitatum*," *Essays: Critical Approaches to Medieval and Renaissance Texts* 1 (1981): 46.

hibits his male authorial rights by manipulating Heloise's discourse, which will be seen in his later letters. Caroline Walker Bynum mentions that male medieval authors were, in essence, identified by their predisposition to authority, command, and judgment.[11] But, as Amsler's article points out, Abelard is also "feminized" because of his physical castration, and this signals only the beginning of a series of theological and secular castrations that will be discussed later on in the *Historia*. Moreover, it is also possible to interpret the recurring theme of victimization in the text as representative of his "feminized" otherness, an idea that is reinforced by the function of the confessional letter. As discussed earlier, Abelard wants to plead his case publicly as the victim wrongly condemned by the church. To portray himself as a "victim," and thus as impotent, is to assume the "traditional" role attributed to women. Furthermore, as Amsler views it, the textual references to Mars in the *Historia* may be read as Abelard's "desexualization" by Venus, the dangerous seductress.[12] Along these lines, one of the most recurrent images is the medieval misogynistic perception of woman as the temptress who sets out to ruin men. In the case of Abelard, punishment in inflicted on the part of his body with which he had sinned under Fulbert's roof. Specifically, Amsler postulates that Abelard's misfortunes culminating in the castration reflect the image of "Mars unmanned."[13] This allusion points to the destruction of his masculinity; Abelard loses his sexual power, and so the remnants of past erotic experiences are subjected to a conversion process, whereby the souvenirs are stored in the obscure recesses of the memory. It is this emasculated image of

---

[11] Caroloine Walker Bynum studies gender differences between male and female writers in late medieval writing, which is based on an inherent dichotomy between men and women. See Walker's essay, "...And Woman His Humanity": Female Imagery in the Religious Writing of the Later Middle Ages," *Fragmentation and Redemption: Essays on Gender and the Human Body in Medieval Religion* (New York: Zone, 1991): 158-179.

[12] Amsler 42-3.

[13] Amsler 45.

Abelard that characterizes his androgynous nature, which becomes all the more visible after the castration. To reapply Aristophanes' theory, Abelard fits into the concept of the androgyne because he is thrust unexpectedly into a state of a monumental lack resulting from his mutilation, an idea that can also be placed in a more modern context as Plato's discourse on loss and lack anticipates Jacques Lacan's theory of desire.

According to Lacan, loss, similar to the myth of Aristophanes concerning the original state of man as a divided being, is also related to the idea of the split. The individual experiences a void because he or she is deprived of the privileged signifier. The moment of rupture refers back to the traumatic separation taking place within the Imaginary order when there is a definitive severing from the maternal bond.[14] The principle of the lack is based on a nostalgic need to return to the harmonious state of fusion with the mother, a search to regain lost fulfillment that recalls Plato's references to the androgyne; the figure who also experiences the pursuit of the whole called love. Plato describes the completed entity as the idealized state preceding the split of the two halves. Lacan elaborates on Plato's notion of the lack, which is highly significant in view of the fact that he builds his theories on desire and loss on the very foundation of this principle of impossible unity. To return to some of Lacan's fundamental principles describing the early stages of the subject's psychoanalytic development, the child leaves the Imaginary Order, the territory identified with the mother, and then enters into the Symbolic order, after realizing that he/she cannot have the mother because only the master signifier, the father, who represents the Law, has the phallus. In the Symbolic order, the child becomes aware that his desire to possess the mother is impossible. He is powerless in the presence of the paternal fig-

---

[14] Juliet Mitchell's introduction on Jacques Lacan is particularly useful in her explanation of Lacan's psychoanalytic theories on sexuality. *Feminine Sexuality: Jacques Lacan and the école freudienne* Ed. Juliet Mitchell and Jacqueline Rose, eds. (New York: W.W. Norton & Company, 1982): 3-10.

ure, the phallus. Therefore, it is fruitless to hope to reconstruct the original state of completeness that he once experienced in the womb of the mother. Like the androgynous being who searches for its other half, the Lacanian subject is forever engaged in the never-ending pursuit to fill the void created by the unattainable Other. However, the parallel that connects the androgyne to the Lacanian subject does reveal some differences.

Francette Pacteau's psychoanalytic work on fantasy and representation studied the problematic question of the androgyne's desire. Pacteau suggests that, like the Lacanian subject, the androgyne is inherently linked to the Imaginary, the region where the desire is unrestricted and free of obstacles.[15] However, there is a fundamental difference between the two that occurs at the point where the Imaginary and the Symbolic orders intersect. The androgyne resists erasure of sexual difference, which means that the construction of gender identity is forever characterized by sexual ambiguity. But the Lacanian subject does not share the androgyne's dual identity because the child undergoes a series of developmental stages prior to acquiring a specific gender association. Moreover, whereas the Lacanian subject wishes to reestablish the maternal bond, the androgyne's underlying pulsion is auto-erotic.[16] The androgyne is caught up in an ambiguous position. He/She does not know what it desires, and so the Other is associated only with the feeling of loss and estranged distance from the missing half. On the contrary, for Lacan, the individual knows precisely that he dreams of returning to the Imaginary Order; freed from the later intervention of paternal law in the Symbolic Order. There is an undercurrent of narcissism in the need to satisfy the self by recapturing the moment when harmony was still intact.

[15] See Francette Pacteau's article, "The Impossible Referent: Representations of the Androgyne," *Formations of Fantasy*, eds. Victor Burgin, James Donald and Cora Kaplan. (London & New York: Methuen, 1986): 62-84.

[16] Pacteau 68-9.

Pacteau's text also refers to the myth of Aristophanes to reemphasize the androgyne's need to search for its deprived part. She also points out that narcissism is the underlying drive that generates the pulsion to regain lost unity, an idea that can be applied to Abelard's narrative technique in the *Historia*.

The text reveals self-centered tendencies, and at the same time concentrates repeatedly on Abelard's personal "loss." In retelling the details of the castration, he deliberately directs the spotlight on his persona without providing the reader with an idea of how this tragedy affected Heloise. He silences her discourse so as not to digress from the emphasis on his own misfortunes. As an author, it is possible that he seeks to persuade his reader that his predicament was far worse than hers. The numerous references pertaining to his "loss" indicate a preoccupation with the mutilation: "Le jugement de Dieu me frappait avec justice dans la partie de mon corps qui avait péché" (*Historia* 69).

At this stage, the text turns to the subject of the disgraceful state of the eunuch in God's eyes. These various theological concerns relating to the castration are analyzed by Abelard in a highly structured way while maintaining the focus on his adversities. In fact, Abelard simply reiterates the medieval doctrine on castration by quoting the 28th chapter of Deuteronomy, directly related to the status of the eunuch. He fears that he will suffer alienation from God because eunuchs are impure beings, and thus are not allowed into the house of God. However, according to Catholic tradition, men who were castrated involuntarily were not subject to be removed from the clergy. Since Abelard was a victim of Fulbert's punishment, his mutilation was not self-inflicted and, therefore, he was not really expelled from the Church. In any case, the official Catholic doctrine regarding the question of castration does not alter the status of the eunuch in relation to God. A man who suffered mutilation was nevertheless considered inferior to a whole being. Abelard was reduced to a more "feminine," powerless state and would later need Heloise in order to further his self-interests and ambitions in the Church. This aspect will be discussed in the analysis of their love correspondence.

The Double Castration

The marriage imposed by Abelard was not the end of his manipulation of Heloise's destiny. At Argenteuil, she had sacrificed herself by accepting the veil before Abelard officially entered the monastery. As he says in the *Historia*, "Héloïse, avait déjà, sur mon ordre, pris le voile" (70). Charrier, Dronke, Muckle and many other scholars have pointed out that Heloise received the veil solely for Abelard.[17] She was never attracted by professional aspirations in the Church. Her own "loss" is directly related to the severing of her intimate relationship with her husband. She sacrifices her "erotic past" in distancing herself from Abelard, behind the walls of the convent. As will be seen in her second letter, what really was transpiring behind the veil that was dissimulating her desire was far from holy meditation, but the notion of her "loss" is highly significant also in the *Historia*. The Lacanian theory of searching for the distant object of desire applies equally to Heloise. Physically, she is brutally separated from her husband, and would be forever doomed to wander in endless pursuit of the unattainable Other in order to fill the void caused by his deliberate attempt to force her to forget her passion. But in the recesses of her memory, Heloise would continue to search, indulging in a Lacanian "replaying of the loss" so as to hold on to the remaining shreds of past remembrances, of time spent together, in order to eternalize the image of Abelard etched deep within her. Abelard, in imposing his will on his wife, was subjecting her to her

[17] As noted, most scholars are of this opinion. See Peter Dronke's book, *Abelard and Heloise in Medieval Testimonies* (Glasgow: Glasgow UP, 1976). The references to Muckle and Charrier are given in note seven.

own wrenching mutilation. Jean-Charles Huchet elaborates on this idea of double castration. He maintains that Heloise's entire discourse is in fact constructed by her loss and abrupt severing from her husband: "Dans *L'Historia,* la castration signe la perte sexuelle d'Héloïse, et ouvre sur le désert absolu du manque. La blessure du corps est amputation de l'être;. . ."[18]

Huchet's critical lens draw on Lacanian loss and gap in order to make a case for Heloise's sexual loss. It is curious that he mimes Abelard by using his vocabulary, "blessure" and "amputation," references found in the passages from the *Historia* cited earlier. These two terms are then applied to Heloise's loss to reaffirm the existence of a double castration. Huchet also ties the castration theme to the overall structure of the narrative of both the *Historia* and the correspondence. Related to Huchet's idea of the double castration is the possibility that Abelard "amputated" Heloise's letters, which will be explored in the analysis of the love correspondence. In fact, this theory reinforces the case for a double castration. The first chapter will show that the correspondence does indeed reveal some instances where Abelard may have intervened in Heloise's original letters. For instance, in the main body of the epistolary correspondence, we will see textual examples of Abelard's technique of borrowing Heloise's voice. The tendency to appropriate her voice indicates, as Huchet, Amsler and Nouvet also affirm, that Abelard's "otherness" is feminine. Howard Bloch's work on medieval misogyny attributes the borrowing of feminine voice to the traditional, Christian antifeminist discourse silencing women's own voice, and thus labeling the female as a passive text to be reworked by males.[19] The significance of borrowing this voice will be considered in depth in the main body of the correspondence, but, in the context of the *His-*

[18] Jean-Charles Huchet, "La Voix d'Héloïse," *Romance Notes* 25.3 (1985): 274.
[19] See Howard Bloch's book, *Medieval Misogyny and the Invention of Western Romantic Love* (Chicago & London: University of Chicago Press, 1991).

toria, it is important to recognize that this literary strategy enables the reader to observe the feminine side of Abelard's "otherness." As noted earlier in the discussion of the myth of Aristophanes, Abelard acquires androgynous characteristics following his castration. He vacillates constantly between his male/female roles depending on the situation. For example, the text reveals numerous depictions of him as a victim, which is associated with his weaker or "feminine" side. When he gives advice, he slips back into his male persona in his attempt to guide others; but as a means of compensating for his impotence and impurity, he will turn to Heloise and use her body and voice, as will be seen again in the fourth love letter, to gain access to God's redemption since Heloise held a more advantageous position in the Church in comparison to his status as a eunuch. Doris Earnshaw and Elizabeth Harvey validate the significance of this masculine technique of borrowing woman's voice. These critics trace the origins and development of woman's voice in literature, and they postulate that feminine discourse was thought to express passion more "naturally" than man's; especially in the Middle Ages and in the Renaissance.[20] In order to borrow Heloise's voice and persona, thus capitalizing on his "otherness" following the castration, Abelard seems almost envious of her position as a nun because she is closer to God than he is, now that he is a eunuch. In the *Historia*, Abelard mentions that they both donned religious habit at approximately the same time. Their entry into monastic life garbed in a similar way allows Abelard to alter the vestimentary code. On a symbolic level, he can assume the role of Heloise, as a nun, by exchanging garments with her. He seems to slip into a dress that disguises, after the mutilation, all of his masculine attributes. Interestingly enough, Heloise and Abelard both include

---

[20] See Doris Earnshaw's work, *The Female Voice in Medieval Romance Lyric* (New York: Peter Lang, 1988), and Elizabeth Harvey's book, *Ventriloquized Voices: Feminist Theory and English Renaissance Texts* (London: Routledge, 1992).

numerous references to St. Jerome and often compare themselves to him. As is well known, there is a famous illustration of St. Jerome in a dress. He was the victim of a joke by his contemporaries who planted a dress next to his bed. The next morning St. Jerome put on the dress thinking it was his church frock, unaware that his enemies wanted him to appear to have spent the night with a woman. In the drawing, St. Jerome is wearing the dress while reciting his vespers. This image bears resemblance to Abelard, who recalls St. Jerome at the precise moment he accepts the monastic attire which veils his masculinity. The referential implications of the garment seem to suggest that he relinquishes his carnal and predatory manly nature in favor of a more feminine, passive role. In fact, Abelard saw himself as a perpetual victim of slander and vicious gossip long after his castration. Similar to St. Jerome, he was constantly attacked and persecuted by his enemies in the clergy because he consorted with women as his enemies said of St. Jerome. But the illustration depicting St. Jerome is also representative of Abelard's feminine "otherness" as a retiring, withdrawn figure in the monastery. The image of the frock serves as a disguise enabling Abelard to maintain a constant fluctuating movement between the masculine and feminine aspects of his being, whereas Heloise's religious garments will serve a different function, as will be discussed in the first letter.

Monastic Life after Separation

The *Historia* also traces the events following Abelard's decision to seek refuge apart from Heloise. After the couple took their vows, he retreated to the abbey at St. Denis to study Scripture and continued to attract throngs of followers and students. In the text, Abelard compares himself to another famous Christian eunuch, Origen, who also interpreted philosophy and studied theology. The narrative reveals a kinship between the two eunuchs . Abelard relates his own suffering to Origen's who was also greatly criticized by the Christian community. Soon after, the text indicates that Abelard became the target of another serious persecution by his rivals in the church who accused him of heresy. He refers to his enemies, Alberic, Lotulphe and Rudolphe. These theologians actively pursued the condemnation of Abelard's book, *On the Unity and Trinity of God,* because he read it in public, and it was considered contradictory to the conception of the Christian trinity. Abelard was summoned to the city of Soissons to meet with a special assembly to study his case. The purpose of the Council was to determine if he had indeed written a document that was contradictory to the Catholic faith. But once again his three enemies carefully exerted their powerful influence against him. According to his account in the *Historia, t*hey carefully devised a plan to attack Abelard by spreading rumors. They insisted that he should be condemned because he was guilty of reading his book publicly before the Pope had granted him permission. Abelard was then called upon to throw his own book into the fire. This destruction of his "subversive" book represents another type of castration. As Amsler reads it, Abelard continued to be threatened by various manifestations of violence recalling the castration, but this time he suffered a spiritual mutilation. Amsler describes this idea by integrating the spiritual castration into the overall narrative structure of the *Historia*:

> In the narrative line, Abelard's seductive teaching at St. Denis and the burning of his book recapitulate his seduction of Heloise and his castration. Throughout the *Historia,* the narrator represents himself as Mars unmanned, whether by a vindictive uncle or envious teachers of philosophy. Abelard's literary castration is the type which the text repeats in other forms as the violation of a virtuous man by a hostile public. (Amsler 47)

The recurring image of Abelard as a victim reappears after the devastating incident at Soissons. After the destruction of his book on the Trinity, Abelard once again sought refuge in the region of Troyes, and devoted himself to building a hermitage known as the Paraclete. Despite his alienation from the theological world, students still followed him and helped in building his retreat. Surrounded by his faithful disciples, Abelard decided to open a school on this parcel of remote land. In the *Historia*, he explains the significance of the Paraclete:

> Au reste, en nommant notre chapelle le Paraclet, je n'ai pas eu l'intention de la consacrer à une seule personne. Je l'ai fait sur le seul motif que je vous ai indiqué: en souvenir de ma consolation. (*Historia* 97)

The text indicates that his choice of name, the Paraclete, is linked to a self-motivated interest or, as he writes, "en souvenir de ma consolation." In fact, the construction of a religious retreat seems to suggest that Abelard builds his own, personal haven, freed from the accusing eyes and scathing tongues of his enemies. This self-serving idea is reinforced by the text: "J'étais, de corps, caché en ce lieu. Mais ma renommée courait le monde et ma parole y résonnait plus que jamais" (*Historia* 97). The passage shows that his reputation did not appear to suffer from his isolation from the public. At least, this is the impression Abelard chooses to convey to the reader. Soon after the construction of the Paraclete however, he had to go to St. Gildas where the monks had elected him abbot. The brothers at St. Gildas were an unruly and dangerous group, and Abelard's life was in peril from the moment he arrived. He deeply regretted leaving the beloved chapel that offered him a peaceful retreat.

Transformation of the Paraclete into a Feminized Space

At St. Gildas, Abelard learned that the nuns at Argenteuil were to be expelled from their cloister. He quickly found a resolution to their dilemma and suggested that Heloise move to the Paraclete since he could no longer look after his property. This move to the Paraclete recalls her acceptance of the veil. Abelard had asked Heloise to take her vows before he did, and once again the decision to live within the confines of the Paraclete represents a manipulation of her will. In providing her with a new place to live, he was also guiding her into another enclosed space, remote and isolated from contact with the outside world. Since the Paraclete belonged to Abelard, in essence, so did the women who were to be confined within his masculine construction.

Under Heloise's skillful guidance, the Paraclete would eventually enjoy success for years to come. The spatial dimension is interesting here because Heloise's direction is directly responsible for the flourishing of Abelard's domain. In his absence, she successfully cultivated his space. It is possible that she wanted to manage the cloister especially well because of the spiritual and physical bond between her and Abelard, as represented by the land on which the Paraclete was erected. Ironically, the Paraclete, a site of germination, was constructed under the supervision of a seemingly not so barren eunuch. The Paraclete evoked the memory of their desire, thus creating a sacred territory where Heloise would spend the rest of her life. In the text, the Paraclete represents the idea of consolation that would always provide a spiritual link between the two lovers. As Abelard describes it, "on peut donc aussi bien l'appeler Paraclet, c'est-à-dire Consolateur"(94). The land glorified their lost love, and united them symbolically by their common misery. The couple was brought closer by the space that had been originally cultivated by Abelard's followers and then successfully managed under Heloise's capable direction. After Heloise moved to the Paraclete, Abelard mentions in the text that he called on Heloise to discuss monastic affairs. But once again, his enemies accused him of visiting the Paraclete for carnal reasons: "J'étais encore dominé, disaient-ils, par la concupiscence de la chair, puisque je ne pouvais supporter peu ni prou l'absence de mon ancienne maîtresse"(*Historia* 104).

Abelard, describing his plight as the undeserving victim of society, compares himself once again to St. Jerome who had also been the target of scathing gossip regarding his relationships with several Christian women, among them Paula and Asella. Like Abelard, St. Jerome was a controversial religious figure. Interestingly, Abelard finds consolation in comparing his destiny to that of other great religious figures, and draws on the power of logic to deconstruct the calumny launched against him: as a eunuch, he claims he is above all suspicion, and poses a rhetorical question in order to stress the intentions of those out to ruin his reputation: "Comment donc le soupçon subsiste-t-il, quand le moyen d'accomplir les turpitudes de la chair m'a été retiré?" (*Historia* 105). The passage shows a deliberate attempt to squelch the rumors. Abelard then proceeds to construct a parallel between his case and Origen's in order to clarify the differences between voluntary and involuntary mutilation. Reiterating the Catholic laws regarding castration, he states that Origen committed a sin because he mutilated himself voluntarily, whereas he was the random victim of an involuntary mutilation, and thus innocent. He finds consolation in rationalizing that Origen was worse off than he is in God's estimation, and the self-serving aspect of the narrative reappears, as indicated by the use of repetition. He is tortured more by the slander to his name and reputation than by the actual physical mutilation. This split between body and soul is evident in his writing: "Mais si mon corps avait moins souffert, la calomnie me poursuivait plus longtemps, et ces attaques contre ma réputation me torturaient plus que n'avait fait ma blessure" (*Historia* 106). The term "blessure" refers back to the loss of his masculinity as well as the damage to his reputation. At this point, Abelard seems to compensate for his multiple amputation by shifting his attention to another empowering symbol: the pen. This is closely tied to his strong belief in the powers of reason that he continued to cultivate in his teaching, long after the castration, but in essence, he redirects his energy towards the spiritual pursuits of the soul as a way of transcending his impure body towards a higher plane: if he is allowed into the kingdom of heaven, he will rise above his flawed status as a castrated man. But while he still remains in the material world, the "phallus" or the pen will also be the emblem of his manipulative nature. In addition to directing Heloise's destiny, prior to her vows, he did so even after he gave her the Paraclete by quoting the apostles and stating that man is ultimately woman's chief: "Le sexe faible ne peut se passer de l'aide du sexe fort." (109). He clearly applies this idea to his sisters in Christ placed in his land:

> Ces réflexions me déterminèrent à aider de tout mon pouvoir mes soeurs du Paraclet, et à assurer l'administration de leur établissement. Ma présence, les tenant en éveil, augmenterait leur respect pour moi et je pourrais ainsi subvenir plus efficacement à leurs besoins. (*Historia* 110-111)

Even though the sisters were well organized and in the capable hands of Heloise, Abelard admits in the passage above that he still felt a strong need to oversee their community. In spite of his mutilation, Abelard attempts to show that he still represents patriarchal law because he is a man, and that he is necessary to validate the "women's" life.

Closure of the Confessional Letter

Abelard exteriorizes his fears at St. Gildas as he nears the end of his life in the unruly monastery where the relentless monks had tried to poison him on several occasions. After relating the list of his adversities to his anonymous friend, he returns to his purpose of penning this long story of his life and to the "consolatio" device of using his own misfortunes as a means of comparison. This cyclical aspect of readdressing himself to his recipient represents an integral part of his epistolary technique, but the closure of the *Historia* is only apparent. The dialogue will be reopened when Heloise receives her copy of this epistle. In essence, this autobiographical text sets the tone for the possibility of initiating another exchange, this time with his distant wife, in a work which will represent the birth of the genre of the love letter, and will contain many of the themes already present in the *Historia* such as Abelard's domineering nature, eunuchism and double castration.

2.

The Genesis of the Love Letter

After ten long years of separation, a copy of the *Historia* supposedly fell into Heloise's hands. Finally, she had news of her husband. As stated earlier, many *Historian*s of the text believe that he intended for his story to circulate within the public domain, and so it is not really surprising that Heloise received the autobiographical account of his misfortunes, but Heloise's reception of Abelard's text cannot be considered without reviewing the various theories surrounding the debate on the authenticity of the correspondence. Muckle elaborates on the issue, stating that scholars like J. G. Orelli believed that someone else, possibly a monk, may have written the letters after the death of Abelard and Heloise. Other specialists such as Ludovic Lalanne suspect that Heloise may have edited the love letters after Abelard's demise. The opposing argument is supported by S. M. Deutsch, Bernhard Schmeidler, and Charlotte Charrier.[1] These scholars share the opinion that Abelard wrote all of the letters himself, and thus created a literary fiction. Moreover, Charrier postulates that Abelard deliberately edited Heloise's text as part of his self-serving strategy, seeking to benefit from the specific part of her amorous discourse that would enhance his rep-

[1] For a brief history of the authenticity debate, see Muckle's article, "The Personal Letters of Heloise and Abelard," *Mediaevel* Studies 15 (1953): 48. For a more recent perspective, see John Marenbon's article, "Authenticity Revisited." *Listening to Heloise: The Voice of a Twelfth-Century Woman,* ed. Bonnie Wheeler (New York: St. Martin's Press, 2000): 19-33.

utation. In turn, Charrier's position is discussed at length by critics such as Benton, Vitz, Nouvet, McLeod, Muckle, Dronke, and Newman.[2] Even if they do not entirely share her opinion, these scholars all concur that it is highly possible that Abelard may have tampered with Heloise's letters. However, Charrier's theory is challenged by Gilson, who defends the position that the correspondence is completely authentic, and thus functions as a historical record of the two lovers' lives. In any event, the controversy does not reveal any substantiated evidence, and so it is more interesting to study the correspondence strictly as a literary text. To support Charrier's position in her monumental work on the legend of Heloise, a close reading of the text will show that Abelard borrows Heloise's feminine persona as well as fragmenting her epistles. The analysis of the love correspondence will also reveal that Abelard engages in pseudo-feminocentrism in order to flatter himself all the more. Numerous examples of Abelard's attempt to veil "feminine" desire, as well as Heloise's erotic pulsions, will be analyzed throughout the course of this study; but, at this point, it is appropriate to consider first some basic characteristics of the epistolary love letter as a preface to Heloise's first letter.

Altman outlines general characteristics of multiple varieties of missives and considers fundamental aspects of epistolary discourse. Altman's theories on amorous correspondence provide insight into understanding the structural mechanics of Abelard's and Heloise's letters. One of the most important elements of the love letter is that the correspondents write in the present, spontaneously addressing themselves to the absent object of their desire and thus creating a sense of immediacy inherent to the style. The pen bridges the distance that separates the couple and impedes them from entering into direct

[2] See Newman's article, "Authority, Authenticity and the Repression of Heloise," *Journal of Medieval and Renaissance Studies* 22.3 (1992): 121-141. Here, Barbara Newman summarizes the positions of John Benton, J. T. Muckle, Peter von Moos and other scholars on pp. 123-7.

physical communication with each other. The writer is often alone, confined to a solitary space, as is the case of Heloise. She writes from the Paraclete, enclosed in the cloister, with a passion for Abelard that is ever present and seemingly undying. Love letters can also function as an instrument of seduction and as a means of dissimulation. Often the writer of the epistle develops a thematics of secrecy that requires the reader to decipher the message hidden beneath the words exchanged between lovers or friends. Above all, the writer who participates in the epistolary pact hopes for a response, especially if he or she is revealing intimate secrets to the receiver. Altman defines this relationship as the "I"/you" dialectic, which is seminal to epistolary structure. The "I" writes in the hope of reaching the "you," the absent receiver. The distant quality of the elusive addressee creates a sense of emptiness inscribed in the spaces and gaps of the missive.

Altman describes yet another aspect of epistolary discourse which concerns the language of letter writers. The language that conveys separation and distance is itself emblematic of absence:

> Epistolary discourse is a discourse marked by hiatuses of all sorts: time lags between event and recording, between message transmission and reception; spatial separation between writer and addressee; blank spaces and lacunae in the manuscript. Yet it is also a language of gap closing, of writing to the moment, of speaking to the addressee as if he were present. Epistolary discourse is the language of the "as if" present.[3]

Even if the addressee is absent and is temporally very far removed, the writer can pretend that he or she is there by relying on the power of the memory to restore presence. Indeed, this is what Heloise practices. Despite the ten-year gap, she has not forgotten her lover. Her recollection is so vivid that the salutation of her first letter reflects her inner focus on Abelard. She

---

[3] Janet Altman, *Epistolarity: Approaches to a Form* (Columbus: Ohio State University Press, 1982): 140.

begins by "à son seigneur" followed by various titles Abelard has, but significantly ends with "à Abélard." The structure of the letter invokes her husband, and gradually moves away from the emphasis placed on God. In fact, the word "seigneur" does not appear to carry a religious significance at all. Heloise retains her focus on the domestic level by stressing her subservience to Abelard. She fluctuates between the social and private spheres, as is illustrated by her selection of titles referring to Abelard, but she tends to emphasize the more personal aspect of her relationship to him. Her focus is directed towards the man, as reinforced by the final "à Abélard," followed by the first line of her letter, the phrase "mon bien-aimé," which establishes the tone for the epistle. From within the Paraclete, Heloise begins to reflect on her life with Abelard inspired by her reading of the *Historia*. As Peggy Kamuf has shown, the motif of the closed space is important for the staging of the amorous epistolary exchange:

> A constant, however, is a focus on the constructions which enclose women with their desire. Whether it is behind the solid walls of the nun's cloister, at the unspoken limit of the hysteric's language, or within the frame set by a parent's desire, the passion that shapes these fictions can only discover itself in transgression of the law which encloses it.[4]

Kamuf refers to the spatial enclosure of the cloister as a transgressive place threatening to undermine the religious laws that provide the structural pillars for the organization of the nunnery. In fact, the architectonics of the Paraclete confine Heloise to an oppressive cell, where she is enclosed with her overwhelming passion. In her isolation, she creates a personal haven in which she can contemplate her desire, transforming it into her own fiction. But at the same time the imprisoning atmosphere hinders her from re-establishing contact with her

[4] Peggy Kamuf, *Fictions of Feminine Desire* (Lincoln & London: University of Nebraska Press, 1982): xvii.

remote object of desire. Her fiction of recalling and retelling the lovers' story in her own version is constructed on the remnants of her carnal desire. Jacques Derrida's concept of the crypt in "Fors" may be applied to Heloise's veiled passion: when this psychoanalytic text delves into the interior self, one discovers a network of inner spaces described as "an inner safe" or a vault hidden deep within the consciousness. The crypt, like the cloister, resembles a tomb, but also functions as a place that conceals buried secrets pertaining to the powerful force of desire.

> What is a crypt? No crypt presents itself. The grounds (lieux) are so disposed as to disguise and to hide: something, always a body in some way. But also to disguise the act of hiding and to hide the disguise: the crypt hides as it holds.[5]

Derrida defines the crypt as a site of absence, which is also reminiscent of the convent, and as a space containing many interior partitions, just as the Paraclete contained cells and various private corners of worship. Within the walls of Heloise's cell, the space holds a secret charged with meaning. The exterior or physical surface is sterile and thus devoid of memories of her passion, but the interior, also represented by the blanks and gaps of her love letters, reveals traces of her desire. The epistle itself functions as a substitute for the beloved. As Elizabeth MacArthur and Janet Altman have pointed out, the missive functions as a metonymy for the lover.[6] The contact with the paper constitutes a seductive subtext in which the writer fills in the empty spaces with the lines and contours of the lover's body. Underneath the flowing ink of the pen, the missive composer is in fact creating a replacement for the lover's presence. In the epistolary process, the letter writer almost seems to reach out and touch the receiver. Altman describes the metonymy of

---

[5] Jacques Derrida, "Fors," *Georgia Review* 31.1 (1977): 67.

[6] On the epistolary narrative, see Elizabeth J. MacArthur's *Extravagant Narratives: Closure & dynamics in the Epistolary Form* (Princeton: Princeton UP, 1990). Also Altman's *Epistolarity: Approaches to a Form,* as cited above. Both scholars emphasize the importance of metonymy in amorous discourse.

the lover as an erotic experience because the epistle symbolizes the body of the receiver.[7] In Heloise's case, the absent body of her husband is resurrected by the act of composing the love letter. It is as if she were writing on his body, therefore engaging in a seductive act. In her opening missive, the first paragraph of her letter to Abelard indicates that she has not forgotten, even after ten years have elapsed. Her spartan cloister transforms itself into an intimate sanctuary where she can devote herself to reaching her remote object of desire. From within the tomb of the Paraclete, Heloise, empowered by the pen, develops a strategy to transcend the walls of her prison by speaking to Abelard in a startling intimate way:

> Mon bien-aimé, le hasard vient de faire passer entre mes mains la lettre de consolation que tu écrivis à un ami. Je reconnus aussitôt, à la suscription, qu'elle était de toi. Je me jetai sur elle et la dévorai avec toute l'ardeur de ma tendresse: puisque j'avais perdu la présence corporelle de celui qui l'avait écrite, du moins les mots ranimeraient un peu pour moi son image. (Letter I, 119)

The reception of the *Historia* by Heloise results in the hope of engaging Abelard in epistolary exchange. The passage clearly indicates that she views the reception of the letter as a metonymy, standing in for the physical presence of her husband. The solitary setting for reading and writing enhances the amorous charge of the language. Her verb choice is forceful, and the rhetoric seems strikingly out of character for an abbess, mainly as Heloise's plume articulates her body's desires. Linda Kauffman's work on the discourse of desire is useful in studying the origin of Heloise's rhetoric, which is reminiscent of Ovid's *Heroides.* After reading the first part of Heloise's letter, the reader recalls that in the *Historia* Abelard mentions that the two of them often read Ovid together under the pretense of studying philosophy and theology in Fulbert's house. To clarify the

[7] See Altman p. 19 for a clear explanation of the letter as a metonymy for the absent lover.

rapport, Kauffman stresses the aspects of abandonment, solitude, separation, absence, and extreme pathos as seminal to the construction of a lover's discourse.[8] As a critical lens, she employs M. Bakhtin to point out that the language of desire is double-voiced, and inherently dialogic. The rhetoric of passion always comes from somewhere else, and mimes someone else's language. In *Problems of Dostoevsky's Poetics,* Bakhtin comments specifically on the epistolary form:

> Discourse here is double-voiced, and in most cases unidirectional [...] The letter, like a rejoinder in a dialogue, is addressed to a specific person, and it takes into account the other possible reactions, the other's possible reply.[9]

Bakhtin also indicates that epistolary form lends itself well to the reflected discourse of another because of the relationship to the absent receiver. The letter anticipates and projects the response directed to the addressee. In writing to Abelard, Heloise attempts to anticipate his response. In fact, she writes under the guise of following the epistolary rules of the day. That is to say, she asks for an *epistola consolatoria,* just as Abelard composed for his anonymous friend. She believes that she deserves a letter of consolation because he owes it to her as his wife and now sister in Christ. However, this is a masked pretense for the intimate letter that she secretly desires. If the love letter is double-voiced, Heloise waits and hopes that Abelard will answer her with a different rhetoric: one of a sensual nature, echoing the opening paragraph of her first letter. This is the true significance of restoring his image for her. The double quality of the missive reveals passion, etched in a palimpsest under the surface of the spiritual language of direction. In light of Heloise's position as an abbess, Kamuf interprets this clandestine pulsion

---

[8] See Linda Kauffman's book, *Discourses of Desire: Gender, Genre, and Epistolary Fictions* (Ithaca & London: Cornell UP, 1986): 30-61.

[9] Mikhail Bakhtin, *Problems of Dostoevsky's Poetics* (Minneapolis: Minnesota UP, 1984): 205.

as an erotic transgression, which Kauffman links to the disorder created by the discourse of desire that marks "woman's" language by signs of dissimulation, doubleness and duplicity.[10] Within the cloister, Heloise engages in a revolutionary act (as will be seen later in her second epistle), by penning her innermost erotic desires. At the same time, she disguises her desire by penning a veiled, neutral rhetoric. As an abbess, Heloise is supposedly writing to Abelard to seek spiritual advice, but her underlying motivation hinges on dissimulation. She addresses him on a more intimate level, calling him "mon bien aimé," and thus her writing shows evidence of a double discourse. Heloise's attempt to restore Abelard's image, through establishment of the "I"/ "you" dialectic, is transgressive because it creates disruption for her as a nun, and it establishes the tone of dissimulation for the course of the love correspondence. Her sensual language shown earlier in the opening paragraph by such words as "dévorai," "l'ardeur," and "tendresse," seems dangerously out of character for an abbess. Above all, the striking description of her reaction upon receiving his autobiographical letter, "je me jetai sur elle," reinforces Kauffman's notion of transgression.[11] Her language is so disturbing that Abelard will completely ignore it in his reply to this epistle. As will be considered later in the next letter, he will attempt to selectively filter out her passionate discourse. But, the power of her memory constitutes a resisting force to Abelard's attempt to redirect her writing away from him, towards God and other spiritual matters. Heloise overrides her master's authority by indulging in the replaying of those passionate memories when the two of them were together in Fulbert's house. In Lacanian terms, she is replaying the loss, which immobilizes the desire, by reliving past moments of rapture so that memories don't

[10] Kauffman talks about the "doubleness" of Heloise's love discourse on page 73. See also Kamuf's book, page 12.

[11] Kauffman elaborates on the textual implications of Heloise's erotic transgressions on page 83.

fade away. In this way, her passion remains an active force, hoping to connect through the letter with the object of her fantasies.

Repaying the Debt

The body of Heloise's first epistle focuses on the theme of debt. Abelard owes her a letter of consolation because he is responsible for her accepting the veil and the vows before he entered into the monastery. In addition to this, Heloise maintains that he should at least recognize their community, since he gave the Paraclete to her nuns. She begins by using "nous" to create the appearance of following the proper form for an abbess writing to a monk. There are repeated pleas not to forget the community of nuns. Given the duplicitous nature of the text, the "us" can be read as "don't forget about me," which is affirmed later in the letter. Heloise shifts from reminding Abelard of his indebtedness towards the Paraclete to a gradual use of "toi." The tone changes abruptly, and the reader suspects that she is really referring to his personal debt towards his wife, abandoned without any communication for a period of ten years.

> Le fondateur de notre établissement, c'est toi seul après Dieu, toi seul le constructeur de notre chapelle, le bâtisseur de notre congrégation. Tu n'as rien édifié sur les fondements d'autrui: tout ici est ton oeuvre. (Letter I, 123)

Heloise is addressing herself directly to her husband. The choice of vocabulary serves as a frame for the architectural construction of the convent. Abelard, the builder, has enclosed her in a space that he has erected, therefore she becomes his "oeuvre." Ironically, the cloistered structure gives birth to a feminized haven in which Heloise transforms her confinement into a sacred place for the creation of the discourse of desire. Inadvertently, Abelard has built her a sanctuary, facilitating a scene of writing which is unrelated to spiritual matters. The language in the passage below reveals sexual overtones linked to the notions of planting and (re)birth. The implication of "cette plantation nouvelle" represents Heloise's hope to reawaken their desire so that it might blossom once again; the idea of enclosure is radically transformed, rewritten:

> Elle est donc à toi, bien vraiment à toi, cette plantation nouvelle qui croît dans l'amour sacré. Elle pousse maintenant de tendres rejetons qui, pour profiter, ont besoin d'arrosage. Elle est formée de femmes; et ce sexe est débile; sa faiblesse ne tient pas seulement à son jeune âge. (Letter I, 124)

Kauffman interprets the germination theme as dual.[12] On one hand, Heloise is perhaps alluding to her pregnancy and the implantation of Abelard's seed. On the other, she may be stressing aspects of spiritual life. The nuns need assistance and guidance in order to grow in their faith. Here, Heloise mimes the cultural construct of "woman" in the Middle Ages by repeating the misogynistic assumption that the weaker sex needs the direction of a man. However, (given the clandestine and duplicitous nature of her missives), another reading is possible. The word "plantation" may indicate a redefinition of the cloister. The refrain of "it belongs to you" designates Abelard as her receiver. Through writing, Heloise is actually allowing herself to cultivate and produce a discourse of desire by engaging in epistolary correspondence. Kauffman emphasizes the wild, untamed aspects of the birth of the "seed" of desire in this section of Heloise's epistle.[13] The architectural construct, the Paraclete owned by Abelard, forms a symbolic bridge connecting the couple despite their separation. Within the walls of the cloister, Heloise is transforming the exterior surface of religious devotion into a closely cultivated, secretive display of the poetics of passion. She is carefully setting the scene in anticipation of re-staging the original scene of passion to be played out

[12] For Kauffman's reading of Heloise's idea of the "plantation," see pp. 66-7.
[13] Kauffman discusses the wild aspects of Heloise's desire on pp. 66-7 in her book cited above.

through the epistolary exchange of amorous desire. She reworks the biblical ideas of the planted seed into a subtle lament or nostalgic longing to rekindle the carnality that was hauntingly familiar, and omnipresent in her memory. This part of the letter is followed by the confession of her unbridled love for Abelard: "tu sais quel lien nous attache et t'oblige, et que le sacrement nuptial t'unit à moi, d'une manière d'autant plus étroite que je t'ai toujours, à la face du monde, aimé d'un amour sans mesure" (Letter I, 126).

Regardless of their physical separation, Heloise emphasizes the nuptial tie between them. The excessive nature of her erotic passion illustrates Kamuf's theory of desire as a transgressive force that oversteps all boundaries and surpasses all limits.[14] Heloise continues this intimate conversation by elaborating on her loss. "tu sais, mon bien aimé, et tous le savent, combien j'ai perdu en toi; [...] je souffre incomparablement plus de la manière dont je t'ai perdu que de ta perte même" (Letter I, 126). Heloise depicts her loss and suffering as immeasurable and wrenching, but her most painful loss is the fact that she is bereft of Abelard's presence as a man. Huchet has considered the effect of this "perte", or in his words, the double castration on Heloise. For Huchet, Heloise's voice is born of the castration, which is illustrated in her first letter. She allows her voice to resound by composing her own autobiographical text in response to Abelard's *Historia*.[15] She will attempt to set the record straight in her first letter, filling in what Abelard has selectively left out. At the Paraclete, she begins to write her version in the aftermath of losing Abelard. To fill in the void created by his absence, Heloise writes from the position of the abandoned woman whose epistle is a metonymy for the absent lover. As mentioned above, there is evidence of a double castration, with misery serving as a catalyst. Heloise refers to her suffering as a

[14] See Kamuf for her commentary of Heloise's transgressive desire, pp. 23-7.
[15] Huchet 282-5.

loss of carnal pleasures as well as an abrupt detachment from her beloved. To interpret this loss in Lacanian terms, the severing from the object of desire results in a interminable search to rediscover the unattainable lover or the distant "Other."[16] Heloise engages in repeated textual, epistolary scenes in which she replays the loss so as to preserve the passion in her memory. Her diatribe of despair and solitude is punctuated by refrains of "toi seul," and culminates in the confession that she only desired Abelard: "Je te prouvai ainsi que tu règnes en seul maître sur mon âme comme sur mon corps. Dieu le sait, jamais je n'ai cherché en toi que toi-même" (Letter I, 127).

The Refusal of Marriage

Heloise elaborates on her undying love and devotion to Abelard, and provides textual evidence that she was against the marriage imposed by her husband. Marriage was contradictory to her heart; the excessive nature of her love for Abelard would only have been squelched by the traditional framework of the marital institution:

> Le nom d'épouse paraît plus sacré et plus fort; pourtant celui d'amie m'a toujours été plus doux. J'aurais aimé, permets-moi de le dire, celui de concubine et de fille de joie, tant il me semblait qu'en m'humiliant davantage j'augmentais mes titres à ta reconnaissance et nuisais moins à la gloire de ton génie. (Letter I, 127)

Selflessly, Heloise did not wish to risk destroying Abelard's ambitions in the Church by marrying him, but above all she desired to be his whore. This passage suggests that her letter was perhaps edited by a third party. As Charrier and Huchet strongly advocate, Abelard may have reworked her letters, thus creating a fragmentation and alteration of her original missives. One notes, for example, that Abelard's version of Heloise's op-

---

[16] Jacqueline Rose interprets Lacan's theory of the "Other" in her critical commentary on Lacan's theory of feminine sexuality in *Female Sexuality*. See pp. 30-38.

position to his marriage proposal in the *Historia,* mentions that Heloise preferred to be his mistress rather than his wife, and the use of mistress (rather than of whore) may have been an attempt to tone down the passionate aspect of Heloise's rhetoric. Nouvet's article on the notion of "whore" in the text attributes the term to Heloise's refusal of marriage so that she wouldn't damage Abelard's career as a philosopher, in an attempt to preserve Abelard's reputation at all costs, and her preference for "whore" would also assure an unbinding love in lieu of the limitations of the conjugal bond.[17] But Nouvet also calls attention to the notion of labels, insisting that Heloise wanted to accept the label of whore in name only, because the unrestricted freedom associated with the whore would also protect and nurture her immeasurable passion. In this way, Heloise could avoid the enslavement of the marital bond. She did not want to become the property of a man. On the contrary, she was primarily concerned with being with Abelard, as a lover, and allowing their passion to rise above and beyond the constraints of marriage. This idea is not in Abelard's version of the story in the *Historia* where the ellipsis of the term "whore" might indicate a deliberate attempt to curb Heloise's unbridled desire by selecting a less obscene word. It is possible that Abelard was determined to rid her of her sexual nature by not acknowledging that disturbing aspect of her passion. Contrary to him, Heloise refers to the decision of the marriage as an unhappy moment in their love story, and she focuses precisely on what is not to be found in his account of her argument against marriage:

> Dans cette lettre de consolation à ton ami, tu as bien voulu exposer toi-même quelques-unes des raisons que j'invoquais pour te détourner de cette malheureuse union. Pourtant, tu as passé sous silence la

[17] For a fascinating discussion of Heloise writing as a "whore" see Nouvet's article, "The Discourse of the Whore: An Economy of Sacrifice," *MLN* 105.4 (1990): 750-773.

plupart de celles qui me faisaient préférer l'amour au mariage, et la liberté au lien. (Letter I, 127)

This passage is highly significant because it is one of the very few intertextual references to the *Historia*. Heloise accuses Abelard of not conveying her version of the story in a truthful manner, as noted above by Nouvet. Heloise also criticizes Abelard for not recognizing her social opposition between wife and whore, for Abelard omitted her arguments against his proposal of marriage. The reason for the deletion was that Heloise stressed the transgressive freedom of desire as an unbinding bond which was in direct contradiction to the marital contract. This passage indicates an aspect of "pseudo-feminocentrism" in the love correspondence, a term used by Miller to refer to male authors who take over the women's place in order to further their own gain. Here, Miller's term can be applied to Abelard's masculine domination and manipulation of Heloise's discourse, a strategy which is, as Miller views it, fundamentally egocentric and inherently homoerotic:

> [...] the founding contract of the novel as it functions in the phallocentric (heterosexual) economies of representation is homoerotic: "woman" is the legal fiction, the present absence that allows the male bond of privilege and authority to constitute itself within the laws of proper circulation.[18]

In the passage cited previously, Abelard alters Heloise's letters and intention as will become evident in his reply to her first letter, when he begs her to address him only on specific questions relating to monastic matters. Because his goal is to see to her spiritual conversion, her discourse is then forced to submit to the editing of his pen, the phallic symbol of patriarchal law. For example, while the numerous textual references to her immense love and desire flatter his ego, he does not answer her on this dangerous and transgressive level; he ignores her passion,

[18] Nancy Miller, "The I's in Drag," *Diacritics* (1982): 49.

deliberately casting a visible veil over it, as he continues to communicate with her on a religious level. He takes full liberty in selectively filtering out what does not concern religious matters. As Miller reads it, this intervention in the female author's text only serves to reaffirm masculine self-interest and narcissistic gain while diminishing the author's presence where she appears to be exchanged between men who constitute the Law. In essence, Abelard hopes to dictate Heloise's discourse, molding her in his image so that she echoes the same religious rhetoric. His reply to this letter will build on this narrative strategy, and later lead into a related yet different form of epistolary transvestism that will be analyzed in the fourth letter. But to come back to her opening letter, Heloise stresses the forced fragmentation of her discourse by Abelard, and reinforces her accusation of being silenced by him when she adds that even if Emperor Augustus wanted her to be Empress she would still prefer to be Abelard's whore than the bride of a famous man. Her overwhelming need to preserve her desire recalls MacArthur's conception of the epistle's ability to function as a metonymy for the lover.[19] Heloise wants this passion to persist, and she sustains the movement of desire through the letters, by continuing to pour out her sensuality. Towards the end of her first letter, she overtly describes her desire to provoke a similar response from her distant receiver:

> Mon coeur m'a quitté, il vit avec toi. Sans toi, il ne peut plus être nulle part. Je t'en conjure, fait qu'il soit bien avec toi! Il le sera s'il te trouve propice, si seulement tu lui rends tendresse pour tendresse, peu pour beaucoup, des paroles pour des actes. (Letter I, 133)

Not only does she remain hopeful in restoring the presence of the beloved, but her plume traces a web of transgressive activity in that she refuses to shift her tone in favor of adopting a

[19] MacArthur refers to Lacan's conception of metonymy, relating to desire and lack. See pp. 26-7. She provides her definition for the use of the term metonymy on p. 33.

spiritual discourse. As she recollects the past, her missive contains other intertextual echoes reminiscent of the first part of the *Historia*. She praises Abelard's talents as a composer of seductive love songs written for her while they were living under Fulbert's roof. She refers to his fame in Paris as both a philosopher and a lyrical composer. She claims that the songs were so well-known that every woman in Paris envied her place in Abelard's bed:

> Quelle femme mariée, quelle jeune fille, ne te désirait en ton absence, ne brûlait quand tu étais là? Quelle reine, quelle grande dame, n'a pas envié mes joies et mon lit? (Letter I, 129)

Unfortunately, none of these songs have ever survived to disclose this more passionate aspect of Abelard as a lover, but Heloise elaborates on this seductive quality and emphasizes that it was very rare for a philosopher to possess such versatile talents. His songs, she insists, made her name famous all across the land, and celebrated their great love. Even though there is no record of these love songs, scholars are fortunate to possess samples of Abelard's lamentations, written in poetic form, and Zumthor has published the first translation of this text which includes a "plainte amoureuse" in which Abelard appears to address himself to Heloise.[20] This idea is supported by similarities with the love correspondence where he begs her to stop complaining (as it resurfaces in the third letter). But here the lyre replaces the spoken word, revealing Abelard's more artistic and sensitive side: "Plutôt que par hauts discours/ je lui

[20] See *Pierre Abélard Lamentations suivies de Histoire de mes malheurs et de la correspondence avec Héloïse* trans. Paul Zumthor (Paris: Babel, 1992). More recent research on the musical legacy of the couple has revealed a surprising discovery. David Wulstan maintains that Heloise also composed music, but her lyrics remain mysteriously missing. However, Wulstan confirms that Heloise composed liturgical dramas, including an Easter drama with a particular focus on the music in the "Song of Songs." See David Wulstan's article, "Heloise at Argenteuil and the Paraclete," *The Poetic and Musical Legacy of Heloise and Abelard: An Anthology of Essays by Various Authors*, eds. Marc Stewart and David Wulstan (Ottawa: The Institute of Medieval Music, 2003): 67-71.

parle avec ma lyre"/. He speaks of the cruelty of love and refers to its powerful force, "l'amour est vainqueur de tout/l'amour est maître de tout"/. But it is also possible that his lyre symbolizes the use of a female construct, and that, interestingly, he already appropriates a female voice. Indeed, to speak of desire in these songs, Abelard borrowed the persona of a woman in love not unlike many (male) troubadours who were later discovered to have impersonated females. Earnshaw and Burns have conducted in-depth studies on the phenomenon of men appropriating women's discourse in the genre of love songs.[21] As Burns pointed out, the troubadour's image of his lady often represented an idealized reflection of himself. The lady represented a state of moral perfection that the man aspired to, but was unable to attain. For a male poet, the erotic potential of women had a captivating and alluring quality. Through his idealized image of his lady, the troubadour acted out a fiction, projecting his own desire onto her.[22] Ultimately this rapport revealed a fragility, a possibly destabilizing, but also troubling aspect. As Burns describes it, the poet views himself as the passive and suffering one, destined to wait for the return of the lover. Once again, the Lady is reduced to a refraction of the troubadour's conception of her, and so is molded after the patriarchal perception of her role where she plays either the role of man's troublesome helpmate or the seductive temptress, the inheritor of the original sin. The male poet's technique of borrowing indicates a violation of feminine voice because it is altered and even distorted by the masculine dominating force. The misogynistic perception of women in the Middle Ages labeled the female as submissive, unable to resist a man's manipulation of his portrayal of her image. Burns argues that the Lady is thus obscured, virtually written out, as a

[21] See Doris Earnshaw's book, *The Female Voice in Medieval Romance Lyric* (New York: Peter Lang, 1988): 1-28. Also, Jane Burns' article, "The Man behind the Lacy in Troubadour Lyric," *Romance Notes* 25.3 (1985): 258-9.
[22] Burns 263-70.

result of the troubadour's infringement of her discourse, which in fact also allows him to express his so-called "feminine" traits.[23] Earnshaw stresses the appropriation of the "Other's" discourse, referring to the female persona, and applying Bakhtin's theory that language is inherently dialogic and thus reflects multiple voices.[24] But this use of borrowing from the Lady diminishes the significance of the female voice. She is nothing but a complement to the controlling force, the male poet. In some instances, the female voice is veiled, ostensibly anonymous in the works of some troubadours. Women become a mere tool for male composers, and thus, as already discussed in Abelard's handling of Heloise's version of the marriage story, fragmentation emerged as the result of their borrowing women's voices. Needless to say, appropriating the female persona tended to also contribute to gender blurrings. The male poet crossed the boundary, and in an unexpected way was in essence exploring his "otherness" or "femaleness." As a seductive composer of love songs, like the troubadours, Abelard (to come back to him), creates some confusion in gender distinctions, just as he does in the letter correspondence, when he projects himself onto his wife by executing a subtle, intricate manipulation of her epistolary technique. In those letters, the fact that Heloise stresses his versatile talents as a composer invites the reader to seek out the expression of his buried carnal desire for his lover. After all, the lyrics celebrated passion and the unveiling of fleshly pleasures, describing those long, sensuous afternoons spent under Fulbert's roof. This area of Abelard's female "otherness", exemplified by his esthetic gift for writing lyrics, will be considered on multiple levels in his subsequent replies to Heloise's epistles.

[23] Burns 268.
[24] Earnshaw 11-14.

Heloise's Devotion to Abelard

Heloise concludes her first letter to Abelard by repeating her demand that he answer her. She admits to having taken her vows only because it was his will, and she adds she would gladly follow him to the gates of hell. His presence is preeminent in her mind, and at the same time essential to sustain the movement and energy of desire so that the correspondence can remain open-ended: "je te conjure de me rendre ta présence, dans la mesure où cela t'est possible, en m'envoyant quelques mots de consolation" (Letter I, 134).

Heloise returns to the idea of consolation, adding that she needs inspiration to improve her spiritual devotion, a religious motivation that is clearly presented as an afterthought. Once again, she transgresses the laws of the cloister by developing the passionate aspect of her epistle to her beloved, and therefore de-emphasizing her need to grow in her faith. This reversal of Abelard's priorities will be important for her confession in her second letter. In writing of her love, Heloise allows herself to divulge her secrets from within the austere walls of the convent. This disclosure of her desire comes from deep within her consciousness. Once again, the spatial complexity of the inner self recalls Derrida's notion of the crypt in Fors where passion is equated with the "vault of desire," in an echo of the abbess's predicament. Heloise seeks, without any qualms, to gradually unveil the innermost secrets buried deep within the crypt-like structure of the Paraclete. But as she resurrects the remnants of her emotions, her concept of this "crypt" transgresses the traditional notion of death as explained by Derrida:

> [...] the cryptic place is also a sepulcher. The topography has taught us to take a certain non-place into consideration. The sepulchral function in turn can signify something other than simply death. A crypt, people believe, always hides something dead. (Derrida 78)

Heloise's crypt, the cloister, represents something other than death. It is through the description of her physical desire that Heloise expressively articulates her nostalgic loss, which is, in fact, resuscitated to live again in the present. Indeed, the secret that she conceals in her cell is strikingly incongruous to the ashes that one would expect to find in the interior of a crypt. The third letter in the sequence of the correspondence, actually Heloise's second reply to Abelard, will continue to unveil other shocking revelations. But the tone wanes in the reply to her epistle as Abelard attempts to curb her disruptive rhetoric.

Letter 2: Abelard's "Brotherly" Epistle

As Abelard addresses his own letter to "Heloise, his sister in Christ, from Abelard her "brother," he immediately shows signs of reading selectively and formulating his own response to her demand of a letter of consolation. As he reaffirms his faith in Heloise as a wise woman of God, he sets the tone of the whole letter. He intends to limit himself to religious matters, attempting to filter out extraneous, personal, and therefore potentially dangerous language for a couple who has taken vows to a life devoted to God. However, in following this spiritual course, he is also breaching the rules of the epistolary exchange as he shifts to a monologue, and completely disregards the "I"/"you" dialectic, seminal to all letters. There will be no real exchange or dialogue here, in an illustration of Abelard's evident egocentric tendencies. His "conversation" consists mainly of a monologue with himself. He responds to Heloise's plea of restoring contact, but strictly on a spiritual level. When he mentions that he will send the Paraclete a psaultier, critics all agree that this offering is rather odd because it is highly unlikely that a convent would not have one or even more than one. Perhaps this religious object simply provides a false pretense for Abelard to ask a favor of Heloise and her nuns. Once again, the overall tone and theme of this epistle will reveal self-serving motivations that are completely unrelated to rekindling intimate memories of love. Specifically, Abelard pleads for the nuns' prayers as a collective group, and he asks that his body be buried at the Paraclete. When he also quotes the Bible in order to emphasize the importance of women's role in the resurrection of Christ, the reader recalls that Abelard is now a eunuch at St. Gildas where he fears for his life, and has even survived numerous attempts by the monks to kill him. Abelard can't be admitted into the house of God because of his impure state, and therefore needs the prayers of the nuns to acquire God's grace after his eventual demise. But, on a symbolic level, this plea is interesting because it demonstrates quite clearly a wish to enter into the sacred territory occupied by the women. Their prayers are so fundamentally important that, in a way, he wishes he could slip into the nun's religious habit to more readily receive the redemption of God. In Abelard's time, nuns and monks dressed in a fairly similar fashion. Both were garbed in dark, long woolen robes, which lends itself well to the idea of gender blurring already present in the eunuch who contains androgynous characteristics of maleness and female "otherness."[25] Once again, the desire to gain admittance into a feminized, privileged, haven is indicative of Abelard's inner longing to borrow a female construct. As Bynum's work on gender and religion in the Middle Ages has shown, God was described at that time in male and female terms. In fact, Christ was often represented as "female" with an emphasis on his nurturing, self-sacrificing, and humanistic characteristics.[26] In order to achieve spiritual advancement in the Church, ecclesiastical males embraced female images of themselves, and thus reversed or exchanged genders. Linked to this idea is Abelard's

---

[25] See Marjorie Garber's *Vested Interests: Cross-Dressing & Cultural Anxiety* (New York: Harper): 212-219. Here, Garber provides details on how it is that religious garments could easily facilitate transvestism, as shown in the Middle Ages.

[26] Bynum, *Fragmentation and Redemption* 157-67.

unconscious wish to project himself on the gender of the "other's" body, as demonstrated by the fact that the entire letter is devoted to the praise of the nun's special and unique role in the house of God. In elaborating on this aspect, Abelard is writing out his desire to exchange places with the nuns in order to get closer to God. To assure this goal, he even asks Heloise to accept him on her land, and above all to pray for him every day. This attempt to gain access to the sacred territory recalls a seminal aspect of Miller's theory of "pseudo-feminocentrism." In this instance, male writers take over the "Other's" place and thus engage in impersonating women by a reversal of traditional roles. Usually, the woman is the one who, for a number of reasons, waits on the man. But, in this text, Abelard presents himself as waiting to see if Heloise will allow him to be buried at the Paraclete, and also if she will devote herself to praying for him. This demand casts him in the feminized, "waiting" role, as quoted by Miller who discussed this specific type of role reversal using Roland Barthes's *A Lover's Discourse: Fragments*:

> Woman gives form to absence, elaborates its fiction, for she has the time for it; she weaves and she sings: the Spinners, the Weaving songs communicate both immobility [...] It follows that every man who speaks the absence of the other, declares himself as belonging to the feminine: the man who waits and suffers from waiting is miraculously feminized. (Miller 55)

Although Abelard is not lamenting the absence of his lost passion with Heloise, he is clearly thrust into a subservient position because he is the one waiting. He heightens the pathos and the drama with his description of the crying nuns preparing for the resurrection of Christ and concludes the epistle by adding that the nuns received a visit by an angel announcing the second coming. On a symbolic level, this angel also typifies the androgynous nature of Abelard, given his present state as a eunuch. The angel fuses the dual images of masculine power and feminine grace into an ambiguous form. As Jean Libis's work has shown, androgyny equates the angel with the feminized side of man as well as with an emblem of divine law, but mainly the angel represents the hopes of restoring the reunion of man's original state of wholeness.[27] Abelard confirms this by saying: "je t'en prie, souvenez-vous de moi dans le Christ" (146), a remark which anticipates the theme that he will develop in his final letter of conversion, to Heloise. Before his reunion with his wife in heaven, it is his deepest desire that Heloise's nuns pray and mourn for him at the time of his death in order to enable him to receive the grace of God. Throughout the letter, Abelard 's repeated emphasis on the nuns' devotions seems, once again, to express a hidden desire to exchange monastic attire with the sisters. The outward appearance of gender confusion could easily be created, given, as we said above, that the shapeless frock adorning the body obscured clear distinctions between the sexes. As Marjorie Garber posits:

> Ecclesiastical or religious dress is particularly fascinating because of the ways in which particular items [...] the word "frock" began as a term for monk's garment, of clothing have tended to cross over gender lines and has only recently become a word for female as opposed to male attire.[28]

The religious garment or "frock" worn by monks and nuns in the twelfth century did tend to resemble a unisex uniform: thus, clothing allowed for the interchangeability of gender (as is also affirmed by Garber), a theory that will resurface later when Abelard's narrative transvestism is discussed.

Letter 3: Unforgettable Desire

Heloise prefaces her second letter by directing her attention to the salutation of Abelard's previous missive. She claims that Abelard violates the epistolary rules of the time by placing her

[27] Jean Libis, *Le Mythe de l'androgyne* (Paris: Berg, 1980) : 86-91.
[28] Garber 212.

name before his own. The reason he reversed the order was most likely linked to Christian doctrine regarding eunuchs as impure beings in the house of God. But on a symbolic level, Abelard's modification of the salutation also indicated that the couple had exchanged places in the hierarchy of the Church. Abelard now presents himself as the "feminized" victim, who suffers constant torment by his fellow monks. In the eyes of God, Heloise is clearly in the more favorable and prestigious position. After these brief remarks on form, she then enters directly into the main content of his letter, commenting from a collective point of view, returning to "us," the nuns of the Paraclete. She assures Abelard that, even after his eventual death, he will remain unforgettable to their community; the contemplation of his demise creates an overwhelming desire to follow him. Heloise finally concludes this subject by asking Abelard not to think of his own mortality. But, gradually, she shifts from us, her sisters, to "I" once again, prefiguring the main part of her second epistle. On the structural level, the transition from the collective is effected by a quote from Lucan's *Pharsalia,* which conveys the idea that man hopes his final moment will come quickly, so as to assuage his fears of death. But after this reference to man in general, Heloise launches into a monologue returning to her personal loss, which reveals an intertextual echo of Ovid's discourse of the abandoned woman. As already noted, the Ovidian heroine typically laments the unbearable pain of her solitude and separation, bereft of her lover's presence. Heloise increases the pathos of this misery by adding that God was cruel to her, and Fortune worked against her. The letter allows her to record the desire of her tormented body and of an unrelenting desire that borders on madness:

> O fortune infortunée! La destinée a épuisé contre moi ses traits meurtriers, au point qu'il ne lui en reste plus pour frapper ailleurs. Elle a vidé sur moi son carquois, et nul autre n'a plus à craindre ses assauts. Lui fût-il demeuré une seule flèche, qu'elle eût plutôt cherché sur moi où faire une nouvelle blessure. (Letter 3, 151)

This passage marks the return to the use of the double-voiced discourse. The use of military or martyr terminology, the idea of arrows plunging into her body, deepening her wounds, also echoes Abelard's mutilation. Heloise affirms the theory that the castration is indeed double, as shown by her strong poetic rendering of the loss inflicted on her own body and soul. The violent image of the arrows piercing her flesh parallels Lacanian theory regarding the abrupt separation from the desired "Other," after which the subject is plagued by the obsessive need to reestablish contact with the absent object of desire. She continues to extrapolate on the injustice of her grief and then enters into a diatribe on adultery as she returns to the period where she and Abelard lived under Fulbert's roof. However, she now refers to their illicit love as debauchery, ironically punished by God after the marriage only.

> Mais du jour où nous avons légitimé ces plaisirs illégitimes et couvert de la dignité conjugale la honte de nos fornications, la colère du Seigneur s'est lourdement abbattue sur nous. Notre lit de souillure ne l'avait pas émue: elle se déchaîna quand nous l'eûmes purifié. (Letter 3, 152)

This passage seems out of character for Heloise, and if, as Charrier supports, Abelard reworded her letters, this letter may have indeed been altered by him. The use of the word fornication is most contradictory for her, and the phrase "notre lit de souillure" is also striking because she has never suggested previously, or even in the context of this specific missive, that she regrets or views her sensuality as sinful. It is possible that Abelard inserted these words to reinforce his goal in writing to her. He wanted to succeed in converting her desire to God's service. The choice of such words as fornication and illegitimate points to the condemnation of lusty appetites in favor of following the only path: the one leading to God's love and thus the renunciation of Heloise's sexuality. This argument is developed in the next part of her letter where she launches into a monologue emphasizing the theme of woman as sinner, beckoning man into temptation and contributing to his eventual downfall. It is very possible that Abelard also edited this part to insist on the importance of salvation. Here, Heloise seems to be simply repeating the accepted discourse of the Middle Ages, which depicted women as the lustier sex who lead men astray.[29] This notion was predicated on the belief that women were biologically predisposed to a more sexual temperament. She even goes on to acknowledge that women can only lure men to inevitable ruin, and interestingly, this misogynistic perception reappears in Zumthor's 1992 edition of the correspondence that includes Abelard's *Lamentations.* His "Plainte d'Israël sur Samson" seems indeed intertextually related to Heloise's second letter when he places the blame on Dalila for bringing about Samson's destruction. "Et toi, Dalila/ que dis-tu de ce crime impie/ dont tu fus cause? (67). He then expands the negative image of Dalila to women in general: "la femme fut créée/ pour notre destruction!/" (69). Indeed, "Heloise's" letter cites various famous women such as Eve, the temptress and once again, Dalila, who are all guilty of destroying great men:

> Déjà la première femme, dans le jardin d'Eden, séduisit le premier homme: créée par le Seigneur pour lui porter assistance, elle fut sa perte. Samson, fort entre les forts, homme de Dieu dont un ange avait annoncé la naissance, fut vaincu par la seule Dalila, qui le trahit le livra, le priva de la vue, et le réduisit à une telle détresse qu'il préféra s'écraser lui-même avec ses ennemis, sous les ruines du temple. (Letter 3, 154)

This part of the epistle culminates in a confession by Heloise, which seems also rather suspect, especially because she never shows elsewhere any indication of converting:

---

[29] See Bloch's *Medieval Misogyny and the Invention of Romantic Love,* especially pp. 17-35. In his discussion, Bloch provides background on various medieval misogynistic conceptions of "woman." For instance, the image of "woman" as sinner and the more carnal sex compared to males.

> Longtemps asservie aux voluptés charnelles, j'ai mérité ce que je subis aujourd'hui; ma souffrance est la juste conséquence de mes fautes passées. Rien ne finit mal, qui n'ait été mauvais dès le début. (Letter 3, 155)

But was her perception of their relationship really rooted in sin, or is this a case of Abelard's reworking her letter to realign her rhetoric with his conversion goal? Underlying the issue of his editing, there is another aspect that is rather curious. Because of its tone, this letter functions as an ode to Heloise's lost love; religious rhetoric is interwoven with the language of desire and abandonment. But the question remains that if Abelard did indeed retouch the text, why didn't he cut out more of her dialogue on the erotic longings plaguing her at the Paraclete? To apply Bakhtin's theory of double-voiced discourse, is it implausible to suggest that, here, Heloise is used, once again, but this time to exteriorize Abelard's clandestine passion onto the paper? The question of gender blurring reappears in this letter. In allowing her to write about her desire, Abelard could be projecting his passion through her. Hiding beneath the ambiguous monastic garment, Abelard could be making the attempt to change gowns with her, symbolically, in order to speak of the illicit yearnings that cannot be expressed when he is dressed as a monk. As Garber has shown in a previously cited passage referring to cross-dressing, the word "frock" was originally associated with monks, but later came to be associated with womanly attire, she also adds that priests were often perceived as feminized, and Bynum confirms that it was common for monks in the Middle Ages to think of their souls as feminine, and to identify themselves with the bride of Christ.[30] Bernard de Clairvaux, ironically, one of the teachers with whom Abelard studied in Paris, even went so far as to call himself a woman. These conceptions apply even better to Abelard given his state of eunuchism, and the uncertainty of the gender construct car-

[30] Bynum 160-173.

ries over into the rest of "Heloise's" letter as it shifts from the idea of sin to penance, and emphasizes the inner torture that threatens to tear her own soul from her body.

The Erotics of the Cell

Gradually, Heloise confesses that she is still haunted by memories of those moments spent together at her home in Paris. She believes she should suffer in order to share the burden of pain that Abelard was forced to bear after his mutilation. But she is caught in the middle of a contradictory situation:

> Peut-on dire que l'on fait pénitence, quelle que soit la mortification que l'on impose au corps, quand l'âme conserve le goût du péché et brûle de ses anciens désirs? (Letter 3, 156)

Underlying the ideas of sin and penance is the repeated torture of her physical desires. Heloise cannot forget the past. Her love will not allow her to move on to the acceptance and transition to the true devotion to her faith. The passage above prefigures the core of her letter in which she completely transgresses the confines of her imprisonment by transforming her solitude into an intimate confession of her true feelings towards Abelard, hoping perhaps to seduce him by the force of her words:

> Les plaisirs amoureux qu'ensemble nous avons goûtés ont pour moi tant de douceur que je ne parviens pas à les détester, ni même à les chasser de mon souvenir. Où que je me tourne, ils se présentent à mes yeux et éveillent mes désirs. Leur illusion n'épargne pas mon sommeil. Au cours même des solennités de la messe, où la prière devrait être plus pure encore, des images obscènes assaillent ma pauvre âme et l'occupent bien plus que l'office. Loin de gémir des fautes que j'ai commises, je pense en soupirant à celles que je ne peux plus commettre. Nos gestes ne sont pas seuls restés gravés profondément, avec ton image, dans mon souvenir; mais les lieux, les heures qui en furent témoins, au point que je m'y retrouve avec toi, répétant ces gestes, et ne trouve pas même de repos dans mon lit. Parfois, les mouvements de mon corps trahissent les pensées de mon âme, des mots révélateurs m'échappent. (Letter 3, 157-8)

Devastated by this lust, Heloise speaks freely of her body's desire. Even in sleep and during prayer, she is tormented by unholy thoughts of carnal pleasures. To live within the cloister is to suffer, deprived of the sensual delights she once shared with Abelard. The powerful memory of the flesh transgresses her monastic vows, and at the same time this inner conflict creates a dual discourse. Concealed under her imprisoning frock, she allows herself to remember what she has lost, while on the outside she attempts to play out the role of the religious abbess devoted to her spiritual life. Peggy Kamuf interprets this confession as the main reason why Heloise fails to move in the direction of spiritual conversion. Her letter allows her to unburden the weight of this unbearable situation, but, at the same time what she admits constitutes a subversive dialogue. Desire is then viewed as a destabilizing force threatening to undo and dismantle the structure of the monastic order. The spartan nun's cell transforms itself into an intimate feminine space, charged with sensuality, in which Heloise launches a final attempt to conjure up Abelard's image while hoping to coax him into a more personal exchange in his next epistle. As Kamuf says regarding the transgressive power of Heloise's discourse:

> There is no sanctuary, no structure which can lock out the invasion of erotic forms, erotic significance. Neither the symbolic activity of the Mass nor the meaningless inactivity of sleep can function to contain or convert the repetition of the erotic scene. (Kamuf 25)

Through the searing expression of her desires, Heloise wishes to draw Abelard out, bringing him back within her field of reach. In order to pull him into her intricately spun web of seduction, she reworks the intertext of the past by supplying details of their amorous encounters:

> Je brûle au contraire de toutes les flammes qu'attisent en moi les ardeurs de la chair, celles d'une jeunesse encore trop sensible au plaisir, et l'expérience des plus délicieuses voluptés. Leurs morsures me

> sont d'autant plus cruelles que plus faible est la nature qui leur est livrée. (Letter 3, 158-9)

Once again, the text shows evidence of the effect of the castration on her as she laments the destruction of her own self, as a result of Abelard's mutilation. Heloise's suffering is dramatized by the metaphor of fire, the flames consuming her body and soul, but the most disturbing result of the castration is the haunting yearning to rekindle what she had before. In succumbing to this persistent obsession, Heloise admits her weakness. This aspect of the letter is significantly developed and anticipates the next phase of her avowal regarding her hypocrisy:

> On me juge pieuse, certes; mais, de nos jours, la religion n'est plus, pour une grande part, qu'hypocrisie, et l'on fait une réputation de sainteté à qui ne heurte point les préjugés du monde. (Letter 3, 159)

Heloise claims that under her saintly appearance, she is undeserving of her pious reputation because her mind is preoccupied by the contemplation of her body's desires, but the idea of hypocrisy is also a further illustration of her dialogic discourse. Within one body and soul, she is engaging in passionate conversation with Abelard, and, at the same time, she maintains a religious dialogue by speaking to Abelard through the conventional channels of spiritual direction. She sustains a dialogic conversation in order to articulate multiple voices. As Bakhtin has pointed out, novels using pathos are often double-voiced:

> A discourse of pathos may also be conditional, and may even be doubled, like double-voiced discourse. In the novel it is precisely as double-voiced that pathos almost inevitably occurs; [...] Novelistic pathos does not have discourses that belong to it alone—it must borrow the discourses of others.[31]

---

[31] Mikhail Bakhtin, *The Dialogic Imagination*, trans. Michael Holquist (Austin: University of Texas Press, 1981): 394.

Pathos never stands alone; it absorbs fragments of other types of discourse. Heloise's discourse of the abandoned woman, suffering in the absence of her beloved, inscribes pathos between the spaces and gaps of the letter. Following the passage on her hypocrisy, she returns to retelling her own version of their story, and recalls the acceptance of her vows as having altered the course of her life:

> C'est sur ton ordre que j'ai pris l'habit, non par vocation divine. Vois donc quelle vie infortunée je mène, misérable entre toutes, traînant un sacrifice sans valeur et sans espoir de récompense future! Ma dissimulation t'a longtemps trompé, comme tout le monde, et tu nommais piété mon hypocrisie. (Letter 3, 160)

The key term in this passage is dissimulation, which reinforces the existence of a double-voiced discourse. Under her habit, Heloise is now admitting that she entertains other thoughts, unrelated to her position in the Church. Garber's discussion of Catholicism and "the erotics of the cloth" applies well to Heloise's predicament. As Garber explains, the veiling of a woman was perceived as a boundary between two opposed worlds.[32] But here the exterior represses desire, whereas concealed beneath the veil, lurk unbridled erotic longings. Mary Ann Doane's psychoanalytic work on veiled desire reaffirms Garber's idea and points out the erotic implications of veiling because hidden under the opaque fabric lies the buried secret of feminine seduction.[33] Doane also views the veil as a dangerous mark of duplicity or deception. Sexual identity is never clearly visible because of the blocked gaze, and so gender distinction becomes precarious. Adding to the concealing significance of the veil, Garber considers the cowl as another part of the vestimentary code of sexual ambiguity. She draws a parallel be-

---

[32] Garber 217-20.

[33] See Mary Ann Doane's "Veiling over Desire: Close-ups of the Woman," *Feminism and Psychoanalysis,* eds. Richard Feldstein and Judith Roof. (Ithaca & London: Cornell UP, 1989): 109-11. Doane offers a fascinating psychoanalytic analysis of veiling from a feminist perspective.

tween nuns and monks by establishing the cowl as borderline garb promoting "the cover-up" of gender crossing. As mentioned earlier, the dark, shapeless garment lends itself well to travesty for monks, but Garber also explains that the cowl is a "figure for repetition as well as for substitution and displacement." (219): "Underneath the cowl and flowing robes the body of the celibate itself is an object of suspicion" (Garber 220).

Eve Sedgwick's commentary on veils echoes Garber in that she associates them with doubleness, and with strong erotic symbolic implications. She accentuates the sexual dimension of covered flesh:

> The veil that conceals and inhibits sexuality comes by the same gesture to represent it, both as a metonym of the thing covered and as a metaphor for the system of prohibitions by which sexual desire is enhanced and specified.[34]

Heloise's veiled "nun's" body conceals her other skin: the vibrant flesh of a young woman unable to bury the memories of lost pleasures. But in writing her confession of this dissimulation, Heloise is perhaps speaking for the two lovers. As a eunuch, Abelard crossed over towards his "feminine" side, and if he did indeed alter Heloise's letters, it is possible, as Nouvet suggests, that he even used Heloise's body as a substitution for his fragmented and impure body in order to reach immortality. In front of God, Heloise must pray, an opportunity Abelard doesn't have as a eunuch. Since mutilated beings were not allowed to show themselves in God's presence, Abelard seeks refuge within the feminine body, seeing his wife as a logical substitute for his flawed body. As Nouvet postulates, Heloise is thus looked upon as an extension of her husband:

> La "femme" ne désignant guère que la chair de l'homme, elle peut donc lui tenir lieu de corps quand le sien lui fait défaut. Dans le corps d'Héloïse, Abélard est ainsi légitimé à voir un corps de substi-

[34] Eve Sedgwick, "The Character in the Veil: Imagery of the Surface in the Gothic Novel," *PMLA* 96.2 (1981): 256.

> tution à sacrifier à la place de son propre corps devenu insacrifiable. A travers elle, il peut encore se sacrifier.[35]

However, through the female body, Abelard may also be projecting his passion into Heloise's discourse, veiled behind her, borrowing her pen to really verbalize "their" nostalgic need to restore sensual communication. Because women were believed to be weaker, naturally predisposed to lust, it would be logical that in attempting to exteriorize his "forbidden desires," Abelard would resort to the technique of borrowing Heloise's voice and using her body as a substitute to gain access to God. In many ways, Abelard himself is veiled, as will be further discussed now.

Veiling the Body-Masking Desire

Before dealing with the question of the function of the veil in the love correspondence, it is essential to retrace briefly some theories on veils as feminine body concealment. In *The Gay Science*, Friedrich Nietzsche established a comparison between the veil and the sail. According to him, woman is like a sail silently gliding, gracefully through the water. Seminal to his hypothesis is the notion of "woman" representing the unattainable:

> The magic and powerful effect of women is, in philosophical language, action at a distance, action in distance; but this requires first of all and above-all-distance.[36]

The main idea emphasized here is that "woman" is always out of man's reach, somewhere beyond the grasp of his capabilities. From Nietzsche's conception of distance, Derrida responded and developed his own theory, and several of his ideas are linked to dissimulation, just as in the love letters. Derrida elab-

[35] Claire Nouvet, "La Castration d'Abélard: impasse et substitution," *Poétique* 83 (1990) : 273.
[36] Frederich Nietzsche, *The Gay Science*, trans. Walter Kaufmann (New York: Random House, 1974): 124.

orates on Nietzsche's idea of distance. "A Woman seduces from a distance. In fact, distance is the very element of her power."[37] Similarly, through the distance of her letters, and by the retelling and reliving of her desire, Heloise hopes to seduce Abelard, from afar, by writing in a "mirror-like" style, expressing his reawakening passion.

Derrida also defines the veil as characteristic of the image of woman as a "dissimulatress" and as an artist. Indeed, Heloise, the artist, possesses a literary talent that may very well mark the emergence of a woman's discourse grounded in the epistolary genre, following in the tradition of Ovid's heroines. As a "dissimulatress," she deftly manipulates her masked discourse under the guise of a religious exterior, but the real purpose of her epistolary exchange with her husband is to entice him into a personal dialogue. In *Spurs,* Derrida stresses the affirmative power of "woman" as originating from her art of dissimulation.[38] In maintaining her discourse of desire, Heloise puts into practice this notion. In essence, she is affirming and reaffirming over and over again the importance of not forgetting the powerful force of love raging within her. But as mentioned earlier regarding Garber's theory on religious attire and gender blurring, Derrida also points out that dissimulation in women also allows for mask switching. He associates veiling with dismantling and undoing so that there is a constant alternating, bipolar movement maintained between unveiling and dissimulation, characteristic of the doubleness that has been mentioned throughout this epistle. This idea is also linked to the gender confusion of the monk behind the cowl and the nun behind the veil. This particular vestimentary code functions like a curtain obscuring sexual distinction, and the inability to see clearly beneath the opaque surface of the fabric also recalls Lacan's

---

[37] Jacques Derrida, *Spurs: Nietzsche's Styles*, trans. Barbara Harlow (Chicago & London: Chicago UP, 1985): 49.
[38] Derrida 47-54.

theory on sexual difference and the phallus. Specifically, he explains in "The Significance of the Phallus" that the "master signifier" can only do its work when veiled. In the text, Abelard and a eunuch and as a monk is cast into a state of ambiguous gender identification. Related to this question of gender instability, Lacan also posits that the veiled attribute of the phallus can also be marked in the feminine.[39] Inscribed within his theory of desire is the idea that women want to "have" what they "lack," and to obtain it, they must masquerade as the phallus. Garber interprets this conception as the third term closely associated with transvestites. Specifically, she says that "having" and "lacking" can both be identified with "seeming." She links this theory to the situation of the cross-dresser. Abelard, as a cross-dresser, disguised beneath the monastic frock, slips into the dress of his "feminized " body image; his lack of "having" is protected by the mysterious, loose garment that masks the secret of his "otherness." According to Garber, the transvestite who enjoys adorning himself in feminine attire is defined as "a powerful agent of destabilization" in the social organization of gender identities.[40] Abelard's eunuchism seems to reflect these various theories concerning gender blurring and instability. Once the body is draped behind the window dressing of the religious frock and cowl, he is free to enter into the travesty of exchanging identities.

Letter Three is thus quite sensually charged, and Heloise will conclude it by modifying its tone slightly. She returns to her plea that Abelard should help her so that she might aspire to a better spiritual life, but she remains honest in adding that she is not purged of her desire. Thus, she still sustains the double-voiced discourse. She begs Abelard to stop praising her and regarding her as a pious, superior being in the eyes of God. In

---

[39] See Mitchell & Rose's interpretation of Lacan's meaning of the phallus on pages 74-85. Their analysis on p. 82. is particularly insightful.
[40] Garber 26-9.

her heart, she does not share his adulation or exalted admiration of her spiritual growth. All that she hopes for is that God will reserve for her a little corner of heaven where she might then find peace, or perhaps be free to pursue her "other," more passionate discourse.

Letter 4: We Are One in God

Abelard begins this final letter by responding to Heloise's remarks concerning his decision to place her name before his in the last exchange. He argues that his salutation is appropriate because she is his superior in the eyes of God. He clarifies the significance of the word superior, referring to her position as Christ's bride, and the fact that he now addresses Heloise as Christ's wife prefigures the core of this letter. His goal is only to persuade Heloise to accept her conversion and redefinition of her role in their marriage as his sister in Christ. Strangely, however, to buttress his arguments, Abelard embarks on an implicit comparison of Heloise with the Ethiopian bride, from the Song of Songs. He describes the exotic bride as "black on the outside" but "lovely on the inside":

> L'Ethiopienne a la peau noire et paraît, extérieurement, moins belle que les autres femmes. Mais intérieurement, loin de leur être inférieure, elle les dépasse en blancheur et en éclat: ainsi par les os, par les dents. La blancheur de ses dents est vantée par l'époux lui-même, lorsqu'il déclare: "Ses dents sont plus blanches que le lait." Noire au-dehors, belle au-dedans (Letter 4, 168)

The passage has multiple implications (including racist ones) but mainly a very strong erotic presence. The black bride functions as a metaphor on two levels. On the one hand, since Abelard selects the image of the black bride from the Song of Songs, and thus from one of the most sensual love songs ever, may this not reflect his own secret, erotic longings, or recall memories of the woman he once loved? On the other hand, the Ethiopian bride is a spiritual metaphor representing the change in Heloise's and Abelard's respective roles in the church. Kamuf interprets Abelard as the guard at the entrance of Christ's bedroom whose task is to present the bride to the Savior.[41] The Ethiopian bride reflects the transformation of their status. As a eunuch, Abelard can only serve God by ushering in the bride, Heloise, to His chambers, so the apparent purpose of the epistle is to convince her of this spiritual reality in accepting her position as Christ's bride. But even though he tries to persuade her of his religious intention, his argument is nevertheless problematic and ambiguous. The barely veiled sensuality of the image of the black bride sharing His chambers is a textual strategy that allows Abelard to speak of his own desire. Hiding behind the Ethiopian bride, he speaks to Heloise through her body. The symbolism of the king' s bed may be read as Abelard's secret wish to project himself into the spiritual scene, and to exchange places with Christ in order to partake of the passion. But the closed chamber also provides him with a cover to conceal his desire. Indeed, the multi-faceted metaphor of the black bride allows Abelard to manipulate two different discourses. First, he reverses the notions of public and private space, seminal to his discourse on Christ's bedroom; then, he can mimic Heloise's rhetoric of intimacy. The Christian idea of spiritual love replaces the personal interpretation of desire, and, ultimately, Heloise's sensual nature must undergo a process of conversion in order to translate this emotion into divine love. Kamuf analyzed the black bride analogy in depth:

> Specifically, the analogy of the black bride replies already to what Heloise has written of her inescapable desire and consequent hypocrisy. In effect, Abelard reinscribes that desire and its force of contradiction in a mode which converts term for term the portrait Heloise sketches of herself. (Kamuf 29)

For Kamuf, Abelard's desire is cleverly shrouded beneath the figure of the black bride. In the letter, Abelard explains that the

---

[41] Kamuf 28-32.

black exterior of the Ethiopian bride is a result of her tribulations in life; however, her interior reveals startlingly white bones indicative of her radiant beauty. If Abelard's own clandestine desire, as Kamuf affirms, is buried deep within the black folds of the bride's garment, he is once again attempting to borrow the female body in order to disclose his own "unspeakable" and shameful passion. He can identify with the black exterior symbolizing his misfortunes as a result of his past sins described in the *Historia*. But his ultimate goal is to reach the "other" side, which is represented by the inner beauty of the bride's purity. Once again, this attribute is also marked in the feminine, and so in aspiring to this spiritual goal, Abelard seems to glide discreetly under the woman's skin. The white image represents the divine and sanctified female body, which he greatly admires in contrast to his flawed, mutilated body image. Above all, Abelard devotes his letter to converting Heloise's transgressive desire, which is a deliberate attempt to destroy her hope of restoring his presence through the epistolary pact. In order to succeed, he must see to it that she reformulates her thinking so as to shift intimate passion, identified with Abelard, towards the spiritual domain, but ambiguously described as God's bedroom. Kamuf adds that Abelard's conversion strategy constitutes an attempt to stabilize desire, ultimately achieved by the redirection of these feelings. Ironically, Abelard as a castrated monk is, in a subtle way, also reinstating patriarchal law and recasting himself in the master role by seeing to it that Heloise curbs her desire. He goes on to remind Heloise that she must not continue to speak of their entry into religion. At this point, he anchors his rhetoric solidly in the present, whereas Heloise's style always reveals a tendency to slip into her nostalgic yearnings of the past. This temporal disparity underlines the fundamental gap in their respective styles. Abelard writes always in the present or the future because he is concerned with his destiny, but Heloise, too miserable, and undevoted to her faith, is not concerned with the present or the future because her ties to life are always rooted in the past. Consequently, she cannot sever herself from her role as a wife in order to embrace her new role as the bride of Christ. However, Abelard employs the persuasive technique of repetition, pleading with her to forget him and their past so as to redirect her discourse on the right path leading to Christ. Bluntly, he tells her that his presence will not be restored to her. He then proceeds to reverse word for word all of her descriptions of their unbridled passion into a condemnatory diatribe on the sins of the flesh. But as he does so, and in order to do so, he confesses quite strangely to a particularly lusty episode which took place at Argenteuil, after they had taken vows, in a corner of the church:

> Peu de temps après que nous eûmes reçu le sacrement, tu t'en souviens, tu étais alors retirée au couvent d'Argenteuil, je vins un jour te voir en secret: ma concupiscence, déchaînée, se satisfit avec toi dans un coin du réfectoire, faute d'un autre endroit où nous livrer à ces ébats. (Letter 4, 182)

This reference does not appear in Heloise's previous letters nor in the *Historia*. In fact, Abelard's confession of their scandalous encounter in the church surfaces for the first time, and this passage sheds new light on the nature of his passion, which, until now, has remained deeply sequestered, and not even alluded to in his other letters. In a sense, he admits that his desire did not fade following the castration. But the fact that he views his desire as contradictory to his Christian faith means that he must find another way to articulate his hidden passion. Once again, he chooses the tactic of appropriating feminine discourse: in the passage directly preceding the confession above, he uses two terms that appeared in Heloise's second letter:

> A quoi bon rappeler nos anciennes souillures, et les fornications dont nous fîmes précéder le mariage? La honteuse trahison dont je me

> rendis coupable envers ton oncle, dans la maison duquel je vivais en familier, lorsque, impudemment, je te séduisis? (Letter 4, 182)

Ironically, the words "fornication" and "souillure" were supposedly penned by Heloise in the previous letter to refer to her version of their amorous meetings that took place under Fulbert's roof. The resemblance might suggest that Abelard retouched her text so as to emphasize the wanton aspects of their relationship, prior to realigning the letter to a moral conversion goal, which is demonstrated by the omission of dangerous and subversive memories associated with their past. As noted above, Charrier strongly supports the theory that Abelard edited Heloise's text, and Gilson, Muckle and Dronke also discuss this controversy. All of them agree that evidence points only to the fact that there are expressions and stylistic tendencies in Heloise's letters that appear more characteristic of Abelard's style. And such is the case with the words "fornication" and "souillure." The condemnatory force behind these terms might in fact indicate Abelard's personal signature. He seems to place himself in a position to judge the moral implications of their unabandoned, carnal pleasures. This attitude also reflects the commonly accepted belief of the medieval period, when the term "fornication" carried a connotation of man's susceptibility to temptation by the lustier sex, "woman." By condemning Heloise's desire, Abelard simply repeats and thus subscribes to the misogynistic perception of women. But this passage also underlines the absence of love, on his part and thus focuses on Abelard's strategy of seduction, prior to the "fornication" episodes. He views their relationship as all the more scandalous because of the predominance of lust over love. As he proceeds to elaborate on their past sins, he denounces their mutual profanation of a church devoted to the Virgin Mary. He also launches into a discussion on divine justice, seeing himself as deserving castration. After his admission of guilt as a willful seducer, he then returns to Heloise's disguise as a nun when he had her carried off to his home in Brittany. He interprets her previous dissimulation as part of God's justice, and he begs her to stop mocking her position, and to accept her entry into the Church by not living a lie. He also advocates that she dedicate herself solely to serving the Savior. Abelard then thanks God for saving them, which anticipates his reprise of the consequences of his mutilation. In the *Historia*, he described the events leading up to the castration, but in this final letter the involuntary loss of his masculinity signifies a newly acquired spiritual cleansing that, in his opinion, is responsible for delivering them both from the temptations of the flesh.

> L'indigne trahison commise par ton oncle fut donc un effet de justice et de clémence souveraines: diminué de cette partie de mon corps qui était le siège des désirs voluptueux, la cause première de toute concupiscence, (Letter 4, 185)

Abelard regards his mutilation as a act of God, freeing him from the original "seat" of his lust. But it is curious that throughout this letter, he never once admits to loving Heloise, but instead employs the word lust over and over again. He seems to repent for his past conquest of her fragile will, adding that she was an easy victim in succumbing to his charms, and at the same time he attributes all of his past seductive tactics to biology and his debased sexual organ. The severing of this sinful organ enables him to serve God and purifies him from the debauchery of man's sensual appetites. For Kamuf, Abelard's references to the castration functions as a warning to Heloise. He wants her to understand that she must not write about her desire, and if she cannot abandon this subject in her letters, she must learn to dissimulate better:

> By directing Heloise "to refrain from speaking like this," Abelard enjoins her to dissimulate her desire more efficiently, so that it leaves no traces on the surface of things, no mark which belies the order to flight and pursuit, no sign which accuses the discrepancy within representation. (Kamuf 35)

And yet, Abelard's epistolary strategy also shows the signs of a double-voiced discourse, very much like Heloise's own. On the one hand, he glorifies the untainted aspect of his castration, but his praise of the mutilation is also an attempt to once again bring Heloise in line with his phallocentric law as he orders her to discontinue her amorous writing. In Abelard's mind (and body), the severing of his masculinity ensured the destruction of the passion. Heloise must also cut her ties with the past, thus "castrating" herself to look ahead to the present and future, or salvation. Again Abelard adopts the misogynistic discourse of the times, as he identifies Heloise as a member of the weaker sex, and thus naturally more susceptible to carnal thoughts. He implores Heloise to rise above this temptation by entering into God's service. However, this command is also underlined by a self-serving motivation. Indeed at that point, Abelard compares himself to Origen, another famous Christian heretic who mutilated himself in order to extinguish concupiscence once and for all. Origen castrated himself in a zealous moment, believing that the Lord reserved a special place for eunuchs in his kingdom. Admittedly Abelard's predicament differs from Origen's, whose very sin was self-mutilation, whereas Abelard was the "innocent" victim of someone else's action. But whether the eunuch is innocent or guilty, mutilation still results in his being labeled as an outcast. As Peter Brown noted, the medieval perception of Origen's eunuchism set him apart from society:

> What Origen may have sought, at that time, was something more deeply unsettling. The eunuch was notorious (and repulsive to many) because he had dared to shift the massive boundary between the sexes. He had opted out of being male.[42]

Brown adds that Origen was in essence "exiled" from any precise gender identification and, in this sense, Abelard's eunuchism strongly resembles Origen's. He comes to fully accept

[42] Peter Brown, *The Body and Society: Men, Women and Sexual Renunciation in Early Christianity* (New York: Columbia UP, 1988): 169.

his mutilation, and at the same time he crosses all gender boundaries, occupying a precarious position between both sexes. Yet, he finds a way to exploit his sexual ambiguity as another part of his argument to persuade Heloise to follow him on the path of divine grace. He assures her that God has not forgotten her:

> [...] il t'a désignée depuis toujours comme devant être sienne, en te marquant, toi Héloïse, de son propre nom d' Héloïm! Tandis que le démon s'efforçait de nous perdre tous deux par l'un seul de nous, sa clémence décréta que notre salut commun serait de même opéré par *un seul*. (Letter 4, 188)

Kamuf interprets the use of "Héloïm" as the name that God gave Heloise, thus designating her as belonging to the king.[43] Abelard forces her to see that her name is unique to God's special calling. Once again, Abelard attempts to deliberately convince her to accept her role as the Bride of Christ. She must answer to his call of "Héloïm," which marks her as His divine wife. The passage underlines Abelard's powerless state. Heloise clearly occupies the more advantageous position; she is closer to God than her alienated husband. But at the same time, Abelard disguises his true intention in singling out Heloise as the chosen nun. He aspires to her rank so as to gain his own salvation in heaven, again, he borrows Heloise's holy body to gain admittance to God's kingdom. Nouvet substantiates the relevance of this idea when she proposes that Abelard 's doctrine of conversion depends on his ability to substitute Heloise's body for his own, slipping inside Heloise's skin as part of his marital rights: "S'attachant à la femme, l'homme s'attache en fait à un autre "lui-même" à un "autre" corps qui n'est guère que l'extension du sien" (Nouvet 273).

In many ways, then, the feminine body functions here as an exterior envelope for Abelard. The female construct represents

[43] Kamuf 40.

an outer garment for the eunuch. Madeline Kahn's views on transvestism are related to Nouvet's theory on substitution:

> The transvestite engages in a kind of gender megalomania when he annexes every female "you" as part of "my own (male) me. He imitates a perceived other and thus makes her a part of himself.[44]

Kahn stresses the narcissistic tendencies of the transvestite's personality. She also elaborates on the double gendered being, as is the case with the eunuch. For religious reasons, mainly salvation, Abelard 's ambition is to adopt Heloise's female persona to assure his chances by also masking himself in her body. Curiously, his final argument uses their marriage as a last resort in his persuasive strategy to convince her to dedicate herself to God:

> Nous sommes un dans le Christ, une seule chair par la loi du mariage. Rien de ce qui te concerne ne me semble étranger. Or le Christ est à toi, qui es devenue son épouse. Et voici que tu m'as pour serviteur, comme je te l'ai dit plus haut, moi qu'autrefois tu tenais pour ton maître. Mais un amour spirituel plus que la crainte m'attache à ton service. (Letter 4, 197)

The passion is converted and redirected towards her other husband: Christ. Abelard renounces his previous role as Heloise's master, and thus recognizes his subservient position to her and to the Savior. However, the refrain of the idea that they are one in God, underlies his persuasive strategy and assures his own salvation. This idea is related to both the concepts of desire and androgyny.[45] According to Plato, the androgyne longs for a state of fulfillment (represented in the text as "une seule chair par la loi du mariage"). It is perhaps Abelard's hope that the couple will meet again as one in heaven, but in the context of spiritual love. Libis interprets the notion of one between lovers as a desire to revert to the original state preceding the initial

---

[44] Madeline Kahn, *Narrative Transvestism: Rhetoric & Gender in the Eighteenth Century English Novel* (Ithaca & London, Cornell UP, 1991): 16.
[45] See Libis, 142-145.

separation. He bases this theory on the myth of Aristophanes, and Nouvet reinforces this proposition in showing that Abelard searches for wholeness.[46] One can compare the ultimate state of the medieval lovers to the androgynous nature of angels, because these celestial figures surpass gender identification, and are associated with a third term defined as a spiritual or eternal sex. The androgynous angel is therefore delivered from corporeal desire and freed from gender constraints. Abelard alludes to the lovers' next meeting in eternity. His closing words in the fourth letter reiterate the notion that their salvation lies in Christ's hands and that he previously had begged Heloise to have his body brought back to the Paraclete to assure their final encounter: somewhere on the other side, in a corner of The kingdom, or her domain, where passion can once again bring them together.

As discussed in the analysis of the text, Heloise's love letters are one of the earliest literary examples of a woman's original love discourse in the history of French epistolary literature. A close reading of Heloise's letters reveals that she is manipulating a double discourse where her religious habit is only a cover-up for her "other" more passionate language addressed to her husband. The transgressive nature of Heloise, dressed as a nun, is, however, checked by Abelard's intervention in her letters. Abelard reworks Heloise's missives in order to curb her desire so that he can persuade her to accept God's calling as the bride of Christ. In forcing Heloise to speak a purely religious language that is not hers, Abelard demonstrates his intention to modify her original passionate style. This violation of a woman's claim to her text also reveals a longing to exchange genders with the stereotypical conception of the weak female. As a transvestite, Abelard borrows Heloise's words and her persona in order to find a voice to articulate his own "angelic" desire that is beyond gender. This pseudo-feminocentric behavior

[46] See Nouvet, "La Castration of Abelard." 276-78.

where the male author fragments the female epistle to further his own self-interest will also be seen in the next chapter, as we look at the early translations of Abelard and Heloise's love correspondence in the thirteenth century, and then at the first seventeenth-century version written in 1642 by François de Grenaille, in which Heloise's love letters are edited, co-authored and once again altered by a man who invades the space of the female textual creation.

3.

Grenaille's Eloize as "La Magdalene Française"

(Very) Preliminary Mappings: Jean de Meun's Translation of the Manuscript

Abelard and Heloise's correspondence in Latin was first translated into French by Jean de Meun around 1290. Leslie Brooks, who has studied the thirteenth-century translation in depth, observed that the prose version of the love letters most likely was written subsequent to the references to Heloise's arguments against marriage inserted in *Le Roman de la rose*. Brooks concurs with Charrier that Jean de Meun produced a clear and faithful translation, closely following the original Latin; a remarkable accomplishment considering that Jean de Meun was working with an incomplete manuscript.[1] In his translation, he included the *Historia,* Abelard and Heloise's four letters, the first missive in the letters of direction, and the epistle written by Abelard on the subject of women's monasteries. The text also contains a translation of Heloise's letter to her friend, Peter the Venerable. But Jean de Meun's translation does contain some differences from the original manuscript. As Brooks points out, every translation implies some original elements of creativity,

[1] See Leslie Brook's article, "Reiterated Quotations and Statements in Jeun de Meun's translation of the Abelard-Heloise Correspondence," *Zeitschrift fur Romanische Philogie* 105.1-2. (1989): 81-91.

emanating from the translator himself, and in Jean de Meun's case his text is renowned for the portrait of Heloise as "la saige Héloïse" or "la belle Héloïse." Above all, Jean de Meun is most celebrated for his version of Heloise's argument against marriage. It is important to emphasize that this initial effort did generate some interest. Jean de Meun's translation attracted the attention of one reader worth noting, François Villon, who later included references to Heloise in his work *Ballade des dames du temps jadis,* which contains stanzas where Heloise is described as "la très saige Héloïse." But, aside from Villon and Jean de Meun's works, Abelard's and Heloise's letters remained relatively unknown from the Middle ages through the Renaissance.[2] As Charrier posits, the medieval lovers' story was virtually forgotten until the dawn of the seventeenth century when new interest in the epistolary genre would announce the birth

[2] Recent scholarly interest has, however, generated around the discovery of a late medieval anonymous correspondence known as *Lettres des deux amants attribuées a Héloïse et Abélard* (Paris: Gallimard, 2005). These letters were copied around 1471 by Johannes de Vepria, a monk and talented scribe. The text contains a collection of over a hundred love letters and poems. In 1974, Ewald Könsgen published a Latin edition of this amorous correspondence between a gifted teacher and an adoring student. Könsgen believed there were many correlations between these letters and the epistolary characteristics of Heloise and Abelard's writing style, mainly the Ciceronian influence attributed to the woman's epistles. Constant Mews, John Ward and Neville Chiavaroli concur that they could have been written by Heloise and Abelard. Mews subscribes to the theory that they could very well have been penned by Heloise and Abelard during the time of their affair between 1116-1117. For a detailed analysis of this anonymous correspondence see Constant Mews' book, *The Lost Love Letters of Heloise and Abelard: Perceptions of Dialogue in Twelfth-Century France* (New York: Palgrave, 2001). Also, Mews' article, "Philosophical Themes in the Epistolae duorum amantium: The First Letters of Heloise and Abelard," 35-52. See as well John Ward and Neville Chiavaroli's article, "The Young Heloise and Latin Rhetoric: Some Preliminary Comments on the "Lost" Love Letters and Their Significance," *Listening to Heloise: The Voice of a Twelfth-Century Woman,* ed. Bonnie Wheeler. (New York: St. Martins Press, 2000): 53-119. Stephen Jaeger also agrees with these scholars. See his article, "Epistolae duorum amantium & the Ascription to Heloise & Abelard," *Voices in Dialogue: Reading Women in the Middle Ages,* eds. Linda Olson & Kathryn Kerby-Fulton. (Notre Dame: Notre Dame UP, 2005): 125-66.

of the legend of Heloise's and Abelard's saga of tragic love and suffering.

Early Developments in the Epistolary Genre

Abelard's and Heloise's original love correspondence in Latin was published for the first time in 1616 in France. It is intriguing that the first published edition became available to the public precisely at a time when the epistolary genre was expanding and attracting greater readership. As Bray notes, the development of the letter in the seventeenth century was directly related to the social system of interaction. Aristocrats were writing letters in order to construct a communication network that would allow them to establish contact with others. To assure their success in the art of penning letters, they relied on epistolary manuals that provided them with models for imitations. These "how to" texts like "Le Parfait Secrétaire" served as examples for writing letters of gratitude, consolation, condolence and compliments.[3] The aristocrats who followed these handbooks could also be assured of respecting the moral conventions established by the court and the salons. Letter writing was widely practiced as a "divertissement" that attracted many women as active participants in such famous salons as Madame de Rambouillet's "chambre bleue," or Mademoiselle de Scudéry's Saturday gatherings. Gradually, the letter was gaining importance and recognition as a genre. The missive was evolving; letters had originally been placed within heroic and pastoral novels, and, by, the end of the century, they emerged as their own entity, moving in the direction of the development of the epistolary novel. The genre was also strongly influenced by the revival and popularity of Ovid's *Heroides*, a text which was instrumental in establishing a predominant "feminine" genre grounded in the trope of the woman in love. But as Bray points

[3] Bray, *L'Art de la lettre* 10-15.

out, after Ovid, the other major sources of the epistolary genre in the seventeenth century were Abelard's and Heloise's letters, and the love letters of the Italian actress, Isabella Andreini.[4] Bray also established a parallel between Heloise's letters and the epistolary circumstances in the seventeenth century. According to him, Heloise practiced the art of writing letters of consolation, compliment and, most of all, love, which appealed to the seventeenth century reader's literary taste. In 1642, the earliest adaptation of Heloise's missives appeared in François de Grenaille's *Nouveau recueil de lettres des dames tant anciennes que modernes*, a collection of many famous, "real" women's love letters. What is interesting, however, is that both Andreini's and Heloise's letters were reworked in order to respect the code of "bienséance" dictating the proper moral decorum of the day. Grenaille's contribution is significant in that his was the first attempt to modify Heloise's text, and this literary project was then adopted by other translators who would follow later in the century with other revisions of Heloise's persona.

Grenaille's (Re)Structuring of Heloise's Letters

Grenaille's collection appeared in 1642, a time when the trope of feminine suffering and abandonment was popular. In fact, he was capitalizing on the wave of interest generated by Ovid's *Heroides*. In his introduction, Grenaille says that he translated these letters from Greek, Latin and Italian to give the women the recognition that they well deserved. He refers to himself as the Secretary of these women, thus serving the "beau sexe," and adds that if he invented some of the letters it is not to be read as an attempt to improve the missives, but rather as an imitation of the ladies' style. In any event, he does depart strikingly from the original Latin manuscript. On a structural level, the key differences from the medieval text are quite clear even

[4] Bray, 16-21.

before the reader encounters the letters. The first important change in the structure is Grenaille's insertion of the rubric "lettres chrétiennes," which is used as an organizational tool to immediately place Eloize's letters in a Christian category. It would seem that he hoped that his readers would look upon Eloize as a model of Christian virtue. To underline his moral intentions, he adds a paratext as a preface to each of the four letters. Here, we find an "Argument," an invented textual space, where the "master" states his purpose for translating the missive. The added paratexts mark the second important difference from the medieval narrative. In the first paratext that introduces the opening letter, one of the key changes is Grenaille's portrayal of Eloize as being more renowned for her intellect than for her beauty. But most of all, Grenaille names Eloize "La Magdalene Française," a calculated strategy to remind the reader that she was debauched and then redeemed. In setting the religious tone for his translation, Grenaille wants the reader to view Eloize as a penitent woman devoted to God's love. The third structural change is the insertion of at least one fabricated, fictional letter that deviates completely from the original Latin text. In the "Argument" that precedes the fourth letter, Grenaille openly admits he invented this missive (as will be discussed later on). There is also a fifth letter addressed to a friend of Eloize, concerning theological matters related to Abelard's reputation, but since it is not classified under the rubric of a love letter, it will not be considered here. The fourth difference worth noting is the absence of epistolary exchange. Eloize's letters are monophonic; in spite of the references to Abelard as a receiver, the letters remain unanswered. This change represents a startling digression from the accepted rules constituting the epistolary pact that governs the relationship between writer and receiver. Grenaille thus immediately alters the textual representation of Eloize who addresses her letters to her distant lover, and the privacy of the pact is also violated in

Grenaille's effort to mold her into a model of Christian virtue. By calling her "La Magdalene Française," Grenaille de-emphasizes the genuine passionate nature of Eloize as seen in her original letters to Abelard, but at the same time the desire is not completely restrained, regardless of the translator's efforts to keep it out of his version. As we will see, the passion resurfaces in many episodes, which creates a contradictory representation of Eloize as a penitent figure. The final structural modification is the shifting of biographical aspects discussed earlier in the *Historia* chapter. Interestingly, Grenaille patches details written by Abelard in the *Historia* onto Eloize's letters to compensate for the absence of a receiver reading her letters. The result of this grafting technique produces widespread fragmentation of certain accepted facts regarding the lovers' background. The sequence of events is at times altered, which can create confusion in following the narrative. In the first letter, for instance, Grenaille deletes and censures some details of Heloise's and Abelard's intimate relationship in order to realign the story in accordance with the moral constraints of the seventeenth-century public. He describes in an ambiguous and vague manner the circumstances leading up to Abelard's marriage proposal. In other words, he leaves out the physical details, (as we will see later on), and then proceeds to Eloize's rejection of marriage, interpreting her decision as her choice of God over Abelard. The analysis of Grenaille's translation will show that he did not in fact carry out his role as a "secretary" translating Heloise's letters, that he altered, fragmented and added to a substantial portion of her epistles, and that, in this 1642 text, the genesis of the legend of Heloise and Abelard was indeed born.

Letter 1: Between "Précieuse" and Penitent

The "Argument" that prefaces the opening letter clearly establishes Grenaille's motivations in appealing to a wider public with a French version. Grenaille flatters the seventeenth-century reader's literary tastes by choosing to translate letters written by women, which interested the "beau sexe" that frequented the salons. In his translation of Eloize's first letter, he constructs a parallel to the medieval narrative, as shown by his focus on her intellectual qualities. Here, she embarks on a lengthy, embellished diatribe against marriage, but the stress on intelligence is used to appeal to Grenaille's precious readers who were also interested in stimulating subjects pertaining to women's issues in the seventeenth century. Grenaille thus retains the medieval premise of Heloise's criticism of marriage, but updates her rhetoric so that she has, in some instances, a precious style in her expressions and point of view. Unlike her medieval ancestor, she carefully controls her word choice so as not to shock the audience. As in the original text, Eloize is not in favor of marriage because she does not want to damage Abelard's reputation as a scholar. She insists, once again, that family responsibility is inappropriate for a philosopher. She also advocates the preservation of her love by remaining his "Amante" instead of becoming his wife, as in the original's first letter that also placed free love above the constraints of marriage. Here again, Eloize fears squelching the passion that has always bound them together, but other disadvantages of matrimony appear in Grenaille's translation. He expands the misogynistic concept of "woman" by inserting new dimensions to the biblical antifeminist argument that Heloise uses in her original second letter to Abelard:

> Mais quand le mariage aurait plus de douceur qu'il n'a d'amertume, & qu'une femme ne soit pas aussi souvent une couronne d'espines que de roses pour son mari, comment pensez-vous venir à bout d'un dessein que ceux qui le semblent favoriser maintenant, empêcheront de tout leur pouvoir?[5]

---

[5] All of the quotations are taken from François de Grenaille, *Nouveau recueil de lettres des dames tant anciennes que modernes* (Paris: Quinet, 1642)

In addition to the marriage arguments, other persuasive reasoning is used to convince Abelard that his true calling is the Church; therefore he should not even think of physical pleasure since it is sinful. Here, Grenaille is turning Eloize's rhetoric around so that she appears to be a model of Christian virtue. As Caroline Lougee noted in her illuminating study on women and salons in the seventeenth century, Grenaille defined an "honnête woman" as the lady who stayed at home and did not get herself seduced.[6] In this way, Grenaille reshapes Eloize to emphasize her spiritual qualities and suppress the physical aspects of her original nature. He also condemns carnal desire as criminal, deviating sharply from the language of passion attributed to the medieval Heloise, and he then proceeds to edit the text in order to (re)create Eloize as a penitent figure. To carry out this strategy, he must also modify the language so that it is considered acceptable by his readers. He incorporates some aspects of precious language to appeal to his public, which was mostly feminine, but it is important to clarify that he was not a champion of "préciosité." He was in fact quite against the salons. Clearly, he borrowed some instances of precious rhetoric and style, and grafted them on Eloize's diatribe against marriage. Like an aristocratic lady, she now declares that marriage is like slavery or servitude, an opinion shared by many "précieuses" such as Mlle de Scudéry, who employed these same terms in her discussions of the topic. His Eloize adds that women lose their glory when they marry, which then leads them into inevitable slavery. Again, this might be read as a precious argument portraying Eloize as a proto-feminist. The text does not, however, develop the courtly, gallant aspect, so we can only look upon this as an example of Grenaille's clever use of "préciosité" to make his readers identify with Eloize through

[6] See Carolyn Lougee's book on women and the seventeenth-century salons, *Le Paradis des femmes: Women, Salons, and Social Stratification in Seventeenth-Century France* (Princeton: Princeton UP, 1976): 82.

familiar language and opinions. He wishes to sway his public over to Eloize's point of view so that later they will more readily accept her newly transformed image as a saint. To lay the groundwork for his revision of Eloize, he deletes aspects of the medieval text and alters the, at times, crude language in order to respect the moral constraints of the day. For this reason, the body is virtually written out, rendered unrepresentable, which constitutes a serious travesty of the medieval Heloise's rhetorical style as she articulated her passion through the body. Furthermore, the details surrounding Heloise's pregnancy are vague and greatly abbreviated, but still of textual significance because her predicament directly influences her opinion on marriage. Grenaille deliberately omits any words that allude to her pregnancy, in the "Argument" as well as in the first letter. Katherine Jensen reads this as part of a narrative strategy taking into account seventeenth-century readers' reception of the scandalous and shocking events surrounding Heloise's love affair:

> Grenaille's suppression of the detail of pregnancy would correspond to his reason for "bienséance" and his desire to represent Heloise as a purified and penitent woman, a reborn "honnête femme."[7]

In considering the modification of Heloise's epistles and persona, Jensen prefaces her ideas on the transformation of Heloise in referring to Gérard Genette's definition of what constitutes "vraisemblance" and "bienséance."[8] Genette established a relationship between these two key terms, which depended greatly on the public's opinion of what was considered appropriate decorum for the classical period. In light of this social convention, Grenaille censures what might be viewed as morally im-

[7] Katherine Ann Jensen, "Rewriting for Vraisemblance: Grenaille's Versions of Héloïse," *Cahiers du Dix-Septième* 3.1 (1989) : 158

[8] Jensen, 155-57. It is also important to consult Gérard Genette's article for a discussion of these two terms, which is also placed within a larger contextual framework for an analysis of key literary masterpieces of the period. See "Vraisemblance et motivation," *Communications* 11(1968): 5-21.

proper, so the details describing Heloise's conception of an illegitimate child are simply left out. Grenaille does, however, find a technique to work the delicate topic of castration into his version without vividly recalling the episode. The castration is introduced in an ambiguous and subtle manner as Eloize now plays the role of a prophetess who predicts inevitable doom for Abelard, with a veiled reference to Fulbert:

> Persuadez-vous, mon cher Abélard, qu'il ne s'adoucit que pour vous traiter avec plus de rigueur, & qu'il ne demande mon retour que pour m'engager dans la peine qu'il vous prépare; (I, 296)

Grenaille uses foreshadowing as a means of reinforcing Eloize's idea that it is not "raisonnable" to marry. Concerned for Abelard's life, she attempts to forewarn him of her uncle's wrath, and alludes to a dark and troubling vision of the lovers' destiny:

> Quoi qu'il en arrive, tenez pour tout assuré; cher Abélard, que si vous vous déterminez au mariage, je prévois que notre destin voudra que la douleur de cet couple d'Amants ne soit pas moindre que leur amour, et qu'ayant été quelque temps heureux, ils soient après malheureux toute leur vie. (I, 299-300)

Eloize's gift of predicting the lovers' future is entirely invented, written into the story by Grenaille, and the insertion of this fictional element sets the tone for the rest of his "translation" of Heloise's epistles. The "predicting passage" also anticipates other instances of "authorial moralizing," as we will see in subsequent letters.

Letter 2: Heloise's Confession

The translation of the second letter includes most of the biographical facts already seen in the medieval text, but the first difference worth noting is the change in the narrative sequence of events. Grenaille deviates from the original text in taking the liberty to combine and integrate aspects of Heloise's original two letters addressed to Abelard. The second key difference is inserted in the "Argument," the preface to the second letter. Grenaille, (instead of Abelard in the *Historia*), narrates the tragic details leading up to the lovers' retreat into separate cloisters. The departure from the Latin text is also underlined by the omission of Abelard and his *Historia*. In his version, Grenaille condenses the *Historia* into an abbreviated prose piece, which is transformed into the "Argument." As a paratext, the "Argument" provides a frame for Grenaille so that he can establish himself as a writer, and it is here that Grenaille alludes to the castration in an ambiguous way, "il quitta les vices, parce que les vices l'avaient quitté" (301). He adds that Heloise's uncle retaliated cruelly by drawing Abelard's blood, but does not point directly to the castration, and thus he respects the moral code of "bienséance." He concludes the "Argument" with an "added on" description of Eloize as a "complaining" woman because she reproaches Abelard 's negligence for not writing to her, which is still his conjugal debt. The final difference from the medieval text is the suppression of Heloise's original erotic and passionate nature, which, this time, is used as the grounding premise for the construction of a confession that is highly significant as it constitutes the main portion of this letter.

Grenaille's second letter opens much like Heloise's original first letter in the Zumthor translation. She has read Abelard's autobiographical epistle addressed to an anonymous friend. Once again, Eloize mentions that having read one of Abelard's letters has conjured up the presence of its cherished author. The missive is described in Grenaille's version as representing Abelard's image. Although this process strongly resembles theoretical epistolary aspects discussed in the Zumthor version, it is interesting that the representation reference only occurs in Grenaille's translation. For Foucault, representation in classical thought is articulated by the edification of a sign system.[9] We can read the letter as a sign representing Abelard's persona. Heloise, in asking Abelard to write to her, hopes that he will send her an "image" of himself. At the same time, she wishes she could also inscribe her own "secret" desire onto the blank space of the page. As Peter Brooks has shown, the body itself represents a place or a scene of discourse. It is a site where one seeks to write clandestine messages that mark erotic desire.[10] Here, Eloize appears to transmit coded messages to Abelard. As Ros Ballaster observed, the letter is the privileged "female" site of passionate expression where women can exteriorize their concealed, amatory desire.[11] Indeed, this is what Grenaille tries to suppress by redirecting Eloize's discourse onto a religious level, but there are numerous instances when she will return to the metonymic conception of the letter, which recalls the medieval text where she freely expressed her passion and desire to restore Abelard's presence by enticing him into amorous exchange. To go back to the text, Grenaille adds minor changes that augment Eloize's persuasive strategy. She expresses concern for Abelard's life, and, as she goes on to say that he might find comfort and solace in writing to her, the therapeutic aspect of writing is stressed. Eloize wishes to restore communication, no matter how disturbing his news might be. She admits that reading her letter to his friend opened up new wounds and reminds Abelard of his conjugal debt, as previously seen in the Zumthor version. One of the new variations in the second letter is the replacement of the "plantation" metaphor that refers to the Paraclete, with the word "Colonie." Eloize says that Abelard established one of his colonies where she now resides.

[9] Michel Foucault provides a detailed discussion on seventeenth-century signs, relating to representation in the third chapter of *The Order of Things* (New York: Randon House, 1970): 47-77.

[10] See Peter Brooks, *Body Work* (Cambridge: Harvard UP, 1997): 20-26.

[11] For more information on the characteristics of the love letter, see Ros Ballaster's *Seductive Forms: Women's Amatory Fiction from 1684 to 1740* (Oxford: Clarendon, 1992): 61-6.

Grenaille thus deletes the erotic details of the plantation and germination metaphor to perhaps reduce the risk of this part of the letter being considered inappropriate or offensive to the sensibility of his female public. However, he does not completely alter the original idea of planting: "Puisque c'est vous qui avez planté cette nouvelle vigne, c'est à vous à l'arroser, si vous voulez qu'elle croisse" (II, 310-11).

Eloize elaborates on the theme of conjugal debt to make her point that Abelard owes it to her to contact her. She reminds him that he is still her husband. But Grenaille shifts the spiritual tone of Abelard's original love letters onto Eloize's discourse: "Vous ne cessez pas d'être mon mari, tout Religieux que vous êtes: & nos esprits se doivent unir davantage par la séparation des corps" (II, 312).

Clearly, Grenaille intervenes in order to recast her as a saint. He suppresses Heloise's "original" carnal desire in favor of this mystical, ethereal reunion of their souls, which goes along with his (re)creation of Eloize as a religious figure. The above passage shows an attempt to curb the passion, reformulating it into an aesthetic conception of spirituality, that could also be more appreciated by Grenaille's readers. As the letter continues on to address the question of love, one notes that Grenaille shifts Eloize's avowal of excessive love into the past tense, then diverts the amorous discourse into remembering the pain of Abelard's affliction. Once again, Grenaille's Eloize alludes to sharing the suffering of the double castration as indicated by the idea, as in the medieval text, of "perte." However, Grenaille carefully deletes any mention of the word eunuch to respect the code of "bienséance." Further along, Grenaille's narrative strategy of portraying Eloize as a penitent woman does however seem to unravel and produce widespread contradiction within the text:

> Or je n' attends point d'autre que de vous, cher Abélard, car comme vous êtes le sujet de ma douleur, je veux que vous soyez aussi ma

> seule allégeance. Il n'y a que vous qui puissiez ou réjouïr, ou affliger, puisque ma vie & ma mort dépendent de vous. (II, 315)

Abelard, instead of spiritual devotions directed towards God's service, clearly dominates Eloize's thoughts. This is contradictory to the saintly image that Grenaille hopes to convey to his readers. The text contains a palimpsest where the translator's pen fails to write over the remains of the medieval amatory discourse that places Abelard as the subject of Heloise's thoughts. On the occasions when the editor doesn't completely etch over Heloise's discourse, the reader is allowed to glimpse, through an aperture in the text, the site of the "feminine" creation of the love letter. Here, he momentarily forgets about restraining Eloize's passion and reverts to the medieval representation of Heloise as a very physical woman in love. As also seen in the Zumthor translation, Eloize repeats that she didn't care about Abelard's material possessions, only about his "personne" and that she merely followed his order to take the veil because he asked her. But as Grenaille continues to patch other fragments that recall the original text onto his second letter, he also alters significantly one seminal theme: the confession.

Although the medieval Heloise openly talked about her erotic feelings to her partner, it was private and without any guilt or regret, and therefore did not constitute a true confession. Heloise poured out her love intimately to Abelard in the form of an epistolary dialogue. But, in the Grenaille version, the situation is transformed on many different levels. On the structural plane, Eloize's letters are monologic, she writes to Abelard, but he acts as a false receiver; no one answers her epistles. Here, the concept of privacy has already been breached. Eloize will speak out, but not privately to Abelard, as Grenaille omits him from the text. Before looking at Grenaille's invention of Eloize's confession, it is useful to preface our analysis by noting that the ritual of confession takes on a different meaning in the seventeenth century. The revision of the procedures occurred after the Council of Trent, in the sixteenth century, had declared that confession was mandatory for every individual, especially women. New techniques of confession were established and new relationships formed between the directed and the director. Michel Foucault's brilliant study of confession in the first volume of the *History of Sexuality* provides further insight into this question. As he observes, the seventeenth century actually transformed sex into discourse and stressed the need for people to reveal their secrets pertaining to sexuality:

> The confession is a ritual of discourse in which the speaking subject is also the subject of the statement; it is also a ritual that unfolds within a power relationship, for one does not confess without the presence (or virtual presence) of a partner who is not simply the interlocutor but the authority who requires the confession, prescribes and appreciates it, and intervenes in order to judge, punish, forgive, console and reconcile.[12]

Confession by its nature is a ritual where secrets are divulged and where knowledge is made public. As Foucault maintains, it is based on a power relationship; the repressive force that dictates the laws governing sexual discourse. Disclosing secrets to the confessor provides him or her with intimate knowledge. This dialectic places the director in an empowered situation. Grenaille, as an editor, alters Eloize's confession by (re)writing it and sharing it with the public. He, then, is placed in the confessor's role as a witness to Eloize's confidential information, and executes an editorial power play violating the privacy of the erotic, confidential secrets that are directed to Abelard in the medieval text. Grenaille is clearly not her partner in sin, but nevertheless he intervenes in Eloize's narrative and joins Abelard in that he takes full liberty to fragment, and transform, her epistles. In silencing Abelard's voice throughout the narrative, (he is unrepresented), Grenaille becomes the one who listens to

---

[12] Michel Foucault, *History of Sexuality, Volume 1: An Introduction,* trans. Robert Harley (New York: Pantheon Books, 1978): 61-2.

her secrets so that he can later publicize Eloize's revelations, and then transmit the moral message to a wider audience:

> Et pour achever de faire ici une confession publique de mes folies; j'avoue que le nom d'Amante m'a toujours semblé plus doux que le nom de femme, quoi que l'un fût profane & l'autre sacré. (II, 316-317)

Although this passage is very similar to the Zumthor text, the aspect of the public "tell all" is completely different. Grenaille's Eloize discloses her preference to be his "Amante" so that she appears to his readers to voice her clandestine desire. He carefully avoids the reprise of "concubine" that followed the original passage in the medieval text, for reasons of "bienséance" perhaps. He also inserts the opposition between sacred and profane love, an insertion that already brings out the penitential quality in this revised representation of Heloise. In any case, Grenaille pushes Abelard out of the text to slip himself into the role of an authority figure. Interestingly, Grenaille appears to perform another travesty. As a priest, he is impersonating Abelard in his attempt to play the role of a religious director who takes people's confessions. But the structure of the spiritual relationship has been radically altered. In the Zumthor version, Heloise carries on a dialogue with Abelard; here the exchange is gone, and rewritten as a "tell-all" presented in monologic form. Here, Grenaille not only exerts his power as a self-appointed monastic figure, but also assumes the role of the judge who evaluates the confession. The emphasis is on listening, which implies that he bears witness, and this process empowers him to re-transmit the knowledge in whatever form he decides. As Jeremy Tambling reads it, listening clearly places the confessor in an active, participating role:

> Confession is both avowal and disavowal, an obsession to know which affects as much the person confessing as the person hearing;

> but the obsession to know is itself a screen, a representation to hide a further representation.[13]

Grenaille's desire to make his Eloize "tell" the truth of her carnal desire is an attempt to produce a valid, convincing recharacterization of her as "La Magdalene Française." This portrayal is seminal to the success of his literary reproduction. His feminine public must find her plausible, and so once they have identified with her, he can then better convince them of his moral message. But Grenaille's intervention as a confessor has serious implications for women. Textually, he imprisons Eloize's persona in the enclosed, darkened confessional and forces her to whisper the secrets of her illicit crimes as well as admit publicly, "j'avoue que je suis fort coupable," (323), instead of privately, to Abelard, as was the case in the medieval text. Interestingly, the ritual of the confessional draws attention to the ear; the key source of the internal message system, directly connected to the power structures at work. In *The Ear of the Other,* Derrida, too, stresses the keen ability of the addressee's ear to decipher the "autos" of the writer's autobiographical narrative.

With regards to Eloize, Grenaille makes her retell her own "so called" scandalous story, and thus places himself in her text. He plays the role of the addressee whose ear strains to listen and transmit her message. But as Derrida notes, ears come in all shapes and sizes; therefore the message can be interpreted in a variety of ways. In any case, it is always the addressee that signs the autobiographical "tell all" with his "ear": "To hear him, one must have a keen ear. In other words, to abbreviate my remarks in a very lapidary fashion, it is the ear of the other that signs."[14] Grenaille, as the "ear of the other" and

[13] Jeremy Tambling, *Confession: Sexuality, Sin, The Subject* (Manchester & New York: Manchester UP, 1990): 199.

[14] Jacques Derrida, *The Ear of the Other,* trans. Peggy Kamuf (Lincoln & London: Nebraska UP, 1985): 51.

the confessor, 'hears" Heloise's confession, and thus there is a transference of power placed in the editor's hand who can now alter freely what he has heard. Moreover, some additional modifications place the confession within a seventeenth-century context. Eloize is no longer writing from a monastic cell, but from a small private space called a "Cabinet." The shift from the religious cloister to the more secularized space of the "Cabinet" provides the grounds for other women to identify with Eloize's dilemma. Joan DeJean's *Tender Geographies,* a monumental study on women writers in the seventeenth century, provides the reader with a description of the Cabinet.[15] She explains that the Cabinet was a room that resembled a small library, a space where precious women could have private conversations or write letters. But, once again, Grenaille invades yet another "feminine" site of creation and transforms this "safe haven," favorable to literary activities, into a false retreat, which is really a prison where Eloize is forced to tell the truth of her illicit passion. In this public confessional box, her persona becomes a victim as she is subjected to a masculine, authoritarian interrogation with no exit out of the enclosed space. It is as if Grenaille has locked the door to the box, obliging her to divulge all of her secrets to the public. She is forced to talk about her desire as if it were a crime of the flesh. As Foucault observes, the confessional ritual bears strong resemblance to the power structure of a "police technology" system or, in other words, the person who confesses has no choice but to surrender to the authority figure, a theory that is also shared by Mike Hepworth and Bryan Turner in their work on religious confession and deviance.[16] As we will see, the confessional theme dominates the body of this second letter.

---

[15] See Joan DeJean's *Tender Geographies: Women and the Origins of the Novel in France* (New York: Columbia UP, 1991): 63-4.

[16] For an interesting study on deviance and confession, see Mike Hepworth's and Bryan Turner's book, *Confession: Studies in Deviance and Religion* (London & Boston: Routledge & Kegan Paul, 1982).

Grenaille develops the unveiling of Eloize's inner thoughts in a way which is similar to the medieval text, but does contain some variations as he seems to lose ground in his attempt to transform Heloise into a Christian figure. At first, the discourse remains quite moral and Christian, but there are also contradictions that resemble her medieval textual counterpart. We have already noted the reference in Grenaille's second letter, where Eloize says that Abelard is the sole author of her conversion. Eloize also views Abelard as her "juge" and "témoin" of her testimony and hopes he will also confide in her:

> Je vois bien que vous ne voulez pas confesser la vérité, mais si vous me cachez vos sentiments je vous découvrirai les miens, avec d'autant moins de honte & d'apprehension, que mes présomptions particulières sont fécondées des soupçons de tout le monde. (II, 324-5)

Grenaille takes advantage of Abelard's absence by rendering Eloize's confession public once again. He is reinforcing his repentance strategy, or, in other words, he is preaching morals to his feminine public through the publication of Eloize's avowal. He has her create the appearance of purging her sins in order to receive God's forgiveness so that other women could imitate her as a virtuous, self-sacrificing figure. But there is a salient contradiction in the text. Grenaille's Eloize, much like her medieval predecessor, is also openly pursuing a discourse of desire. In the passage following the one cited above, she recognizes that Abelard didn't love her, but rather lusted after her, as already seen in the medieval text. But, she still wants news of Abelard, and once again, there is an echo of the familiar refrain that he is her one and only source of devotion:

> Je ne sers Dieu que pour vous servir suivant vos ordres. Ce n'est pas tout un sentiment de religion que votre exprès commandement qui m'a fait consacrer ma jeunesse à un Monastère et changer la douceur des contentements du siècle à l'austerité d'un Cloître. (II, 327)

Here, Grenaille actually embellishes the portrayal of Eloize's undying devotion to honor Abelard's orders, instead of adhering to his initial plan to (re)create her as "La Magdalene Française." This more secularized Eloize, who writes from her Cabinet, uses a long, logical and rational argument to persuade Abelard to write her. She invokes him, addressing him as "juge," in the hopes that he will be moved by her honesty and loyalty and, therefore, honor his duty to resume epistolary contact. This appeal to the absent Abelard creates a contradiction in Grenaille's revision of her as a Christian figure. Once again, the palimpsest reappears and Grenaille does not completely obliterate all of the remains of Eloize's desire. The "amorous" Heloise resurfaces, which creates an obstacle in the intention to convert her passion into austere redemption. There are moments, as seen in passages previously cited, where Grenaille's pen cannot erase the traces of Heloise's "original" letters where she was clearly engaging in amatory dialogue with her receiver. In spite of Grenaille's additions to the text, Eloize remains nevertheless attached to the excessive force of her passion, and it appears that there are several judges listening to her confession. Every mention of her unforgettable desire is directed towards her absent, silent beloved, and so even from a distance he faintly hears her avowal. As noted previously, Grenaille plays the more significant role in his guise as a priest who takes her confession first-hand. In this translation, a mute judge, Abelard, remains in the background of the text; he is brought to the foreground by Eloize's repeated effort to address her letter to her husband in order to articulate her desire.

It is during these passionate moments that tend to interrupt Grenaille's repentant revision of her persona that the text seems to get away from his control. However, he always reasserts his authority by his manipulation of her speech, diverting it from her passion to a more spiritual level. On several occasions, one notes that he begins, suspends, and then comes back to his role as a priest and resumes listening to Eloize, along with Abelard; so there is in fact a double displacement in the text. Abelard is passively listening while Grenaille is actively listening and reworking Abelard's role as well as Eloize's rhetoric. Together, both male authors share the task of fragmenting Eloize's discourse: Abelard, as seen earlier, borrowed from Heloise to benefit his own self-interests while Grenaille alters, edits and inserts in order to assure that his moral message will be conveyed to his public. The two men act as "judges" or "confessors," and they exercise their authorial power to alter Eloize's language and thus subjugate her to the inferior, powerless position reserved for the "beau sexe." Hepworth and Turner have looked at the historical developments in the confessional ritual, and they have observed that it was originally implemented as an instrument of social control, as a means of policing behavior.[17] Therefore, it is not surprising then that the confessional relationship here is not grounded on a relationship of equality, but rather inequality. By confining Eloize to her "Cabinet," Grenaille and Abelard, through their respective authorial intervention, use their power to keep Eloize in her "place." As DeJean's work has shown, women, especially women writers, were very frequently placed in a similarly powerless position. Their very authorship was considered a political, even subversive, activity that threatened to dismantle and overturn the foundations of the nation. But nonetheless women were gathering and composing letters in the salons.[18] (Mlle de Scudéry, for instance, wrote rules and guidelines to follow in the art of penning love letters). Above all, the style had to be spontaneous and natural, closely resembling the acquired art of talking about love in salon conversations. The emotional freedom and ease of women's epistles was an attractive quality to male writers who borrowed "feminine" rhetoric to suit their own purposes. Yet, as Jensen

[17] Hepworth & Turner 1-15.

[18] DeJean 94-126.

reads it, Grenaille goes even further in that he subverts gender categories by writing himself through Eloize's literary persona:

> It is then in the space of this "feminine" textuality that Grenaille finds his own space for writing. While one of his forays into fiction concerns women's disempowering effect on physical man, the other concerns the self-empowering force of feminine force. (Jensen 62)

Grenaille violates Eloize's space in occupying her site as a writer. He veils her textual presence so that he can take over and stage his masquerade as Eloize. In addition, this impersonation of Eloize also allows him to profit from the reception that her "Christian" letters will bring him as an author. Grenaille commits the most serious violation of her discourse by signing in her name, which, to put it in Miller's words, constitutes another form of "pseudo-feminocentrism." He seals and completes his act of appropriation every time he closes one of Eloize's letters with this transgressive signature.[19] Interestingly, in the Zumthor translation, Heloise's letters are not signed, which creates an open space in the text for Grenaille to intervene. Every time he signs a letter "Eloize," he is disguising himself as a woman, using her name as a "cover-up" in order to benefit from his retouched version. But, at the same time, there is a paradox that points to a loss of authorial manipulation. Once again, Grenaille seems to introduce a striking contradiction into the text. By signing in her name, he is actually reintegrating Eloize into the text and reaffirming her textual presence instead of repressing or casting a visible veil over her persona, as he had previously shown in his revision of her. As Kamuf opines, women's names were often interrupted, repressed, and, to use Virginia Woolf's words, "broken in on."[20] Heloise's signature appears to be interrupted or "broken in on" by the editor who takes full liberty in

---

[19] For a fascinating discussion on signature and how it relates to authorship, see *Signature Pieces: On the Institute of Authorship* (Ithaca & London: Cornell UP, 1988): 1-20. Kamuf's remarks are especially useful in looking at the travesty that takes place behind the name Eloize.

[20] Kamuf 163-4.

writing his name through hers, which, in turn, albeit paradoxically, partially erases her signature. Grenaille's pen intrudes upon her claim to her text, and consequently Eloize's literary production is severely altered by the male writer, the dominating force behind the fragmentation of her letters that forces her into the silence and the darkness of a locked-up chamber, the omnipresent confessional box.

Letter 3: The "Honnête" Heloise

The "Argument" that introduces the third letter shows overt evidence of Grenaille's revision of Heloise's textual persona: he states that he wants his Eloize to speak more "honestly" in French than she did in the Latin text. This could be read as another strategic power play to rework her rhetoric so that she appears to be confessing: "On observa encore que je n'ai pas offensé Eloize, en la faisant parler plus honnêtement en Français qu'elle ne parlait en Latin" ("Argument," III, 334).

Grenaille begins the letter with the familiar Ovidian trope of the abandoned woman in love, moved to tears by the separation from the object of her desire. He alters the structure of the Latin text by grafting the theme of Abelard's inevitable death and its consequences for Eloize's nuns onto this third letter. We recall that these incidents were originally seen in Heloise's second letter in the Zumthor translation. The sequence of events has been fragmented, switched around and lengthened to further embellish the Ovidian trope that introduces this third epistle. Grenaille enriches the Ovidian model with the insertion of the wound metaphor that augments Eloize's "perte." Here, Eloize's pathos suggests that her sensuality would inevitably destroy her happiness; and she, like her ancestor, blames Fortune for her miserable destiny . Since we have already seen a similar idea in the medieval text and have already discussed the Ovidian intertext, it is more interesting to focus on the differences presented in the letter. Firstly, Grenaille returns to the original portrayal of Eloize as the penitent Christian figure, and then he goes on to retrace the lovers' illicit sins. Eloize accepts all blame and responsibility for the tragic events leading up to their separation. Her suffering is intensified by the fact that, as in the original, the two of them sinned, but only one was punished: "Il n'y a eu qu'un criminel bani, ou deux avaient commis même crime, & celui qui l'avaient moins mérité a souffert pour l'un et l'autre" (III, 346).

Grenaille modifies the language, the words "criminel" and "crime" are more in accordance with his revision of Heloise. The medieval Heloise does not refer to herself as a "criminel" nor to their desire as a crime; instead we find the word "faute" in the Zumthor translation. Grenaille seems to hope that his readers will recognize that Eloize's illicit love is criminal, and constitutes a fatal flaw in her travesty as a false nun, which can only be rectified by repentance. As in the medieval text, here Grenaille's misogynistic conception of "woman" as the lusty temptress that leads men into ruin is perpetuated. Grenaille builds this idea up to the point where the sin becomes a "crime;" an interesting choice of words because it is equally associated with a legal or judicial vocabulary, thus placing Grenaille in the position, once again, as a judge listening to Eloize's confession. He places her on the "right" path that leads to God by forcing her to narrate and reconstruct the detailed circumstances that characterize the "crime." He deftly weaves the penitence theme into her confession, which allows her to convey the moral message that sensual, concupiscent love can only end tragically. Thus, Grenaille's Eloize warns other women to guard against the dangers of carnal desire. In the text, Eloize goes on to say that she wants to suffer all of her life as a compensation for Abelard's misery and great pain during the mutilation. She then moves into the erotic confession originally directed to Abelard. The sequence has been altered, but the basic elements resemble the medieval text. Once again, Eloize's sleep is tormented, plagued by disturbing memories of desire. Grenaille updates the vocabulary to appeal to his seventeenth-century audience by inserting amorous rhetoric. Thus the translator, once again, encroaches on Eloize' s discourse and scrawls over her words to rework the medieval version. The goal is to persuade his readers' that through Eloize other women could also be converted:

> Les pensées qu'il me suggère m'inquiètent dans le repos du sommeil aussi bien que dans la fatigue des veilles. Ses profanes désirs me suivent quoi que malgré moi jusque dans les lieux sacrés & lorsque mon esprit doit être le plus épuré, c'est lorsqu'il semble être le plus enseveli dans la chair. (III, 354)

Grenaille's Eloize is torn between haunting "profane désir" and her arduous struggle to redirect the passion into sacred love. She admits that she fears losing her reason as a result of replaying in her mind over and over again the memory of previous conversations with her beloved. In the medieval text, we do not find such a conflicting battle between sacred and profane desire.

The addition of this tension does, however, take on different meaning in the seventeenth century. Grenaille inserts this opposing angle to create the appearance that Eloize tries to overcome these troubling thoughts for the sake of repentance, but he fails to produce evidence that she ever forgets the souvenirs of these moments of carnal ecstasy. In fact, he shows that she is still tormented by the flesh. The language has simply been toned down in comparison to the vivid, erotically charged confession of her medieval sister. Grenaille alters the personal memory of the illicit episodes while redefining the representation of the erotic for his readers. According to Jacques Solé, in the seventeenth century, spiritual love and religious ecstasy were considered to be highly erotic experiences for the soul as opposed to the dangerous disorder that physical desire produced on the body.[21] Sacred love was looked upon as a substitute for the flesh, given the sexually repressive atmosphere of the times. Here, the erotic is by no means suppressed, but, as is the case with Grenaille's Eloize, it is reformulated. The erotic is directly interwoven into the spiritual aspects of the divine pursuit of love where souls can reunite and be brought closer to God's radiating love. It is possible that Grenaille's intention was to gradually realign Eloize with this elevated and ethereal image of the spiritual, lifting her above the debauchery and baseness of corporeal passion. However, he fails to persuade his readers that his Eloize can rise above her passionate memories. In the Zumthor text, Heloise was disturbed almost to the point of "oublier la raison" (354), and as seen before, she wished that she could commit such illicit acts again. Once again, the palimpsest is made visible, revealing the original amatory discourse in spite of Grenaille's efforts to erase "woman's" excessive display of boundless passion. Instead of encountering passages that point to her repentant nature, we find strong textual evidence of amorous language that allows the reader to locate the "female" in the text:

> C'est vous principalement cher Abélard, qui êtes trop avant gravé dans mon coeur pour pouvoir être éloigné de ma pensée. Quoi que je sois séparée de vous je suis toujours avec vous. Ces imaginations me troublent si fort qu'on voit à mon extérieur ce qui se passe au dedans. (III, 355)

Eloize remains undeniably devoted to Abelard, and thus overrides Grenaille's authorial attempt to portray her as a self-sacrificing, devout Catholic who abandoned her passionate memories in order to serve God's calling. Furthermore, she confesses that she is a hypocrite, which undermines Grenaille's literary goal and creates a problematic contradiction. Like her

---

[21] For a general history on love and spirituality in the seventeenth century, see Jacques Solé's book, *L'Amour en Occident à l'époque moderne* (Paris: Editions Complexe, 1976).

medieval sister, Eloize openly sees herself as an impostor playing the role of the holy nun. The recovery of the "hypocrite" theme only tends to invalidate Grenaille's revision of Heloise's persona as "La Magdalene Française." At the same time, he reintegrates the misogynistic conception of "woman" as a moral index to weakness, that hinders Eloize from dedicating herself to God: "Outre que plus son sexe est faible, plus son ennemi est puissant. Ainsi plusieurs me tiennent pour sainte qui ne voient pas mon hypocrisie" (III, 356).

As Eloize says, one should not be deceived by the external appearance of her nun's attire as it only dissimulates the truth of her hypocrisy. She reiterates, like her predecessor, that her vocation was purely a sham:

> Reconnoissez donc maintenant que ma dissimulation vous a trompé aussi bien que beaucoup d'autres, & que vous avez pris mon hypocrisie pour une dévotion sincère. (III, 358)

But Grenaille also reworks the false facade of the saint into a more contemporary context by shifting the language around. The term "dissimulation" adds emphasis to the game of deception and appearances. Grenaille's Eloize is a saint only on the surface. Her nun's attire is merely a "cover-up" for her one and only object of devotions, the memory of Abelard as a lover. She goes on to confess that she just wanted to please Abelard and so, now that she has unveiled the truth of her hypocrisy, she wants Abelard to stop praising her. Yet once again, Grenaille forces her to tell the truth so that he can guide her in the "right" direction that leads to redemption. As seen earlier, the attention of this confession is drawn to Grenaille's ear since he actively replaces Abelard. Eloize appears to address her erotic confession to Abelard, but his textual presence shown by the repeated use of his name is only an illusion, an empty facade masking his absence. So what happens to the woman's position? Eloize is textually placed between two males, one active and the other passive. She has become an object, trapped between two masculine poles, and then exchanged between these two editors, who, in turn, rework her original words to serve their own self-interests. In a larger social context, we can also consider this concept of "passing women" in the literary marketplace in the light of Gayle Rubin's informative work on sex and gender. She refers to the relationships in patriarchal, heterosexual societies as "trafficking in women." Rubin traces the origin and the tradition of exchanging women, using Claude Levi-Strauss's theories on the sociological organization of kinship relations.[22] Levi-Strauss studied primitive societies where women were looked upon as gifts, exchanged among men who could give and take them as they so desired. As the oppressed gender, women were then placed in a context of a circulation network. Other feminist critics such as Luce Irigaray also deal with the issue of women as a commodity, exchanged in a male economy:

> Autrement dit encore : tous les systèmes d'échanges qui organisent les sociétés patriarcales, et toutes les modalités de travail productif qui y sont reconnues, valorisées, rétribuées, sont affaire d'hommes. Femmes, signes, marchandises, sont toujours renvoyés pour leur production à l'homme (quand un homme achète une fille, c'est le père ou le frère qu'il "paie," non la mère [...]), et ils passent toujours d'un homme à un autre homme, d'un groupe d'hommes à un autre groupe d'hommes.[23]

In many ways, this concept is also relevant to women's literary production in seventeenth-century France. As early as the Renaissance and well beyond the seventeenth and eighteenth centuries, women's literary creations were often circulated without their knowledge or permission. Men controlled the circulation and the marketing of women's writings. DeJean's remarkable

---

[22] For more information on sexual inequality and oppression with a focus on Freud and Lévi-Strauss, see Gayle Rubin's article, "The Traffic in women: Notes on the 'Political Economy of Sex," *Toward an Anthropology of Women,* ed. Rayna R. Reiter (NY & London: Monthly Review Press, 1975): 157-210. Rubin refers to Lévi-Strauss's *The Elementary Structures of Kinship* (Boston: Beacon Press, 1969): 171-175. Here, she examines the idea of women as gift transactions, mainly in marriages.

[23] Luce Irigaray, *Ce sexe qui n'en est pas un* (Paris: Minuit, 1977): 168.

work on women's writing in the seventeenth century provides insight into this important question on female authorship. She cites examples of men who intervened in a woman's textual creation. Madame de Villedieu, for instance, had her personal correspondence stolen and published by her lover without her knowledge. But this was not an isolated case, as Mlle de Scudéry's brother had published more than one text that was actually written by his sister. Many women's texts mysteriously vanished and were published without their signature or someone else's was written over theirs, thus invalidating the women's claim to the work.[24] In short, all of these male interventions underline the fact that historically women were excluded, and viewed as outcasts from the production of literary works; and this aspect can be applied to Heloise's epistolary text. Her letters were first thrust into Abelard's hands and then into Grenaille's control, who then joined Abelard in using his power to alter, modify and fragment her "original" discourse. As we have shown, there is clear evidence that Grenaille did not honor his role as a mere Secretary to literary ladies. On the contrary, he wrote at least one of Heloise's letters and fabricated a substantial part of the preceding epistles in his translation. Under his power as an editor, Heloise's correspondence becomes a commodity which brings Grenaille recognition and fame among his male peers. But Rubin's important essay on trafficking in women has other ramifications on Grenaille's translation. As Rubin notes, the exchange of women is directly linked to gender relations. She points out that gender can be looked at as a category or a socially imposed system that divides the sexes.[25] In other words, there is a difference between the genders, which relates, perhaps, to the tension that existed between the sexes in the seventeenth century. Women who were writing at the time created gender tension because of their difference,

[24] DeJean 94-126.
[25] Rubin 173-77.

which, in turn, created male sexual anxiety. Men, the empowered gender that had always held the pen, feared that women would usurp their literary dominance if permitted to publish alone without their assistance. As DeJean observed, men had to find a way to keep women dependent and therefore marginalized as a fringe group.[26] One way of assuring masculine power was to disguise themselves as "literary" women. Miller also supports this idea. According to her, female impersonation provided a way to guarantee that the power structure remained intact. For Eve Sedgwick, who concurs with Miller, the goal of men in any sexual discourse has political implications and is directly related to the power relations between genders, which is essentially "homoerotic."[27] In other words, masculine writers wanted to bond with other males to be recognized and praised for their success in carrying off their impersonation. Once again, women's literary creation, like Heloise's love letters, provides the "goods" to be exchanged within the male economy. Miller describes the erotics of "pseudo-feminocentrism" practiced by male authors:

> [...] the erotics erected by female impersonation is a mirroring not of female desire but of a phallic pride of place, a wish-fulfillment that ultimately translates into structures of masculine dominance and authority.[28]

In his translation, Grenaille, who replaces Abelard, appears to slip into Eloize's monastic attire; he steals her pen and edits her love letters. Impersonating Heloise may be an erotic experience that enables him to investigate freely his more "sensitive" side as noted by Jensen who constructs her argument on Miller's "pseudo-feminocentrism":

---

[26] DeJean 1-16.
[27] See Eve Kosofsky Sedgwick's book, *Between Men: English Literatue & Male Homosocial Desire* (NY: Columbia UP, 1985): 21-27.
[28] Miller 54.

> In other words, to write through the feminine allows a Grenaille or Guilleragues to explore his own "femininity", an exploration which, were it taken on " as a man," would be tantamount to admitting effeminacy. (Jensen 163)

Like Abelard symbolically dressed as a woman in the medieval text, Grenaille carries on a literary masquerade and crosses over to a more "effeminate" side, associated with the love discourse, an instance of "pseudo-feminocentrism," that is also visible in the signature. Grenaille dissimulates his masculinity by signing "Eloize," and thus further settles into a "feminine" role in the text.

Letter 4: "Born Again" Eloize

The "Argument" that precedes the fourth letter indicates that Grenaille not only fabricated this missive, but tried his skills at mimicking Heloise's style without selecting one of her Latin letters as his basis for imitating and embellishing the text. To put it in Miller's terms, Grenaille is clearly and openly engaging in "pseudo-feminocentrism" here. He takes the liberty to actually become the Other by writing in Eloize's place. In the "Argument", Grenaille says, "j'ai supposé cette lettre pour rendre Eloize aussi sérieuse qu'elle paraît libre dans les autres" (364). The fourth letter must, however, resemble Heloise's style in order to be considered in accordance with the previous letters he translated and co-authored. His goal is to make her appear austere and so, to carry out this mission, Grenaille borrows elements from the medieval correspondence and reattaches the fragments to create this fictitious letter. He redirects her discourse to the subject of religion so that she will appear to be a devout woman, but once again, the text shows contradiction and his redefinition of her is already unraveling at the beginning of the letter: "je ne crois pas être toute à Dieu, la plus chère moitié de moi-même étant encore dans le monde." (IV, 366) Here, Eloize is clearly divided between Abelard and her religious devotion, which undermines Grenaille's idea of Christian virtue. Yet, Grenaille soon abandons Eloize's dilemma (perhaps because it does not show evidence of spiritual conversion) and completely alters the course in the rest of the letter.

From this point on, he will fabricate the events in the epistle to further communicate a moral message to his readers. Eloize implores Abelard to seek solace and comfort in his spiritual life and to dedicate himself completely to God. Here, the shift in sequence is surprising, as Grenaille borrows Abelard's discourse in the final letter he wrote to Heloise. As we recall, he ordered her to forget him as a man, only address him as her brother in Christ and seek out his advice on monastic affairs. Grenaille grafts this spiritual aspect onto Eloize's invented letter to conclude his translation with a convincing representation of her persona as "La Magdalene Françaíse." Eloize begs Abelard to forget her by elevating himself spiritually as God's servant, and she advocates retreat, a term that has important connotations in the seventeenth century. Interestingly, Grenaille places her back in the confines of a cloister, which would be a familiar scenario to many of his readers. This enclosure of women in convents brings to mind the restricted choice that women had at the time; it was often marriage or monastic life, the convent was a place where women had to go if they were too poor to marry; some actually chose the convent if they were widows, or separated from their husbands, and still others elected of their free will to live in the cloister as a place of refuge. Spatially, this creates a brutal reversal in Grenaille's text. Eloize goes from the secularized site of the Cabinet back to a religious cell, but, once again, it is an imposed prison. This time it is Eloize who says that she finds solace in waiting to be reunited on the other side with her beloved, whereas, in the medieval text, it was Abelard who had expressed hope to rejoin Heloise in heaven. Eloize goes on to ask Abelard to abandon his study of scholastic theology in favor of practicing "la Morale."

She wants to persuade him that spiritual mysticism is the highest form of meditation, and she adds that they can learn the most in silence. She then launches into a diatribe in which she enumerates the virtues of sacred love:

> Après tout, persuadez-vous que nous n'avons jamais été plus intimes l'un à l'autre que si nous sommes à Dieu. C'est en lui que nous pourrons nous voir & nous saluer même dans notre absence mutuelle. (IV, 370)

Grenaille uses spiritual language, and thus deviates completely from the medieval Heloise's passionate tone. The original text was grounded in corporeal symbolism, but because Grenaille omits this aspect, the readers become convinced that Eloize has converted her carnal desire into sacred love, reinforced by the mystical style he is now using. It is Eloize who says "Adieu," which is astonishing in comparison to the original where she clearly indicated that she would never relinquish Abelard and was unable to convert her passion from the present into the past tense, indicating closure of the intimate relationship. Her use of the present tense was a sign that she still hoped Abelard would honor the pact by resuming dialogue on an amorous level, not a spiritual plane. As MacArthur reads it, passion in the epistolary narrative usually remains open-ended, which explains the widespread and strategic use of the present tense in the love letter.[29] The discourse of desire is not a fixed form intended to pursue meaning; it is discontinuous, free-flowing like passion, without borders or limits. The writer fights against closure or switching to the past tense because it would extinguish the passion that sustains the narrative and propels it forward throughout the course of the epistolary exchange. Grenaille, on the contrary, completely ignores this nuance in Heloise's writing in his endeavor to invent this last epistle. His final image of Eloize depicts her as a religious model of Chris-

[29] MacArthur 7-12.

tian virtue and self-sacrifice. He draws the letter to a close by striking a balance between the original, borrowed from Abelard's last letter to Heloise in the love correspondence, and his own version, thus shaping his feminine public's sensibilities, and at the same time he tells them what constitutes proper, Christian behavior, which is displayed by "La Magdalene Française":

> Adieu donc, cher Abélard, & si je ne mets point ici le nom d'Eloize, c'est que je veux que vous ne soyez proprement qu'à Dieu. Je me sers d'un terme d'Adieu, non pas par complement comme les autres, mais pour vous porter à vous mettre avec moi dans un état, où nous ne nous séparerons jamais. (IV, 370-371)

The lovers are thus predestined to a mystical reunion which is more in line with one Christian conception of the "couple" as well as Grenaille's idea of the "serious" moral representation of Eloize. The suppression of her "original" desire transforms her into a sober, holy figure. Other noteworthy modifications include the omission of Eloize's signature at the end of this letter, whereas previously all the missives were signed. As stated in the previous passage, she belabors the point. On one hand, this creates added credibility to the revision of her as "La Magdalene Française." Grenaille forces her to relinquish Abelard as a proof to his readers that she belongs to God. As a saint, she has become disembodied, disassociated from her original sensuality and overt carnal nature. But there are more subtle and serious textual implications of this omission. The underlying question is what the editor hopes to accomplish in leaving out her name. Once again, there is evidence pointing to the fragmentation of Heloise's persona by Grenaille's (re)invention of her epistles. As Grenaille erases her name from the missive, he gradually breaks her down from the vital, complete woman that she originally was to an inconsequential fraction; it is as if he were pronouncing her dead. Here, Grenaille seems to be following a textual progression that he created in his narrative construction. As noted earlier, he encloses Eloize in a cell and then proceeds to bury her within these ominous cloister walls. Kamuf's fascinating work on signature reads this from a Derridian perspective:

> It is an unnerving remainder or reminder, a fragment that was never wholly of the whole, be it author or work. Reading signature pieces cannot, therefore, offer a method of exorcism, restitution, or any other rite performed in view of some eternal life. The wager is of another order which puts on the line not life & death but, precisely, the line of their separation, the "single line divided."[30]

Here, a "single-line divided" refers to the concept of the cleavage between writer and text. Eloize is reduced to a mere "remainder," or shadow of her own signature; she is left out of her creation by Grenaille's authorial intervention. The distance from the text, underlined by the absence of her signature in this fourth letter, or even by Grenaille's technique of signing in her name as a "cover-up" for his masculine identity, points to, as Kamuf observed, the separation between the woman writer and her literary production, which ultimately leads to the question of the death of the author.[31] The erasure of Eloize's signature removes all traces that reflect her "original" letters. In writing her out, Grenaille relegates Eloize to the margins, and he, in turn, takes over. Consequently, Heloise gradually becomes a ghost of her own writing. To put it in Barthes' terms, the modern scriptor buries the author who is associated with the past. In Grenaille's translation, the burial process begins by introducing additions to and modifications of the original. His manipulative power play concerning her signature is but one example of "pseudo-feminocentrism": as he slips behind her desk, the site of the Other, and seizes control of her pen to invent a letter falsely attributed to her. Heloise's medieval persona fades into the background, and becomes a mere fragment of a lost whole

[30] Kamuf 10.
[31] Kamuf 145-73.

that is reworked in order to close the text with a convincing image of her as a penitent figure. With Grenaille, she now portrays a Christian model that readers should emulate, drawing inspiration from her great courage, suffering and sacrifice. From the moment that the medieval text is transformed into a confession by Grenaille's translation, Heloise's textual persona is set on a course determined by men who will revise her for their own benefit and self-interest. For the public, especially the female reader, the transformations of Heloise in the various translations and versions of her story points to a difficult and often complicated search in which one attempts to locate the woman's "original" discourse of desire that constitutes her literary claim to the birth and rise of the love letter as a genre. But before leaving Grenaille, it is intriguing to point out that this first modern French translation may not have been widely known, at least by critics: Charrier's extensive research on the various editions and versions still mentions Bussy-Rabutin as the first seventeenth-century translator who set out to translate Heloise and Abelard's love correspondence, probably because his version was widely circulated, and attracted greater readership.[32] Yet, Grenaille's contribution is highly significant not only as the first transformation that exists in the history of the legend of the medieval lovers, but also for his moral, Christian revision of Heloise into "La Magdalene Française."

[32] Charrier 411-17.

4.

Bussy Rabutin's Letters

The first prose rendering of the legend of Heloise and Abelard was written by Jacques Alluis, a lawyer from Grenoble who published his version in 1675. His text appeared long after Grenaille's partial translation, but it marked the (re)emergence in activity of other fictionalized accounts of the lovers' misfortunes. The most striking aspect of Alluis' literary production is the modifications of the structural framework. The work consists of an abridged short story that eliminates all medieval traces of the original love correspondence, including Abelard's *Historia* as an introduction to the love story. Although this abbreviated version did not attract great readership, I will look at some of the key changes in this rewriting of the tale, as they can be considered as a preface to Bussy Rabutin's later translation. Since the text contains no letters, and therefore falls outside of the theoretical, epistolary boundaries of studying the seventeenth-century translations of the legend, I will focus only on aspects of the (re)creation and (re)invention of Abelard and Heloise's personas which will resurface in Bussy Rabutin's text.

Alluis' Authorial Intentions

While brief, Alluis' preface may prove interesting to the reader, since the author states his intention in choosing to (re)tell Heloise's and Abelard's story. He advises the public to view the text not as a translation, but as an imitation. Like Grenaille, Alluis openly admits he has altered the historical events for his seventeenth-century audience, which he clarifies with an example. For instance, he has suppressed whatever may have physically transpired between the lovers at Argenteuil, and he alludes to having censured other carnal aspects of the twelfth-century story in order to respect the code of "bienséance." The focus on the couple's courtly relationship shows that the author wants to place love at the locus of his textual production; hence his title, *Les Amours d'Abailard et d'Héloïse*. Therefore, he will not deal specifically with the misfortunes (a veiled reference to the castration), which were the cause of the tragic course of events leading up to their separation. In this version, the sequence of events is inverted and restructured to focus on happier, imaginary episodes prior to Abelard's tragedy, the moment that concludes this brief prose narrative. Alluis may well say he wants to convey the truth to his readers; his idea of truth is far removed from the medieval text since he portrays Fulbert as Heloise's father. Already the stage is set for a fictionalized account of the couple's amorous adventures in which Fulbert's persona is more significantly developed. Here, he plays the role of Abelard's adversary who poses an obstacle to the couple's happiness until the closure of the love story, and their retreat into separate cloisters.

Restructuring: The Body of the Narrative

Alluis begins his imitation with a very loose abbreviation of the *Historia*, omitting Abelard's autobiographical point of view. The first few pages summarize Abelard's family background, and the events that actually led to his teaching position in Paris where he became a renowned theologian, professor and scholar. Abelard is described as a contemporary seventeenth-century man: "sa taille était riche, sa mine haute, son air & sa démarche d'un homme de qualité" (12). A few pages later, Alluis presents Heloise who, therefore, enters almost immediately in the narrative. It is stated that she was Fulbert's daughter, but to avoid any possible scandal, Fulbert, (who was also in the church), said she was his niece. Early on, Abelard recognizes Heloise's beauty and intellectual merit, a salient feature because in later seventeenth-century versions, the erudite or "savante" qualities of her personality will be diminished. Here, Alluis marks a transition between two extremes. He retains some of the medieval traits, while inventing new aspects of the lovers' personas. For instance, Abelard's charismatic, intellectual qualities are preserved as is Heloise's gift for languages and science, but at the same time Alluis draws our attention to her beauty:

> Heloïse avait la taille très bien prise, tous les traits de son visage étaient dans une juste proportion; mais surtout sa bouche & ses yeux étaient la plus belle chose du monde."[1] (11)

This seventeenth-century Heloise possesses the delicate refinement and grace characteristic of the aristocrats who frequented the salons. Even though Abelard is charmed by her beauty, he does not accept becoming her tutor immediately, whereas in the medieval text he does so practically from the beginning. Many social encounters are presented in dialogue form where the gallant Abelard is clearly flirting with Heloise, but she coyly resists his courtly advances and admiration. Alluis adds "precious" aspects to their conversations. His Heloise blushes, Abelard compliments her on her beauty and "bel esprit," but she receives his flattery in classic precious style, remaining cold and distant. As she even fears she could become the cause of Abelard's troubles, she unexpectedly leaves Paris to get away from him. Alluis creates a fictional, family home, Corbeil, that Fulbert had bought for Heloise's mother. At this point, Alluis has already introduced one of the most important modifications in the seventeenth-century revisions of Abelard's and Heloise's

---

[1] All of the quotes are taken from Jacques Alluis, *Les Amours d'Héloïse et d'Abélard* (Amsterdam: Chayer, 1695).

love story. Abelard is clearly in love with her from the start, but most of all he is less serious in his commitment to the Church than was his medieval counterpart. He speaks more often of love to Heloise than of other intellectual or spiritual topics. Although Alluis retains Abelard's theological and religious identification as background, he shows him actively pursuing his passionate intentions to have Heloise as his own. The text contains a great deal of physical movement as Abelard follows Heloise in and around Paris, hoping to win her affection and devotion. Alluis' fictional construction, the house at Corbeil, becomes the clandestine site of other meetings. When Abelard finally catches up with Heloise at Corbeil, she confesses to him a great secret concerning her birth. (The secret confession appears to be a common romanesque element in the seventeenth century.) Alluis fabricates a detailed subplot in which Heloise is Fulbert's illegitimate child. As a chanoine, he fell in love with Geneviève, Heloise's mother, who became pregnant and later had the baby at Corbeil in seclusion. The story is told by a third person, Heloise's maid, who increases the intrigue as her confident. She advises Abelard to keep the story a secret, due to its potentially scandalous repercussions. Heloise had hoped the story would discourage Abelard's interest in her, but on the contrary, he decides to make Fulbert an offer to tutor her. Here, the narrative reverts back along the lines of the medieval text, but the amorous interludes between the two lovers are already transcribed in "mondain" terms:

> [...] sous pretexte de s'adonner aux sciences, ils s'adonnaient aux plaisirs que cause une réciproque amitié. Comme l'étude & la méditation demandent des retraites & des lieux écartés, leur amour en profitait, sans que ceux qui s'en apercevaient y puissent trouver à redire. (47-48)

Other gallant language is used in the game of love, constructed upon the lively art of "badinage." We will see significant textual development of this aspect in Bussy Rabutin's later version, but, as shown in the medieval text, Alluis establishes himself as an innovator in suppressing Heloise's desire. The physical play of desire shifts to a more public space where passion is commonly described as "plaisir," "amitié" and "ardeur." These conversational, seductive terms were often heard in the salons to express flattery and admiration exchanged between "honnête" men and women. Alluis includes other elements that will reappear in Bussy's translation. For instance, he uses the word "prétexte" to introduce the double game of appearances. The lovers would use their lessons, as a pretense, to abandon themselves entirely "aux plaisirs que cause une réciproque amitié" (47). As we know, the idea of "réciproque amitié" was also valued by the "précieuses" as the ideal love relationship. The term was often used by Mlle de Scudéry and was very fashionable in the salons of literary women.[2] But, the "réciproque amitié" between Heloise and Abelard did not last long, and Alluis builds up the intrigue in the narrative by creating a purely fictional theme of jealousy with the addition of Alberic, a student of Abelard's, who also falls in love with Heloise.

The Triangular Structure of Desire

Alluis does not stop with Alberic who pursues Heloise throughout most of the story. There is an interior, structural modification in this text based on the creation of triangular desire. On the one hand, Fulbert is jealous of Abelard perhaps because he secretly loves Heloise too much, but he is not alone. Her three admirers, Alberic, Abelard and Fulbert, are all positioned at different points of the triangle. At the intersecting angles of each line of the triangle, Heloise is caught between two masculine poles, as the object of the two men's desire. Once again, the woman is the gift or the commodity exchanged be-

---

[2] For detailed information on the salons, see Lougee's, *Le Paradis des femmes*.

tween males, which also promotes a form of homoerotic bonding. Alluis plays with the romanesque implications of triangular desire in an exaggerated, melodramatic fashion. For instance, Alberic spies on the couple and then reports back to Fulbert; he subsequently competes with Abelard for Heloise's hand in marriage. As in the medieval text, Heloise's marriage plans are delayed as the author preserves her original argument against matrimony, looking upon it as inappropriate for a philosopher, but Abelard's persona is altered and significantly weakened. He is overwhelmed by jealousy, and threatened by his young student. The drama is heightened by a scene is created in which Abelard, hidden outside Heloise's door, overhears Alberic ask her to marry him; he, in turn, becomes infuriated. It does not take long for the young student to realize that his professor is also in love with Heloise, but the lovers' happiness is further jeopardized by Fulbert's decision to order Heloise to marry Alberic. Although Fulbert forbids her to see Abelard, Heloise arranges to meet Abelard secretly while her father is away at morning and evening vespers. The intrigue is increased through the fictional insertion of the "billet." Alberic receives word that he must return home because of a sick family member, and thus the marriage is delayed. His absence allows Heloise and Abelard to see each other more often, but always clandestinely, never openly. Abelard reasons an acceptable, social strategy in part to console Heloise and to persuade her to continue their relationship, saying that married women can still maintain "un commerce gallant." Precious women and gallant men in the seventeenth century were strong believers in (or reduced to) either extramarital or non-marital amorous relationships.[3] This inserted aspect modernizes the lovers, rendering them appealing to contemporary aristocrats' literary tastes.

---

[3] On the subject of seventeenth-century gallantry, see *Coquettes et précieuses* Ed. Eva Avigdor. (Paris: Nizet, 1982). Also, Dorothy Backer's *Precious Women* (New York: Basic Books, 1974) and Maurice Magendie's *La Politesse mondaine*

After Fulbert eventually finds the lovers together, and packs Heloise off to Corbeil, she sends a "billet" to Abelard forewarning him of Fulbert's anger. As a fictional element, the "billet" augments the intrigue in the plot. It circulates in a public context, which marks the transition between the private space of the medieval text and the more public sphere of this fictionalized seventeenth-century version. As we know, in the salons, these short messages were frequently circulated to arrange meetings between lovers and to relay other brief messages containing personal information. Here, Abelard answers Heloise's brief note and arrives, in disguise, at Corbeil to see her, slipping into her room secretly in a circuitous way through the garden. Heloise tells him she is pregnant, but her familiar stance against marriage is reworded and shifted into the context of the times: she says she would rather be his slave than his wife and she would prefer him as her master instead of her husband, a choice of words which seems to privilege the seductive relationship identified with Abelard's role as her tutor, and, in turn, relegates her to a submissive, subservient position. At the same time, the disparity in the power relationship underlined by the dialectic of master and slave also favors the illicit aspects of the lovers' desire, outside the legal constraints of the marital bond. We recall that Grenaille also used the idea of slavery, but the wording was presented differently as a result of his monophonic translation that did not include Abelard as a partner. This reference to the slavery of marriage will also reappear in Bussy's text, and so, once again Alluis insertion sets the tone for other versions. Other aspects of Heloise's diatribe against matrimony are more in line with a more contemporary rendition of the medieval text. She describes matrimony as "le tombeau de l'amour" and a "tromperie," which could be read as a precious attack. Her reluctance anticipates her "en-

---

et les théories de l'honnêteté en France au XVIIe siècle de 1600-1660 (Paris: Felix Alcan, 1926).

lèvement" from Corbeil by Abelard so that she can have her baby in hiding. Alluis' text is colored with a series of adventures involving physical movement, also popular with aristocratic readers, and following the tradition of the heroic novel. Narrative progression is delayed by adding numerous romanesque episodes. For instance, Alberic, who arrives at Corbeil after Abelard has carried Heloise off with him, finds a message addressed to her mother in her room. As he intercepts the message, and learns the secret of Heloise's birth as well as the real identities of her parents, he is revolted by the knowledge that Fulbert is her father. Once again, the public aspect of the "billet" is brought out. Alberic goes public with the fact that Abelard has taken Heloise with him, and he does not hesitate in transmitting this information to Fulbert. The privacy of the message is violated. Eventually, Abelard returns to confront Fulbert and to strike a compromise of marriage on the condition, as previously seen in the medieval text, that the marriage will be kept secret in order to protect his reputation. Alluis intervenes in the text as a narrator to tell the reader that matrimony was not the end to their love story. Fulbert pursues his plan to destroy Abelard, and admits publicly that the two were man and wife. Here, Alluis reverts back to the events of the medieval text, and, as we recall, Abelard decided to place Heloise at Argenteuil to protect her from Fulbert's wrath. But the plot similarity ends here as Alluis embellishes the original text and adds new characters in the central part of his work, which builds the intrigue and amplifies the fictional dimensions of the text.

Amorous Adventures and Monastic Life

The first important modification in the narrative is the introduction of Luce, Abelard's mother, whom Heloise fortuitously meets at Argenteuil. Luce acts as a confidant forewarning Heloise of the discipline and hardship of religious life. She hopes to persuade Heloise to think twice before committing herself as a nun. Alluis casts Luce in the role as the older voice of reason. Heloise soon begins to confide in her about her adventures with Abelard. Here, we find a striking difference from the medieval text as Abelard continues to visit her at Argenteuil: "Ils se communiquèrent leurs désirs, & Héloïse fut chargée du soin de chercher quelque invention pour les satisfaire." (103). Alluis' representation of religious retreat transforms it into a mere appearance of devotion. One of the key modifications is the fact that Heloise does not take the veil, which allows her the freedom to leave the cloister: "[...elle y prît tous les habits de Religieuse, hormis le Voile, afin qu'elle pût en sortir quand l'occasion favorable s'en présenterait..]" (97).

The change in Heloise's monastic attire also reflects Alluis' architectural restructuring of the convent. In sharp contrast to the medieval text, Heloise's cell is not an oppressive prison, separating her from her lover, but rather an open space, an escape hatch allows her to flee once the night falls, and rejoin Abelard outside. It is not long before Heloise finds another nun with a lover, and they devise a plan to escape at night so that they can meet their suitors on the other side of the wall. These fictional episodes recall the heroic and courtly adventures of the lengthy, frequently tedious novels that were popular at the beginning of the century, yet with a more overtly sexual bent quite typical of the end of the century's fascination for "chroniques scandaleuses." Alluis embroiders the medieval narrative in his fictionalized description of Heloise's clever plot to deceive the nuns. She and the other sister leave a light on in their rooms to create the illusion of late-night prayer, but it is only a cover-up for their adventures. The staging of their nocturnal flight reminds the reader of the twelfth-century damsel in the tower rescued by her gallant knight. Heloise and her friend escape "a l'aide d'une échelle de soie que leurs amants leur tenaient" (106). The seventeenth-century reader would probably find this elaborate sequence of events appealing and be amused by the web of ruse and deception concocted by the two young women. Once they meet their lovers on the outside, the following events of the evening are structured along the lines of a game of "être" and "paraître." The other nun's lover, Baudoin, takes Heloise for a real nun. He does not know that she is neither religious nor available, since Abelard never reveals that she is a married woman. Charmed and intrigued by Heloise, Baudoin proposes that they change partners. But Abelard is inwardly against the idea even though he does not say anything. As a jealous and sensitive lover, he is totally repulsed by the thought of sharing his wife. He finds a way to forewarn Heloise of Baudoin's plan and plays along with the young man. Baudoin leads Heloise into a "cabinet" to seduce her, but she discourages him. In a melodramatic way, Alluis places Abelard at the door where he overhears the conversation, which only increases his jealousy. Soon after they part ways with Baudoin and his nun, Heloise and Abelard devise another plan to see each other in private.

This fictional addition above resembles some of La Fontaine's *Contes*. The reader recognizes the familiar signs: the clever game of mistaken identity, the secret doors, and the amorous intrigue that takes place in the dark. Heloise has Abelard enter through a secret, back door, but another nun sees her as she, too, awaits the clandestine, nocturnal visit of her suitor. Her lover enters as Abelard exits and, in the dark, the other man takes Heloise for his beloved. Suddenly, the lights go on, the nuns deduce that someone had let this man into the convent, and the other nun who had seen Heloise and Abelard is surprised to see her own lover there. Alluis exaggerates the plot even further by the revelation of the unknown lover's identity, none other than Abelard's student, Alberic, who was courting another nun in Heloise's order. Heloise finally admits that she is married, and the sisters let Alberic go; but the scandal doesn't stop there. It reaches the "abbé" of the church who decides to visit the convent:

> il découvrit tant d'intrigues amoureuses, tant de débauches, tant de prostitutions, qu'il resolut dés alors d'anéantir entièrement ce Monastère, dont les débordements étaient si excessifs. (120)

When Fulbert learns of the possible damage to Heloise's reputation, he comes up with a plan to have Abelard castrated. Alluis' description of the castration is based on the medieval narrative, but he obeys the seventeenth-century code of "bienséance" and thus avoids the direct use of the word itself:

> on le punit dans la partie qui avait péché, & on le mit de ne pouvoir jamais devenir père: enfin on exerça sur lui cette horrible cruauté dont les siècles suivants ont tant parlé. (122)

As in the original text, Abelard's shame is his overall motivation in choosing monastic retreat. In concluding his abridged narrative, Alluis focuses on the marriage as the seminal source of the couple's epistolary correspondence. He draws his story to a close by adding that the lovers had the pleasure, until the end of their lives, to persuade one another of their love and fidelity. Here again, the revision of Heloise is in part constructed upon her medieval predecessor, as she blames God for the misfortunes caused by their marriage. According to her, it was only after their "plaisir" became "honnête," that God let them suffer and punished their matrimonial state with pain befitting an adulterer's sin. Alluis paraphrases this idea as he reformulates it as the subject of Heloise's "plainte" in her missives, and the text closes at the moment the separation is imminent. Alluis has modified the structure in that his version precedes the love correspondence and concentrates on the couple's amorous adventures prior to the castration. As his title suggests, he rewrites the love narrative instead of dealing with the other tale, the tragedy that he leaves for Bussy Rabutin.

Bussy Rabutin's "Free" Translation

Bussy Rabutin's translation of Abelard and Heloise's love correspondence was published in 1687, twelve years after Alluis' romanesque rendition of the lovers' story. Many critics actually consider Bussy's version as the first epistolary translation as one more complete since it included both of the lovers' letters, whereas Grenaille only worked on a partial translation of Heloise's epistles and excluded Abelard's missives. In fact, Charrier's monumental study on the legend ignores Grenaille's initial effort, but C. Rouben's more recent work on Bussy Rabutin as a letter writer acknowledges Grenaille's translation as a preface to Bussy's version. Rouben considers Bussy's translation important because he expanded the genre and paved the way for the next literary wave, the letter novel that arose at the end of the century.[4] Bussy seemed to have intended the text to be an amusing read for his friends who enjoyed the epistolary genre. He worked on this translation during his years in exile, (for subversive and slanderous writing on many famous, public figures in his novel, *Histoire amoureuse des Gaules*), from Louis the XIV's court. At his country chateau, Bussy had the time to devote to his writing and to choose whatever literary project he wished. He had prior experience in translating Ovid's *Heroides* and was well versed in the trope of the "plainte," or the familiar topos of the abandoned heroine consumed by the pathos of her solitude. As Bray noted, Ovid was one of the key sources in the development of the overall epistolary genre in the seventeenth century.[5] As for other literary influences, we cannot say that Bussy actually read *Lettres portugaises*, but it is highly plausible since the work attracted enormous public attention. His cousin, Madame de Sévigné, even coined the phrase writing letters "à la portugaise," as a reference to the art of composing

---

[4] C. Rouben offers an insightful study of Bussy Rabutin's life and career in his *Bussy Rabutin, Epistolier* (Paris: Nizet, 1974).
[5] Bray 14-16.

love letters. As Rouben suggests, it is most likely that Bussy was familiar with Guillerague's work, whose style is reflected in the translation of the medieval couple's tragic missives.[6] So far, the few critics who have looked at Bussy's text have not taken the work very seriously. Charrier insisted that the gallant adventures and courtly aspects were far removed from the medieval narrative.[7] Rouben is less harsh, but prefaces his remarks by clarifying that Bussy's version is extremely unfaithful to the Latin text (as were many other translations of other texts in the seventeenth century).[8] He also placed it in the aristocratic, gallant tradition and underlined the importance of Bussy's contribution in creating widespread interest in the lovers tragic tale, which would continue to attract more readers well into the eighteenth century. Above all, Rouben pointed out the combination of novel and love letters intertwined in the form. Other critics like Robertson labeled the text a comic version, and another Bussy scholar, Gérard-Gailly, read it as deviating radically from the medieval story.[9] Bussy's attitude towards the text perhaps sheds more light on how he hoped his public would receive his version. In the description of his project to Madame de Sévigné, he provides insight on his motivation in choosing the text:

> Je me suis amusé à en traduire quelques-unes {les lettres} qui m'ont donné beaucoup de plaisir. Je n'ai jamais vu plus beau Latin, surtout celui de la Religieuse, ni plus d'amour & d'esprit qu'elle en a.[10]

Writing for pleasure not only reflects authorial intention, but also sets the tone for his audience in the late seventeenth centu-

---

[6] Rouben 111-116.
[7] Charrier 411-12.
[8] Rouben 116-17.
[9] See D.W. Robertson's book, *Abelard and Heloise* (New York: The Dial Press, 1972). Also, Emile Gerard-Gailly's *Bussy-Rabutin, sa vie ses oeuvres et ses amies* (Paris: Honoré Champion, 1909): 294-387.
[10] Bussy Rabutin, *Les Lettres de messire Roger de Rabutin, comte de Bussy,* XV, I (Paris: Florentin et Pierre Delaulne, 1697): 49.

ry. Rabutin adapted his translation in accordance with the literary taste of his readers. Consequently, Abelard and Heloise differ greatly from their medieval ancestors. Bussy's characters play out their desire through the exchange of language, whereas their medieval predecessors (mainly Heloise) articulated their desire through the body. Like Alluis, Bussy begins by displacing them, taking them out of their intimate ambiance and placing them into a more public sphere. The couple now appear as social participants in the luxurious and elegant interiors of the salons where aristocrats gathered to engage in conversation, and the games of sophisticated banter and mutual admiration. Like his fellow seventeenth-century translators or imitators, Bussy respects the code of "honnête," "bienséant" behavior and modulates the passionate elements of the original text that would have been considered too shocking or explicit for his public. Once again, as in Grenaille and Alluis, the words castration, mutilation and concubine are eliminated from the text. Bussy focuses on the gallant code of etiquette and polite conversation that were considered essential skills for the successful "honnête" aristocrat.[11] But before looking at his translation of Heloise and Abelard's love letters, it is necessary to preface the discussion with a preliminary outline of Bussy's structural changes placed within the context of the importance of spoken dialogue that is then transferred into the written epistle.

Structural Modifications: Creating a Frame for Free Translation

The most striking aspect of Bussy's text is that it restores a significant, structural element of the medieval text. Epistolary dialogue is reconstructed between the lovers so that the couple can

---

[11] Domna Stanton elaborates on the specific traits of "honnêteté in her book, *The Aristocrat as Art: A Study of the honnête homme and the Dandy in Seventeenth and Nineteenth-Century French Literature* (New York Columbia UP, 1980): 119-146.

engage in a mutual, amorous conversation which is developed throughout the exchange of letters. Altman comments on the importance of the addressee's role in the epistle:

> In letter language, moreover, the addressee plays a role; he is able, & is expected, to initiate his own utterance. Such reciprocality whereby the original you becomes the I of a new utterance is essential to the maintenance of the epistolary exchange.[12]

Unlike Grenaille, Bussy respects the general narrative form of the medieval correspondence. In other words, he constructs his free translation on the organizational principle of balance and reciprocality between the two lovers. Elizabeth Goldsmith discusses this idea in her enlightening *Exclusive Conversations,* in which she elaborates on different aspects of dialogue in "mondain" circles. For example, the "honnête" man or woman had to be talented and able to sustain an intriguing conversation as well as possess the ability to transpose this spoken skill into written form. At the locus of conversation, the reader finds a highly codified set of rules that governs the spoken pact adhered to by aristocrats frequenting the salons. Grenaille and Méré are examples of the vast group of moralists proposing written rules or virtual "how-to guides" for the ambitious socialite who wanted to "make it" in the elite circle of those seasoned in "honnête" conversation. Grenaille believed that one should express oneself naturally, and with ease. The "honnête" man was not supposed to be too serious or too brilliant, and he had to be careful not to appear too pedantic or affected. Méré agreed with Grenaille but stressed that the "honnête homme" should always be aware of his social goal, which was to amuse his listeners. Other principles of conversation included sensitivity to the interlocutor, proper moral etiquette, and the selection of light subjects that would give optimal pleasure to the other

---

[12] Janet Altman, *Epistolarity: Approaches to a Form* (Columbus: Ohio State UP, 1982): 117.

participants in the conversation.[13] The most scintillating topic was of course love, which we will return to later. Furthermore, balance and modulation, (as well as prudence, civility and discretion), were important rules to respect in the art of developing successful conversational skills. Like Goldsmith, Jean Starobinski also underlines the idea of balance and reciprocity as a fundamental principle of the aristocrat's way of interacting with others: "[...] l'idéal de l'honnêteté; c'est la réciprocité parfaite: l'individu qui se met en évidence s'expose dans son mérite."[14] In restoring the reciprocality between Heloise and Abelard, the reader must bear in mind the social importance of polite, harmonious conversation. This structural modification is seminal to the interpretation of the translation. Elizabeth Goldsmith, Erica Harth and Domna Stanton all point out the importance of polite conversation in the seventeenth century.[15] They insist on the nexus between writing and conversation for the "honnête" man or woman who wished to gain admittance to the most elite salons of the period. Their position is affirmed by Mlle de Scudéry, who, in her *Nouvelles conversations sur divers sujets,* often referred to the fundamental, social necessity of the two social skills, which, in turn, applies to Bussy, whose text combines these oral and written conversational elements.[16] The lovers create the illusion of conversing together, which is then reproduced in written form, the love letter, and sent off to the interlocutor, the reciprocal object of desire. As Altman ob-

---

[13] For more information on the conversational aspects of "honnêteté," see Goldsmith *Exclusive Conversations* pp. 41-54.

[14] Jean Starobinski. "Sur la flatterie," *Nouvelle Revue de la Psychanalyse* 4 (1971): 132.

[15] In addition to Goldsmith's *Exclusive Conversations,* already noted, see Erika Harth's, *Cartesian Women: Versions and Subversions of rational Discourse in the Old Regime* (Ithaca & London: Cornell UP, 1992) and Stanton's *The Aristocrat as Art,* cited above. These scholars all elaborate on the specifics and importance of polite conversation in seventeenth-century culture.

[16] See *Nouvelles conversations sur divers sujets par Mlle de Scudéry, I* (La Haye: Guillaume de Vays, 1710).

serves in her theoretical work on epistolarity, this model is a characteristic of the genre:

> As a written dialogue, epistolary discourse is obsessed with its oral model [...] the epistolary dialogue attempts to approximate conversation of the "here" and the "now." (Altman 135-6)

The reader recognizes the talky aspects of Bussy's epistolary dialogue, whereas Grenaille's monophonic translation was more auricular in nature. It is also possible that the verbal aspect is more highly developed in Bussy's translation because the body language is erased. The couple is pursuing a less immediately physical discourse of desire, one that can be talked about in the presence of others because it is gallant and polite instead of explicitly carnal as in the medieval text. We will, however, see moments when Bussy, (he was after all a libertine), does preserve such authentic fragments of the medieval narrative as the erotic dream sequence, but he will tone it down for his readers. In respecting the decorum of the day, Bussy will remodel Heloise as a precious woman; however, she is not the same as in Grenaille's portrayal of her as a moral role model. In this version, the reader can easily imagine her in the public space of the salon, engaging in polite dialogue, coyly concealed behind her fan, blushing as she listens to Abelard's flattery and enticing words of love and devotion. Abelard will appear as an "honnête home," more interested in declaring his "tendresse" and admiration to Heloise than talking about religious matters, and thus once again differing radically from his medieval counterpart. Moreover, Bussy's Abelard will play the role of a man in love. As in Alluis' prose version of Abelard, he will pursue his object of desire from the start. But he will go back to using the epistolary form to correspond with Heloise, voicing his passion through the courtly code, befitting of a seventeenth-century gallant suitor who seeks to win the esteem and respect of his lady.

Letter 1: Imitating a (Supposed) Woman's "Plainte"

In his work devoted to the legend of Heloise and Abelard, D. W. Robertson observed that Bussy's first letter closely resembled the medieval text.[17] Thematically, we find indeed the same subjects as in the Zumthor translation. Heloise receives a copy of Abelard's letter to a friend, relives her love for him, asks him why he doesn't write to her, and hopes to restore communication. Bussy's Heloise is older, however, in her late teens, and much more beautiful than her more austere predecessor. The first line refers to the "hasard" of receiving Abelard's autobiographical epistle, a word which takes on new meaning in the seventeenth century. This "hasard" is in fact the unexpected catalyst that allows the couple fortuitously to participate in epistolary exchange. Heloise's reading of Abelard's epistle immediately releases a flow of memories and a renewed experience of longing. The addition of "tears" reflects the Ovidian influence on Bussy. It is also possible that Guillerague's portrayal of the Portuguese nun's suffering is used here as a generalized model for feminine suffering. Kauffman considers tears an integral component of the "feminine" discourse of desire:

> Through such signs, the heroine transmits a part of herself, the corporeal, to the textual, implying that the body's message is truer than speech; tears are irrefutable evidence. Tears prove-both to the lover and the beloved—that grief is not an illusion.[18]

As a reader and translator of Ovid, Bussy's use of tears shows an imitation of "feminine," "natural" expression of pain, which equally reveals his authorial intentions. Like Ovid's heroines, his Heloise moistens her letters with tears as a means of transmitting her interior, sincere pathos. As Kauffman reads it, tears in epistles are more important than words because they measure the disparity between what is signified and the manner in

[17] Robertson 159.
[18] Kauffman 36.

which it is signified.[19] Throughout this excessive display of suffering, Bussy also transforms Heloise's spatial surroundings into a prison similar to that of the Portuguese nun. In the medieval text, Heloise's tears are less frequent and she does not allude to the convent as a prison in her opening missive. This seventeenth century-version immediately sets the stage for a sentimental construction placing love at the core, and therefore downplaying the religious dialogue of the original circumstances. One of the initial major changes appears almost at the beginning. Bussy's Heloise clearly establishes the purpose of telling their story:

> Puisque le temps, qui vient à bout de tout, n'a point usé leur haine contre vous, et que votre vertu est toujours persécutée, je suis résolue de publier en toutes les langues nos disgrâces, pour faire honte au siècle injuste qui ne nous a pas connu;[20] (I, 56)

Erica Harth's recent work (*Cartesian Women*) provides insight on the idea of "going public" in the seventeenth century. She observes that revealing information publicly means recording spoken language, and then divulging private secrets to the society.[21] This applies to Bussy's will to have Heloise set the record straight. As Charrier indicated, the medieval text remained virtually unknown until the seventeenth century when Bussy decided to translate it, making it more accessible to the contemporary literary taste of his readers. By this time, Bussy was capitalizing on the popularity of the letter as people were developing an ever-increasing fascination with amorous narratives written in epistolary form. In telling the lovers' story publicly, Bussy could then attract the attention of many readers in order to bring back to the original text the justice it well deserved.

---

[19] Kauffman 36-7.

[20] Quotes are taken from Bussy Rabutin, *Lettres d'Héloïse et d'Abélard* (Paris: Lacrampe Fils et Co., 1847).

[21] Harth 15-63.

But in order to market his own version, Bussy added and incorporated other popular elements that the seventeenth-century "mondain" reader appreciated in novels. For example, Heloise elaborates on the joy of looking at Abelard's portrait, which Guillerague had previously used with the image of the soldier in Mariane's cell:

> En attendant que vous me donniez le même plaisir, je goûte celui de regarder souvent votre portrait: je le néglige quand je vous vois, votre absence le rend meilleur; mais si la peinture donne tant de plaisir, quelle joie n'inspirent point les lettres; elles qui parlent, qui allument et qui nourrissent le feu de nos passions! (I,57)

The painted representation of the beloved functions as a metonymic substitute for Abelard's presence. But the portrait had other significance for the aristocrats, especially in the salons. For the "précieuses," the portrait was an index to interior analysis of the sentiments contained within the representation. John Lyon's work on painting in the seventeenth century looked upon the image as a sign that could bridge the gap between presence and absence, but yet never fulfill it, and this theory seems to apply quite well to the epistolary genre.[22] The portrait is a stand-in for Abelard as well as a constant reminder of his absence. Susan Stewart's more recent work on longing opens up new possibilities for Bussy's use of the pictorial image. She regards the portrait as a miniature of the person or as a mirror of the absent other; the reduced representation of the lover allows for possession of the face by the beholder. In gazing at the portrait or reflection of Abelard, Heloise is able to recall the contours of his face. As a result, she then restores partial presence of her beloved. If we apply Stewart's idea of the face functioning like a mirror, we could say that in talking to Abelard, through the combination of oral and written dialogue, Heloise

---

[22] See John Lyon's "Speaking in Pictures, Speaking of Pictures: Problems of Representation in the Seventeenth Century." *Mimesis: From Mirror to Method, Augustine to Descartes,* ed. John Lyons and Stephen Nichols (Hanover & London: New England UP, 1982).

repairs the communication gap. Textual evidence of this idea will be found in Abelard's reply to her first letter. Stewart describes the importance of the face by comparing it with the text:

> Behind the appearance of eyes and mouth lies the interior stripped of appearances. Hence we "read" the expression of the face with trepidation, for this reading is never apparent from the surface alone; it is continually confronted by the correction of the other. The face is a type of "deep" text, a text whose meaning is complicated by change.[23]

Bussy plays with the surface or the appearance of the lovers to create a different reality that Stewart calls "the deep text" or, to put it in other words, the image that is revealed underneath the painted exterior. To apply this to Bussy's version, the mouth is the part of the body that leads the reader into the interior behind the face or mask of the characters. In reading this translation, the oral quality of the words flowing from the mouth constitutes the focal point of Bussy's narrative. As we will see later on, it is the mouth that manipulates dual dialogues. Although Bussy's tone is predominantly light, he does color the text with more serious moments when he invites the reader to delve beneath the surface of the code of gallantry into the deeper space of the interior. Here, we find another hidden discourse revealing the Ovidian influence constructed on the discourse of amatory pathos.

In her first letter, Heloise goes on to talk about how she would wear Abelard's letters like an emblem, crushing them to her breast and showering them with kisses. Here, the letter as a "sign" for the absent lover becomes exaggerated and even comical, as she says she would never stop kissing Abelard's letters if he would write to her. Heloise orders him to write from the heart, as salon women who believed love letters were to be written naturally and spontaneously from the heart. According to Scudéry and Sévigné, the heart should speak in the love let-

[23] Susan Stewart, *On Longing* (Durham & London: Duke UP, 1993): 127.

ter, and Scudéry also proposed other rules for composing love letters: "il faut qu'une lettre d'amour ait plus de sentiments que d'esprit, que le style en soit naturel, respectueux & passionné."[24] In imitating Heloise's love letters, Bussy seems to abide by these stylistic conventions. In the text, Heloise tries to persuade Abelard that they could still see each other. The clandestine meeting was also a common romanesque seventeenth-century element that appealed to readers (as previously seen in Alluis' prose version):

> [...] le sacrement a rendu notre commerce hors de scandale; vous pouvez même me voir sans danger. Quand nos voeux ne seraient pas un obstacle à nos plaisirs, et que nous pourrions les oublier, la cruauté de mon oncle à votre égard ne nous laisse rien à craindre de notre tendresse. (I, 59)

The possibility of the secret, stolen interlude differs from the medieval text and also points out the striking suppression of the religious discourse in Bussy's version. As in Alluis' prose translation, the convent creates only the appearance of austerity and devotion, but behind the surface Heloise actively pursues amatory dialogue. But Bussy curbs Heloise's desire in order to realign her sentiments with the appropriate decorum of the times. He veils the reference to the word castration by rephrasing the events:

> Mon oncle a cru que, semblable aux autres femmes, je n'aimerais que votre sexe, il s'est trompé en vous l'ôtant, je me venge bien de lui, en vous accablant de toute ma tendresse. (I, 60)

Unlike her medieval sister's diction, her love and undying devotion are modulated and shifted into precious "tendresse." Interestingly, there is no mention of the body. She then launches into a "precious" diatribe against marriage, shown by the words often used by Scudéry and other "precious women," to emphasize the slavery of the institution:

---

[24] Scudéry, *Nouvelles conversations* 43.

> Combien vous ai-je témoigné de répugnance pour le mariage! Quoique je connusse bien que le nom de femme était auguste parmi les hommes et saint dans la religion, je trouvais plus de charmes dans celui de votre maîtresse. Les chaînes du mariage portent un attachement nécessaire qui ôte la gloire d'aimer. (I, 60)

The "précieuses" were reputed champions of women's rights and greatly criticized the enslavement of the marriage bond. As Jean-Michel Pelous observed in the third part of his *Amour précieux amour galant,* the "précieuses" envisioned utopian reforms that would free women from the tyranny of marriage.[25] Precious women were strong advocates of "l'amitié tendre" as an alternative to the physical entrapment of matrimony. Heloise is speaking like a "précieuse," as she, too, prefers "tendresse" to marriage and wants to protect her love at all costs so that it will not be destroyed by legal bondage. Here, Bussy's Heloise takes the same position as her medieval sister, but the language has been altered. As we know, while the medieval text uses "concubine" the seventeenth-century version substitutes "maîtresse" in order to avoid the vulgar connotation of the original wording. In contrast to the medieval text, Bussy's version is distinguished by a striking absence of the female body's articulation of desire. On the contrary, Heloise goes on to envision a spiritual union constructed on a pure concept of reciprocal love, also a salon ideal. Pelous suggests that the "précieuses" also believed in a utopian concept based on equality between the sexes.[26] In favoring reciprocal love, Bussy's Heloise appears to be searching for that balance. Thus, she integrates the precious ideal, or the public influence into her personal dialogue with Abelard. At the same time, she uses the idea of reciprocity as a persuasive strategy, hoping Abelard will answer her with a letter. She wants him to actively participate in the game of love

---

[25] Jean-Michel Pelous offers a very detailed section on the cultural history of precious women in his book, *Amour précieux, amour gallant* (Paris: Klincksieck, 1980). For his comments on their position on marriage, see pp. 250-63.
[26] Pelous 330-52.

and to flatter her by responding in the tone that becomes a gallant suitor. Bussy affirms this idea further on in his "mondain" allusion to a powdered, courtly Abelard. Heloise describes this image of Abelard in her epistle, coaxing him to write to her by flattering him:

> Le moyen de n'être pas touché de votre air, de vos manières, de la vivacité de votre esprit, du brillant de vos conversations?[. . .]Avec quelle facilité faites-vous des vers les plus galants du monde! Persone ne badine comme vous! (I, 61)

Here, Bussy has completely transformed Abelard's persona. There are no references to his "serious" side as a theologian and philosopher, aspects that would be incompatible with the portrayal of Abelard as a gallant lover intent on impressing Heloise by his skill at manipulating the spoken word, later committed to paper. Religious subjects would be considered too pedantic for a "mondain" who sought to please and amuse his lady with his conversation. Only the courtly elements characteristic of gallantry are woven into the narrative. Abelard's original songwriting talents are also shifted into the aristocratic context. In the medieval text, the songs were originally composed and shared in private at Fulbert's house. But in the seventeenth century, the context is redirected towards a more public space. The songs and verses are delightful and flattering to Heloise's beauty and grace. The "précieuses" greatly appreciated verse and poetry as a topic of discussion in their salons and as a forum for oral presentation in front of others. Heloise talks about the fact that Abelard's songs were celebrated by others, and she mentions that she even had rivals, jealous of her lover's devotion to her. Bussy transforms Abelard's "esprit"; he is no longer described as a charismatic orator who attracted droves of students to his religious lectures, but as a clever, gallant suitor, skilled in the fine art of courting a lady. In the "mondain" context, the verb "badiner" is very significant since it is an acquired art and index to one's success in society. Like Alluis, Bussy further enhances the aristocratic transformation of the couple by inserting "billets," thereby altering the medieval description of Heloise's entry into monastic life: "En prononçant mes voeux j'avais sur moi un billet de vous, par lequel vous me juriez que vous seriez toujours à moi" (I, 62).

In "mondain" circles, the "billet" was circulated to pass on brief information typically pertaining to meetings between lovers or friends. *In Conversations nouvelles sur divers sujets,* Scudéry suggested that the love letter had to remain secret because of its intimate nature, but the" billet" could be passed around publicly if it contained information that would not violate one's privacy. Here, the fictional "writing in" of the "billet" differs from Scudéry's rules of social etiquette. Even as a contemporary addition to the text, it is clearly associated with the legend as it brings intrigue to the narrative. The insertion of the "billet" also tends to diminish the serious tone of the original scene where Heloise took her vows, which marked the eternal, tragic separation of the lovers. But the "billet" is also a sign of doubleness in Bussy's text. On the outside, Heloise pronounces the vows of her profession, but this is a deceptive appearance because underneath the religious attire is the other discourse, symbolized by the "billet" or the emblem of sentimental love. "Je ne dois penser qu'à Dieu, et je ne parle que d'un homme" (63). Bussy embroiders and enriches Heloise's duplicitous speech and transforms her language into that of a "précieuse":

> Au travers des feux dont je brûle, je me vois quelquefois comme une pécheresse qui devrait pleurer ses péchés: et, misérable que je suis, je ne pleure que mon amant: je rappelle sans cesse le souvenir de ces péchés; mais ce n'est pas de les avoir commis que j'ai de la douleur, c'est de ne les plus commettre. (I, 63)

Jean-Michel Pelous and Roger Lathuillère identify "feu," and "flamme" as precious jargon linked to the ornamental, embellished descriptions of love appreciated by these women. As Pelous noted, these poetic terms were substitutes for carnal passion.[27] In general, precious women were prone to excessiveness in their expressions, and the passage above shows a clear example of Heloise's exaggerated sentiments. Bussy also plays with the word "péché"; here it takes on a secularized connotation. Instead of suffering because she sinned against God, she is tormented because she can no longer commit the same sins. As seen in the medieval text, Abelard is, once again, placed at the center of her epistle, but in this updated version Heloise's love shifts away from the physical to a more spiritual, purified love. It is an ideal shared by the "précieuses." Bussy's Heloise also asks Abelard to cure her of her love for him, "par pitié aidez-moi à me guérir de vous" (64), which does not occur in the medieval text. As in Grenaille's transformation of her persona, Bussy's Heloise differs radically at the end of her first letter. She abruptly changes the tone and direction of her epistle and asks Abelard to find a new path for them, which, as we recall, was Abelard's original strategy in the medieval text:

> Sans changer de coeur, changeons d'objet; élevons nos esprits à Dieu; n'ayons de transports communs que pour sa gloire; j'attends cela de sa miséricorde. (I, 65)

Bussy further alters the medieval text by substituting the word "coeur" for "chair" and adding "transports," common seventeenth-century terms referring to violent passion, as noted in Richelet's dictionary. He further modernizes the passage by adding "gloire," which Richelet defines as "honor," in the classical age. Bussy carefully shifts the medieval, passionate text into a moral, "bienséant" context that would be acceptable to his readers. The letter closes with Heloise's confession that she battles with herself to try to conquer her love for Abelard. Like Grenaille, Bussy signs in her name, but the closure of the first letter shows that he reproduces a convincing imitation of a

[27] Pelous also offers an analysis of precious terms in amatory discourse; see pp. 421-25.

woman's amatory discourse. As Ballaster observed, "feminine" style in the love letter is based on spontaneity and a natural style of expression, which Bussy achieves by enhancing the narrative with these stylistic qualities:

> Amatory passion in the letters is signified typographically, through the use of parentheses, exclamation marks, inverted word letter, abbreviated sentences; and finally lexically the language of religious experience and spiritual autobiography.[28]

Bussy's translation shows a high frequency of exclamation marks, inverted sentences, and contradictory thoughts, all highlighting the spontaneous quality in his imitation of Heloise's style. The carnal text is deleted and the emphasis on writing from the heart replaces the idea of viewing the missive as a blank space upon which the medieval Heloise attempted to inscribe her physical desire. Here, the reader encounters a more veiled erotic presence in her writing, perhaps because Bussy's imitation of her style is placed on a more abstract, spiritual level combined with the conversational aspects of his version. As a "précieuse," Bussy's Heloise talks a great deal, which tends to diminish the original desperate, plaintive tone of her medieval sister's letters to Abelard. The transition of this version into the social salon atmosphere calls for a total restructuring of her persona, and, once again, separates the woman, as author, from her textual production. In the following letters, Bussy, as an imitator of Heloise's amatory style, will intervene in her textual space, and like Grenaille, he will infringe on her site to write through her.

Letter 2: Revising Peter Abelard as a "Woman in Love"

The most striking change in Bussy's free translation of the love correspondence is the reworking of Abelard's persona. As mentioned earlier, gallantry did not favor conversing on serious

[28] Ballaster 63.

subjects or indulging in pedantic displays of knowledge. To create the image of Abelard as a courtly aristocrat, Bussy transforms him, disassociating him from philosophy and overt religious conversational topics. The distance from his medieval brother's devotion to God leaves space for Abelard's confession of his love for Heloise. We recall that in the Zumthor translation, Abelard never acknowledged Heloise on an amorous level: such an acknowledgement would have been contradictory to his goal of persuading her to accept God's service. This significant modification represents a radical step in the process of creating the legend. At the beginning of the second letter, Abelard echoes the sentimental tone of Heloise's previous letter. In some instances, he even appears to be repeating her words, combining the spoken and written elements, in order to find a voice to confess his love for her:

> Héloïse, je vous adore avec plus d'ardeur que je n'ai jamais fait. Il faut vous ouvrir mon coeur: j'ai caché ma passion au monde depuis ma retraite par vanité, et à vous par tendresse; je voulais vous guérir par mon indifférence affectée. (II, 67)

Like Heloise, Abelard seems to actually be talking from the heart. In the passage above, he expresses his "ardeur" and "tendresse" for his beloved. Bussy creates a textual echo revolving around the idea of "guérir." Heloise had also said previously that she wanted to try to cure herself of him. The two share the turmoil of a dilemma, dividing their allegiance between their professions and their love. It is interesting that Bussy introduces Abelard's conflict on the first page of his response to Heloise's first letter. In Bussy's revision of Abelard's letters, the legend is born from the very moment that Abelard professes his love and clues the public into the fact that he cannot disregard his feelings, no matter how hard he tries. As a "mondain" gentleman, he puts love at the core of his speech. Bussy renders him more convincing as a suitor as he continues to enlarge the field of his futile efforts to forget Heloise. Like Ovid's heroines, Abelard describes the deception of solitude:

> La solitude, où jai cru trouver un asyle contre vous, désoccupé de tout le reste du monde, vous laisse seule remplir mon coeur et mon esprit, et je suis convaincu que c'est un soin inutile de travailler à ne vous plus aimer. (II, 67-68)

Separated from Heloise, he has the time to reflect on his personal life; and his religious concerns are clearly not the focus of his reply to her first letter as he goes on to talk about his unsuccessful attempt to distance himself from his wife: "je fis deux cents lieues pour m'éloigner de vous" (69). This amplifies a previous spatial reference, "je mis la mer entre vous et moi" (69). Other parts of his speech duplicate Heloise's Ovidian "plainte" of the abandoned woman. Abelard confesses, "j'ai beau m'éloigner de vous, votre idée et ma passion me suivent partout" (68). Like Heloise, he says he searched for ways of forgetting her. Philosophy and religion could not conquer his passion, which echoes her battle in the previous letter. As Bussy suppresses other references to Abelard's illustrious career as a scholar, he builds on the final echo of Heloise's previous epistle where she describes her constant struggle with her heart. This sentimental version plays up the solitude that plagues Abelard with perpetual thoughts of Heloise. He differs radically from his medieval predecessor, who would never confess in this personal manner because of his spiritual strength and intellectual devotion to the Church. Here, most of the traces of the medieval Abelard have been erased. Bussy's Abelard is more spontaneous, he seems to speak in a monologue, also shown by the insertion of a stanza of verse that reinforces his physical distance from Heloise. There are numerous refrains of "faible" or "faiblesse," completely out of character with Abelard's medieval ancestor. Like Heloise, he burns with love, he cannot forget her, and he is in a state of emotional turmoil. He adds that when he was writing the *Historia*, it only served "pour m'enflammer" (69). In other words, Bussy grafts Heloise's passionate display of desire onto Abelard's speech and writing. If the signatures were erased, we could even attribute the following sentence to her pen, "mais mes désirs, qui ne peuvent être satisfaits, n'en sont que plus violents" (68), or "je m'allume en vous parlant de mon amour" (70). In the restructuring of Abelard's persona, Bussy transposes Ovidian epistolary traits of the "feminine" "plainte" onto Abelard's spoken and written discourse, which produces an iterative effect in the text. As Alain Roger's work on the love letter has shown, the masculine display of passion may be read in gendered terms. Citing a study on gender and identity by Stoller, who postulated that one can always hide one's sex and even disguise it in writing, Roger claims that the (male) author of a love letter is like a transsexual, who slips into another gender:

> [...] une femme écrivant une lettre d'amour correspond ordinairement à son sexe. Un amant, en revanche, pour peu qu'il s'y passionne—et cela n'est possible que par intermittence, dans l'hystérie de l'écriture—s'adonne à un genre qui s'oppose, non seulement à son sexe, mais aussi au gender qui lui est habituel.[29]

As Roger also observed, the epistolary genre is stereotypically feminized because it is grounded in love as the source of its occidental origins. As he notes, the man who writes love letters is fascinated by his own femininity, as seems to be the case in Bussy's revision of Abelard. Like an Ovidian woman, Abelard's abandonment is misery, his solitude is not peaceful but tormented, and he cannot stop thinking about Heloise. From the loneliness of his cell, it is almost as if he, too, gazes at an imaginary portrait of Heloise, engraved within his memory. Abelard addresses her as she had addressed him in her previous epistle. From her mouth to his pen, she provides him with the essential

---

[29] Alain Roger, "La Lettre d'amour et l'effémination épistolaire," *Ecrire, publier, lire les correspondances*, ed. J.L. Bonnat and M. Bossis (Nantes: Publication de l'Université de Nantes, 1983): 98.

amorous script in which he can, as Derrida would say, "mime" a similar discourse of desire. For Derrida, Plato provides one of the fundamental models of mimesis, which is grounded on imitation, copy and duplication of living simulacrum.[30] Bussy's superposition of Heloise's amatory discourse onto Abelard's epistle is constructed on this principle of copying. In confessing his love, Abelard duplicates Heloise's spontaneous, natural, (living) style to find a voice similar to hers. In order to "mime" or "copy" Heloise's discourse of desire, Abelard must also search the "remainder" of his memories. In an example of what Derrida calls "anamnesis," Abelard goes back to an anterior "amorous," temporal point in his memory before the castration. His imitation of Heloise's style will then be transferred to the present, which means that he is "miming" the past in the present of his writing time. Like Heloise, Abelard must initially resurrect distant memories that enable him to relive his passion in order to preserve it from dissolution. In *Dissemination,* Derrida reads this as part of the mimetic process:

> What announces itself here is an internal division within mimesis, a self-duplication of repetition itself; ad infinitum, since this movement feeds its own proliferation.[31]

Following Derrida's idea of endless repetition in miming something else, Bussy's Abelard duplicates Heloise's master narrative. To put it in gendered terms, he is copying from the original script of passion, which was already marked in the feminine in the medieval text. The following passage in Abelard's letter evokes the medieval Heloise, when she blamed her bad fortune and alluded to the struggle between God's service and her love, a conflict now transferred to Abelard's letter:

---

[30] Jacques Derrida talks about mimesis and duplication in *Dissemination,* trans. Barbara Johnson (Chicago: University of Chicago Press, 1981): 190-193.
[31] Derrida, "The Double Session" 191.

> Mais, s'il faut mourir, ô mon Dieu! pourquoi ne pas mourir pour vous, tant de souffrances seront-elles perdues pour le temps et pour l'éternité?[...] Enivré de mon amour, je n'ai pleuré jusqu'ici que ma maîtresse. (II, 70)

Here, Abelard manipulates the religious and the love discourse but, (like Heloise), he is more torn by the passionate one. In fact, the passage reads like an Ovidian "plainte," drenched in tears, which, as Stanton pointed out in *The Aristocrat as Art,* is a direct violation of the code of the "honnête home."[32] Abelard has overstepped the boundary of the "bonne mesure"; he exhibits excessive emotion that was frowned upon. As Stanton also noted, gloom, tears, and complaints were considered unattractive for the aristocratic gentleman, who was supposed to please others all the time. In other words, the "honnête homme" had to be very careful not to let his mask down to reveal his authentic self in front of others. Here, we seem to have more of a case of a precious woman's exaggerated sentiments than of a "honnête homme" who had a carefully controlled language of love. Abelard appears to switch genders in order to facilitate the articulation of his desire. As we recall, his "feminized" side as a eunuch enables him to more readily convey the "plainte" of his misery. According to Barthes' comments on the feminization of the love discourse:

> It follows that in any man who utters the other's absence something feminine is declared: this man who waits and who suffers from his waiting is miraculously feminized. A man is not feminized because he is inverted but because he is in love.[33]

Bussy begins Abelard's response to Heloise's first letter by reiterating her dilemma of the battle between love and God, but it is expressed slightly differently, "je vous trouve toujours entre Dieu et moi: quel obstacle pour aller à lui!" (71). In order for

[32] Stanton 119-45.
[33] Roland Barthes, *A Lover's Discourse: Fragments,* trans. Richard Howard (New York: The Noonday Press, 1978): 14.

Abelard to serve God, he must forget Heloise, which remains problematic because Bussy does not provide textual evidence of Abelard's personal sacrifice. Instead, Bussy changes registers and builds up other fictional elements. Abelard speaks in an ambiguous way about the castration, saying that Fulbert wanted to make an example of him for other lovers. Abelard admits that he was jealous and didn't want Heloise to find another lover, and so he forced her to take her vows to assure him that she would not find someone else. And yet Bussy ends the letter by restoring the persuasive rhetoric of the original Abelard who reverts back to the public sphere, and away from the intimate confession of love that dominated the body of the letter. Abelard says their repentance should be as public as their crimes had been because they were the bad example of " la mauvaise conduite" of youth. This moral Abelard may be conveying a moral message which would be considered in accordance with the values of the appropriate "bienséant" decorum of the day. But the other possibility is that Bussy decided to remain closer to the Latin text, thus concluding with some of the medieval Abelard who signs off begging Heloise to cry in order to extinguish the fire of their passion.

Letter 3: Pre-romantic Desire?

Heloise's second letter, the third in Bussy's text, combines many elements previously seen in the medieval text. As in the Zumthor translation, she devotes a significant part of her missive to the future contemplation of Abelard's death and the consequences it will bring to her nuns' welfare. For her, separation is linked to death, which is underlined by the recurrence of tears: "Abélard, vous deviez arrêter mes larmes, et vous les faites couler" (76). Again, the absence of her beloved is also translated into precious language, when she compares her loss to dying "mille fois." As Lathuillère observed, precious women had a tendency to use numerical references in their writing and speech to exaggerate their emotions.[34] Here, Heloise confesses that she only lives for Abelard and then launches into a lengthy "plainte" like the Portuguese nun, but Bussy does not develop the pathos to the extent of Guilleragues's sustained outpouring of suffering in his portrayal of Marianne. Instead of focusing on the tragic aspects he alters the reciprocal aspect of the previous two letters. The earlier conversational style in which each participant repeated what the other had said is now reformulated into a more somber, introspective tone. The shift is marked by the textual reference to the loss of Abelard's heart: "je suis sensible à la perte de votre coeur" (79). We have already shown that the heart is at the center of the language of love as well as the common point that allowed for the mutual and sincere exchange of passionate discourse. Here, Heloise goes on to lament the loss of Abelard, which destroys the balance; the couple will no longer speak to one another on a reciprocal amorous level. Instead of having her respond in dialogue form to Abelard, Bussy reworks her discourse into a monologue; he translates more closely to the Latin text in this epistle, but prolongs her diatribe. There is a transition between the introductory theme of death and Heloise's role in Abelard's misery. She takes responsibility for his suffering, and she also establishes herself as the source of his pain. This is not a new aspect. This misogynistic conception of "woman" is simply reworded in "mondain" speech, "Qu'il est dangereux à un grand homme de se laisser charmer par notre sexe" (81). Bussy embroiders the medieval text by inserting other precious linguistic features such as flowery comparatives and superlatives. After saying that death is less dangerous than the beauty of a woman, Heloise enters into a personal confession, saying that she cannot repent for her crime. Once again, Bussy reworks the twelfth-century text re-

[34] See Roger Lathuillère's article, "La Langue des précieux," *Trauvaux de Linguistique et de Littérature* 26.1 (1987): 243-269.

shaping her words into the "plainte" of a seventeenth-century heroine:

> J'ai cherché à vous plaire aux dépens de ma vertu; j'ai par-là irrité les peines que je ressens. Mes coupables transports ne pouvaient avoir qu'une fin malheureuse et tragique [...] Il m'était trop glorieux d'être aimée d'Abeilard. (III, 83)

Like a romanesque heroine in one of Scudéry's long novels, Heloise vocalizes her excessive feelings of guilt and violent emotions leading up to the tragic turn of events. Here, Bussy embellishes the medieval text and adds to this original idea of glory which, as we know, was popular with precious women: they appreciated heroic qualities in their novels, as is reflected in the arduous "chevaleresque" novels from the beginning to the mid-century. Bussy rewords and updates the vocabulary with words like "transports," "gloire," "vertu" and "plaire," common expressions to his "mondain" audience. At the matrix of Heloise's guilt, love is a privileged over the Church:

> Je sacrifiai tout à mon amour, et je les fis céder au désir de rendre heureux le plus aimable et le plus savant de tous les hommes. (III, 83)

Once again, Bussy's Heloise's tendency to articulate her desire in the style of a precious woman is shown by the use of the superlative intended to flatter and express her admiration of Abelard. The theme of love is sustained in the body of the narrative as Bussy moves toward his reworking of the erotic sequence. The dream episode is introduced by her confession where she returns to speaking genuinely from the heart, and thus restores the spoken conversational aspect of the text:

> L'amertume du coeur doit suivre l'aveu de la bouche: c'est ce qui se rencontre rarement. Pour moi qui ai trouvé tant de plaisir à vous aimer, je sens bien malgré moi que je ne pourrai jamais me repentir de l'avoir goûté, ni cesser d'en jouir autant qu'il m'est possible, en les rappelant dans ma mémoire. (III, 84)

Bussy re-stages the scene to prepare the dream confession, triggered by the power of her memory. Instead of talking about her vows, Heloise is worshipping her beloved's souvenir, and underlines the "plaisir" of loving him. Although Bussy respects the events of the medieval narrative, he amplifies the sentimental, glorified aspects of her devotion to Abelard as a replacement for the original carnal desire. The overall erotic effect is preserved, but expressed more through the language than the body. As with her medieval sister, Heloise's sleep is disturbed and tormented, but presented in a more vivid and striking form:

> [...] je ne saurais éviter les illusions que mon coeur fait naître. Je crois être encore avec mon cher Abeilard. Je le vois, je l'entends, et je lui parle. Charmés l'un de l'autre, nous abandonnons les études de la philosophie, pour nous entretenir plus agréablement de notre passion. (III, 84-5)

As she reflects upon their moments together, the visual image transforms the dream into a more clearly focused reenactment of her memories. Unlike in the medieval text, Bussy's Heloise appears to internalize the image of the portrait in her cell in order to concentrate on the reinvented image of her beloved. Once she has restored his silhouette, she imagines that she is conversing with him in her sleep. She relives that pleasurable time when they were together at her uncle's home, but the scene is devoid of the medieval sexual desire. But as Bussy diminishes the physical presence of passion, he builds up the fictional intrigue to maintain his readers' interest: Heloise imagines that she was present at the time of the "entreprise sanglante," (a barely veiled reference to the castration), so that she could heroically put up a fight and protect Abelard from his enemies. In this scenario, she fills his room with her resounding screams, only to awaken, "noyée de mes larmes;" unlike in the medieval text, she travels further back in time, remembering the first instance when Abelard declared his "tendresse"; she clings to the memory of him as if it were the emblem of her love, "je porte le souvenir criminel de nos plaisirs passés" (85). This lengthy section in which Bussy prolongs the dream sequence culminates in a sudden return to precious language where the battle motif is now directed towards Heloise's personal dilemma: "Je suis plus à plaindre que vous; j'ai mille passions à combattre: il me faut résister à ces feux que l'amour allume dans un jeune coeur" (III, 85).

From her private struggle, Bussy transforms the battle into a public one. The next section of the epistle is a variation on the Latin text where Heloise divulged the truth about her piety. Once again, Bussy has her speaking from the heart, the presumed source of sincerity. His Heloise says that if only her nuns could see into her heart, the place where there is no veil that masks her desire, they would uncover the secret of her false virtue. The original, shocking drama of her confession in the medieval version is reworked here by the insertion of a series of oppositions, common to the seventeenth-century reader. Bussy plays with the illusion of "paraître" and "être," vice and virtue, and the revelation of Heloise's disguise, dressed as a nun. She confesses her masquerade publicly, a cover-up for the inner weakness of her unforgettable love for Abelard. She finds grace in a secular way, based on her ability to dissimulate her "penchant" from the nuns:

> J'ai assez de force pour leur cacher mon penchant, et je regarde cela en moi comme un effet puissant de la grâce. Si elle ne me porte pas à embrasser la vertu, au moins elle m'empêche de commettre le mal. (III,86)

Like her medieval sister, Heloise manipulates two discourses, but she favors the sentimental one. Like Alluis, Bussy reverses Grenaille's textual strategy as he shows no evidence of conversion in his revision of Heloise's persona. On the contrary, his Heloise is skilled in the art of "trompe-l'oeil." She takes pride in being able to play her role as an abbess convincingly, and it is not long before she admits publicly that Abelard is still the center of her devotion:

> Je n'ai de souci que celui de vous plaire[. . .] Ma fausse piété vous a longtemps trompé ainsi que les autres: *vous* m'avez cru tranquille, et j'étais plus agitée que jamais. Vous vous êtes persuadé que j'étais attachée à mes devoirs, et je n'avais d'autre occupation que celle que l'amour me donnait. (III, 87)

Heloise abruptly changes the tone of her diatribe to address the subject of praise, how one can be blinded by a seducer's words, and she goes on to apply this to her own case, adding that Abelard's praise and admiration of her is dangerous because she took his words too seriously, and actually believed that she deserved his flattery.

As in Abelard's previous letter, she oversteps the boundary of the gallant code. Her desire to please her lover is excessive. As Stanton noted, one of the "honnête" rules of conversation stipulated that the participants in the exchange never believe the praise a flatterer would bestow upon them.[35] Heloise admits this is her weakness in her effort to please Abelard. She signs off repeating that she is weak and cannot renounce this "funeste passion," emphasizing the pathos of her dilemma. At the end of the letter, Bussy goes back to the medieval text, where Heloise said she did not expect to receive the crown of glory, but the seventeenth-century Heloise closes her letter on a heroic note: she can only hope to avoid danger, and therefore her glory is not in the victory, but in the battle that she stoically wages to protect herself. This military terminology could appeal to the aristocrat's literary taste for adventure, and it was very popular at that time in many genres, but, for Bussy, it also creates more intrigue and therefore embellishes the drier medieval version.

---

[35] Stanton 139-46.

Letter 4: Brotherly Love

Abelard's reply to Heloise's previous epistle signals a return to the medieval portrayal of his persona as he begs Heloise not to write to him anymore and tries to persuade her to accept Christian life. Abelard switches to "vous" to break from the personal exchange, addressing his remarks to Heloise and her nuns as a collective group. As in Heloise's letter, the reciprocal link appears to be severed; Abelard now privileges the spiritual over their prior intimate conversations. Here, Bussy seems to restore the image of Abelard as a spiritual director, coaxing Heloise to pursue the perfection of her soul. The role transformation appears on the second page of his letter, "je serais votre maître et votre père" (90). But the next section of the letter reveals a startling turn of events as Bussy does not develop the spiritual-guidance aspect of Abelard's persona. The resounding echo of Heloise's closing words describing her "funeste passion" resurfaces in his letter. Like Heloise, Abelard says he will open his troubled heart for the last time. The appearance of the devout Catholic is deceptive however because his heart, like hers, has no inner peace. Once again, Bussy grafts fragments of Heloise's previous public confession onto Abelard's discourse. He even repeats the military motif of his combat against his tender thoughts in order to express the pathos of his Ovidian "plainte," which, like hers, is drowned in tears:

> Vos lettres, je l'avouerai, m'ont ému; je n'ai pu lire avec indifférence des caractères tracés par une main si chère. Je soupire, je verse même des larmes, et toute ma raison suffit à peine à cacher ma faiblesse aux yeux de mes disciples. (IV, 91)

Here again, his confession mirrors Heloise's in the previous letter. In front of his monks, Abelard puts on a masquerade and struggles to dissimulate his desire. Like Heloise, he wages an ongoing battle with his feelings as the source of "faiblesse." Even an emotional expression of his dilemma is an imitation of Heloise's. Bussy portrays her as sighing and weeping, lamenting the fact that she can no longer play out her desire with her partner. He transfers Heloise's erotic dream sequence to the letter, as a stand-in for Abelard's beloved. For him, each reading of Heloise's epistle, sketched by her hand, is a way of retracing the contours of her body, which in turn restores her silhouette to his field of vision. The erotic rereading of her love letters parallels Heloise's dream of visualizing Abelard's face in the portrait.

Other echoes of her style include his confession that he too has cleverly deceived everyone around him. His monks think that his soul is tranquil, but this is only a cover-up for the truth. He has not forgotten her, and this thought leads him into a reflection on what her uncle has deprived him of in the past. Once again, Bussy inserts a veiled reference to the castration, calling it an accident, but Abelard dramatizes his suffering, and the persecution subtext is enriched as he shows himself threatened by his enemies in the church. The text then reverts to a persuasive strategy, as he tries to convince Heloise to pursue a state of grace. This reprise indicates the transformation of the dialogue into a monologue. Abelard insists on the glorious aspect of fighting temptation. Borrowing Heloise's military expressions, he envisions a stoic battle that leads towards the victorious goal of Christian virtue, but he wishes to achieve a spiritual elevation different from Heloise's more secular battle. Abelard welcomes the religious challenge of redemption, whereas Heloise's previous letter indicated that she was undeserving of salvation. On this question of penitence, Bussy translates fairly closely to the medieval narrative. Abelard goes on to say that he wants to conquer all obstacles standing in the way of heaven's gate. The Christian difference in their monologues is marked by Abelard's speech on spiritual temptation directed more at man in general in comparison to Heloise's diatribe on a personal battle that divides her heart between the Church and her love. In his closing remarks, Abelard comes back to Heloise and advises her to destroy "le funeste penchant" in order to honor her vows to God. The language has been altered, but the message remains the same as the one delivered by his medieval brother. He begs her to erase the image of him as her lover:

> Que l'image d'Abeilard amoureux, à votre esprit toujours présente, prenne désormais la figure d'Abeilard véritablement pénitent, et puissiez-vous autant verser de pleurs pour votre salut que vous en avez répandu durant le cours de nos malheurs. (IV, 94)

It is interesting that Bussy concludes with yet another visual element. Abelard's last words to his wife could be read along John Lyon's lines of pictorial interpretation (noted earlier). For example, Abelard appears to ask Heloise to replace the portrait of him in her cell as her lover with a religious, nonsexual reflection. But he is veiling his epistolary strategy: in substituting the image of himself, he hopes for a mimetic outcome in which Heloise will copy his original example, and then model herself after him in devoting herself to God.

Letter 5: The Malady of Love

Heloise's last letter appears to have been purely invented. As in the original text, Bussy maintains the absence of dialogue. In the introductory remarks, Heloise is angry because Abelard hasn't replied on an amatory level. He has blocked the exchange of conversation by not answering her as her lover. Bussy convincingly imitates her spontaneous, highly punctuated style by inserting numerous exclamation points and contradictions that point to her state of turmoil and frustration. He produces this fictionalized epistle by selecting elements that appeared in Heloise's final letter in the medieval text, and then reworking them into his translation. He embellishes the sentimental intrigue in this supplemental scene where Heloise becomes ill as a culmination of her emotional disorder. She says that she was so sick that she thought her love, which she had always considered innocent, had actually seemed criminal to her, a sudden change which instills the fear of God in her. She reflects on how she has spent her time in the convent, filling the enclosed space with her tears of pain and loneliness. But suddenly, in her weakened state, she has a revelation. The main body of this final letter is clearly fictional as Bussy leads the reader to believe that she has actually taken Abelard's spiritual advice. The illness serves as a catalyst for her abrupt devout change and her realization that she must relinquish her passionate memories. This is not the first time we have seen this moral conversion. Grenaille used this idea in his final letter to convey a moral message, and Bussy seems to be doing the same thing for his audience. However, his revision of Heloise's moral conversion is very different from Grenaille's because Heloise, here, remains very sentimental, and melodramatic. The deviation from the medieval text is extremely striking, as the twelfth-century Heloise would never relinquish her passion in order to publicly acknowledge Abelard as her spiritual father. In Bussy's text, Heloise tells Abelard she can forget him as her lover and husband. Later on, she even confesses that she has been touched by grace, and Bussy describes her confession in an exaggerated precious style as if she were performing a heroic sacrifice in front of an audience:

> Il faut l'avouer, je l'ai acheté au prix de mon amour. J'ai fait un sacrifice violent, et qui passait mes forces. Je vous ai arraché de mon coeur; n'en soyez point jaloux [...] (V, 101)

This state of grace, however, does not last very long. Bussy curbs her newly acquired religious fervor in the next paragraph where she suddenly alters her tone again. Cleverly, Bussy weaves être and paraître in a subtle strategy. Heloise only appears to be converted, but underneath the deceptive "trompe-l'oeil" of her speech, she has not overcome her passion; she has just found a better way to conceal it. After saying that she has placed God in her heart, she contradicts herself in the next line: her heart may belong to God, but that still leaves room in her "esprit" to store her memories of Abelard. Heloise has discovered another way to preserve his memory. "Je me ferai un plaisir secret de penser à vous" (101). Yet, once again, she returns to manipulating double discourses as she recognizes Abelard as the official father of her community of nuns, and assures him that his daughters will carry out his spiritual orders. In this part of the letter, Bussy reverses the image of the convent. At the beginning, Heloise's illness accentuated the cloistered, oppressive atmosphere of her prison. But this sudden acceptance of her service to God restructures the space of her enclosure. In the peaceful surroundings of the Paraclete, she appears to have found a spiritual sanctuary where she even performs her role as abbess in a serious capacity. This religious revision of Heloise shows a reversal of roles, and she even criticizes Abelard for bemoaning his misfortunes. This time, it is Abelard's space that is described as a "woman's" prison in which he is locked in with his tears:

> Que dirait le monde, s'il lisait comme moi vos lettres? Il s'imaginerait que vous ne vous êtes renfermé que pour pleurer votre impuissance. (V, 103)

Interestingly, Bussy also reverses the consoling roles. In the original narrative, Abelard is always the one consoling Heloise in an attempt to elevate her soul. Here, Heloise performs his role in trying to console him and lift him out of despair. She wants him to realize that burying himself in his unhappiness is futile because he cannot change his destiny. She reminds him that it is a shame if a philosopher cannot console himself for an accident that could have happened to anyone. Bussy enhances her persuasive words with a return to her heroic confession that she, herself, fights stoically everyday to triumph over her "mouvements trop tendres" (104). She wants him to forget all of the negative persecutions and go back to charming his followers with his charismatic gift of speech. Yet, once again, Bussy alters Heloise's tone in the last part of her letter as she prepares a lengthy adieu to Abelard, addressing him this time as her husband. Again, the monologue is dramatized by the use of exclamation points, questions marks, and accelerated rhythm. Heloise evokes the pictorial image of Abelard as she pays attention to his mouth, the "deep text," which creates the illusion of gazing at his portrait:

> Cette bouche qu'on ne peut regarder sans désirs, ces mains si propres à piller les trésors de l'amour, enfin toute la personne d'Abeilard ne peut être envisagée par une femme sans péril. (V, 105-106)

The passage uncovers the "other" discourse concealed beneath the appearance of her religious speech on grace. Once again, Heloise confesses that the greatest pleasure of her day is the refuge of sleep where she can abandon herself to the cherished memories of seeing her lover in her dreams. Every night she returns to the time when they were together before the accident destroyed their happiness. But the magic of her reverie always fades away at the onset of dawn; when she opens her eyes she can no longer find Abelard, he slips out of her arms, and when she calls him he does not answer. She begs Abelard to excuse a wife who momentarily strays from her profession, haunted by the pain of her loss. Although Bussy's fictional addition of the visual aspect of the erotic dream sequence is invented, he restores an important part of the medieval abbess's discourse. Her continuing struggle between faith and love follows the original narrative, so he imitates her style convincingly. To put it in Derrida's words, Bussy is amplifying the "remainder" or "reminder" of her desire that lives on.[36] Since the medieval text never produced proof of her conversion, Bussy actually reconstructs the original conflict that divided her heart. But, at the same time, he is paving the way for the next wave of Heloise imitators in inserting a closing image of her as the weeping

---

[36] See Jacques Derrida's "Living On: Border Lines," *Deconstruction and Criticism* trans. James Hulbert (New York: The Seabury Press, 1979): 75-176.

abbess, eternally tortured by this unresolved inner battle. He transfers the "plainte" back to her as Abelard had previously appropriated the feminine trope to convey his despair and loneliness:

> Héloïse seule est à plaindre. Toujours la triste Héloïse versera des torrents de larmes, sans être assurée qu'elles serviront à l'ouvrage de son salut. (V, 107)

In a melodramatic style, she describes a destiny that does not hold the promise of salvation. This tearful portrayal of Heloise is pre-romantic and also recalls the excessive emotional display of Guilleragues's Portuguese nun. Yet after this confession, she changes the subject again. Bussy inserts another invented episode in which she informs Abelard that one of her nuns fled the cloister to go to England to be with her lover, that she ordered the nuns to keep this scandal a secret, and she insists that if he had been there no one would have strayed from the path leading to God. This invention may be another deceptive illusion, intended to appeal to the readers' imagination. It is possible that Bussy's Heloise secretly hoped that Abelard might be tempted to plan their escape, like the nun's valiant departure from the convent. But this digression does not alter her conflict as she signs off openly admitting that she had tried to persuade Abelard of her acceptance of God, but that this was a cover-up. As she says, she must burn her epistle because she has experienced too much pleasure in writing to him, and the letter closes reminding Abelard that she is still torn between her duty and her passion.

Thus, Bussy Rabutin's version of Abelard's and Heloise's correspondence marks the revival of the medieval version. Charrier and Rouben concur that he is responsible for the development of the legend that would explode in the eighteenth century.[37] Bussy may have borrowed from Guilleragues's por-

---

[37] See Rouben 116-36 and Charrier p. 411.

trayal of Marianne's emotional display of illicit passion in order to satisfy his public's literary tastes. In any event, he chose to translate a letter text that was becoming a fashionable genre, and so his timing was well planned. Bussy's talent as a translator and an imitator of women's amatory discourse was so seemingly "feminine" that Bayle, believing, like many others, that women could more naturally express the emotions they had actually experienced, though the text had actually been written by a woman. This reception of the text is interesting because Bayle alludes to the question of authorship. Bussy's imitation of Heloise can be read as another textual example of pseudo-feminocentrism. As Miller would put it, he has become the "other," not only by appropriating Heloise's discourse, but also by mastering a highly convincing imitation of her amorous style. Like Grenaille and Alluis, he has embellished the original text by integrating romanesque elements (his own contribution to the plot), in order to entertain his readers, and, in some places, to convey a moral message. His recasting of Abelard as an "honnête," gallant gentleman and Heloise as a "precious" woman could appeal undoubtedly to an audience that appreciated the seductive, "conversational" game of love. In altering the medieval personae of the two lovers, he intervened not only in Heloise's discourse of desire, but in Abelard's portrayal as a serious philosopher and theologian. Interestingly, the seventeenth-century Abelard is acutely sensitive, weakened by his emotions; he mimics Heloise's over-dramatized feelings. While all of this could be fascinating to his readership, Heloise's literary creation has become, once again, the target of masculine manipulation. As a result, she recedes even further from her claim to the correspondence, and is almost erased by the plume of the imitator who borrowed from her to reproduce a prototype of authentic "feminine" writing. Once again, a male author/translator attempted to marginalize a woman's rights to the love letter by stealing her pen and sitting in her space in order to imitate her amatory style, and market a melodramatic, embroidered version of the medieval story. As Barthes noted in "The Death of the Author," a writer can be killed several times over in his own textual creation.[38] Here, the connection to the medieval Heloise's voicing of desire is becoming more and more obscure, practically erased. Above all, Alluis' and Bussy's translations have suppressed Heloise's physical language, and, to put it in Barthes' terms, they enacted the death of the author, reducing her presence to a fragment. Yet, paradoxically, this did not rule out the possibility of her recovery in a different guise. We will see evidence of this in other versions of the lovers' story that will appear in the eighteenth century, a time when the epistolary novel entered into a period of great success and popularity all across Europe. At the very least, Bussy's text was very important in promoting interest in this story of tragic love. His contribution inspired many other translators to work on the text, and by the end of the seventeenth century other minor translations had appeared on the market.

The Imitator Imitated

Bussy's version started a trend for other "translators" and launched the birth of the cult built on the popularity of the medieval lovers' saga. Other translations appeared, but mostly as plagiarized versions of his text. Remond des Cours also produced a "precious" revision of the lovers' saga, an *Histoire d'Eloïse et d'Abélard* which came out in 1693, together with a "la lettre passionnée qu'elle lui écrivit, traduite du latin." Des Cours published a second edition in 1695, and as Charrier noted, his work announced the pre-romantic, tearful portrayal of Heloise that would be developed more fully in Pope's version in the eighteenth century.[39] Also in 1695, Dubois's *Histoire des*

[38] Barthes, "The Death of the Author," *Image, Music, Text,* trans. Stephen Heath. (New York: Hill and Wang, 1977): 145-8.
[39] Charrier 418-24.

amours et infortunes d'Abélard et d'Eloïse appeared on the market, with another text attributed to him and known as *Le Philosophe amoureux* that included letters supposedly published at the Paraclete. Again, Dubois follows Bussy's text, placing Heloise and Abelard in a gallant, "mondain" context, emphasizing language in the game of seduction, and thus differing radically from the original Latin text.[40] By the end of the seventeenth century, the epistolary genre was clearly entering into its most active period. The public relished love stories composed in letter form. At the dawn of the eighteenth century, the lovers' legend expanded further, gaining more and more readers. This, in turn, would inspire other translators to publish different versions of Heloise's and Abelard's love story, altering it again to meet new literary tastes and social conventions.

[40] Charrier provides historical information on Dubois on pp. 424-7.

5.

Fictional Transformations of the Lovers

At the dawn of the eighteenth century, the story of Abelard and Heloise continued to attract more and more readers, and writers who composed countless imitations. Interested in the couple's tragedy and personal experiences, Pierre Bayle included Heloise and Abelard in his *Dictionnaire historique et critique* published in 1697. As Charrier has noted, Bayle remained the only *Historia*n of Abelard and Heloise until Charles de Rémusat, who studied the medieval couple towards the end of the eighteenth century. Bayle approached the biographical details of the couple's lives in a "scientific" manner, paying close attention to the facts, to theological questions and to controversies that touched Abelard's life. His goal was to produce a truthful reading of the available biographical documentation on the couple. One of the most interesting aspects of his articles on Heloise and Abelard focuses on Abelard's castration, a subject that sparked considerable attention in the eighteenth century. Since Bayle deals with this topic in several of his articles, it is useful to initially place the castration event in a historical context in order to conduct a detailed analysis of the numerous references to Abelard's mutilation and the subsequent tragic repercussions on Heloise.

World Views of Eunuchs

Many eighteenth-century intellectuals were intrigued by the anomaly of the eunuch for a variety of reasons, one which was most likely associated with the spread of orientalism during the Enlightenment. These ambiguous beings were originally identified with exotic places in Asia and the Middle East. It is widely believed that the practice was first carried out by the Persians who performed castration to use eunuchs as palace guards and protectors of holy places of worship.[1] There were also instances of practicing castration to use eunuchs as slaves; thus many ancient rulers enforced mandatory amputations.[2] As Piotr O. Scholz posits, Semiramis, an Assyrian Queen, was the first ruler to order that castration be performed. In fact, she promoted the popularity of eunuchs by surrounding herself with a group of mutilated servants and was involved in the business of selling eunuchs. Semiramis even disguised herself as a man by donning men's clothing to pass as her own son. As a man, she could more easily demand that all servants in her kingdom be castrated to serve at the court.[3] Many of these historical facts

---

[1] Shaun Marmon's work *Eunuchs and Sacred Boundaries in Islamic Society* (NY & Oxford: Oxford, UP) offers an extensive study of the important role of eunuchs in upholding the social order in medieval Islamic society. The book looks into the seminal function of eunuchs as guardians of the harem as well as of the sacred space of the sultan's private compound. One of the most interesting aspects of the discussion is the exploration of the relationship between eunuchs and the sultans, especially the eunuchs who were the guardians of the Prophet and his family as well his tomb in ancient Egypt.

[2] See Victor Cheney's *A Brief History of Castration* (Bloomington: Author House, 2006) for a detailed historical account of castration practices in the ancient world.

[3] Piotr O. Scholz's *Eunuchs and Castrati: A Cultural History* (Princeton: Markus Wiener Publishers, 2001) provides an inclusive cultural study of eunuchs which spans the course of history around the world. In the third chapter, he looks at the myth of Semiramis, the Assyrian Queen who supported the practice of castration. She went so far as involving herself in the business of selling eunuchs. Scholz's perpective is valuable in studying the historical origin of castration, as he highlights the widespread popularity of the practice in the Middle East and such ancient civilizations such as the Greek, Roman and various exotic empires in the Far East.

were discussed in the Enlightenment by notable intellectuals like Montesquieu. He was intrigued by the history of the Far and Near East and even based his view of the eunuch's role on the oriental tradition. For him, eunuchs were associated with despotism and surrogate power. The eunuch was designated as a substitute for the absent ruler of the harem whose job was to maintain order in the seraglio amongst the sultan's wives. In these exotic kingdoms, eunuchs also carried out the function of acting as guardians of the marital bed. Kings relied on their eunuchs for personal service and in turn, their loyalty was richly rewarded. As a result, eunuchs enjoyed many benefits from assisting their rulers, which enabled them to gain social acceptance. In the Roman empire, eunuchs often served as escorts for ladies and some even attained powerful status in the courts. But it was during the Byzantine Empire that eunuchs flourished, as they occupied prestigious positions in high offices and even served in the military. They were thought to be diligent and sharp; thus kings delegated military campaigns to them. Ottoman sultans were known to have chosen eunuchs as generals and conquerors. During the Ottoman empire, it was not uncommon for eunuchs to rise to political power as governors.[4]

During the Enlightenment, the popularity of the opera was yet another expression of fascination for castrated men. The phenomenon of the castrati's voices sparked great enthusiasm for opera lovers. At the time, castration was also performed on young boys to ensure that they would retain the high-pitched quality of their voices, which produced an unworldly, angelic sound. Consequently, their sexual development was stunted, which extended their childhood and adolescence. On the physical level, they often gave the appearance of remaining eternally young. The castrati practice began in Italy but spread across Europe. European women pursued operati castrati mainly because their voices were mysteriously seductive, and they were

[4] Scholz 228.

appealing as lovers. Eunuchs could achieve erection and perform sufficiently; thus many engaged in carnal relationships with artistocratic ladies. Women could indulge in extramarital affairs without taking the risk of becoming pregnant. The historical context concerning the castrati inspired a protestant thinker to write about eunuchs. In 1707, Charles Ancillon published his *Traité des eunuques*. Although the text contains historical and medical information about eunuchs, the goal of the treatise was to warn women against the dangerous seduction of Italian castrati.[5] At the same time, Ancillon focused on the importance of upholding the traditional heterosexual model of the family, one which advocated procreation to ensure the survival of subsequent generations.[6]

Since Ancillon was an advocate of the family model, he investigated the eunuch's sexuality through a critical lens to better reinforce his position on the couple. To clarify this idea, it is useful to look at Ancillon's definition of a eunuch: "Un Eunuque donc, est une personne qui n'a pas la faculté d'engendrer, par la faiblesse, ou par la froideur de la nature, ou à qui on a retranché les parties propres à la génération" (57). Similar to the Far Eastern view of eunuchs discussed above, Ancillon's belief was that the castrated being constituted the "third sex." In other words, the body of the eunuch was classified as ambiguous. This idea was most likely perpetuated by the idea that eunuchs had an effeminate appearance. Their male development was halted at puberty; thus they never grew facial hair. In fact, their skin remained smooth, and they supposedly never lost their hair. Ancillon tended to equate eunuchs with homosexuals, even referring to them as sodomites, thus main-

---

[5] Charles Ancillon alludes to this goal in the preface to his *Traité des eunuques* (Paris: Ramsay, 1978): 15.

[6] For a critical reading of Ancillon, see Lise Leibacher-Ouvrard's article, "L'eunuque anathema et prétexte: économie libidinale et construction de l'hétérosexualité," sous la direction d'Olga B. Cragg *Sexualité, marriage et famille au XVIIIe siècle* (Laval: UP, 1998): 17.

taining a critical view of their inherent sexual difference. Furthermore, Ancillon maintained the idea of exclusion, which is explained by Lise Ouvrard-Leibacher: "le lien de la castration à l'exclusion est établi dans des catégories déjà bien définies: l'hérésie, la jalousie, la maladie, la folie et la criminalité suicidaire" (16). Another view of these amputated beings, which reinforces their marginalized status, is the portrayal of them as monsters. Once again, the idea was to isolate them from the prevalent model of the family in the eighteenth century, so as not to threaten the hierarchy of societal values. Leibacher affirms this idea in her comments on Ancillon's treatise: "il sert à imposer l'hétérosexualité, à définir masculinité et féminité comme deux pôles opposés. Rejeter l'ambiguïté "contre nature" permet que deux sexes seuls soient légitimés, ancrés dans une dualité prétendue naturelle" (19).

The multi-dimensional aspect of Ancillon's treatise on the subject of eunuchs also delves into other reasons for castration. In his analysis of some of the medical documentation, Ancillon noted that some beings were just born as eunuchs.[7] Matthew Kuefler also considered some of the medical reasons for castration, which were associated with certain ailments. For instance, medieval scientists believed that castration was a viable treatment for leprosy, gout, satyriasis, elephantiasis and epilepsy.[8] There were also some fundamental differences in the ways the operation was performed. The first procedure was the removal of the penis. Another common surgical process was the removal of the testicles, which left the penis intact. The less common method was the complete removal of both the testicles and the penis.[9] From the physiological description of the surgery, the

[7] Ancillon 69-71.
[8] See Matthew S. Kuefler's article, "Castration and Eunuchism in the Middle Ages," *Handbook of Medieval Sexuality,* ed. Vern L. Bullough and James A. Brundage (New York & London: Garland, 1996): 286.
[9] Kuefler 285-6.

subject also engendered discussion on a more spiritual level and was of interest to many religions, including Christianity.

In ancient times, castration was carried out as punishment by rulers, especially for political crimes. It was also considered a form of torture for crimes like rape and adultery.[10] In addition, the idea of punishment carried into religious reasons for castration, but it was really associated with some form of sin. As Victor Cheney observes, Christianity viewed castration as a means of cleansing man of his sexuality. The removal of the testicles not only constituted a brutal physical procedure, but had spiritual implications: it was a means of eradicating the lustful part of man. Cheney also points to Jesus' supposed belief that castration was one way of attaining a more divine spiritual state. Jesus also subscribed to the idea that evil was rooted in parts of the body.[11] This connection between punishment and sin reappears in Ancillon's references to Abelard. He specifically explains Abelard's misfortune as punishment while simultaneously categorizing it as an act of vengeance: "Les parents de cette fille lui firent couper les parties viriles avec lesquelles il avait deshonoré leur famille, ils allérent jusqu'à la racine du mal et l'arrachérent de telle sorte qu'ils ôtérent au coupable le pouvoir de la rechute" (77). Read from a Christian perspective, the removal of Abelard's sinful part of his body represents the punishment for Abelard's scandalous crime of getting the young Heloise pregnant. At the same time, the medieval cultural context is more complex. Scholz postulates that castration was tied to the idea of chastity and divine punishment. For Scholz, Abelard was haunted by the idea that his castration was the result of a divine punishment, which overwhelmed him with fear.[12] Thus, it was not unusual for an emasculated theologian to seek refuge in a monastery. The medieval view of castration regard-

[10] Scholz 22-8.
[11] Cheney 172-3.
[12] Scholz 246-50.

ed eunuchs as universally despised beings, once again, relegating these "amputated" men to a marginal status.

The parallel between the eighteenth-century perspective on eunuchs and the medieval view of them, itself strongly grounded in Christian ideology, is retained in some of Bayle's key passages found in his articles on Abelard, Heloise, Foulques and Combabus.[13] In his reading of Bayle's articles on Heloise and Abelard, Eric Walter highlights the illicit nature of the couple's relationship. Here, he adds depth to the castration question by underlining the tension between the philosopher's imposed celibacy and the inherent sexual nature of the correspondence. For Walter, Bayle places Abelard at the center of his study; thus Bayle's articles are inherently phallocentric. In his own essay, Walter elaborates on Abelard's true motivations:

> Abélard est homme de désir; pédagogue, il substitue les baisers aux leçons et remplace le fouet par attouchements; poète et chanteur, il boute le feu au coeur et au corps d'Héloïse; castré mais toujours désirant, il reste, dit-on capable de volupté. (135)

The passage describes Abelard as a eunuch with an active libido. Walter also points to Bayle's fascination with the more infamous and scandalous details of Abelard's life.

Bayle's Portrayal of Abelard

In its overall organization of the article on Abelard, Bayle's text appears to closely resemble Abelard's *Historia*. He proceeds chronologically by retracing Abelard's early career as a philosopher and theologian, including extensive references to his conflicts with his professor, William Champeaux, concerning complex questions of logic. Since these details of Abelard's early career as a theologian and philosophy professor have already

---

[13] All of the articles are included in a relatively recent edition. See *Personnages de l'affaire Abélard et considérations sur les obscénités* (Lausanne: L'Age d'Homme, 2002).

been discussed in the *Historia,* it is more useful to focus on Bayle's account of Abelard's encounters with Heloise, events prefiguring the castration incident.

While Bayle does not overlook Abelard as a man of God, he does, however, emphasize Abelard's passionate nature in descriptions of his tutorial sessions with Heloise. One of Bayle's most striking passages is his version of Abelard's seduction of Heloise. Here, he emphasizes Abelard's vanity as a poet and composer of love songs.[14] Interestingly, the references to Abelard's love songs appeared in Heloise's first letter of the medieval correspondence. But Bayle shifts the focus over to Abelard, thus suppressing Heloise's praise of his lyrical talents. Bayle also tends to underline the fictional aspect of Abelard's gift as a clever lover. In Bayle's article, Heloise is easily seduced by succumbing to the beauty of Abelard's verses and songs. However, the seduction of Heloise is shifted into the eighteenth-century context of using reason as part of a calculated strategy of attaining the object of desire, Heloise. Bayle includes this in note "g" to the article: "il ne raisonna pas en malhabile homme sur ces matières, lorsqu'il espèra que la conquête d'Héloïse serait plus aisée que celle d'une autre; qu'il l'espèra, dis-je, par la raison que le savoir d'Héloïse donnerait lieu à un commerce réglé de lettres" (65). For Bayle's Abelard, writing is privileged over conversation because the couple can freely express their secret longings, which they can't do within the formal context of Heloise's lessons in her uncle's home. Also, the importance of writing to one another underscores the interest in epistolary novels that would become increasingly popular later in the eighteenth century. For instance, Bayle embellishes the text by insisting on the romantic aspect of Abelard's seduction, but at the same time Abelard also seems to be undone by his own seduction strategy. It is through his study of amorous sonnets with Hel-

[14] See Bayle's article on Abelard, note "i" pp. 66-7.

oise that he loses sight of his professional obligations, prefiguring the act of vengeance by Heloise's uncle Fulbert.

Bayle's version of the castration scene also remains relatively close to the medieval text, but he highlights in a supplemental note the shocking repercussions of Abelard's mutilation. On a structural level, Bayle's notes enable him to criticize and comment on specific biographical and historical details relating to the couple's tragic love. The abundance of footnotes tends to create a fragmented and discontinuous form in the overall organization of the articles, a writing style that resists closure. However, the notes often contain revealing information that add intellectual depth to the interpretation of the articles. For example in the article on Abelard, Bayle's note "t" recounts the malicious gossip that was rampant in society in the wake of the castration. At this point, Bayle enters into the Enlightenment discussion on eunuchism. As he puts it, "on sût qu'il n'avait plus de quoi contenter une femme, on ne laissait pas de dire qu'un reste de volupté sensuelle le tenait attaché à son ancienne maîtresse" (76). Here, Bayle not only fictionalizes the text but revises the discourse on the eunuch's potency. It was believed that a castrated man, who still had a penis, had the ability to perform to a certain extent. A eunuch could most certainly satisfy a woman. Gary Taylor discusses this idea:

> A penis-being who has freed himself from the biological demands of his testicles, who no longer limits his sexual identity or imagination to sperm delivery, can create and sustain spirals of excitement, vortices of reciprocal engagement. That is not impotence, but power. (10)

Taylor also posits that castration does not suppress eros, an idea also confirmed by Cheney who adds that castration does not necessarily erase a man's sexual urges. These cultural *Historia*ns offer insight into reading Bayle's text, especially since he includes references to the couple's supposed secret visits after the castration, an aspect already noted in the medieval *Historia.*

In the same note," t," he includes other references to a more general status of eunuchs. Bayle begins with the familiar comparison to St. Jerome, as seen in the medieval text. This parallel is significant because the two theologians shared the common fate of enduring social slander after their misfortunes. As eunuchs, they were particularly vulnerable to scathing social criticism. In the supplementary note section, Bayle shows that he was quite familar with the historical documentation on eunuchs by pointing to the fact that wealthy and powerful men often entrusted their wives to the care of eunuchs, for it was believed that they had no reason to be jealous. Evidence of Bayle's knowledge of this idea can be seen in his article on the Syrian eunuch, Combabus.

Bayle's Textual Adaptation of the Eunuch Combabus

Bayle's article on Combabus is particularly illuminating because it shows some striking similarities to Abelard's social marginalization as a eunuch. The ancient story of Combabus could also be read as a partial allegory of Abelard's plight in life after his tragedy; the details of the intrigue revolve around a lord's duty and loyalty to his ruler. Combabus was chosen to accompany the King's wife, Queen Stratonice, on a journey. Since Combabus knew his handsome appearance might create jealousy, he decided to voluntarily mutilate himself. For safekeeping, he stored his testicles in a box and asked the King to keep the mysterious container until he returned home. As Combabus anticipated, the Queen fell in love with him and, in a drunken state, attempted to seduce the young lord. To resist her, he showed her his wound, thereby providing evidence of his impotency. The Queen's love was, however, unwavering.[15] Here, Bayle questions the harmless nature of their conversations plus the legitimate context for their subsequent social in-

[15] Bayle note "b" p. 140.

teractions. He warns his readers that men who entrusted their wives to eunuchs for protection should nevertheless be wary: "Ils crurent qu'en mettant leurs femmes sous la garde des Eunuques, je veux dire de certains hommes à qui l'on avait coupé les génitoires, ils n'avaient qu'à dormir en repos; mais ils trouvèrent qu'ils s'étaient trompés" (140). Bayle suggests that eunuchs were not only good for something, but in some places in the world actually held preferential status. To return to the story, the King eventually heard what was going on and ordered Combabus back to the kingdom. The young eunuch was imprisoned and condemned for execution, but he insisted on his innocence and asked that the box be presented to the King. After Combabus had explained his motivations for self-mutilation, the King exonerated him and then entrusted him with a mission of supervising the construction of a temple. A statue was erected in the temple to honor Combabus, but the bronze figure did not reflect a true likeness of the young lord. As Bayle describes it, " On avait donné à cette statue l'air d'une femme, et les habits d'un homme; et néanmoins on a conté que par compassion pour les femmes il avait quitté l'habit d'un homme et s'était habillé comme elles" (139). Bayle includes another note to the statue incident in which a woman supposedly fell in love with Combabus. When she heard he was a eunuch, she killed herself. Bayle inserts a moral interpretation of the tragic death of the woman by offering an explanation for this historical example of vestimentary transvestism.[16] He asserts that Combabus chose to abandon male garb, symbolized by the feminine silhouette of the bronze figure, so that women would not be deceived by his external appearance as a man.

Several of these facets discussed in the article on Combabus are pertinent to Bayle's portrayal of Abelard as a eunuch, for this safe status of the loyal eunuch is directly grafted onto Abe-

[16] Bayle note "f" p. 144.

lard's persona. He supposedly was able to offset gossip when it came to being alone with Heloise. Bayle weaves the historical facts about eunuchs into Abelard's justification of his chaste behavior, suggesting that he had consulted ancient documents on eunuchism.[17] Like Combabus, Bayle reiterates the idea of the eunuch's inherent innocence, offering him a legitimate pretext to engage in conversation with Heloise. This notion also harkens back to the ancient idea that eunuchs were considered so trustworthy that they often acted as guardians of the harem. Moreover, the idea of escaping jealousy exemplified by Combabus' voluntary mutilation resembles Bayle's treatment of Abelard as a eunuch liberated from social suspicion. The question of castration stands out in Bayle's dictionary, as he expands the importance of the incident into several articles which can be read simultaneously with the one on Abelard's life.

Philosophical Views on Castration

The article on Foulques reveals a more philosophical attitude on the subject of castration. To situate the context, Foulques was a friend of Abelard who supposedly penned a letter of consolation to him after his misfortune. The goal of his missive was to persuade Abelard to accept his mutilation and to even recognize some of the advantages of his condition. In the opening parts of the article, Bayle's Foulques seems to adopt the medieval misogynistic position on women; however, he broadens his argument by alluding to the fact that all women are dangerous temptresses. His friend condemns women in general without

[17] Bayle's details in the dictionary concerning the castration question are filled with references to ancient documents and even contemporary sources, which strongly supports the theory that he consulted a variety of available sources to add dimension to his discussion of castration in this series of articles on Heloise and Abelard. In particular, he demonstrates an avid interest in the biblical, scientific and historical facts surrounding the castration procedure. See pp. 139-148. Interestingly, Bayle's name appears several times in Ancillon's treaty on eunuchs, indicating that the two were most likely familar with each other's work and philosophical perspectives.

placing the blame specifically on Heloise. Bayle's presence as a critic manifests itself; he inserts the fact that Abelard's reputation as a ladies' man was hearsay, an interpretation that seems to increase the reader's curiosity regarding Abelard's tragedy. Once again, the notes contain key information about Abelard's castration. Bayle informs his reader that Foulques reminded Abelard of an unforeseen advantage. The mutilation is isolated from the rest of his body, recalling the medieval idea of cutting off the most sinful part of man's anatomy.[18] Foulques believed that Abelard would gain much by losing the part of him that had brought him the greatest damage to his life and reputation. Since many of these ideas are embedded as Latin in the French text, the English version of Bayle's dictionary is useful because it provides a translation of the Latin passages. It comes as no surprise that Foulques strongly condemns the lewd sexual pulsions of women, whom he refers to as rapacious beings.[19] For this reason, he tries to persuade Abelard that he is free of "that troublesome member, which by God's will and favor you have now lost" (71).[20] This idea is further developed in Foulque's argument on freedom. He supports his case by noting that Abelard can now seek lodging in any home without arousing suspicion, but one of the most interesting points is Foulque's erasure of passion. As he puts it, "il pourrait passer et repasser au milieu des femmes les mieux parées, et regarder les plus belles femmes sans aucun péril et sans craindre les criminelles tentations" (152). As a mutilated being, Abelard's loss of his member

[18] Cheney interprets Abelard's castration from a medieval point of view. For religious reasons, the practice of castration was thought to be befitting as punishment for the part of the male body that had committed the sin. Interestingly, this idea is also alluded to in the medieval love correspondence, but Abelard sees it as freedom from lust. See pp. 170-75.

[19] See the English translation of Bayle's dictionary, specifically Bayle's article on Foulques, note "c" p. 71.

[20] The English translation of Bayle's historical dictionary is particularly useful because it provides a translation for the Latin passages, which is not included in the French version. The edition consulted here is the 1984 reprint by Garland.

signals his textual transformation into an androgyne. Foulque's representation of the androgyne is expressed in his claim that Abelard's liberation from lascivious thoughts can open up a new path towards discovering the secrets of nature, a supposed allusion to a philosophical attribute of castration.

Bayle's Foulques underlines the importance of uninterrupted meditations that are devoid of emotions, thus enabling Abelard to fully utilize his powers of reason. Bayle also includes a note on the subject of Abelard's liberation from corporeal desires. Interestingly, he constructs a parallel between Foulque's argument on the advantages of the castration and the discourse on celibacy in the eighteenth century. For Bayle, Foulques looks upon the mutilation as one of the most positive aspects of a theologian's life:

> C'est le chemin de la chasteté non seulement le plus commode, mais aussi le plus sûr; car ceux qui ne peuvent se maintenir dans cette voie que par de fréquents combats; sont forts à plaindre: ils vivent dans l'agitation et dans l'inquiétude; leur état est toujours douteux, la victoire est quelquefois chancelante. (160)

According to Foulques, the imposed celibacy on a eunuch signified that he could surpass the turbulence of carnal desire and thus aspire to a superior spiritual state of existence. This ascending tone in his line of argumentation is further amplified by another reference in note "e" to Abelard's loss. Bayle's Foulques reminds Abelard that this loss is irreversible and implores him not to grieve for something that cannot grow back. Bayle constructs a rational argument for Foulques in which the latter tries to persuade Abelard that, since his loss is permanent, he must accept it and eventually come to bear the burden with patience.[21]

Bayle includes other consolation rationales that Foulques supposedly used in his letter to Abelard, but he criticizes one of

[21] Bayle's article on Foulques, see pp. 160-4.

Foulque's weaknesses in the latter part of the article. He specifically accused Foulques of exaggerating the social repercussions of Abelard's misfortune. In note "h," Bayle expresses doubt that the theologians of Paris were greatly afflicted by Abelard's social mutilation. This is another textual example of Bayle's attempt to correct flaws in the historical documents that he consulted. Thomas Lennon observes that Bayle did not only intend to eliminate these flaws, but rather to disclose these misconceptions to his readers. As an author, Bayle also asserts his critical stance by interjecting his presence into the text in order to skeptically assess the facts. The reference to the reaction by the clergy of Paris is qualified in a universal lamentation by the Parisians in general and, in particular, Parisian women: "Elles versèrent d'aussi chaudes larmes, que si elles avaient perdu chacune dans une bataille son mari ou son galant. Il n'y avait pas eu mort d'homme, il est vrai; mais néanmoins elles avaient perdu leur champion" (168). Here, Bayle prefigures the sentimental tone of Pope's poetic version of Heloise that would become very popular in eighteenth-century English fiction. At the same time, the tears of these women widen the suffering to a level of universal grief, which Bayle attributes to Foulque's words. Bayle compares this rampant lamentation to the loss of the women's Adonis; he also includes a criticism in note "i" in which he states that Foulques should have been more careful in his rhetoric. As he puts it, "il fallait donc dire, ou que les autres ne pleurèrent point, ou que si elles pleurèrent, ce fut moins par quelque amitié pour Abélard, que par la crainte des conséquences" (168-9). Here, Bayle explains the tears as a sign that women fear the implementation of the barbaric practice of castration as a punishment for lewd behavior.

Bayle also supports this larger public fear of castration in his reference to an ancient Greek war in which the Marquis of Spoleto, an ally of the ruler, ordered the castration of many of their prisoners because the Greek emperor loved eunuchs. One day, one of the prisoner's wives came to the Marquis to protest against the mutilation of their husbands. In speaking to the Marquis, she said: "peut-on nous faire une guerre plus cruelle, que de priver nos maris de ce qui nous donne de la santé, du plaisir, et des enfants? Quand vous en faites des eunuques, ce n'est pas eux, c'est nous que vous mutilez" (169-70). The woman was successful in persuading the Marquis not to castrate her husband. When asked what she should do if her husband took up arms again, the woman replied that they could take other parts of his body, but they should leave her the part that belonged to her. Bayle interjects to say that this woman most likely would have preferred that his life be taken instead of seeing him cut, and thus condemned to live as a eunuch.

The related theme of grief for Abelard's mutilation is also treated on a more personal level. Bayle informs the reader that Foulques does not refer to Heloise in his letter of consolation to Abelard because it was widely known that she grieved for her husband's loss. The comments on Heloise's loss reveal the authorial presence of Bayle as a critic. At first, he acknowledges the facts. At the time, Heloise was in a convent: 'Il est vrai qu'elle était alors dans un couvent, mais elle n'y avait que l'habit de religieuse, et les visites secrètes qu'elle y recevait de son mari n'étaient point un simple verbiage, ils avaient l'adresse de se retirer dans quelque coin pour s'entretenir tout à leur aise" (171). Although other versions allude to these supposed encounters which have already been discussed, it is important to situate this scene within the fictional framework of the lovers' legend. In the passage cited above, Bayle seems to point to the reversibility of the nun's frock, suggesting it is a mask facilitating the illicit encounters between the two. Once again, he shows that he was most likely familiar with the medical research on eunuchs, whereby the ability to perform was not ruled out by the amputation. This is significant because these amorous encounters are presented in the light of what people knew in the Enlightenment about eunuchs, so it was not just a fantasy but also medically feasible. While the scene is firmly grounded in the legend of the couple, the author also foreshadows the extreme anguish of the young Heloise. Bayle includes a comment on her grief in his reading of a translation of the love letters that came out in 1693: "Aussi bien y a-t-il de l'éloquence à se taire, quand la grandeur des malheurs, ne peut plus être exprimée" (171). He projects a critical eye on this anonymous translation by praising Heloise's silent reaction. For Bayle, the power of her silence shows a voice of experience and sensibility. The emphasis on sensibility marks the shift to an eighteenth-century interpretation, a reading that would be developed further in Jean-Jacques Rousseau's novel, *Julie ou La Nouvelle Héloïse,* which was published in 1761. Moreover, Bayle questions whether their love was chaste or driven by lust, but nonetheless he reverts to the phallocentric position by describing her as a deluded woman. He maintains that she never ceased to love Abelard, thus never deviating from carnal desire. Bayle suspends his discussion by abruptly concluding his remarks.

The final argument on consolation reveals a repetition of other points that Foulques used to console his friend. Bayle reads Foulques' conclusion as a reminder to Abelard not to lament his past happiness. Foulques attempts to bolster his friend's spirits by telling him that he will be rewarded on Judgment Day. Bayle also inserts his own assessment of Foulque's rationale; he confesses to his readers that if Abelard had replied to his letter of consolation he would of made it clear that Foulques was not highly skilled as a comforting friend.

Bayle's Fiction Representation of Heloise

The final article to be considered here is the one on Heloise, which highlights Bayle's critical view of women. At an overall glance of the structure, this article can be read as an intertext to the one devoted to Abelard, especially given the textual repetition pertaining to the biographical details leading up to the castration. Bayle begins the article by saying that, since one had spoken so much about Heloise in the past, she at least deserved an entry in his historical dictionary. He recognizes her prowess for learning, but he points to a deviation from her intellect, privileging her more romantic penchant. He describes her uncle's disappointment with her private lessons: "elle n'apprit qu'à faire l'amour" (182). This is significant because Bayle sets the tone for his revision of Heloise, yet he is careful to document, in note " b," the fact that she had the reputation of being one of the most erudite women of her time. Although he acknowledges her intellect, he casts a skeptical eye: "Dans ce siècle-là, une jeune fille pouvait passer pour un miracle, avec une très médiocre érudition" (188). It is after Bayle documents the inevitable act of her uncle's vengeance that the biographer enters into a more fictional portrayal of the subsequent events of the couple's lives. Above all, he insists on the use of the word "scandal," prefiguring the genesis of the lovers' legend. In a recent translation of this article, Deborah Fraioli analyzes Bayle's objective as an attempt to provide the reader with an amusing and disparaging portrayal of Heloise.[22] She, too, confirms that the article can be read as a fiction, especially given the dramatic exaggeration found in his descriptions.

The first example of this heightened dramatic aspect of the article is Bayle's description of Heloise's love. To support the prevalence of her love over religious duty as well as conver-

---

[22] Deborah Fraioli's recent translation of Bayle's article on Heloise is germane to this discussion as she supports the theory that Bayle contributed significantly to the fictional legend of the couple. See "Pierre Bayle's Reflections on a much discussed Woman: The Heloise article in the *Dictionaire Historique et critique," Listening to Heloise: The Voice of a twelfth-century Woman,* ed. Bonnie Wheeler. (New York: St. Martin's Press, 2000): 341-360. In particular, Fraioli maintains that Bayle's portrayal of Heloise is in essence overly dramatic and inherently mocking. Thus, he does not provide a faithful representation of the learned Heloise.

sion, he cites the medieval correspondence, Jean de Meun's translation, and Bussy's version. However, his account of the marriage argument deviates significantly from these previous versions. For instance, he maintains that Heloise would rather be Abelard's concubine instead of his wife. Bayle goes as far as to say that Heloise would rather be known as Abelard's "putain" to assure the liberty of love over conjugal bonds. In his revision of the marriage argument, he includes a lengthy argument against marriage for philosophers. In note " h," Bayle outlines Heloise's main points against marriage, revolving around the danger and dishonor that it would cause for Abelard. It was thought that celibacy was essential for philosophers, so that sex would not interfere with their meditations and professional obligations. As Walter points out, Bayle was very critical of the conjugal institution, and this could shed light on his extreme, exaggerated rewriting of Heloise's criticism of the marital state. At the same time, Bayle builds up the unreasonable nature of her love for Abelard, to such an extent that she appears to lose touch with her reason, overstepping the boundary between rationality and hysteria. He illustrates this idea in note "m":

> Ils prouvent, non seulement que l'amour de concupiscence dominait la pauvre Héloïse; mais aussi qu'elle était un peu démontée car une personne bien sage n'aurait jamais parlé de la sorte. Il est apparent que l'étude avait commencé de la détraquer; et que l'amour fut un grand surcroît de désordre. On voit dans ses écrits beaucoup de marques d'une imagination déréglée. (204)

Here, we note the striking difference with the medieval, erudite representation of Heloise as an exceptional woman, abbess and scholar. Bayle would seem to suggest that knowledge, dangerous for a woman, contributed to Heloise's extreme, irrational behavior. He analyzes her through a critical, masculine lens; locking her into the subjugated stereotype of the "hysterical" woman who not only loves too much, but is too intelligent for her own good.

He embellishes her passion further by stating that Heloise was never "cured" of her eternal passion, as traces of her "madness" remained. As an appendix to this idea of never being "cured" of her love, Bayle again inserts a reference to the castration in note "k," reinforcing the theory that Abelard's mutilation caused great suffering for Heloise. In essence, Bayle's Heloise claims that her husband's amputation was a swift accident, whereas her internal wound never healed. To add dimension to her suffering, Bayle cites the popularity of the *Lettres portugaises* to show that nuns were quite capable of producing genuine displays of excessive passion.[23] According to Bayle, love is viewed as a malady, and, as noted earlier, Bayle claims that Heloise was an eternal victim of her infirm nature. Once again, he appears to forewarn the reader that Abelard's castration did not render him completely impotent, but this time points to Heloise's seductive ploys to indulge in amorous encounters at the Paraclete:

> Ceux qui médirent des frequents voyages d'Abélard au Paraclet (45), furent sans doute téméraires, puisqu'ils ignoraient les dispositions intérieures d' Héloïse: mais s'ils les avaient sues, ils auraient dû craindre qu'il ne fût inévitable, humainement parlant, que cette femme ne se portât à des actes d'impureté avec cet homme. (202)

In this manner, he builds up the legend by embellishing Bussy and Guilleragues's Ovidian vision of love driving the heroine to the brink of illness, and he sets the precedent for a theme to be significantly developed in later eighteenth-century versions of Heloise's persona. Once again, the male author or, in this case, historical biographer, re-writes the woman: he presents her as a hysterical victim of male seduction, which, inevitably, invalidates her claim as a serious writer because she is viewed as irrational. The woman as a "victim" to her passions is clearly

[23] See Bayle's article on Heloise, p. 183.

represented as not in her "right" mind and unable to measure up to the masculine conception of reasonable, controlled emotions; thus Bayle's Heloise is reduced to an inferior position.

Bayle also contributes to the growth of the fictionalized legend in his description of the miracle that supposedly took place at the time of Heloise's death. After he researched various documents, he comments that when they opened the tomb to lay Heloise's body to rest next to Abelard, who had already been dead for at least twenty years, his arms reached out to receive her so that they could be reunited in eternal peace.[24]

Bayle should be recognized not only as the innovator of this famous melodramatic aspect of the cult that surrounded the couple, but as a visionary who would, inadvertently, inspire many British writers to create their own fictional heroine, constructed on the pre-romantic image of the passionate, melancholy nun who clung to the memory of Abelard. Bayle would later influence the French imitators of Alexander Pope (mainly Pierre Colardeau) and others who would amplify the sentimental representation of Heloise in addition to dramatically altering the form of the text. Before looking at Pope and Colardeau, it is important to explore another prose version which has recently become available to scholars. Dom Gervaise's translation will be considered in the next chapter, focusing on his portrayal of Abelard's castration and other fascinating eighteenth-century philosophical ideas.

---

[24] See Bayle's article on Heloise, p. 185. Here, he provides his account of the couple's burial together.

6.

Dom Gervaise's Repentant Translation of Heloise and Abelard

In 2002, a recent edition of Dom Gervaise's 1723 translation of the correspondence came out, facilitating the study of a rare text which was not readily available to scholars of the famous couple. Dom Gervaise was a theologian and philosopher who was a rather controversial figure in the Church. His religious career was overshadowed by a series of turbulent political problems in the Carmelite and Trappist orders. In his private life, the theologian was also plagued by numerous scandals. For instance, it was rumored that he was bisexual, and an intercepted love letter by Saint-Simon revealed that he was not only debauched, but in love with a nun.[1] To escape from his problems, Dom Gervaise eventually retired to a life of religious solitude much like Abelard's later years. The introduction to the edition suggests that Gervaise identified with the adversities Abelard had in the Church, including personal enemies and conflicts with his colleagues, which may have inspired him to embark on the project of translating the medieval correspond-

[1] Roland Oberson's introduction to Dom Gervaise's edition contains the details of Gervaise's controversial relationships. *Lettres d'Héloïse et d'Abélard,* Version Dom Gervaise avec Vie d'Abailard par M. de L'Aulnaye. (Lausanne: L'Age d'homme, 2002): 281.

ence. Since the text is similar to the medieval one, it will be considered only in regard to certain eighteenth-century ideas on castration and philosophical ideas, placing it in dialogue with Bayle. On a philosophical level, Gervaise refers to the fact that he wanted to search for moral truth in carrying out the project. Like Bayle, he, too, wanted to restore the lovers as they supposedly were in the twelfth century.

Before considering the translation, it is valuable to look at the main reason Dom Gervaise decided to undertake the project. Charrier maintains that he was against the popular wave of the gallant legend of the medieval couple's story. To put it in Gervaise's words:

> l'on ne pourrait les regarder que comme un commerce de galanterie, où deux jeunes personnes de différent sexe, expriment mutuellement les sentiments de la plus vive passion qu'il ressentent l'un pour l'autre. C'est l'idée que nous en donnent les Lettres qu'on voit courir dans le monde, sous le nom de ces deux beaux génies. (315)

In the preface to the translation, Dom Gervaise criticizes the unfaithful versions that were circulating, insisting on his commitment to produce a more accurate representation of the couple (318-321). Charrier's position, however, is less than laudatory, and she views the translation as unfaithful to the medieval love correspondence. Her critical evaluation of his work characterizes it as a paraphrase of the medieval text.

Revising the Lovers

It is not surprising that a first glance at the 1723 prose translation reveals several structural modifications. The *Historia* is replaced by a biography of Abelard's life attributed to M. de L'Aulnaye. In the paratext to this 2002 edition, the editor states that this text, the *Vie d'Abailard,* serves as the introduction to Dom Gervaise's translation. The body of Gervaise's text contains six letters instead of the original four of the medieval text, so, by creating supplementary epistles, he immediately deviates from his intended goal of restoring them. In his critical notes to the edition, Roland Oberson comments that Gervaise wanted to conduct a "tell-all" revealing portrayal of the couple. To achieve this goal, he alters Abelard significantly by representing him, as Oberson puts it, " un amoureux repenti."[2] Oberson emphasizes the fact that Gervaise places the lovers in a textual confessional in which he positions himself as the one who listens to their confessions and ultimately grants them absolution for their sins. But in listening to what the two divulge, he interprets what they say and, in turn, fictionalizes their words. In this manner, Gervaise, too, does not remain faithful to his stated intention of searching for truth in his translation. Although the confessional idea has already been seen in Grenaille's revision of Heloise, Gervaise carves out his own originality by restoring Abelard's presence, then placing the couple into a locked confessional. Abelard is portrayed not only as the familiar erudite theologian and remarkable philosopher, but as a "wounded" man in love, with particular emphasis on his mutilated manhood. However, he is not gallant, as already seen in Bussy or Alluis' versions, but is plagued by an overwhelming sense of sin. Abelard appears inherently powerless, thus reinforcing the omnipresent image of him as a marginalized eunuch. At the same time, Gervaise clearly shifts the context into the eighteenth century by describing Heloise as, "une religieuse mécontente et libertine" (317). Here, Gervaise appears to mirror Bayle's harsh view of Heloise and is a bit more negative by categorizing her as a libertine. Once again, the critical perception of women places Gervaise in accordance with misogynistic conceptions of the times. In Heloise's second letter, Gervaise inserts Enlightenment perceptions of women expressed by the invented diatribe of his Heloise, alluding to gender disparity:

[2] On page 281 of the apologue, Oberson characterizes Abelard's letters as a repentant series of confessions.

> c'est ainsi que nous devenons tous les jours le jouet ou la victime de l'inconstance des hommes! Faut-il que notre sexe, un sexe si faible et si fragile, leur apprenne à n'être point volages, et leur fasse, par notre exemple, des leçons de constance et de fidélité (II, 157)

The contrast between fickleness and faithfulness as well as the differences between the sexes smacks of aristocratic libertine rhetoric. Gervaise's Heloise is clearly espousing an eighteenth-century discourse on men's natural tendency towards infidelity, whereas women are simply cast in the predisposed role of the passive victims of their physical pleasures. Since there are only isolated instances of retouching the medieval text, Gervaise's Heloise is more commonly forced to confess her sins, and having her doing so, Gervaise imposes a symbolic hairshirt upon her.[3] Obserson affirms this notion in his critical remarks, underlining the image of the penitent, suffering Heloise.

Recasting Heloise as Mary Magdalene

To add dimension to these prevalent images of suffering, it is valuable to look at a key biblical source of suffering to compare it to Heloise's portrayal as a penitent figure. It is possible that Gervaise developed the archetype of the sinful Heloise, which can be traced back to a popular devotional and confessional figure in the Middle Ages, Mary Magdalene.[4] Although the more familiar images of Mary Magdalene are identified with tears and mourning, one of the most interesting comparisons is to Mary Magdalene as the embodiment of perfect penance. Katherine Jansen has observed that Mary Magdalene was known to have carried out certain severe penitential practices, mainly after her conversion to Christianity. She supposedly wore a hairshirt, or sackcloth, and engaged in self-mutilation

---

[3] In the apologue, Oberson refers to the idea of Heloise wearing a hairshirt on page 296. The hairshirt is associated with the confessional gesture of atoning for one's sins both orally and physically.

[4] See Katherine Ludwig Jansen's book, *The Making of the Magdalen: Preaching and Popular Devotion in the later Middle Ages* (Princeton: Princeton UP, 2000).

on a daily basis, battering her body in a dramatic way. The repeated flow of blood led to her eventual elevation to the status of spiritual martyrdom. Jansen points out an unexpected historical, medieval fact associated with the ritual of penance in which Abelard played an influential role in implementing changes governing the practice of penance: he also advocated the mandatory practice of private confessions (202). Interestingly, it would seem that Gervaise seems to exchange roles with Abelard; he becomes the confessor who transcribes in writing the illicit story of his sinful relationship with Heloise. In any event, the historical and biblical parallels cannot be overlooked, as Gervaise states that he was supposedly striving to produce a genuine portrayal of the medieval lovers. A review of the medieval text reveals that are numerous references in Heloise's letters pointing to committing sins or crimes as well as engaging in penance, but the difference is shown by her amplified open wound or "plaie," as seen in Gervaise's revision of Heloise. As he writes her, "Héloïse n'étant qu'une plaie" (IV, 179). On a symbolic level, it is as if Abelard's mutilation had become superposed onto her body, so that she could partake of the pain.

In his fourth letter, Gervaise expands the theme of penance by inserting some supplementary passages. For instance, his Heloise writes: "Je me croirai soulagée quand je pourrai partager avec vous la peine due à un péché dont nous sommes également coupables" (IV, 184). Heloise, however, wants to carry the burden of the tragedy by engaging in ongoing penance, which is best exemplified by sustained confession: "Ce n'est pas une chose fort difficile d'ouvrir la bouche pour confesser ses fautes, ni même d'affliger son corps par quelque pénitence extérieure" (IV, 184). The implied idea of self-flagellation buttresses the association with Mary Magdalene, and, at the same time, deviates from the medieval text. Most of the medieval textual emphasis is on internal suffering, but Gervaise preserves Heloise's internal suffering, but supplements it with the original idea of a more physical, external penance. This exterior penance remains, however, on a symbolic level, as he deletes any references to practicing self-flagellation. In his translation, Gervaise places the blame of the castration on Heloise. Heloise's allusions to the wound are reminiscent of Abelard's tragic event, creating an original aspect in this translation that underlines the omnipresence of Abelard's brutal punishment, and thus reveals an intertextual link to Bayle's emphasis on the significance of the castration incident.

Gervaise's Portrayal of Abelard's Castration

The most important part of Gervaise's translation of Abelard's fifth letter highlights Abelard's mutilation and its subsequent repercussions on Heloise. Abelard's letter contains several references to the incident, focusing primarily on the body. In one of the references to the castration, Gervaise's Abelard describes it as an incision and as an "insulte sanglante" (V, 212). Within these same lines, the words punishment, crime and sin reinforce the unforgettable misfortune. Although much of this same rhetoric appears in the medieval text, the accumulation of these terms in the same paragraph serves to heighten Gervaise's representation of Abelard as a man plagued with sin that not even his physical suffering can alleviate. For instance, Gervaise embellishes the text with some Enlightenment ideas in Abelard's fifth letter: 'L'amour dont je brûlais pour vous était si ardent, et avait tellement obscurci toutes les lumières de ma raison, que je ne savais plus ce qui me convenait" (V, 215). One striking modification is the fact that Gervaise's Abelard deviates from the medieval text in overtly acknowledging his love for Heloise. The translator inserts some more contemporary eighteenth-century philosophy by alluding to the fact that Abelard's overwhelming passion dominated his reason, thus causing him to engage in carnal sins with Heloise. The moral aspect is further sustained by the references to violating justice. Since Dom Gervaise was a theologian, it is possible to read this description of Abelard's seduction as inherently evil, another moral aspect highlighting the opposition between purity and virtue as opposed to the darker side of man's sinful nature. This section of the epistle also serves to introduce the justification for the castration. A careful review of the medieval text reveals that Abelard considers the castration as a partial purification process, but Gervaise emphasizes the word "purity" a bit more frequently and views the wound as part of a spiritual and corporeal cleansing process in which he can ultimately transcend his mutilated body. In this same letter, Gervaise seems to insist on this image of spiritual cleansing. He alludes to the castration as "cette punition corporelle" (V, 231). In the medieval text, the language is more general and is restricted to the idea of pain. In spite of his mutilated body, Gervaise's Abelard discovers a divine attribute: "il retranche un membre pourri, afin de nous laisser un corps pur et net" (V, 231). From the removal of the sexual essence of his sin, Abelard is ostensibly reborn as a pure man. It is as if the body were reconfigured in an abstract, but nonetheless more pure form, one that is possibly androgynous and not marked in the male gender. Gervaise points to the difference between Heloise and Abelard towards the end of this missive. His Abelard recognizes God's goodness and he says his justice is revealed by sparing Heloise's life. The theme of cleanliness is augmented, shown by Abelard's reference to Heloise as being more chaste than he. It is possible that Gervaise's Abelard locates the source of his newly-discovered purity by receiving it symbolically through the saintly body of Heloise, especially as the embodiment of Mary Magdalene. Furthermore, there is more textual emphasis on Heloise as a paragon of virtue, which Gervaise's Abelard highlights in the third letter.

Reclaiming Virtue

This notion of chastity is reinforced by another revised aspect of the medieval text. In Gervaise's translation, it is important to consider his portrayal of Heloise as a martyr, especially noting the comparison, once again, to Mary Magdalene. As Jansen posits, the image of the post-conversion Mary is often identified with chastity, which is affirmed by Janet Schaberg's study of the legend of Mary.[5] It is as if she became a virgin again in the spiritual sense. Interestingly, the crown was placed upon Mary. As Jansen postulates, "her humility, patience, and love earned her the same crown as the virgins" (243). In his dramatic fifth letter, Gervaise, too, includes allusions to the crown. Gervaise's Abelard suggests that the tribulations of their passion are substantial reason for Heloise to deserve the crown. For him, she should wear it, "afin de vous procurer ensuite la couronne du long et pénible martyre que vous souffrez" (V, 232). Although the medieval love letters contain references to the crown, this eighteenth-century translation differs in that the crown is the emblem designated for the penitent female martyr. Abelard observes a series of differences between them, pointing to the "wound' as the source of their spiritual deviations. In one swift blow of the knife, he was spared eternal suffering from his sins for the rest of his life. In the medieval text, the emphasis is placed more on the amputation delivering him from burning lust. Since Gervaise includes numerous references to the castration in his fifth letter, he echoes Bayle's emphasis on the event for the eighteenth-century reader. Gervaise also uses the diminished spiritual status of the eunuch within the Church to realign his translation with the medieval text. Gervaise points to the superior position of Heloise by adding in the idea that Abe-

[5] Janet Schaberg's recent book, *The Resurrection of Mary Magdalene: Legends, Apocrypha, and the Christian Testament* (New York & London: Continuum, 2002), offers a fascinating study of the discussion of various legendary aspects of Mary's persona.

lard is only her slave and no longer her master. The word "slave" underscores the pivotal presence of the eunuch and again places the translation in dialogue with Bayle's emphasis on castration in his historical and philosophical reading of the love correspondence. Here, the role of the slave recalls Bayle's historical tracing of the eunuch as the servant of the sultan's wives in the harem, which is discussed in the previous chapter. Moreover, the fact that Abelard refers to Heloise as a martyr is part of his persuasive, religious strategy. As in the medieval text, Heloise must forget her love for Abelard and devote herself to Jesus, especially since she is represented as a saintly figure.

The image of Heloise's additional role as Christ's bride also reveals an intriguing biblical comparison. The reference to the Ethiopian bride from the Song of Songs in the medieval correspondence was already discussed in the second chapter. Here, Gervaise modifies the text by altering the image of the black bride. The familiar contrast between her exterior blackness signifying tribulation and her interior whiteness embodying virtue is found in the medieval text, but Gervaise grafts the image of penitence onto his version of the black bride: "Sa noirceur est l'effet de la vie pénitente qu'elle mène, et des afflictions de cette vie" (V, 201). Once again, it is possible to identify a comparison between Heloise and the black bride, one that revolves around the idea of penance. To place this in a larger biblical context, Jansen postulates that the Ethiopian bride was also associated with tears; thus she evokes Mary Magdalene (209-212). Supposedly, the black bride was transformed from blackness to whiteness through the cleansing flow of tears, linking her to the saintly figure of Mary. The main idea is that one's innocence could be restored.[6] In addition, this interpretation relates to Heloise, for she was once a sinner who has risen in Gervaise's

---

[6] See Jansen for details on the representation of tears and spiritual cleansing on pp. 209-213.

translation to a saintly status, and thus her purity or innocence is textually reborn from the pen of the male translator.

Doing Penance in the Fictional Confessional

The overall tenor of Gervaise's translation portrays Heloise as a sinner engaging in continuous penance, which creates a bond with Abelard. As a eunuch, Abelard openly confesses his sins and looks to his spiritually superior wife to ensure their eternal union. As in the medieval text, Abelard insists on the transformation from carnal desire to spiritual love. Although Gervaise forces Heloise to do penance for her role in an illicit love, he nonetheless carries out a textual strategy of putting her and Abelard together to openly atone for their respective sins. While Heloise often addresses innocence, Abelard speaks of his punishment and eternal pain. In the third letter, the word "innocence" is repeated several times. Susan Haskins identifies another link to Mary Magdelene, which not only underlines the association of Mary with female sexuality, like Heloise, but can be traced back to Eve's fall from grace. As Haskins points out, it is through confession that innocence can be regained.[7] It is as if Heloise's sustained penance restores the purity of their bond: "Notre union était sainte et innocente" (IV, 184). It is the translator himself who takes the power into his hands and ultimately absolves them of their crimes, so as to represent them in a moral light as tragic incarnations of goodness and the human susceptibility to evil, or the carnal temptations that plague mankind.

If Dom Gervaise's version places him in the position of listening to Abelard's and Heloise's confessions, the rare 1796 edition is valuable because it enables modern readers to study

[7] See Susan Haskins book, *Mary Magdalen: Myth and Metaphor* (New York: Harcourt Brace & Company, 1994): 229-230. Haskins offers an interesting discussion of the depiction of Mary Magdalene as a weeping iconic figure, which is placed within the biblical context of the fall of Adam and Eve and the possibility of regaining innocence through the act of penance.

visually some of the famous scenes associated with Heloise's and Abelard's love story. The text was published in three volumes and contained the Latin version of the medieval text along with the French translation published alongside. Charrier finds that it is not a faithful version, but rather permeated with the fictional legend. She also maintains that Dom Gervaise produced a paraphrase of Heloise's and Abelard's love story.[8] This elaborate edition was published by J.B. Fournier le Jeune et fils and contained eight engravings sketched and directed by Moreau le Jeune, a successful book illustrator in the eighteenth century. The artists who executed the drawings were Dambrun, Halbon, Langlois Jeune, Lemire, Pauquet, Romanet et Simonet. At the close of the Enlightenment, it was a common practice for novels to contain engravings. Due to the growing popularity of the illustrated text, readers even came to expect drawings.[9] Recent internet technology has made it possible to obtain access to the engravings contained in the 1796 edition, thereby facilitating an analysis of the engravings related to the important issue of castration in the eighteenth century, as well as to the development of the sentimental legend of the lovers' tragic love story.[10]

Theories of Iconography

Before analyzing at some key engravings, it is important to provide some basic approaches to interpretating the drawings. Phillip Stewart has carried out extensive research on eight-

---

[8] On pp. 486-8, Charrier refers to the 1796 edition and also provides comments on some of the engravings directed by Moreau le Jeune.

[9] Philip Stewart provides an extensive history of book illustrations in his article "L'Illustration du roman aux dix-huitième siècle." *The Eighteenth-century now; Boundaries and Perspectives* (2005): 226-228.

[10] I would like to acknowledge the webmaster, Henri Demangeau, who has given me permission to cite his website, *http://www.pierre-abelard.com/docu-moreau.htm*. Although these reproductions of Moreau's drawings are accessible to the public, Mr. Demangeau, on behalf of the Pierre Abelard association, should be recognized for making these rare reproductions available to international scholars.

eenth-century engravings. He points out that illustrations can be viewed as intertexts and even performances or readings of a text.[11] The task of the reader is to decode the drawing, while taking into account the verbal account of the narrative. For instance, in many engravings a caption provides the verbal frame for the specific illustration. It is up to the reader to construct his own interpretation, one that fuses the visual with the written word, the frame with the drawing. Stewart also provides other elements that are useful in deciphering an illustration, such as examining facial expressions and gestures, the play of light and shadow, and study of symbolic objects within the drawing. Another book-illustration scholar, Edward Hodnett, has also looked at the significance of engravings. He posits that illustrations are "always to in some degree supplementary rather than reproductive images" (14). In another words, drawings do not need to be faithful representations of the novel's events. A drawing can also be viewed as a translation of some key textual event in the novel. As Hodnett puts it, "An illustration translates what is being said in written words into graphic images" (15). He then targets the specific function of drawings by adding that illustrations are intended to represent, interpret and decorate.[12]

Illustration as a Textual Supplement

These illustration scholars shed light on the idea that a drawing can serve as a highlight to the text, and thus is not always a faithful representation of textual events. Furthermore, since the eighteenth century became the most important period for the

---

[11] Philip Stewart's book, *Engraven Desire: Eros, Image & Text in the French Eighteenth Century* (Durham & London: Duke UP, 1992), is an invaluable source, offering a comprehensive study of how to interpret eighteenth-century drawings in a variety of texts.

[12] See Edward Hodnett's book, *Image & Text: Studies in the Illustration of English Literature* (London: Scolar Press, 1982). He provides some basic facts regarding the function of book illustrations, information very useful in formulating an interpretation of the book illustrations. See especially p. 13.

dissemination of the popular legend of the couple's tragedy, Hodnett's theory seems to be highly plausible. Putting illustrations into perspective, Christophe Martin echoes Stewart's theories on the importance of the theatricality of gestures.[13] The task of the reader is to decipher the expressions on the characters' faces. Therefore, the face is similar to a text that must be decoded and then interpreted. Stewart provides further insight by studying the lighting in the Moreau le Jeune drawings, a striking feature of the illustrations. For Stewart, the dramatic use of light underlines the tragic elements of the couple's story and seems to emphasize either the late medieval or gothic reinvention of their legend.

It is important to initially study the drawings in order, since the sequence points to the most notable events of the couple's lives. The first one shows the famous seduction scene in which Abelard is tutoring Heloise in the privacy of her bedroom in her Uncle Fulbert's home. Interestingly, the context is immediately shifted into the eighteenth century, as the lovers are dressed in more modern attire, which deviates radically from the medieval context. Abelard is recast as a much younger man and conversely Heloise is not a teenager, but appears to be a bit older, effacing the dramatic age difference that existed between them in the medieval text. Charrier also subscribes to the shift to an eighteenth-century context. She describes Heloise's bedroom as luxurious, focusing on the alluring ambiance of the master tutoring his student in a private setting: "C'est le soir ou la nuit. La pièce, hautement lambrissée, ornée de quelques chaises gothiques et d'un bahut sculpté 'à la cathédrale,' est toute baignée d'ombre, mais une lampe projette sa lumière vive sur le couple enlacé" (487). Although the couple is surrounded by open books and ostensibly engaged in intellectual activity,

[13] Chris Martin's book, *Dangereux suppléments: l'illustration du roman en France au dix-huitième siècle* (Louvain & Paris: Peeters, 2005), concentrates on the theatrical aspect of human gestures, offering seminal insight on deciphering the theatrical aspects of the Moreau engravings. See pp. 94-6.

the deeper, more subtle text is that of amorous overtures. Charrier's reading of this engraving points to sentimental eighteenth-century rhetoric. For instance, she describes this famous scene as "voluptueux," "extase," and "doux soupirs." Moreover, Charrier considers this drawing as completely unfaithful to the original representation of the seduction scene in the medieval text. It is important to note that the clothing and the portrayal of Abelard are clearly rescripted to represent an Enlightenment image of the tutor who is intent on teaching his student about love instead of cultivating her mind. Stewart has studied the meaning of objects in drawings, and he posits that reading could point to an erotic connotation.[14] In the drawing, the couple is seated at a desk with an open, disorderly array of books before them. A paper has fallen to the floor, thus illustrating Stewart's theory of an erotic context. There are also books, arranged in a haphazard manner, partially visible under the desk. In fact, Stewart maintains that often a novel lying on the floor was the outcome of erotic activity (96). The caption is a quote from Abelard's *Historia* and coincides well with the scene of passion in the illustration. At the center of the drawing is the couple embracing, and the light on the desk highlights their amorous display

The second illustration sketched by Langlois is also framed by a quote from Abelard's *Historia*. This engraving is of particular interest because it is of the castration and, as previously discussed, is a most important event for the eighteenth-century audience. As noted above, the theatrical aspect of the art of engraving is very much relevant for this drawing. The use of dramatic lighting in the center of the drawing highlights the facial expression of horror on the group of people gathered around Abelard's bed. The participants to the castration appear to have frozen expressions on their faces, as if they were captured performing a brutal scene in a play. The drawing reinacts

[14] Stewart, *Engraven Desire*. See pp. 94-6.

the scene as described in the medieval text. Abelard's tragic misfortune occurred in the dead of night in his bed when he was surprised by several men hired by Heloise's uncle, Fulbert, to carry out the castration. Stewart's reading of this specific illustration underscores the violence by pointing out that, not only is the light focused on the victim at the center of the bed, but also shows the man intent on performing the castration deliberately brandishing the blade before the helpless victim, Abelard (60). In sharp contrast to Abelard's illuminated form in the bed, the person who is supposed to perform the castration is concealed in a dark, shadowy half light. Abelard, in turn, appears to block his gaze behind his hands to block out the heinous vision before him prior to the castration. Stewart also characterizes this drawing as an example of the sentimental exploitation of Abelard's story. His perspective is further buttressed by the fact that this illustration was produced at a time when the legend of the medieval couple was at its peak, especially the sentimental and pre-romantic versions that flooded the European book market.[15] It would seem that a violent, disturbing scene like this portrayal of the castration may have appealed to readers, who were eager to own these illustrated editions.

The third illustration by Delvaux and Pauquet shows Heloise taking her vows at Argenteuil. The caption is also from the *Historia*, which is important because it corresponds to Abelard's version of Heloise's willingness to become a nun and devote herself at his request to a religious life. However, as already seen in my discussion of the love correspondence in the medieval text, Heloise was never intent on leading a religious life and never relinquished her love for Abelard. This is important as the engraving is not faithful to Heloise's version of the events,

---

[15] See Charrier on the explosion of the sentimental legend of the couple in Chapter Three on pp. 439-492. Her inclusive tracing of the fictional legend of Abelard and Heloise includes information on the European dissemination of the couple's love story in a variety of literary genres.

but only coincides with Abelard's autobiographical account as told in the *Historia.* The engraving seems to capture Abelard's request, as Heloise is positioned at the center of the drawing and the dimensions of her body are larger than the other nuns' in the drawing. Her eyes are directed towards the heavens, ostensibly sealing her devotion to God's service, and her arms are slightly uplifted in a dramatic gesture of religious faith. In her outstretched hand, she is holding the veil that she will wear from that moment on as she takes her vows to become the Bride of Christ. In the fifth drawing, the religious theme is sustained in this illustration showing Abelard receiving Heloise at the Paraclet, the refuge he gave her for her exiled nuns. As in the previous drawing where she is taking her vows, her body is positioned at the center of the drawing where she kneels in a subservient pose before Abelard. The devote, austere aspects of this encounter are highlighted by Heloise's hands which are crossed on her chest, while Abelard's hands are outstretched in a gesture of religious conviction, alluding to his power.

The next drawing is the one created by J.B. Simonet, depicting the infamous poisoning scene in which a fellow monk at St. Gildas ingested a lethal substance intended for Abelard. The caption is also from Abelard's *Historia.* As noted in the castration drawing, the horror is shown on the face of the young monk, and the light is focused on the deathly pallor of his face. Abelard is cast as the shadowy figure who discovers the dead monk. The dark contours of his body create a mysterious, eerie presence in the engraving which highlights the sharp contrast between life and death, as underscored by the use of light and shadow. The next drawing sketched by L.M. Halbon sustains the death theme, while focusing on Heloise's pain as she grieves on Abelard's tomb. The caption is taken from the famous letter written by their friend, Peter the Venerable, announcing the death of Abelard. He played a key role in sending Abelard's body to Heloise's convent, as it was Abelard's wish to be mourned by Heloise's nuns. The light is directed on Heloise, and she is placed at the center of the drawing; but her face is turned away from the viewer. It is possible that the angle of her face is turned away from the spectator to create a scene of private grief, thus intensifying her passion for Abelard. The reclined position of her body lends itself to an outpouring of unrestrained emotion as she receives the body of her beloved Abelard. This display of pathos and the gothic elements of the room in the convent suggest a pre-romantic representation of this elaborate display of emotion.

The final engraving was created by A. Romanet and depicts the death of Heloise. This drawing is of interest because it insists on the devout aspect of Heloise. In contrast to the preceding drawings, there is more light, which lends a brighter aspect to the overall atmosphere of the drawing. The dying Heloise is surrounded by her nuns, whose faces express their devotion and grief at the thought of losing their cherished spiritual leader. Interestingly, this drawing also corresponds to Abelard's representation of Heloise in the *Historia* as a devoted nun who over time adapted brilliantly to her role as a director of her convent. This drawing seems to celebrate her importance as a spiritual leader. Her elevated body occupies the center of the drawing, and her hands are crossed in a devotional gesture, as she is prays before her demise. Another interesting feature of this drawing is the intertextual portrayal of Jean-Jacques Rousseau's Julie. *La Nouvelle Héloïse* is also depicted as a saintly, maternal figure at the time of her death. The difference is that this illustration insists on the religious aspect of Heloise's career, whereas Rousseau's Julie remains in a secular context as an embodiment of maternal perfection. Nonetheless, the two representations of Heloise highlight her saintly qualities and point to the widespread emotion of love at the time of her demise. Charrier maintains that all signs of her love for Abelard are erased, as well as any trace of profane gestures (489). Once again, this engraving corresponds to Abelard's portrayal of Heloise, especially in the *Historia.* At his command, Heloise was supposed to lead a life devoted to God, and thus relinquish her love for Abelard. This final illustration underscores Dom Gervaise's intention in his translation project, which was to restore the medieval portrayal of the couple. However, the analysis of the key engravings point to many instances of pre-romantic elements that create a deviation from the translator's intended goal. Thus, Gervaise, too, infuses his textual production with many fictional elements which were very popular in the eighteenth-century versions. Dom Gervaise's translation anticipates the next wave of popular sentimental versions which would be shifted into poetry, creating international fascination with the couple's famous tragedy.

7.

The Hysterical and Pastoral Heloise

The eighteenth century also charted the success of the couple's tragic love story internationally. In fact, Heloise's fame was expanding, as the epistolary genre was approaching the era of its most significant development, extending beyond France, across the channel into England. One of the most important versions was Alexander Pope's verse translation of Heloise. He re(invented) Heloise as the prototype of the nostalgic, wistful woman in love who is driven to the brink of hysteria in the absence of her lover, a feature which would prove to be the most popular revision of her in the eighteenth-century poetic versions.

Pope: Eloisa in Verse Form

Pope's version of "Eloisa to Abelard" was based on John Hughes 1713 English translation of Bussy's letters, whose correspondence was not the first to attract international readership since Guilleragues's *Lettres portugaises* had already been translated into English and had been well received abroad. Now, as the genre was becoming increasingly more popular, British writers were looking to other French epistolary texts to appeal to their readers' literary tastes. To that effect, Hughes translated Bussy's French letters and added two fictional letters in his own version of the lovers' tragic story. Inspired by Hughes' rendition, Pope decided to work on a new variation.[1] Even though he had never read the original Latin text, he was not a stranger to the genre as he was very well acquainted with Ovid; he had previously translated several epistles from the *Heroides*, and among them Sappho's, and it is this masterpiece that is the most significant influence in his (re)invention of Heloise. The Ovidian prototype also provides the structural groundwork for the poetic version of Eloisa's lengthy epistle, written in verse form to Abelard. Other direct influences include Pope's overt textual borrowing from Hughes' prose epistles. As Foster noted, Pope's textual borrowing is best explained as a close paraphrase of Hughes' English translation, yet ironically, there is a third "influence": the medieval text.[2] Inadvertently, Pope restores some aspects of the Latin text. Not only do we find recovery of the spiritual struggle with Christian faith, but his erotic portrayal of Eloisa closely resembles that of her medieval counterpart.

Creating a New Form for Eloisa's "Plainte"

One of the initial impressions left by Pope's heroic creation is its strikingly abbreviated form. In order to compose a poem grounded in the Ovidian tradition, Pope had to begin by radically reducing the content of Heloise's letters so that he could rework her words into a carefully controlled couplet form. Borrowing from Ovid, he uses the heroic couplet, which consists of pentameters rhyming in pairs, a verse form that was very popular in the late seventeenth century, and continued into the early part of the Enlightenment. As Gordon noted, Pope's lines are usually balanced with a single caesura in the middle of each

[1] See Charrier p. 446 for more information on Pope's connection to the Hughes version.

[2] For a comparison of the Hughes version with Pope's poem, see Edward Foster's article, "Rhetorical Control in Pope's *Eloisa to Abelard,*" *Tennessee Studies in Literature* 13 (1968): 64-5.

line.[3] Other general structural characteristics of Pope's heroic epistle include antithesis, paradox and parallelism; he uses a closed couplet verse form, thus altering the spontaneous feature of the "feminine" epistle. It is the systematic, precise order of the verse lines that tends to diminish the discontinuous feature of the love letter, which, in turn silences the voice of Heloise, the original epistolary writer. Pope broke away from the tradition of recording extemporaneous thoughts, which would conflict with his creative and technical process of composing verse. In order to maintain balance in the poem, Pope compressed the sequence of events, and grafted a substantial part of Abelard's phrases and words onto Heloise's discourse, as previously seen in Grenaille's version. The most notable change in the process of shifting the epistle into verse form is the modification of the letter exchange. Pope eliminates Abelard from his adaptation, and thus reconstructs monologic discourse, as in Grenaille's version. As a seasoned poet, well trained in the composition of Ovidian heroic form, Pope concentrates on rewriting only the woman's experience of abandonment, suffering and betrayal. However, Pope does not completely efface the love letter in his work; he creates an artificial function for it, which consists of placing the epistle into the background as a passive form. Thus, he creates a deceptive illusion of communication between Eloisa and her lover. His Eloisa is supposedly in the process of writing one long letter, which is composed in verse, but is never sent to Abelard. Devoid of a receiver, this epistle has no real reciprocal value. Ironically, Pope preserves the original circumstances that pertain to Heloise's decision to initiate contact with Abelard. Even though he had never read the Latin text, his Eloisa writes to Abelard after having read the *Historia,* and there is just a brief mention of it in the paratext to

[3] I. R. F. Gordon analyzes the form of Pope's poem in depth, characterizing the work as an heroic epistle. See *A Preface to Pope.* (London & New York: Longman, 1976): 140-1.

clarify the circumstances that precipitated her response. This is the only instance where Pope directly refers to Abelard as a letter writer. Subsequent to this mention of the *Historia,* Pope completely destroys all traces of Abelard's letters, and this exclusion marks one of the most radical structural changes in the text. As Foster observed, other significant stylistic characteristics include omission, compression, addition and rearrangement or substitution.[4] This technique recalls Grenaille's narrative reformulation of the Latin text, but Pope introduces a new, fictional revision of Heloise influenced by the times in which he lived. The poem, written in 1716, contains certain pre-romantic traits that are assimilated into his (re)invention of Eloisa. She is a gloomy heroine who shares her misery with the outside landscape such as the trees, the wind that envelops the Paraclete, the water and the darkness of night. But we must be careful not to characterize Pope's portrayal of Eloisa as a purely romantic, sentimental figure. She does not transcend her suffering through a communion with nature in the later tradition of romanticism; rather, the landscape is worked into the poem as a visible and material means of magnifying the depths of her inner torment. (This could also be read as a close imitation of Ovid, who also included background landscape into his *Heroides.*) Pope's Eloisa could, however, be considered preromantic as well as Gothic since Pope inserted many Gothic elements into the narrative frame, which created a new direction for the eighteenth-century versions. Not only does he anticipate a form of Romantic sensibility that would become very popular later in the century, but he also interpolates a form of despair, melancholy and architectural confinement commonly found in Gothic Revival literature that would become very popular, mainly in the novel, at the end of the century. These two influences will be considered in the discussion of Pope's poetic (re)creation of the abandoned heroine.

---

[4] See Foster, pp. 65-69.

Gothic Influence on Pope's (Re)Creation of Eloisa

Although we have already noted that Pope's heroic epistle was written in the early part of the eighteenth century, Pope can be seen as anticipating the Gothic in many ways. In general, Gothic Revival literature looked to the medieval period for its inspiration, and was particularly interested in twelfth-century architectural constructions. Vaulted pillars with tremendous heights pointing upwards toward heaven were commonly used in Gothic cathedrals as were complex, intricate labyrinths, underneath churches. It was on this subterranean level that crypts and burial vaults were located. As Bayer-Barenbaum has shown, Gothic architecture is marked by fragmentation and division within divisions in the foundation of the churches' structure.[5] We will see evidence of this in Pope's reconstruction of the Paraclete, the place where his poem is situated. Other general characteristics of the Gothic include a fascination with tombs, convent scenes, mysterious corridors, uncanny appearances by ghosts, wild, untamed physical landscape, flickering candles, inexplicable, disembodied voices, dream states, encounters with the living dead and an overall attentiveness to the internal workings of the mind. Differing from the Romantic, the Gothic heroine does not aspire to a higher state of comprehension, but ultimately revels in the lugubrious bleakness that points to her profound discontent and misery. There is no aspiration toward transformation or resolution, as the Gothic heroine views herself solely as a victim destined to a plight of eternal suffering. Trapped by her own sense of irreversible melancholy, she is enclosed psychologically and physically within herself. Some of these aspects derived from the Gothic

[5] Linda Bayer-Barenbaum offers a fascinating study of the relationship between Gothic architecture and literature in a comprehensive way. See *The Gothic Imagination: Expansion in Gothic Literature and Art* (London & Toronto: Associated UP, 1982): 52-69.

are found in Pope's (re)invention of the physical landscape that encloses Heloise in her agonizing solitude, bereft of her lover. Linda Bayer-Barenbaum's description of a typical, Gothic convent captures the ambiance that Pope creates in his heroic epistle:

> The castle (or the convent) in Gothic literature is a good study in contrast. Usually situated in a wild forest or uninhabited mountain range where the sky is unsettled & the wind howling, the calm & the stable are set amid the wild & the dynamic. God's creation is pitted against man's in the clash between nature & architecture.[6]

Here, Bayer-Barenbaum describes the locus of Pope's (re)creation of Eloisa's principal conflict. Once again, Pope restores the standard image of the convent, which does not offer Eloisa the calm of refuge, but forces her to confront her ongoing, turbulent battle between God and her love for Abelard. This emotional conflict is illustrated by the structure of her isolated cell, and as Margaret Doody and Gillian Beer concur, these pre-Gothic traits built into the decor reflect the heroine's state of mind.[7] In addition, reverie is significantly developed as it is based on Bussy's original seventeenth-century innovation of the dream state, but Pope goes even further and writes in a form of Gothic apparitions where the dead seem to come back to life. Other disturbing aspects (such as a type of hallucination that borders on madness at times), are integrated into Eloisa's troubled sleep. Here, Pope contributes to the legend by representing Eloisa as a tragic heroine with an overactive imagination that almost causes her to lose touch with her reason. It is this use of "female" hysteria that clearly brings the fictional

---

[6] Bayer-Barenbaum 23.

[7] See Gillian Beer's article, "Our Unnatural No-Voice": The Heroic Epistle, Pope, and Woman's Gothic," *Yearbook of English Studies* 12 (1982): 121-151. Also, see Margaret Ann Doody's article, "Deserts, Ruins & Troubled Waters: Female Dreams in Fiction and the Development of the Gothic Novel," *The Eighteenth-Century Novel,* ed. Harold Bloom (Philadelphia: Chelsea House): 71-111.

expansion of the story into the "age of reason," and this feature will be even more fully developed in the nineteenth century. Even prior to the eighteenth century, European women were quite often believed to be defective simply because of their sexual difference. The society in which they lived was a repressive one that advocated the domestication of the female sex. As we shall see, Pope will use these social conventions to create the overall oppressive, physical atmosphere in which his Eloisa tells her story.

The Transformation of the Paraclete

Pope prefaces his epistle "Eloisa to Abelard" with a brief "Argument" that is a highly compressed, abridged substitute for the *Historia,* which, in turn provided his audience with some of the more noteworthy details that touched Heloise and Abelard's lives. Pope appears to ignore all of the philosophical and rational aspects of the lovers' original manner of presenting arguments in their epistolary correspondence. In this short paragraph, Pope also suppresses all of the events that led up to their retreat into separate cloisters by simply saying that they suffered a series of well-known calamities: "they were two of the most distinguished persons of their age in learning & beauty, but for nothing more famous than for their unfortunate passion."[8] Here, Pope clearly establishes the direction that his poem will take and then introduces his translation by admitting that he extracted certain details from Hughes' text or, as he calls it, "those celebrated letters." He also informs his readers that he intended to portray Eloisa's conflict or struggle between "grace and nature." In the first section, there is a description of the Paraclete, which immediately portrays Eloisa as a lonely woman who is left only with the treasured memories of her past life with Abelard. In classic Ovidian style, Eloisa evokes the past as

[8] All of the quotes are taken from Alexander Pope's poem "Eloisa to Abelard" (Miami: University of Miami Critical Studies, 1965).

an attempt to re-animate her passion even in light of her present predicament of desperation and dubious piety:

> In these deep solitudes and awful cells,
> Where heav'nly-pensive, contemplation dwells,
> And ever-musing melancholy reigns;
> What means this tumult in a Vestal's veins?
> Why rove my thoughts beyond this last retreat?" (1-5)

From the onset, Pope's Eloisa is entrenched in her loss, or, in Lacanian terms, she hopes to bridge the distance between herself and her beloved. As Ellen Pollak reads her in *The Poetics of Sexual Myth,*[9] Pope's Eloisa embodies lack, and this image of her reflects the contemporary view of women in English society. For instance, women were often presented as men's ornaments and extensions of them. Eloisa's lost plenitude is a prototype for the image of the woman as an incomplete entity, unlike a man. This is useful in looking at this revision of her persona as Pope reduces her to a shadow of a completed being, one that revolved around the harmony of the couple. As S.H. Clark reads it in *Sordid Images: The Poetry of Masculine Desire,*[10] Pope depicts Eloisa as living in a vast void, deprived of the sense of fulfillment that she once knew. Alone with only her thoughts to pass the time, she is trapped in an abyss of despair since there is no real possibility of repairing reciprocal epistolary contact with Abelard. Differing significantly from the seventeenth-century "cabinet" atmosphere where she was brought closer to Abelard through the contemplation of his portrait, she is bereft of any emblem conjuring up the soothing presence of her beloved. Indeed, Pope has removed almost all traces of her object

[9] Ellen Pollak, *The Poetics of Sexual Myth: Gender & Ideology in the Verse of Swift & Pope* (Chicago & London: University of Chicago Press, 1985): 184-7. Pollak insists on the lack which Pope represents as predominantly female, especially in the rhetoric of emotional excess that Pope's Eloisa displays in the poem.
[10] S.H. Clark, *Sordid Images: The Poetry of Masculine Desire* (London & New York: Routledge, 1994): 120. Clark maintains that Pope's portrayal of Eloisa suggests a rejection of the female desiring body.

of desire, which, in turn, allows him to create the melancholy atmosphere described in the opening lines of the poem. Here, Pope creates a "Gothic" ambiance as the dark, gloomy atmosphere of the convent provides an outer frame for Eloisa's inner sense of misery. His innovation manifests itself in this first stanza, as he paints the physically unstable environment that reflects Eloisa's inner conflict, the wrenching battle between God and her love for Abelard. Although Pope preserves the original theme of the medieval story, he radically alters the Paraclete into a "Gothic," claustrophobic, ominous structure. Within these dense walls sealing her off from all that she once knew and cherished, his Eloisa is immediately cut off—not only from Abelard—but from the creation of her own epistolary production. The fact that Pope substitutes verse for prose eradicates the spontaneity of her original words and subsequently locks her into the confining rigidity of the male poet's tightly balanced heroic lines. In this first section, Eloisa travels further back into the past as she contemplates Abelard's name. As Lawrence Lipking noted in *Abandoned Women and Poetic Tradition*,[11] Abelard's name appears to be always already indelibly written in the poem, as if Eloisa transferred her thoughts directly from her heart to the page. Although she tries to combat her passion, Abelard's name always overpowers her weakened will. She finds her hand scrawling it across the page, and the etching of his name seems to drive her more deeply still into a hypnotic state.

With this representation, Pope builds a complex trap. His captive, weeping Eloisa is locked up with herself, spiritually and physically, and thus forced to live in the timeless world of nostalgia. As Stewart reads it, nostalgia is "the desire for de-

[11] Lawrence Lipking, *Abandoned Women & Poetic Tradition* (Chicago & London: University of Chicago Press, 1988): 148-151. Lipking points out that the sight of Abelard's handwriting in Pope's poem rekindles Eloisa's desire. Lipking's reading of Pope suggests that Pope hopes to to resurrect Eloisa's undying desire.

sire," and it is described as an acute state of sadness in which the captive attempts to reconstruct the bridge that will connect her/him with the object of desire.[12] Above all, it is a repetitive process that knows no closure or resolution. In Lacanian terms, what is actually repeated is an absence, or the distance from the object of desire. Indeed, Pope's (re)creation of Eloisa appears to be constructed on this model, but we might add that he casts Eloisa as a trapped nostalgic whose pain is not assuaged even by the comfort of her sanctuary. Strikingly, Pope restructures the Paraclete, as he declares it dispossessed from its historical significance for the lovers. In the medieval text, we recall that Abelard was the founder of the convent and had later given it to Heloise and her nuns. In Pope's introductory verses, the Paraclete is not represented as a spiritual, sentimental place that had been treasured by the medieval Heloise; it is transformed into a cold, austere cell, a subterranean space beneath the Gothic gloomy church that accentuates the distance between the two lovers:

> Relentless walls! whose darksom round contains
> Repentant sighs, and voluntary pains:
> Ye rugged rocks! which holy knees have worn;
> Ye grots and caverns shagg'd with horrid thorn! (17-20)

Like Grenaille, Pope carves his own opening into Eloisa's narrative; writing Abelard out, he becomes the architect who decides to "wall her in" the "darksom round" with her memories. His recreation of the archetypal, suffering, Ovidian heroine is destined to wander in this Gothic labyrinth where she exteriorizes her frustration and loneliness, with tears and sighs. Another key spatial innovation is also shown above with the insertion of the "round" dimension, which pertains to the repetition of the loss that is used as a principal structural element. As Wallace

[12] Susan Stewart 23.

Jackson reads it in *Vision and Re-Vision of Alexander Pope,*[13] the "darksom round" is not only a place, but a reference to Eloisa's frame of mind and inner erotic turmoil. Like her medieval counterpart, Eloisa will relive the past, time and time again, and thus traces a circular pattern in the poem. But the futility of her contemplations also creates a sense of emptiness. As Richard Stamelman posits in *Lost Beyond Telling,*[14] loss and grieving lead to emptiness; the pain penetrates the grieving individual and gradually tends to efface the body and soul. In Pope's version, Eloisa's loss is inscribed upon her anguished silhouette, and the poet expands her misery outwards through an innovative use of landscape. Outside the church, the physical surroundings are described as wild, "rugged," often untamed and unstable, reflecting Eloisa's tormented state of mind as she is plagued by erotic thoughts and an overwhelming desire to persuade Abelard to return to her side. Here, Pope borrows directly from Ovid whose heroines often integrated the depiction of rocks and caves into their missives to illustrate the shaky turbulence of their emotions in the wake of betrayal and abandonment. As Beer posited, the physical landscape in Ovidian discourse is also supposed to increase the profound sense of the heroines' claustrophobia, as well as underlining the impossibility of reunion between estranged lovers.[15] Here, the reference to yet another natural structure, that of the cave mentioned above, represents the journey that takes place inside of Eloisa's consciousness as she travels down the murky, obscure paths. It is a journey leading to the rekindling of faded memories that will, in turn, allow her to reenact the events of her own tragedy. Inside the cave of her own consciousness, she will uncover and

[13] Wallace Jackson, *Vision and Re-Vision in Alexander Pope* (Detroit: Wayne State UP, 1983): 54.
[14] Richard Stamelman, *Lost Beyond Telling: Representations of Death and Absence in Modern French Poetry* (Ithaca & London: Cornell UP, 1990): 3-14. Stamelman offers a highly relevant commentary on loss and grieving from a postmodern perspective.
[15] Beer 135-145.

recover her buried desire, and attempt to regain the lost erotic dialogue that she once shared with Abelard. But will she succeed in breaking the silence that encloses her in solitude and, if so, will the reader be able to identify traces of the "original" Heloise's pen behind the poet's hand? At this early point in the text, Pope has already taken considerable liberties in transforming Eloisa into a silent, trapped victim. As Jackson also postulates, the repetition of Abelard's name is another form of entrapment that binds her to the "round" and is ultimately as emotionally imprisoning as the physical confine.[16] But Pope goes further: Eloisa's hand trembles as it clutches a copy of the *Historia,* which triggers an outpouring of pain:

> That well-known name awakens all my woes.
> Oh name for ever sad! for ever dear!
> Still breath'd in sighs, still usher'd with a tear.
> I tremble too, where'er my own I find,
> Some dire misfortune follows close behind.
> Line after line my gushing eyes overflow,
> Led thro' a sad variety of woe: (30-36)

This emotional response to the reading of the *Historia* is used to introduce Eloisa's confession that she too, (ironically, like her medieval predecessor), is a hypocrite. Pope underlines the conflict with a repetitive opposition between her duty to God and her undying love for Abelard, and she now asks him to write to her. As noted earlier, Pope modifies the original order of the prose epistolary correspondence. As he abbreviates it, he maintains the focus on Eloisa's struggle between God's grace and Abelard. Every stanza is dramatically punctuated by a constant flow of tears. This may be classic Ovidian style, but the reader has the strong impression that Pope also borrowed from the portrait of the weeping Portuguese nun. The result is a combination of the Ovidian weeping heroine, and the Portuguese nun's excessive emotions as well as intertextual echoes of Gre-

[16] Jackson 56-58.

naille's precious version of the weeping Magdalene and Bussy's sentimental, gallant Heloise. Barthes explored narrative functions of tears that help shed light on this eighteenth-century rendition of Eloisa:

> I make myself cry, in order to prove to myself that my grief is not an illusion: tears are signs, not expressions. By my tears, I tell a story, I produce a myth of grief, & henceforth I adjust myself to it. I can live with it, because, by weeping, I give myself an emphatic interlocutor who receives the "truest" of messages, that of my body, not that of my speech: "Words, what are they? One tear will say more than all of them.[17]

This notion of tears telling a story seems to apply to Pope's reworking of the narrative. Eloisa 's tale of misery is drenched in her tears, a device which would also enable Pope to appeal to his public's tastes, since, at the time, pathos was very popular in literature. Eloisa goes on to ask Abelard to enter into her grief by sharing her pain. She wants him to pour out his heart to her so that they can form a harmonious bond founded on suffering. But Pope inserts a novel erotic element into her plea:

> Excuse the blush, and pour out all the heart,
> Speed the soft intercourse from soul to soul,
> And waft a sigh from Indus to the Pole. (56-58)

Here, Eloisa confesses her wish to recreate their severed, erotic union, but, since Abelard has been mutilated, she can only retell the events of their past in order to try to fill the void of impossible love.

Once again, Pope compresses, reorganizes and omits numerous biographical details as his Eloisa reflects on courtship, love, tragedy and separation. As in the Latin text and in Bussy's seventeenth-century versions, Pope advocates free love over marriage. Again, his Eloisa proclaims she would rather be Abelard's mistress than his wife, but interestingly, Heloise's origi-

---

[17] Roland Barthes, *A Lovers' Discourse: Fragments*, trans. Richard Howard (New York: The Noonday Press, 1978): 182.

nal argument—that Pope only knew through Hughes—is embellished by a lengthy stanza devoted to the restoration of this significant element of the Latin text. The opposition between love and marriage is carefully balanced at the caesura of each line to emphasize Eloisa's devotion to her lover as a free, libertine woman who clearly does not want her passion to be extinguished by the bondage of the conjugal state. However, this lyrical, heroic exaltation of her love is radically transformed in the next section: while it continues to retrace the events of their past relationship, the atmosphere changes abruptly as Eloisa describes the castration. Here again, Pope borrows from Hughes (who borrowed from Bussy's version), as his Eloisa repeats that she suffered tremendous guilt because she was not present at the time of the tragedy. She looks upon the "crime" as double and feels that the punishment should have been more equitable. Pope amplifies Bussy's fictional insertion of the couple sharing the sin:

> The crime was common, common be the pain.
> I can no more; by shame, by rage suppress'd,
> Let tears, and burning blushes speak the rest. (104-106)

We note the deviation from the medieval discourse as the original Heloise would never have used the word "crime" to describe the lovers' concupiscence. At this point in the first section, the narrative is highly compressed as Pope jumps ahead, and omits the events between the castration and the decision to place Heloise at Argenteuil. There is no mention of Fulbert, of his anger, or of the other social and political problems that the couple confronted. As Fulbert is written out, the focus is on the conflict between God and Abelard. The description of Eloisa's vows in the church concludes the first part of the poem, which contains the invention of an original Gothic atmosphere that is ominous and mysterious, enriched by the use of personification:

> As with cold lips I kissed the sacred veil,
> The shrines all trembled, and the lamps grew pale:
> Heav'n scarce believ'd the conquest it survey'd,
> And Saints with wonder heard the vows I made.
> Yet then, to those dread altars as I drew,
> Not on the Cross my eyes were fix'd, but you: (111-116)

The taking of the veil marks the closure of this first section at line 116 as Pope underlines her devotion to her beloved. At this point in the famous altar scene, Eloisa abruptly ceases to relive the past, the period that was more commonly known as the lovers' calamities. Pope embellishes the medieval veil ceremony with the use of the Gothic, and the insertion of some fantastic elements to highlight Eloisa's false piety. He plays with the light: the flickering of the candles at the altar reveals a variation on Eloisa's hypocrisy never seen in previous versions. Eloisa cannot fool the Saints who register their disbelief and reservation with a gasp of astonishment or "wonder" as she pronounces the words. The fact that holy objects "tremble" points out the problematic nature of her new vocation as a nun. In a rewriting of Heloise's simulated piety, this Gothic heroine kisses the veil with "cold lips" because she is forced to embrace Christ and not her lover. This idea is shown in a new light in the last line of the text cited above. Here, the atmosphere of the scene is bleak, Eloisa's vision of the altar is colored with an aura of Gothic "dread," which forecasts inevitable doom and interminable enclosure in her cell. Although Pope enriches the scene with Gothic elements, he remains surprisingly close to the Latin text because he emphasizes Eloisa's false piety and dubious faith. She ends the scene by dramatically proclaiming that love was her only devotion; bereft of her passion she is reduced to complete loss. Once again, fulfillment is represented as wholly invested in the man. In this way, the repetitive structure, symbolized by the "darksom round," reappears and brings Eloisa back to her memories of the loss, and to her eternal search for the elusive "other."

Falsifying the Present

Whereas the opening section of the poem is situated in the past, the main part deals with the present as Pope's Eloisa addresses herself desperately to her lover. The transition is marked by the erotic plea, "come!." Eloisa implores Abelard to free her from her solitude and misery, but most of all she yearns to relive her life as she once knew it:

> Come! with thy looks, thy words, relieve my woe;
> Those still at least are left thee to bestow.
> Still on that breast enamour'd let me lie,
> Still drink delicious poison from thy eye,
> Pant on thy lip, and to thy heart be press'd;
> Give all thou canst- and let me dream the rest.
> (119-124)

Eloisa acknowledges that her vows were completely false, and here, in the present, she turns to what is real: her desire. She wants Abelard to allow her to experience, once again, the sensual pleasures of drinking "the delicious poison," of "lying on that breast," and of panting with love. As Murray Krieger suggests, the last line cited above is a pseudo-consummation, which is undeniably charged with eroticism.[18] Eloisa attempts to restore Abelard's true image as her lover but still recognizes his limitations as a eunuch, and the division at the caesura underlines the pause. Interestingly, the fact that Abelard is a eunuch does not detract from the her longed-for desire to be reunited with him. What Abelard cannot physically complete can be fulfilled or played out in Eloisa's dreams; she will compensate for his "lost, impotent part" through her imagination (as we will see in the middle of the poem). The sensual takes over the spiritual completely in this fictional, romanticized vision. But at the same time, Pope restores the original conflict in that

---

[18] See Murray Krieger's article, "Eloisa to Abelard: The Escape from Body or the Embrace of Body." *Eighteenth-Century Studies* 3.1 (1969) : 28-47.

Eloisa is still depicted as vacillating constantly between God and Abelard through numerous antitheses from one stanza to another. As an expression of her inconsistent nature, Eloisa suddenly asks Abelard to help her embrace God, clearly contradicting the previous erotic, intimate plea that was directed to her lover. When she reminds Abelard of his duty to her nuns, Pope goes back to the medieval story, and as she points out his obligation to them, the description of the convent is transformed once again:

> Ah think at least thy flock deserves thy care,
> Plants of thy hand, and children of thy pray'r.
> From the false world in early youth they fled,
> By thee to mountains, wilds, and deserts led.
> You rais'd these hallow'd walls; the desert smil'd
> And Paradise was open'd in the Wild. (129-134)

The medieval description of the Paraclete is embellished. Abelard takes on a paternal role; he represents the savior for Eloisa's nuns, and he is called upon again to assume the responsibility for his "flock." Yet Pope integrates pre-romantic landscape into his renovation of the Paraclete. The medieval representation of it as a site of consolation is reworked into a paradise, with strong erotic connotations, when his Eloisa describes the monastery as a sanctuary, a veritable Eden erected in the middle of untamed country. But further down Pope abruptly tempers the pastoral, airy, open tone with an antithesis that signals the return to Gothic claustrophobia as the Paraclete, once again, enfolds Eloisa in the imprisoning labyrinth of the "darksom round":

> In these lone walls (their day's eternal bound)
> These moss-grown domes with spiry turrets crown'd,
> Where awful arches make a noon-day night,
> And the dim windows shed a solemn light;
> (141-144)

The previously open, natural description of the erection of the Paraclete and the physical surroundings is strikingly modified in the passage above as Eloisa reenters the dark. As noted by Bayer-Barenbaum, arches and vaulted ceilings were common in Gothic cathedrals, as the one Pope described above.[19] But in contrast to the verticality of Pope's interior restructuring, Eloisa's soul does not appear to attempt to rise upwards toward God. On the contrary, she resists the call to heaven, and thus wages a war within her mind. Pope depicts the battle through the balanced opposition between light and dark imagery, a motif that is maintained constantly in the poem. Eloisa's soul cannot rise in harmony with the verticality of the church's arches because her body is an obstacle to her faith. Her world is colored by the darkness that blocks out even the brightest daylight, as she is entrenched in the depths of misery and despair. In her suffering, she calls out to Abelard to come and save her from her loneliness. Once again, Pope expands the depths of her torment through natural landscape. Outside the Paraclete, the physical elements reflect the unrest and instability of her mental state of constant conflict. She cannot pray because she only thinks of her beloved. Pope composes a very original scene in Eloisa's imagination in which she alludes to the veiled, ghostly presence of Abelard that hovers beyond the walls of her prison:

> The darksom pines that o'er yon'rocks reclin'd
> Wave high, and murmur to the hollow wind,
> The wand'ring streams that shine between the hills,
> The grots that echo to the tinkling rills,
> The dying gales that pant upon the trees,
> The lakes that quiver to the curling breeze;
> No more these scenes my meditation aid,
> Or lull to rest the visionary maid. (155-162)

In this passage, Eloisa's erotic yearning is alluded to by the movement of the waves, the rhythmic lilting motion of the

---

[19] Bayer-Barenbaum 52-8.

wind, the "lakes that quiver," and the "dying gales that pant." In the "grots," there is a suggestion that the echo she hears is Abelard's voice resounding in her mind. She knows no peace because it is these longed-for erotic scenes that she wishes to participate in actively as she once had been able to do before their separation. Yet in the following part of the section, Pope suddenly does away with the disembodied ghost of Abelard. In the darkness of night, Abelard's personified presence fades out, and the ominous figure of Black Melancholy takes over his place. The agitated movement reflected in the natural elements above is astonishingly contrasted with a death-like calm that seeps into the narrative with an impeding sense of doom. As Black Melancholy appears, an unexpected plunging movement in Eloisa's heart is represented by a forecast of dread that invades the poem in classic Gothic style:

> Black Melancholy sit, and round her throws
> A death-like silence, and a dread repose:
> Her gloomy presence saddens all the scene,
> Shades ev'ry flow'r, and darkens ev'ry green,
> Deepens the murmur of the falling floods,
> And breathes a browner horror on the woods. (165-170)

The Gothic atmosphere accentuates Eloisa's horror and isolation in a mystical and spiritual way. Gradually, she begins to resign herself to confronting her own demise, which is also a fictionalized creation of the poet's, so that he can embellish the representation of her as a tragic victim.

For Pope's Eloisa, death is the only way out of prison. It is in the Paraclete that she will remain and eventually die as she begins to resign herself to her fate. This portrayal of a melancholy Eloisa is also part of Pope's technique of fragmentation. Breaking her down emotionally gradually destroys her validity as a writer. Already, there is a clear absence of the rationality and highly developed intellect that was evident in her medieval epistles. Pope's Eloisa does not appear to reason her imposed vocation as a nun. In this bleak version, there are no quotations from Seneca or Lucan, and no other philosophical or religious references, and she hardly mentions her monastic duties or her nuns. In other words, Pope eliminates the original background that pertained to Heloise's administrative acumen and exceptional talent as an abbess. On the contrary, the poem moves in the direction of emotional disorder. As Julia Kristeva posited in *Soleil Noir: Dépression et mélancolie,* the state of despair is also linked to the loss of the erotic object, and this impossible fulfillment cannot be articulated in language:

> Depuis cet attachement archaïque, le dépressif a l'impression d'être déshérité d'un suprême bien innommable, de quelque chose d'irréprésentable, que seule peut-être une dévoration pourrait figurer, une invocation pourrait indiquer, mais qu'aucun mot ne saurait signifier.[20]

Like her medieval counterpart, Pope's Eloisa suffers a double castration. She is cut off from contact with Abelard as Pope does away with the epistolary dialogue in favor of monologic discourse, which, in turn, allows him to control her discourse. In fact, Eloisa's voice is castrated by the poet; she bears very little resemblance to the original Heloise from the moment Pope alters the epistle to rework it into verse. Her voice becomes progressively weaker as she is reduced to hopelessness, and then a depressed state of mind. She fades gradually into silence. As Kristeva described above, Eloisa cannot articulate what is "unrepresentable;" she always goes back to the broken amorous bond. Words simply could not articulate what was inherently "unspeakable," beyond speech. In the classic style of Gothic women, Eloisa is ensconced and trapped in a helpless state of passivity. This fictional resignation is developed as a closure to this second section, line 176, with a contemplation of death which offers the tragic victim a refuge.

---

[20] Julia Kristeva, *Soleil Noir: Dépression et mélancolie* (Paris: Gallimard, 1987) : 23.

Trapping Eloisa into a Forced Confession

The most striking section within this main part of the poem begins with a reprise of the Ovidian "plainte." Like Grenaille, Pope traps his Eloisa into an invented textual space and then forces her to "tell all." The prison, her monastic cell, is transformed into another enclosure, the confessional, which sets the stage for the forced repentance for her so-called "crime." Once again, this section contains fragments that actually appeared in the Latin text, without authorial intention since Pope was not familiar with the original correspondence. For example, he restores the medieval theme of the Bride of Christ, an aspect that was more or less forgotten in the seventeenth-century versions. But Pope only mentions this in passing as he focuses on the perpetual battle between Eloisa's love and monastic career. She begins by asking God to help her and then confesses that her prayers are devoted to her love and not the pursuit of grace. The dilemma is skillfully balanced through even divisions at the caesura that mark the bipolar, fluctuating movement in her heart as she swings back and forth between Abelard and God. She should grieve but cannot, and this dissimulates her inner joy of contemplating what she knows in her heart is wrong. Pope adds in the words "crime, "sin," "past offense," and "fault," a textual manipulation that condemns her illicit concupiscence. (Her medieval counterpart never used these moral terms to describe her passion for Abelard). After Pope has her repent her sins of the flesh, he then has her ask Abelard to help her turn to God for direction and strength:

> Oh come! oh teach me nature to subdue,
> Renounce my love, my life, my self— and you.
> Fill my fond heart with God alone, for he
> Alone , can rival, can succeed to thee. (203-206)

Pope thus maintains her vacillation as she swings back and forth between God and Abelard, suggesting that only God can substitute for her lover's role. In the next stanza, as she unexpectedly praises the Virgin Mary, Pope tempers the tenebrous ambiance and creates an abrupt opposition in the form of a celestial, luminous atmosphere, a serene, utopian vision of what religious life should be for those who know how to pray, and are ultimately freed from impure thoughts. The movement of the passage lifts Eloisa out of the murky depths of her prison with a vertical push towards a loftier elevation, up near the Angels where she would be closer to God:

> Tears that delight, and sighs that waft to heav'n.
> Grace shines around her with serenest beams,
> And whisp'ring Angels prompt her golden dreams.
> (214-216)

Pope redirects her focus from Abelard to God through this intrusion of a mystical state of mind. Here, we note the intertext to Grenaille's version as he too had set out to portray Heloise as "La Magdalene Française," a model of Christian sacrifice and virtue for other women to emulate in their pursuit of moral piety. Pope, Grenaille and the original Abelard all are guilty of locking Eloisa into a fixed position in which she is virtually powerless to voice her objections, in this case, to the marriage to God she had originally fought against in the Latin text.

In this eighteenth-century pre-romantic version, one notes that the legend is becoming increasingly fictionalized and contains only remote shards of resemblance to the original text. Pope builds up the sentimental, ethereal tone of this passage as he describes an imaginary marriage, accompanied by the songs of the Angels as his Eloisa is ushered (or is it dragged?) into heaven to take the Spouse's "holy" ring. The ring could be read as another form of bondage, a chain that locks her into more masculine entrapment, which, in turn, pushes her into obligatory redemption and irrevocable separation from Abelard. At this point, Pope even transforms the tears that had previously marked her misery and despair. They become signs of rapture as she assumes her divine role with praises flowing from the Angels who envelop her in a halo of warmth and light. The legend takes on new dimensions as this saintly Eloisa is forced into accepting her glorified, heavenly role as Christ's bride. Ironically, Pope grafts Abelard's mention of her as the Bride of Christ, (originally in his third letter), onto her discourse. But here, Eloisa narrates her own vision of mystical union, parallel to Abelard 's medieval description of the Ethiopian, black bride. This reworking and this textual graft are significant because Pope not only erases Abelard's presence, but also suppresses the original erotic imagery that the Ethiopian bride evoked in the Latin text. And yet, in the next stanza, this Christian "show of faith" is abruptly abandoned as unexpectedly as it had been written into the poem. Once again, Eloisa does not succeed in converting her illicit desire into a love of God. She now regresses back to a cyclical return to the impure, tortured heroine who longs to be reunited with Abelard.

Erotic Dreams or the Ravings of a Hysterical "Woman"?

The lengthy verse that explores Eloisa's tortured, repressed desire is linked intertextually to Bussy's insertion of the dream sequence. But differing sharply from the seventeenth-century imitators of Heloise, Pope's Eloisa is represented as possessing an overly active imagination; she is even recast as an irrational woman. This revision of Heloise is also Gothic since mental disorders and delusions were commonly found in Gothic narratives. As Michèle Plaisant reads it, Pope's Eloisa experiences mutilation, and, once again, the dream sequence provides the reader with an example of fragmentation of Heloise's persona.[21] In some ways, Pope had prefigured the erotic reverie scene with Eloisa's melancholy state that (re)invents her as an hyp-

[21] Michèle Plaisant discusses Heloise's mutilation in the Pope version in her article, "Eloisa et Belinda: Les Désordres de l'âme et du corps." *Bulletin de la Société et d'études anglo-américaines des XVIIe et XVIIIe siècles*. (1985): 75.

notic, somnolent captive whose thoughts are focused on another time and place that evokes wistful nostalgia. He now exploits her sadness and disorder to break her down further which, in turn, suppresses her authorial presence, and forces her into silence. The previous stanza's upward movement is reversed as Pope descends into Eloisa's soul to reveal another dialogic discourse, the passionate one that eludes her during daylight. In this section, Eloisa's dreams free her from the harsh, cold reality of her isolation. As Doody puts it, Pope's heroic poem is Gothic since women in eighteenth-century English Gothic novels were often represented as dreamers.[22] If, as Sigmund Freud would have it, dreams are expressions of a longed-for desire that haunts the dreamer's wishes, for Eloisa, sleep is a welcome refuge that allows her to act out her own erotic fantasies. Once again, the pendulum swings back from God to her beloved:

> For other dreams my erring soul employ,
> Far other raptures, of unholy joy:
> When at the close of each sad, sorrowing day,
> Fancy restores what vengeance snatch'd away,
> Then conscience sleeps, and leaving nature free,
> All my loose soul unbounded springs to thee.
> (223-228)

In the nocturnal refuge of sleep, Eloisa narrows the gap that separates her from Abelard, which also unveils her yearning for plenitude. Pope follows very closely Bussy's dream, for Eloisa imagines that she talks to and sees Abelard in her sleep. As in Bussy's version, when she wakes, her beloved fades away, slowly drifting out of her arms, and leaving her in a state of fear that she will never see or hear him again. But Pope embellishes Bussy's erotic dream as he uses a Gothic, wild landscape to create an impending sense of dread. The eighteenth-century stereotype that women were tragic victims of their own weaknesses is thus reinforced, grounded in sexual difference and the

---

[22] Doody 73.

postulate that women belonged to a sex that was inherently predisposed to a highly developed sexual imagination. But Pope goes even further as he creates an image of Eloisa that borders on the hysterical:

> Thro' dreary wastes, and weep each other's woe,
> Where round some mould'ring tow'r pale ivy creeps,
> And low-brow'd rocks hang nodding o'er the deeps,
> Sudden you mount! you beckon from the skies;
> Clouds interpose, waves roar, and winds arise.
> I shriek, start up, the same sad prospect find,
> And wake to all the griefs I left behind. (242-248)

Pope seems to be visually amplifying Bussy's dream. Providing a vivid illustration of what the libertine translator could have sketched, he uses Gothic landscape to represent the wild, abandoned nature of Eloisa's erotic desire. Her soul is as tormented and restless as the natural elements that surround the Paraclete. Her imagination rises to the brink of delusion; her emotions are so strong that she is driven to shrieking, and this hysterical dimension destroys her credibility as a rational woman, which is another disempowering device, a way of keeping "woman" in her place. Pope creates an hallucinatory representation of Eloisa; she appears to hear voices and even has a vision of an exalted, majestic Abelard in the clouds. Foucault's work on passion and the relationship to delirium is useful in looking at the fragmentation of Eloisa's persona:

> Love disappointed in its excess, and especially love deceived by the fatality of death, has no other recourse but madness. As long as there was an object, mad love was more love than madness; left to itself, it pursues itself in the void of delirium.[23]

Although Pope's Eloisa is not mad, she is remolded into the suffering victim of an extreme passion that practically pushes her over the edge of reason. As Foucault suggested above,

---

[23] Michel Foucault, *Madness and Civilization,* trans. Richard Howard. (New York: Vintage Books, 1965): 30.

Eloisa, too, seems reduced to a delirious dream state as her "disappointed" love is deprived of an object. The pain of separation can be compared to a fatal incarceration where she is forced to replay the loss, as if she were grieving throughout the poem for the death of her beloved "other." As Janet Beizer has pointed out in her fascinating work on gender, hysteria may be marked in sexual difference, but, above all, it renders the heroine incapable of narrating her own story.[24] Because of her gender, Pope seems to say, Eloisa is thus "not in her right mind" to convey the events of her life. She is disinherited; she no longer possesses the rights to it as Pope reduces her intellect to the ravings of a deluded woman in love. Here, the departure from the original text is astonishingly evident as Pope eliminates the rational, highly developed, logical style that is a fundamental, stylistic element of the medieval Heloise's letters. In this way, the poet not only destroys her plausibility, but paves his own entry into the text. By casting Eloisa in a state of confusion and disorder, he may then step in to elucidate her incoherence, to fill in the blanks, to rework her words so that they become plausible. Beizer's work on hysteria provides intriguing, historical perceptions on the subject, and, although she mainly deals with the nineteenth century, her general comments also pertain to the eighteenth century:

> Figure of femininity, label of disorder and difference, hysteria was available for a wide and often contradictory range of differentiation, magnet diagnosis of society's multiple ills, emblem of creative frenzy, identification of the writing self as Other, designation of the century's marginalized symbolic center.[25]

Indeed, Pope's use of the dream marginalizes the woman's writing even further by suggesting that she borders precariously on the edge of raving. Once again, the winds roar and the

---

[24] Janet Beizer provides a history of the medical discourse on hysteria, pertaining to both genders. Her emphasis is, however, directed to women. See *Ventriloquized Bodies* (Ithaca & London: Cornell UP, 1993): 3-12.

[25] Beizer 8.

waves rock to underline dramatically the extreme delusion of Eloisa's hallucination of Abelard looking down upon her from the heavens. Reflecting stereotypical conceptions about women in eighteenth-century England that are also present in Gothic fiction, this dream accentuates the heroine's portrayal as weak and vulnerable, superstitious, enraged and repressed. Pope adheres to the patriarchal paradigm of his times. Like Ovid, he depicts his Eloisa as an anguished, over-sexed, tragic victim. As Doody posited:

> Women, weaker than men, not in control of their environment, are permitted to have dreams. The censorship of dreaming doesn't quite apply to them. Officially, in the eighteenth century, women are thought of as weak and superstitious; they have something of an archaic consciousness, not enjoying the full benefits of masculine reason and masculine knowledge of reality.[26]

Indeed, this "masculine" conception of women is at work in Pope's revision of a pre-romantic Eloisa. The following stanza contrasts the agitated dream sequence with a brief, deceptive calm before the rhythm of the poem is increased, further contributing to the point of view that Eloisa is hysterical. Once again, she calls out to Abelard with the plea, "come!" that points to her spiritual turmoil. As she repeats that the torch of Venus lives on, she dramatizes the heights of her passion. Ironically, however, Pope slips up here; he loses control of his poetic (re)creation temporarily, as he allows the reader to view a palimpsest of Heloise's original writing. Under the "master" pen of the poet, the reader catches a momentary glimpse of the plume that had once articulated Heloise's passion to Abelard. Pope opposes the cold, dead image of Abelard with the astonishing warmth of Eloisa's desire as she attempts to revive him. Her flames represent the hope of rousing or "lighting" him from the grave in the warmth of her love; she wants to bring him back to her to rekindle the passion. Yet, Pope returns to the

[26] Doody 531.

delusion theme as Eloisa launches into another hallucination in which she sees Abelard step valiantly between her and God. Once again, Pope enriches the false piety theme of her unstable Christian faith, and now builds up her monastic hypocrisy. Eloisa confesses that she hears voices during hymns and adds that the angels tremble. It is suggested that the plummeting of her soul into the depths of shame and misery causes the tapers to flicker as she can only think of Abelard. This time the loss is represented in a highly theatrical style by the display of an overwhelming grief that borders on delirium, and is reflected in her body language. Prostrate with suffering and overcome with tears, Eloisa prays by rolling on the ground as if she had lost all control of her reason, and then is overcome by her misery. She boldly appeals to Abelard to oppose himself to God, to block out God's view so that he can free her from her "fruitless penitence and pray'rs" (line 286). As Marilyn Francus observed, Eloisa uses terms of illegal acquisition in the imperative form; words such as "take," rob," snatch" and "consume" overtly welcome the intrusion of her lover as she begs him to carry her off with him.[27] The language also adds an erotic dimension to her appeal to Abelard, which culminates in the words "tear me from my God!" (line 288). The sexual tension is significantly increased in this section. Eloisa is depicted as a rebellious woman attempting to overthrow the bastion of Christian order, the power that threatens to repress permanently her illicit desire. Her request that Abelard break down the wall and deliver her from her monastic prison is even further amplified. However, as Krieger noted, these lines are her last call to Abelard, since she turns around (once again illustrating Pope's hysterical revision of her), and suddenly honors her commitment to the church, as the word "no" indicates:

[27] Marilyn Francus discusses the sexual tension in the poem, highlighting the use the imperative. Francus reads Abelard as Eloisa'a divine lover. See "An Augustan Metaphysical Poem: Pope's *Eloisa to Abelard*," *Studies in Philology* 87 (1990): 488.

> No, fly me, fly me! far as Pole from Pole,
> Rise Alps between us! and whole oceans roll!
> Ah come not, write not, think not once of me,
> Nor share on pang of all I felt for thee.
> Thy oaths I quit, thy memory resign;
> Forget, renounce me, hate what'er was mine.
> (289-294)

The vertical, erotic thrust at the beginning of the stanza climaxes with "fly me"; the direction is abruptly changed by her unexpected plea of "come not." The descending movement is shown by the sudden resignation and abandonment of her previous wish that Abelard save her from God. The conflict reflected in the bipolar fluctuation between love and religion begins to waver precariously. For the first time, she tells Abelard not to come, as this final section of the poem begins to curb her defying, passionate nature, ultimately subduing her erotic nature, and here too, Pope intervenes and revises the text to suit his own purpose. As Krieger reads it:

> I have so over simplified it at this point in order to exaggerate Pope's apparent intention to overcome "passion by virtue," to reduce Eloisa's ill-advised emotional rebellion to painful but calmly reasonable acceptance. In effect, this exaggerated view sees Pope as overriding her unruly fervor with his classic calm, as imposing his rage for order upon her rage.[28]

As a majority of Pope's critics would concur, he was a strong advocate of order, and this is clearly evident in the concluding section of the poem as Eloisa is forced to proclaim her resignation and willingness to renounce her passion. Here, the deviation from the medieval text is truly astonishing. Pope appears determined to separate once and for all Eloisa's body and spirit so that he can convincingly recast her as dedicated to her faith. To achieve this goal, he erases Eloisa's corporeal desire and brings the focus back to the "round," spartan emptiness of her prison cell.

---

[28] Krieger 33.

Closing the Circle: From the Cell to the Grave

The concluding section of the poem begins on line 303 where Pope amplifies a fictionalized aspect of the legend that was also present in Bayle's historical articles on the famous lovers' tragic demise. As noted above, Eloisa is now resigned to her fate as a nun, and so, in harmony with the structure of the poem, she has now come full circle back into the "darksom round," the Paraclete. She had begun her "plainte" by retracing the traumatic events of her past. He had suffered in the present, and she had escaped from her misery through dreams of an imagined reunion with Abelard; she has now come to an acceptance of her future situation through surrender. Since she is still "behind bars," in the cell where Pope had her begin her "plainte," the circle is complete. Interestingly, the poem does contain some contradictions and another unexpected turn of events that shows, once again, that Pope loses ground in his endeavor to restore order to her "unreasonable" desire. Alone in her cell, Eloisa imagines another scene, one of pseudo-consummation. She finds what Pope did not intend for her to discover: the exit out of the labyrinth that enclosed her. She sees herself as love's victim and seeks out, once again, the refuge of sleep to free herself from despair. In the calm of her mind, Eloisa imagines the two reunited in a divine, purified vision where the couple is laid to rest in the same tomb. Once again, a place of confinement plays a significant role here as the austere cell is transformed into a sacred crypt that will eventually receive the two lovers' bodies. Eloisa imagines her own death scene in which Abelard plays the part of the divine priest administering the last rites. But even the imagined scene of her saintly demise contains strong erotic tones as she contemplates seeing him face to face again:

> Thou, Abelard! the last sad office pay,
> And smooth my passage to the realms of day;

> See my lips tremble, and my eye-balls roll,
> Suck my last breath, and catch my flying soul!
> (321-324)

The sacred moment of her imaginary death scene continues to mount in an ascending movement as Eloisa points out that it is Abelard who presents her with the Cross. Pope adorns the atmosphere with Gothic elements: she enters into a mystical ecstasy, and an altered, trance-like state as the angels receive her and she is ushered into heaven by the saints. Her hope now is that the two be remembered as immortal lovers. The fictionalized opening of the gates into heaven where she finds Abelard also transforms the dark prison of the Paraclete into a celestial sanctuary with white walls and silver springs. In this holy place, the cold, marble-like atmosphere has now been transformed. The foundation is laid for the eventual creation of two majestic statues that will eternalize the memories of the lovers so they can serve as an inspiration for others who wish to love as they had loved. Eloisa hopes other couples will be profoundly touched by her great passion and devotion. She wants other lovers to shed tears that will fall on their tomb; she finds comfort in this sentimental, ethereal vision of eternal rest next to Abelard. This emotional display of passion at the grave site marks the conclusion of the poem. Once again, Pope restores order and virtue to Eloisa's conflict, and he executes this by erasing her body and highlighting her spirituality. He intervenes in Eloisa's monologue and even refers to himself in the last lines as the future "Bard" that will see to the couple's remembrance through the immortality of his poetic creation. But before the dust settles on the lovers' tomb, the final suppression of Eloisa's persona is completed through other means.

Burying Eloisa Alive

Pope contributed greatly to the immortal aspect and the sentimental romanticism of the legend that is rooted in the eighteenth century. As noted above, Eloisa's final wish is to be remembered by others after she has passed on. This resigned, tearful Eloisa looks forward to her imagined scene of death so that she can rejoin her lover in spiritual reunion. In his conclusion, Pope appears to have succeeded in subduing or "exorcising" Eloisa's subversive desire, privileging her soul over carnal concupiscence. Like Grenaille, Pope infringed on Heloise's epistolary production by converting it into a monologic form, which placed him immediately in a manipulatory position. But he went further than Grenaille as he breaks down Heloise's rational, logical persona into hysterical delusions that destroy her credibility as a writer, which, in turn, enable him to steal from her at times, albeit inadvertently given that he was unfamiliar with the Latin text and (as noted earlier) was imitating Hughes. Yet at the end, Pope even silences Eloisa's ravings as he writes out her body. Pope appears to reduce her to absence or an empty name. He has deprived her of her original speech so that he can appropriate her voice for his own self-gain. To put it in Miller's terms, Pope, like other male authors in the seventeenth-century versions, resorted to a pseudo-feminocentric strategy to profit from other male readers' accolades at the expense of erasing the original (woman) author's signature from her own text. It could also be argued that he has ostensibly buried Eloisa's desire alive and her authorship along with it in the crypt where she now lies next to Abelard. There is, however, another plausible explanation for Pope's orderly austerity of the 'supposed,' spiritual grave site. As Derrida pointed out in "Fors," the crypt is a structure that contains infinite partitions; inside these divisions, secrets are retained in what he calls the "vault of desire." In other words, this structure can also be hiding something else than a body:

> Thus, the cryptic place is also a sepulcher. The topography has taught us to take a certain non-place into consideration. The sepul-

> chral function in turn can signify something other than simply death. A crypt, people believe, always hides something *dead.* ("Fors," 78)

Indeed, Pope has buried Eloisa's secret desire alive in the Gothic restoration of the Paraclete's burial vaults. Yet, as Clark reads it, Pope, who has repudiated and despised the woman's desire, does not succeed entirely in his misogynistic plan to eliminate it; it remains buried in the discourse, and thus, the text resists what Pope had set out to do in writing his poetic version.[29] It could be argued indeed that within the marble confines of the crypt, Pope seals up her desire, yet the passion lives on in the spiritual revival, and is recovered over and over again in subsequent, fictionalized versions of the legend. Heloise's discourse of desire is not completely dead. Rather, it has become obscured and more difficult to locate. It has faded into invisibility through the intrusion of male imitators. The authoritarian pen has erased her signature as well as the "remainder" of her desire. But in the burial vault, the dead body does not conceal totally the other discourse, the passionate, "spontaneous" one written by Heloise that is now articulated by Pope dressed as a woman. The poet ventriloquizes for her, and his travesty is performed by borrowing her soul (since he has effaced her body) and writing himself though her spirituality, which is another way of assuring the lovers' eternal memory. Disguised as a mystical nun waiting for the peaceful, harmonious reunion with her loved one, Pope veils his own "masculinity." As Eloisa says in the final lines, she will be comforted by someone else immortalizing their tragedy, and it will "soothe" her "pensive ghost" (line 365). The Gothic closure of her ghost lingering on through eternal remembrance supports the theory that recovery might be possible within the labyrinth of the crypt that preserves and nurtures the desire so that it might, as Derrida

[29] Clark 119-20.

would put it," live on" to be recovered at another point in time.[30]

Colardeau's Pastoral (Re)Invention of Heloise

Pope's successful version inspired many other renditions in France that helped to promote the growth of the legend's popularity. The English version rapidly began to evolve and affect the epistolary genre as it expanded into the fictional letter novel, a highly prolific literary form that appealed to a wide audience. As Anderson observed, Heloise's and Abelard's tragic story became quite influential during the Enlightenment, at a time when the visual and verbal portraiture of fictional characters was developed, and the themes of victimization, impotence, or the exploration of imagination grew more common.[31] As Charrier has argued, all of the versions that followed Pope's rendition were mostly fictional, clearly invented and falsified, and the story became more and more distorted with the publication of multiple versions. At least twenty-five translations would appear by the end of the eighteenth century in France, and one of the most important imitations was Pierre Colardeau's poetic version.[32] Published in 1750, it followed a text by François Godard de Beauchamp that appeared in several editions published between 1717 and 1737. Colardeau was considered to be the foremost interpreter of Pope and had clarified that he was not a translator, but an imitator of Pope's tearful, tragic epistle. Like Pope, Colardeau wanted to renew the legend and engender popular interest in the medieval couple's story. Structurally, he preserved Pope's verse and monologic, epistolary discourse, transcribing it into an alexandrine form

[30] Derrida, "Living on": Border Lines," ed. Harold Bloom *Deconstruction and Criticism* (New York: Seabury Press, 1979): 75-80.

[31] David Anderson studies the motif of the famous couple in his article, "Abélard and Héloïse: Eighteenth-Century Motif," *Studies on Voltaire & the Eighteenth Century* 84 (1972): 7-10.

[32] Charrier 424-66.

that included a great deal of "rimes riches" in order to accentuate the pathos of Heloise's speech. In this poetic response to Abelard's *Historia,* he also inserted numerous examples of self-questioning, exclamations, and interjections that created the illusion of skillful "woman's" epistolary traits in this poetic response to Abelard's *Historia*. Like Pope, Colardeau states that the letter is "supposedly" being written at the Paraclete. The 1779 edition contains additional information that sheds light on his authorial intentions. It also includes a fragment, attributed to Colardeau, in which Abelard answers Heloise's epistle, but since this is purely fictional and bears little resemblance to the medieval text, it will not be discussed here.

The paratext, however, merits some looking into as Colardeau states that he wished to restore the beauty of the original letters, and his poem was also created so that his readers could become familiar with the lovers' style and spirit. Colardeau appears to have well researched the biographical details of their lives, since he cites the Latin text assembled by François d'Amboise and published in Paris in 1616. The paratext is followed by a summary of the biographical events that led up to the lovers' monastic retreat into separate cloisters. The poem then begins in the style of an Ovidian "plainte," and Colardeau adopts Pope's structural divisions of the text. As we recall, Heloise talks about her past, bemoans her fate as a nun, then moves into the present, dreams in order to bridge the distance between her and Abelard, and then contemplates her death. A superficial reading of Colardeau's text seems to show few modifications, but to go back to Anderson's point concerning the literary contribution of the legend to literature in general, it could be argued that an author can never exactly imitate another version. There is always a variation or a difference. Colardeau's text appeared at least thirty years after Pope's; other literary influences and themes had become popular during that time. As Anderson noted, visual or verbal portraiture was evolving, and Colardeau created a still-life portrait of Heloise, inscribed in the narrative, that focuses on her amorous contemplation in her monastic cell.[33] This interesting aspect warrants further exploration, and it is, in fact, linked to the most original aspect of Colardeau's poetic rendition, the (re)creation of Heloise's erotic fantasy. In a clear split from Pope's version, Heloise is not portrayed as a delirious, irrational woman torn between God and her love for Abelard. Colardeau tones down the spiritual dilemma, and reintegrates Abelard into his text in a passive, silent role, which, in turn, diminishes the numerous references to God as previously observed in Pope's poem. Instead of amplifying Eloisa's delirium, Colardeau paints an aesthetic, erotic image of her, which transforms the dream state into a pastoral still-life of a woman in love. Other salient differences include the suppression of some of Pope's key Gothic elements. Although Colardeau's Heloise is also writing from her cell, the Paraclete is never described as a "darksom round;" it is not such a bleak, ominous structure, although it retains the image of the prison and the barrier that separates her from Abelard. Interestingly, Colardeau redefines his conception of the Gothic to include the dream state and a disembodied, mysterious voice that entices Heloise to come to the grave, as Pope had done, but there is no reference to an exalted, majestic, ghostly Abelard who appeared in the clouds and performed the last rites. On the contrary, Colardeau (re)invents on an erotic level; he explores the fantasies of a woman hopelessly and impossibly in love. Although he says that he set out to imitate Pope, Colardeau actually creates a simulacrum of a woman in love. Since one of the most significant characteristics of the amorous epistle is to create the illusion of real, lived desire, it could be argued that the "supposed" letter provides the author with a mask or a prop with which he can stage his masquerade as a woman in love recording her emotions on paper. It is through

[33] Anderson 21-23.

this optic that I will limit the discussion of Colardeau's rendition in order to avoid rephrasing what Pope had already accomplished in the prototype for this imitation.

Colardeau's Fictional "Woman"

Bray's study of the epistolary genre in the eighteenth century raises a pertinent issue directly related to the opening of Colardeau's imitation of Pope. We recall that the tearful Heloise is reading Abelard's *Historia,* kissing the page, and lamenting her fate as a nun. Colardeau augments the outpouring of her tears to remain faithful to Pope's Ovidian model. But, as Bray has shown, the use of tears is also more than just a signifier of sadness; an additional function is to erase the original letters traced on the paper, which, in turn, creates an illusion.[34] Thus, Colardeau eradicates the imprint of the original Heloise's pen expressing her misery, and the blurring caused by the tears wipes away the remainder of the genuine author to produce a simulacrum of the prototype.

Colardeau casts his Heloise as the quintessential captive lover dedicated to Abelard. The first section focuses on her past experiences with Abelard, and de-emphasizes Pope's constant reminder of her struggle between God and Abelard. As Colardeau amplifies the tears, he builds up the sentimental aspects and he can delve gradually into her private fantasies. Whereas Pope tended to alternate between her outpouring of emotion for Abelard and her duty to God in order to (re)invent Eloisa as irrational and confused, Colardeau's Heloise says that she cries only for Abelard, and that she found complete satisfaction in him. As also seen in Pope's poem, there is a calculated suppression of the learned, scholarly intellect that colored the medieval missives, and Colardeau omits any references to famous phi-

[34] See Bernard Bray's article, "Héloïse et Abélard au XVIIIe siècle en France: une imagerie épistolaire." *Studies on Voltaire & the Eighteenth Century* 151(1976) : 394-6.

losophers or biblical figures. This Heloise places Abelard's heart at the nexus of all of her worldly goods, titles and grandeur. The marriage argument is altered in a way that would appeal to the libertines' literary taste. Marriage is condemned in favor of the "plaisir" of free love alluded to by the word "volupté." Far from the intellectual pursuits of her medieval predecessor, Colardeau's fictional character advocates learning the art of loving. The original philosophical argument that firmly supported Heloise's stance against marriage is placed in a more secular context. Colardeau's Heloise maintains that even if a king offered her his crown, she would place her throne in Abelard's heart. Pope had retained the medieval reference to Caesar, and even included a mention of God. But Colardeau builds up only the secular aspect of the legend, and it is strictly grounded in Heloise's memory of her husband as a lover:

> Je porte avec orgueil le nom de ton amante;
> S'il en est un plus tendre et plus digne de moi,
> S'il peint mieux mon amour, je le prendrai pour toi.
> Abélard, qu'il est doux de s'aimer, de se plaire
> C'est la première loi; le reste est arbitraire.[35]

After Colardeau's Heloise has exalted the pleasures of love, the castration is described in a highly melodramatic style. There is a variation on the medieval text as Colardeau's character says that love is her crime, whereas, in Pope's poem, Eloisa said that the crime was common. Colardeau's Heloise considers the consequences of the castration as she laments the destruction of their "plaisirs." Once again, the pleasure of love is privileged over any religious ramifications that had originally affected Abelard's career in the church after the mutilation. The vow episode follows and here, too, is a difference. Colardeau preserves the Gothic atmosphere, but this time Abelard is present

[35] All of the quotes are taken from Pierre Colardeau's "Epître d'Héloïse à Abélard" in *Oeuvres de Colardeau de l'académie française,* vol 2 (Paris: Ballard, LeJay, 1749).

and accompanies Heloise to the veiling ceremony. As in Pope's description of the scene, the lights are dim, and the heavens gasp at Heloise's simulated display of monastic faith. Yet, Colardeau tones down Pope's Gothic use of ghosts, the personified presence of angels and saints, and he omits the haunting voices. But most importantly, he deletes Pope's use of the Cross. The episode becomes more secular as Heloise gets caught in a slightly different trap. The sentimental discourse is more highly developed as she poignantly states that the day she took her vows to God, although she was torn from Abelard, in her heart she remained completely dedicated to her lover. Pope ostensibly had a more religious soul than Colardeau's, which might account for the latter's lighter tone. Influenced by French pre-Romanticism in preserving many of Pope's natural and nocturnal elements, Colardeau does, however, transform the atmosphere so that is less bleak than Pope's tenebrous, menacing, and Gothic portrayal. The heavy cloud of religious culpability is lifted in favor of a romanticized, sentimental ode to nostalgic love that already anticipates some aspects of Rousseau's *La Nouvelle Héloïse*. But Colardeau also expands the erotic passage in Pope where Eloisa wished she could still lie on Abelard's breast. The French Heloise uses sensual imagery; she burns with love and longs to drown herself in the pleasures or the "volupté" of the flesh. Pope's Eloisa was content with a fantasy: Abelard should give all that he could and she would dream the rest. Colardeau's Heloise wants to be covered in kisses and then she will invent the rest. In addition, the revision of Pope's similar scene is more visually enhanced. As previously discussed, the reference to Abelard's eunuchism received increased popular appeal in the eighteenth century, and it became the subject of widespread discussions, as readers were fascinated by the curious, mysterious, mutilated beings. In Pope's poem, the theme of impotence surfaces at a pause in the line between the kisses and the dream, the compensation for

Abelards's impotence which concludes the scene. Here, Colardeau seems to perpetuate the misogynistic stereotype of the times that women were the gender more prone to erotic fantasies. Like Pope's Eloisa, Colardeau's Heloise begs Abelard to help her prefer God to his memory, but while the following section also describes the Paraclete as previously shown in Pope's poem, Colardeau combines the Gothic image of the monastery with original pre-Romantic elements. He inserts a light/dark motif constructed on the luminous image of the Paraclete when it was inhabited with the holy, glorious presence of Abelard as a brilliant theologian. But the light fades to darkness when Abelard leaves his monastery. In traditional Gothic style, Heloise says that the dark has enveloped her and her nuns in a veil of shadows. Here, Colardeau creates a stanza in which Heloise adds that her sisters ask for Abelard, the founder and creator of the holy site, and then she reverts back to the personal message, begging him to listen to her. At this point, Colardeau inserts an original element in his poetic imitation of Pope. We recall that Pope had included a Gothic description of the natural landscape that surrounded the Paraclete. Colardeau deviates from Pope's religious suggestion of Gothic gloom that enshrouded the Paraclete, which, in turn, shifts Colardeau's poem into a more secular context. Although Colardeau also deals with a lengthy description of nature, he omits the personified, ominous presence of Black Melancholy, and the reference to tombs. As Charrier pointed out, Colardeau inscribes another still-life of Heloise in the narrative that suggests a Antoine Watteau- or François Boucher-like Rococo ambiance.[36] Also, Colardeau does away with Pope's vertical church's arches, and shifts the architectural focus onto the natural landscape. His poem abandons arches for trees that extend upwards toward the heavens. In Colardeau's revision of the scenery outside of the Paraclete, there are several references to the forest, which

[36] Charrier 460-2.

Watteau often used in his pastoral scenes where solitary female figures were portrayed in a hazy wooded area that exuded strong erotic tones. The ambiance suggests Watteau's pre-Romantic mood of languid melancholy:

> Viens, ces arbres touffus, ces pins audacieux,
> Dont la cime s'élève et se perd dans les cieux;
> Ces ruisseaux argentés fuyant dans la prairie;
> L'abeille sur les fleurs cherchant son ambroisie;
> Le zéphyr qui se joue au fond de nos bosquets:
> Ces cavernes, ces lacs et ces sombres forêts;
> Ce spectacle riant, offert par la nature,
> N' adoucit plus l'horreur du tourment que j'endure:
> L'ennui, le sombre ennui, triste enfant du dégoût,
> Dans ces lieux enchantés se traîne et corrompt tout.
> Il sèche la verdure; et la fleur pâlissante
> Se courbe et se flétrit sur sa tige mourante:
> Zéphyre n'a plus de souffle; Echo n'a plus de voix,
> Et l'oiseau ne fait plus que gémir dans nos bois. (327)

Another important pre-romantic theme, "l'ennui," is also inserted here and creates a leisurely mood. Heloise is transformed into a languorous, sensual figure completely liberated from any serious religious contemplation. On the contrary, Colardeau has carved out a new space in his poem, one located in a secluded, perfumed, wooded area that allows Heloise to abandon herself freely to her desire. But beyond the obvious aesthetics of this invented scene, there is a trace of authorial intervention in this metafictional representation of Heloise. Colardeau acts as a male voyeur who, along with other men, is captivated by the seductive allure of this painting. Heloise becomes the object of his secret fantasies. On the one hand, the painting could be interpreted through a Lacanian lens that would classify the gaze and the desire as male, but the scene could also be reversed. Using Boucher's women as an example, Erica Rand postulated that these sensual figures cast an erotic spell on men.[37] Here, Colardeau has become bewitched by Hel-

[37] See Erica Rand's article, "Agency, the French Revolution, and the Art of Boucher and David," *Genders* 7 (1990): 49-51.

oise's charm. It is as if he had listened to the English Eloisa's monologue, and, little by little, he had been seduced by the titillating details of her story. In overhearing her narrative in Pope's epistle, Colardeau adapted it, shifting it more along the lines of the erotic discourse. Ironically, he allows the reader to catch a glimpse of the "real" lived desire present in the medieval text. In Colardeau's poem, Heloise's words take on images; they are enhanced in a visual transformation as reflected in the two principal still-lifes that were invented. The earlier one depicted a more traditional Heloise as a tearful, reluctant nun; the more original one represents the swirling, sensual, dreamy woman in love. Her passionate nature is captured in this secular version in a movement away from the religious Heloise that would continue to flourish as the legend became increasingly popular.

The Representation of the Moral Heloise

After the pastoral interlude comes yet another abrupt change of tone. Heloise contemplates her nuns' destiny, and her role as the Bride of Christ. She communicates a personal message to her nuns, based on her own struggle so that the sisters can be spared the pain of a divided heart. Here, Colardeau invents and finds a replacement for the hallucinatory dream sequence in which Pope's Heloise has a vision of becoming the Bride of Christ. Colardeau's fictional sequence is more grounded in reality, and even reads like the medieval Heloise's account in that the passage is highly rational, offering her personal philosophy and advice to the women she lives with in the convent. As Peter Cryle pointed out, the eighteenth-century erotic narrative is in fact grounded in the topos of instruction, and in Heloise's case, it is moral education that she is passing onto her nuns so that they can avoid the suffering that she has endured.[38] She changes roles from the lover to the teacher, an aspect never really emphasized in other imitations. Differing strikingly from Pope's more delirious Eloisa, this rational Heloise begs her nuns to listen to her and to take only God as their lover. She advises them to close their hearts to love if they wish to be happy, an admirable quality that she herself cannot acquire. Heloise envies her nuns' serene sleep because they are not troubled by a passionate reverie that draws her inevitably to thoughts of her lover. From her general moral diatribe, Colardeau then creates a bridge into another monologic, sentimental speech in which he contrasts the heat of Heloise's passion with Abelard's cold, dead, inert form. The use of opposition is borrowed from Pope to introduce the dream in which Heloise relives their "plaisirs" or past amorous encounters. But in Colardeau's version, the interlude is abbreviated and she says unexpectedly that reason tugs at the curtain of her waking consciousness, rudely jolting her back to reality. She then considers her lover's predicament, and hints that Abelard's plight is easier to bear since he is no longer alive. The poem remains rooted in more material imagery. Colardeau does not imitate Pope's hallucinatory episode in which Eloisa has a vision of Abelard rescuing her from God in a remote corner of heaven. There is no use of personification, or overly dramatic Gothic images, and Colardeau erases the intervention of the angels and other religious figures who participate in Pope's embellished, theatrical battle scene when God and Abelard struggle over Eloisa's weakened, malleable soul. Above all, Colardeau adds in an original element; his Heloise mumbles a quiet "adieu" to Abelard, and thus marks the transition into the final stage of the poem. The abrupt decision to cut off all contact with her lover could be read in the contemporary

[38] Peter Cryle explains the "modern" view of learning, mainly women's erotic learning in the eighteenth century in his book, *Geometry in the Boudoir* (Ithaca & London, Cornell UP, 1994): 71-91.

context of a transitory "égarement." In eighteenth-century novels, lovers who temporarily strayed from reason were not uncommon, and their meandering was not really frowned upon as the hero or heroine always learned from experience so as to profit morally or draw conclusions from the lesson learned. This was often the case in the Marquis de Sade's libertine novels, or the seductive "apprentissage" texts written by Claude-Prosper Jolyot de Crébillon. In any event, the addition of the good-bye scene here is a fictional creation; Heloise deviates completely from the medieval prototype who would never definitely break the emotional connection to her lover. What remains to be seen is whether Heloise reaches a moral conclusion from her "égarement" of the heart, and, if so, whether this indicates further authorial intervention in the closure of the poem.

Eternal Rest or Authorial Burial?

The final section of the poem begins with a passage borrowed directly from Pope, but the scene is abbreviated. The mysterious, disembodied voice that entices Heloise to the grave is included, but the theatrical Gothic effects are deleted. The lights are not dimmed, and there is no reference to the Spirits or the Saints calling Heloise from a distance. Most of all, Abelard is not there to perform the last rites with the Cross in his hand. Interestingly, there is a startling absence of religious symbols in this version. Heloise begins her final monologue by responding to the voice that she hears; she valiantly welcomes the coming of "repos." It is in death that love ends, and God will now assuage her constant pain with his generous pardon. Colardeau goes back to Pope in that his Heloise also wishes to become immortal, calling out to Abelard to receive her last kiss and breath. Yet, once again, the demand is transformed in a more secular way, devoid of any religious signification:

> Dans ces derniers moments, viens du moins recueillir
> Et mon dernier baiser et mon dernier soupir.

> Et toi, quand le trépas aura flétri tes charmes,
> Ces charmes séducteurs, la source de mes larmes,
> Quand la mort de tes jours éteindra le flambeau,
> Qu'on nous unisse encor dans la nuit du tombeau.
> Que la main des amours y grave notre histoire;
> Et que le voyageur, pleurant notre mémoire,
> Dise: Ils s'aimèrent trop, ils furent malheureux;
> Gémissons sur leur tombe, et n'aimons pas comme eux. (332)

Heloise's wish is to be reunited with Abelard in the same grave after the flames have been extinguished, and thus fade slowly into a distant memory. Whereas Pope had transformed the Paraclete into a celestial burial site that was prepared to receive the lovers' bodies in eternal peace, Colardeau develops the sentimental discourse. The scene is abridged. There is no suggestion of redemption or regret, and most importantly no direct intervention of the poet as the one who will see to their immortality. Colardeau does not imitate Pope's blatant self-flattery as the poet who will ensure the lovers' future remembrance. On the contrary, the poem is more abstract as Heloise only hopes that the hand of love will inscribe their story. The last two lines retain a trace of Pope in that she wants others to remember them, but Colardeau concludes with a universal moral directed to all potential lovers, a message from Heloise that perhaps people will shed tears on their grave and remember not to love too much in order to avoid the suffering that she and Abelard had endured. Yet, Colardeau concludes his poem by signing Heloise's name, and under her name he adds the words "par Colardeau." He then superimposes his name onto hers and allows the reader to view, once again, a palimpsest that contains a fragment of the original Heloise's signature. Yet for the most part, as already seen with Pope, the legend is perpetuated at the expense of burying the original author. Colardeau capitalized on the melodramatic aspects of Heloise's love story and built it up so that he could appeal to the public's literary taste. Inadvertently, Colardeau conserved Pope's portrayal of Heloise as a hysterical, over-sexed woman, but in a dissimulated way, one that is not immediately perceptible. The most salient difference is that Colardeau does not imitate the irrational representation of Heloise, but he does embroider Pope's passionate revision of Heloise through his innovative use of still-life portraiture that provides sensual images, which, in turn, embellishes her amorous speech. In Colardeau's poem, the original Heloise is almost completely invisible; fading from sight; her body and soul are, as Derrida would say, written and signified upon. The desiring body has become an empty site that has been transformed into a metaphor. In the tenebrous shadows of the tomb where the field of vision is restricted, Colardeau and Pope have stolen Heloise's clothes to stage their masquerade. As Béatrice Durand noted in "Diderot and the Nun: Portrait of the Artist as a Transvestite,"[39] male authors who engage in female impersonation are probably fulfilling their own erotic fantasies; they hide behind female attire to see how it feels to be a "woman," and thus the "woman" in the text is but a mere projection of the male writer in drag. Durand's recent and insightful work on transvestism and female impersonation posits that gender borrowing in the eighteenth-century is a game in which authors such as Diderot participated less as a means of exploring their own femininity than as a means of breaking into female domains (like the convent). Pope and Colardeau play the gender game and thus are not only cross-dressers, but performers in their own versions of the amorous tragedy. Pope loses himself in his representation of a theatrical, Gothic Eloisa and ventriloquizes for her the verses he composed. Colardeau goes even further in adding sensual images to Pope's lyrical words. Together, the male authors have written convincing discourses of desire, and they have gone under cover as copy-scriptors engaging in mimetic poetic inventions that produce a simulacrum

---

[39] Béatrice Durand, "Diderot and the Nun: Portrait of the Artist as a Transvestite," ed. Thais E. Mogan *Men Writing the Feminine* (Albany: State UP of New York, 1994): 89-105.

of the master "female" prototype. Colardeau and Pope stage a masquerade as "feminine" ghost-writers who have succeeded in burying the real author, and the question is whether or not Heloise will ever rise again from the depths of the grave to reclaim her text. However, if as Derrida reads it, ghosts always live on, Heloise may come back in the form of yet another narrative voice:

> This living on is also phantom revenance (the one who lives on is always a ghost) that is noticeable (re-markable) and is represented from the beginning, from the moment that the posthumous, testamentary, scriptural character of the narrative comes to unfold.[40]

But before the "ghost" of Heloise could resurface, another epistolary novel emerged, renewing the couple's popularity with the French public However, Jean-Jacques Rousseau would radically revise the couple, shifting the focus to a more spiritual representation of desire in harmony with Enlightenment ideology pertaining to conjugal love.

---

[40] Jacques Derrida, "Living On: Border Lines," *Deconstruction and Criticism,* ed. Harold Bloom (New York: Seabury Press, 1983): 138.

8.

Julie or the Devout Heloise

After the success of the sentimental poetic versions, the public continued to demonstrate an avid interest in Heloise's and Abelard's tragic love story. In 1761, Rousseau published his monumental epistolary novel, *Julie ou la Nouvelle Héloïse,* which contained fragments of some familiar themes found in the medieval text. To create his work, Rousseau partially restored the epistolary form of the twelfth-century love letters, but he radically modified the original private pact between Heloise and Abelard by amplifying their correspondence with his invention of fictional characters. The shift towards multi-voiced narrative was a distingushing mark of his contribution to the dissemination of the legend and was also significant for the expansion of the epistolary genre. By the middle of the Enlightenment, the letter novel was approaching the height of its popularity in France and abroad. As more and more writers began to experiment with letter composition, the genre continued to evolve, expanding the range of diversification. The theme of passion still sparked public interest, but it was integrated into the novel and fused with other subplots. Structurally, the form of the missive was more technically sophisticated; the construction of the epistle's narrative elements were strengthened in order to sustain the movement of the main plot throughout the development of the novel. In the style of Samuel Richardson and Choderlos de Laclos, Rousseau's *Julie* is a work in which the reader follows the unfolding intrigue through the key textual event, the letter exchanges.

Rousseau's use of the polyphonic epistolary form also focuses on the establishment of an intimate, communicative bond among Julie, St. Preux, Claire and Wolmar. Their close network, grounded in friendship, allows them to freely participate in reflecting and commenting on the most critical events in their lives. It is the personal tone of their epistles that enables readers to participate in the letter exchanges. Positioned outside the text, the reader has the opportunity to gaze over the characters' shoulders in order to gain insight by reading Julie's account of her love for St. Preux, the intervention of her father in her romantic life, and her marriage to Wolmar. Although there are several letter writers who often digress on a variety of subjects, Rousseau creates a central structure in the text by organizing their correspondence around Julie's love for St. Preux and her spiritual philosophy. Within this narrative frame, the related themes of conjugal love, family, and virtue are also integrated and comprise a significant part of their correspondence. Since the novel contains 163 letters and is too lengthy to adequately discuss in one chapter, I will concentrate on Rousseau's (re)invention of Heloise. His novel will be comparatively analyzed with other famous imitative versions of the period in order to see if Rousseau establishes a new direction in the fashionable trend of fragmenting and transmutating the medieval nun's epistles.

To begin this discussion, it is necessary to establish a structural framework in order to explore how the novel fits into the revisionist perspective of the present study The text can be divided into two main sections: the scandalous love story and the moral discourse, which provide the foundation to study Rousseau's (re)invention of Heloise. Despite the differences in philosophy and religious ideology, Julie resembles the medieval Heloise. She, too, is an erudite, strong woman. Ironically, Heloise's devotion to Abelard creates a bridge spanning several centuries, linking her to Julie, whose dilemma retains some fragments of Heloise's original struggle between monastic faith and love. It is interesting to consider how Rousseau reconciles feminine desire; he veils Julie's body with virtue, thereby purging her flesh of romantic passion. Yet, as we will see, Julie's desiring body has a way of invading the text to unveil another amorous discourse, which echoes more closely Heloise's Ovidian "plainte" of immortalizing her passion for her beloved Abelard.

In his version of the tragic love story, Rousseau deleted the original religious context in which the medieval lovers' illicit desire was born in order to appeal to the sentimental and more secular tastes of Enlightenment readers. His revision process is set in motion by shifting the location from the urban center of corruption, Paris, to a pure, pastoral setting in Switzerland. Like Heloise, Julie d'Etrange, a young woman with a superior intellect, falls in love with her tutor, St. Preux, fully aware that her father would never sanction a marriage to a commoner. The first two books focus on Julie's clandestine romantic correspondence with St. Preux.

From the opening pages of the novel's first part, the reader finds echoes of the medieval love letters. Similar to Fulbert, Julie's father hires St. Preux to instruct his daughter in their home, but, in comparison to Abelard and Heloise's ambitious program of study, the material for Julie's education is significantly reduced. St. Preux restricts the study of languages to Italian; he eliminates algebra, geometry and physics, and he also confines the subject of history to their own country, Switzerland. St. Preux carefully avoids the study of romantic poetry or novels, with the exception of Petrarch, Tasso, and Metastasio. He explains to Julie that romantic love should be moderated so as not to taint her morals. Rousseau outlines his ideas on education in the twelfth letter of the first part, which deviates significantly from the medieval couple's balanced pedagogical curriculum. One of the most striking contrasts is this particular missive smacks of Enlightenment anti-clericalism, as shown by the curious omission of religious instruction. Yet, Rousseau retains the original association between Heloise and Abelard; St. Preux and Julie's teacher-student relationship parallels Abelard's infamous role as the seductive tutor. However, St. Preux's sensitive nature varies greatly from Abelard's callous demeanor. He is presented as an honorable, sensitive hero who wholeheartedly respects Julie's moral qualities. He truly loves her, so it is not surprising that he is attracted to the sentimental appeal of the medieval Heloise's love; he even encourages Julie to read the nun's heart-wrenching love letters while reproaching Abelard for being a miserable creature, deserving of his fate. Borrowing from the medieval plot, their lessons soon lead to amorous diversions despite Julie's extraordinary efforts to keep their relationship innocent in order to ensure their happiness. Here, Rousseau significantly alters the popular image of the vile seducer. St. Preux differs from Abelard because his romantic advances are less calculated and their union appears more spontaneous. But after the first night of passion, Julie's idealized view of love changes abruptly. After this incident, the novel digresses from the medieval text as Rousseau prepares to radically revise the narrative, reformulating his novel into a philosophical reflection.

Abject Female Desire

If St. Preux's sentimental missives deviate markedly from Abelard's ascetic letters, Julie's passion also differs from Heloise's desire. In the medieval love correspondence, we recall that Heloise's letters reveal a pressing desire to be physically reunited with Abelard. In sharp contrast, Julie's letters deliberately avoid reliving the immediacy of her sexual encounter with St. Preux. She even violates the epistolary characteristic of writing to the moment, which, as discussed in preceding chapters, allows the correspondents to permanently preserve that defining moment of sealing their love. On the contrary, she avoids active contemplation of the night of passion. Her first experience with her lover is oddly described; it is reported in a letter to her confidant, her cousin Claire, and thus tends to lack the sensual "lived" qualities seen in the medieval love letters. Although Julie loves St. Preux, her missive does not celebrate the fulfillment of her physical desire. Rather, her passion has an ominous effect on her mind, "Il semblait que ma passion funeste voulût se couvrir, pour me séduire, du masque de toutes les vertus."[1] Moreover, the night of passion results in agitation, turbulence and emotional disorder. The missive further highlights her self-reproach; she admits to not knowing what she has done

> J'oubliai tout, et ne me souvins que de l'amour: c'est ainsi qu'un instant d'égarement m'a perdue à jamais. Je suis tombée dans l'abîme d'ignominie dont une fille ne revient point; et si je vis, c'est pour être plus malheureuse. (I:XXX, 70)

In Julie's opinion, she has strayed from purity and her only recourse is to block the memory by forgetting the incident. As Michael O'Dea reads it, forgetfulness often appears in Rousseau's works; it is a condition of sexual intimacy (40). For Rousseau, sex is a complex and problematic phenomenon, but here Rousseau elides the portrayal of feminine passion. The sudden memory lapse allows the author to dismiss Julie's passion, and thus Rousseau is guilty of intervening in a woman's discourse of desire. He denies his heroine the right to articulate her passion, as remembered through her body. This authorial stance recalls other male (re)visionists discussed in previous seventeenth-and eighteenth-century imitations of Heloise's missives. Here, feminine desire is thus repressed by burying the recollection. It is declared unrepresentable because Julie cannot express

[1] All of the quotations are taken from Jean-Jacques Rousseau's *Julie ou la Nouvelle Héloïse* (Paris: Garnier, 1988).

her feelings in words or corporeal gestures; she can only convey confusion and regret. But even if the female body seems invisible, Julie's passion does not completely fade from the locus of the text's intrigue. It hovers in the background, relegated to the margins of the characters' letters to reappear again, carefully disguised behind the emerging dominant moral philosophy. At times, the discourse of desire adds to the complexity of Rousseau's ambivalent attitudes towards sexuality, which will be further explored.

St. Preux's View of Carnal Desire

In response to Julie's troubling missive discussed above, St. Preux enters into the discusion after Julie has shared her conflicting feelings with her cousin Claire. At this point, Claire has already responded to Julie's letter and St. Preux now comments on Julie's sudden change of heart. In Letter 31 of the first book, he admits to noticing the torment in her eyes:

> Ces yeux touchants peuvent-ils dérober quelque secret à l'amour? Je vois, je vois, sous une apparente sérénité, les déplaisirs cachés qui t'assiègent; et ta tristsese, voilée d'un doux sourire, n'en est que plus amère à mon coeur. (I: XXXI, 74)

Here, her gaze is analogous to a text. From the eyes, he studies her lips, revealing a sweet smile. However, St. Preux is a discerning observer, for he senses her sadness. Julie's smile resembles a mask, which conceals her real internal anguish. After recognizing her true feelings, he proceeds to try to persuade her that their union is not a crime, but a sacred bond, one comparable to the legitimate institution of marriage. In St. Preux's opinion, they are joined in a natural harmonious manner, and he hopes that she can truly unite her soul with his, as he readily does in confiding his most private reflections to her in his missives. This particular letter is noteworthy because it introduces the theme of dissimulation, which will play an increasingly significant role in the development of the couple's love story.

But Julie's response to St. Preux's letter reveals strong opposition to his point of view. She laments the loss of innocence they once shared before committing the fatal mistake of consummating their desire. For her, the sins of the flesh have profaned the noble, singular qualities of their pure love; they have succumbed to common base instincts. At this point, she only hopes to seek a solitary space in which she can contemplate her irreversible mistake. In this retreat from corporeal contact, she can, however, retain the image of her lover in her mind and soul. She is already in the process of preparing for their inevitable separation. Throughout the rest of the first part and the second part, the lovers' dissolution, albeit imminent, is, however, delayed by Claire's persuasive tactics. To protect Julie's secret love from her father, Claire convinces St. Preux to leave with their friend, Lord Edouard. The couple's epistles are now written from a distance, a familiar situation seen in epistolary narratives. They write to reduce the gap caused by the physical separation as well as to preserve their sentiments. In a polyphonic letter novel, geographical separation between the lovers also tends to slow the rhythm of the narrative; it delays the development of the intrigue, and allows the secondary writers to enter into the exchange in the absence of the core couple's dominant textual presence.

St. Preux's departure not only establishes the thematic focus of the second part, but also marks a transformation of the couple's love. In Letter 11, the tenor of Julie's missives predicated on absence and romantic longing is characteristic of the sentimental discourse of the Enlightenment, as previously illustrated in Pope's and Colardeau's versions. She maintains that the couple must endure separation if they want to be happy in the future. However, Rousseau's Julie differs from the verse imitators, in that she begins to espouse a philosophical position. The main part of her epistle shows a significant change in her writing. The references to her sinful body fade; her emphasis shifts toward the soul reinforced by the seminal words: virtue, heart and soul. Her language is abstract; the majority of this letter deals with her reflections on human passions. Rousseau reverses the persuasive style previously seen in St. Preux's epistle in praise of their sexual union. This time Julie plays the role of the instructor. She wants to teach him to accept another conception of love; one that is strikingly devoid of sensuality. Julie also wants to elevate their love to a higher plane so that it represents a simulacrum of her idea of the "vrai beau" (II: XI, 199). For her, true fulfillment resides in the soul and in the contemplation of goodness. In this embrace of purity, she wants him to see that happiness lies not in man's physical gratification, but rather in the spiritual union of the couple's hearts grounded on the principles of sensibility. It is important to clarify that Julie does not ask St. Preux to forget their love, but she endeavors to redefine their feelings. She wants St. Preux to return to the innocent state of their love before their physical union. To illustrate her position, her speech, at times, shifts tenses from the present to the past. As a result of her retreat, which afforded her the opportunity to contemplate her predicament, she wants St. Preux to view their desire from a different perspective since, he, too, is now venturing into new territory far from home. Julies hopes that his travels will not obliterate her image from his mind; their love is inimitable in its superior communication of their hearts:

> le souvenir de nos premières amours te poursuivra malgré toi; mon image, cent fois plus belle que je ne fus jamais, viendra tout à coup te surprendre. A l'instant le voile du dégoût couvrira tous tes plaisirs, et mille regrets amers naîtront dans ton coeur. (II: XI,202)

Here, Julie advocates leaving their corporeal pulsions in the past to replace it with the indelible image of her purity. Once again, the image of the veil resurfaces, but the ambiguous signification contains multiple interpretations. From a linguistic point of view, the veil could represent an emblem of Julie's rhetorical style. It highlights Julie's skill at maneuvering several discourses at once. Her moral style is subtle, she never overtly denounces or condemns, but rather tends to direct her rational argument on a course of gentle persuasion until her interlocutor intellectually grasps the validity of her argument. In this way, her missives resemble Heloise's epistolary style. Julie, too, employs double-voiced language, an aspect of Bakhtin's dialogic discourse. To clarify, she deftly combines and manipulates more than one type of language. Specifically, she weaves the romantic recollection into her moral maxim. Here, Julie tries to convince him to see that their unique love differs from other relationships he may develop in more urban settings. Since St. Preux is now abroad, Julie suspects he may be frequenting coquettes, and so the reference to the veil could also be read as a moral warning. She hopes he does not succumb to societal evils and physical temptation. Perhaps she hopes that the memory of her, embodying an exalted conception of romantic love, will serve to shake him into recognizing that his reason could become momentarily blinded by his sexual appetite, which could, in turn, veil his true inner essence or, to put it another way, his inherent disdain for gratuitous physical pleasures. A close reading of the letter reveals signs that Rousseau deploys a persuasive strategy through Julie. She wants St. Preux to shift his desire to the inner confines of his conscience, the memory zone, where he can always remain with her. Here, Rousseau appears to erase sensuality from this modern moral Julie, and thus she differs radically from the medieval Heloise, who never could forget physical desire. He performs a textual mutilation by purging desire both from her mind's recollection and from her erotic pulsions of the flesh. At this early point in the narrative, she is gradually moving towards sacrificing passion so that she can experience redemption for her sins. Interestingly, she begs him not to forget "cette Julie qui fut à toi" (202), which introduces the idea of body fragmention. Once again, by the empowering pen of a male rewriter, this modern Heloise symbolically splits into a dual woman: the carnal Julie of the past and the new Heloise (yet to to be born) who is a spiritual philosopher.

Replacing Julie's Body

Although St. Preux is now physically separated from Julie, he continues his correspondence with her throughout the second part. Similar to Bussy's Heloise and Guillerague's Marianne, Rousseau's Julie sends St. Preux a talisman containing a miniature portrait, a metonymical substitute for herself. But here the woman plays the role of the active sender and the man acts as the passive recipient, which poses salient gender implications, with St. Preux recalling the Princess of Clèves and the Portuguese nun. The portrait functions as a fetish conjuring up his distant lover's body, which establishes an erotically charged ambiance in his solitary quarters. Also, the epistolary characteristics usually attributed to women are curiously reversed. Writing like a woman, St. Preux demonstrates a spontanous outpouring of emotion onto the paper of his missive, as illustrated by the abundance of exclamation marks, highlighting his jubilation in receiving a pictorial replacement for his beloved's presence. Once again, he plays the feminine role; he locks himself in his room to privately abandon himself to the pleasure of unwrapping his package:

> Je m'asseye hors d'haleine, je porte une main tremblante sur le cachet. O première influence du talisman! j'ai senti palpiter mon coeur à chaque papier que j'ôtais, et je me suis bientôt trouvé tellement oppressé que j'ai été forcé de respirer un moment sur la dernière enveloppe. . . Julie!. . . ô ma Julie!. . . le voile est déchiré. . .je te vois. . .je vois tes divins attraits! (II: XXIII, 257-8)

The reference to the torn veil containing her portrait reveals an intricate visual illusion. At a first glance, St. Preux is elated to study her reflection in the portrait, but the joy of recovering her symbolic presence soon fades, underscored by his shift to a nostalgic troubling speech associated with her physical absence. The portrait evokes his vivid recollection of how she was as a lover in the past, and so the image of her within the frame embodies the vision of the other more remote woman: the carnal Julie. At the same time, the portrait disturbs St. Preux because he begins to recognize the transformation of the woman he loved to the new, evolving Heloise; the virtuous saint who endeavors to distance herself from her sexuality in order to convert their passion to a superior, spiritual level. To mark this change, her body is symbolically veiled. It is beginning to fade from his field of vision, affirmed by the fact that there are few references to her body; his gaze focuses mainly on her face. St. Preux reads her face as if it were a text. Its contours lead him towards her inner soul, the seat of sensibility. In addition, the attention placed on her face allows him to create an imaginary, substitute interlocutor for Julie. St. Preux addresses his love to this painted stand-in for his beloved in the hopes their love will triumph over the obstacle of separation.

In her response to his letter, Julie's Letter 25 deals with the portrait too. In a reciprocal gesture, she also physically isolates herself in order to envision her lover holding and caressing her portrait. That her imagination actively bridges the distance between them and allows her to recapture the lingering sensuality between them also indicates that her desire is not yet squelched. It momentarily resurfaces, reinforcing her ambivalent and, at times, enigmatic position concerning her love for him. St. Preux answers this missive, but this time he attacks the artist because he does not accurately portray her physical and spiritual attributes. Once again, Rousseau creates an erotic ambiance in this epistle, as St. Preux elaborates on the intimate parts of Julie's body. The attention to detail could be convincingly remembered only by Julie's lover who retraces the lines and curves of her body. Indeed, St. Preux asserts that the portrait does not capture her true likeness and then turns his attention to pointing out the various flaws of the canvas. His idea of how Julie's portrait should be created is inadvertently related to the transformation of her love:

> Le portrait de Julie doit être modeste comme elle. Amour! ces secrets n'appartiennent qu'à toi. Tu dis que le peintre a tout tiré de son imagination.Je le crois!, je le crois! Ah! s'il eût aperçu le moindre de ces charmes voilés, ses yeux l'eussent dévoré, mais sa main n'eût point tenté de les peindre. (II: XXV,271)

In St. Preux's view, Julie's image should be depicted modestly in order to accurately reflect her true essence. Here, Rousseau introduces a key idea—modesty—a common philosophical theme in pre-romantic literature. Janine Rossard elaborates on this conception:

> La pudeur enfin tend vers la Beauté, spirituelle et esthétique. Elle est le fondement de la pureté de l'imagination en détournant l'intérêt des choses basses. Elle est donc source de grace, en particulier chez la femme.[2]

In Rousseau's work, modesty is also associated with his belief in man's inherent goodness and aesthetic conception of virtue. This, in turn, signals the preliminary passage towards the development of Julie's own moral philosophy (as the text will reveal). To look at this idea visually, the painting suggests that modesty may also be an influential factor in St. Preux's objections to the artist's depiction of his beloved's features. Perhaps what the artist's brush is unable to capture is this abstract virtuous quality she is gradually acquiring, illustrated by St. Preux's harsh criticism of his failure to represent her "veiled charms." The significance of "veiled charms" presents a prob-

---

[2] Janine Rossard examines the theme of modesty from a pre-romantic and romantic perspective in *Une Clef du romantisme: la Pudeur* (Paris, Nizet, 1974): 14. In particular, Rossard delves into the fascinating relationship between modesty as a veil, and charnal desire, which is germane to our study of Julie's struggle with her desiring and desired body.

lem of ambiguity. The term implies an elusive, hidden trait in Julie's nature, which highlights her movement away from material, corporeal passion. As Rossard suggests, modesty "canalise le désir pour le spiritualiser"(10). Here, she refers to Nietzsche who posited that true love privileges the soul over the body. Indeed, St. Preux's letter seems to indicate some recognition of a profound tacit change already taking place in Julie's body and soul. In criticizing the artist again, he uncovers an important contradiction in the painting:

> Oui, ton visage est trop chaste pour supporter le désordre de ton sein; on voit que l'un de ces deux objets doit empêcher l'autre de paraître; il n'y a que le délire de l'amour qui puisse les accorder; et quand sa main ardente ose dévoiler celui que la pudeur couvre, l'ivresse et le trouble de tes yeux dit alors que tu l'oublies et non que tu l'exposes. (II: XXV,271)

As the text illustrates, there is a conflict between Julie's modesty and her previous sensuality. The "désordre" of her breast positions the body as a site of disarray; it clashes with the chaste expression on her face. The artist's illustration of love reinforces this emotional turbulence also reflected in her eyes and further underlines the contradiction between the innocent face and the transgressive breast. The reference to "pudeur" is related to Rousseau's symbolism of the veil. The opposition between what the artist discloses and what modesty veils seems to impose another mask upon the body. To clarify, the term "pudeur" also veils the erotic pulsions of the female body. Rousseau casts a veil over Julie's sexuality in order to prepare his conversion of her character from a passionate woman to a devout and desexed wife. Before this defining moment, St. Preux continues to severely criticize the artist. At the conclusion of this missive, he elaborates on how it is that Julie could be more accurately portayed. In his opinion, the portrait would be much improved if her soul were more harmoniously aligned with her facial expression, in order to accentuate her modesty.

Interestingly, the missive's final lines contain another allusion to the veil : "On sent, en regardant ton ajustement, que c'est partout le voile des grâces qui couvre la beauté" (II: XXV,272). St. Preux seems to anticipate Julie's rebirth as a spiritual figure incarnating virtue, as suggested by the veil of grace obscuring her sensual beauty and, above all, distancing him from viewing her body. This seminal event occurs in the next part.

The Birth of the "New Heloise"

At the close of the second part, Rousseau suspends Julie's private correspondence and returns to the body of the narrative to direct the reader's focus to the developments in the compelling plot. The third part opens with the discovery of Julie's secret love letters. Her epistles are intercepted by her mother who soon takes ill and dies after the discovery of the shocking behavior of her daughter. Her father decides to marry her off to a family friend, the Baron de Wolmar, a paternal replacement figure who is cold, rational and authoritative. The arranged marriage to a man of the right class seems to announce the inevitable death of the love story. However, some scenes in the novel tend to show a fluctuating, contradictory movement between virtue and desire, and thus suggest that Rousseau, at certain points in the text, struggles with reconciling Julie's amorous body and her commitment to conjugal marriage.

Before looking at the letter describing her marriage, it is useful to consider the importance of conjugal love in the eighteenth century. In his second preface to the text, Rousseau elucidates his personal vision of Julie as a spokeswoman for companionate marriage. Here, he imagines couples reading his novel together, discovering new courage to carry on their mundane daily tasks. It is is his hope that married couples will view Julie and Wolmar's marriage as a positive state, providing them with a model to imitate in their own pursuit of happiness. While his comments may predict that his character Julie will truly honor her arranged union, it is also useful to consider some of the attitudes towards women and marriage in the eighteenth century.

As previously noted in my discussion of the seventeenth-century imitations, women were often physically separated from men, who had free access to more public spaces. By the eighteenth century, confinement was even more predominant; women were relegated to performing the domestic role at home. Like his peers, Rousseau subscribed to popular biological and social determination theories which clearly defined women's role in society. As Mary Trouille posits, Rousseau's view of women is grounded on his masculinist ideology in which he underlines the importance of nature. For him, man is naturally free and equal, whereas woman is dependent, unequal and inferior on intellectual, physical and moral levels. He further establishes his position by supporting the procreative function of women. Many of these philosophical ideas are transcribed into the text. In Trouille's opinion, this novel exemplifies Rousseau's most glorified view of motherhood and domestic bliss. Julie embodies the ideal wife and mother and also served as a fictional role model for women readers.[3] Absorbed by domestic chores, women, endeavoring to imitate Julie's extraordinary talents, would clearly recognize that proper dedication to their families would leave them virtually no spare time to pursue activities outside their homes. Here, Rousseau also asserts his belief in the separation of the sexes. Frequenting public spaces, men were concerned with war and politics and women, confined to interior spaces, were supposed to occupy themselves with the organization of the household. Rousseau interpolates these ideas in the third book of the novel, which

[3] For an insightful discussion on Rousseau's views of domestic responsibilities for women, see Mary Seidman Trouille's *Sexual Politics in the Enlightenment: Women Writers Read Rousseau* (Albany: State New York UP, 1997): 28-38.

will be comparatively discussed with the medieval love correspondence.

To Love and Honor: Julie's Marriage with Wolmar

In Letter 18 of the third part, Julie pens a long epistle to St. Preux in which she informs him of her wedding plans. This lengthy confesssional missive also contains the astonishing news of her miscarriage, a detail that was quite scandalous for the times. In the paratext, Rousseau forewarns young girls that reading even just one page of his novel might pose a moral threat to their innocence. The reference to the illegitimate pregnancy, however, mirrors the medieval love correspondence and marks the first in a series of striking intertextual reversals. The letter focuses on Julie's description of her marital vows, an episode which recalls Heloise's monastic vows imposed by Abelard, but the circumstances are altered to fit the conjugal contract. She begins the epistle with a reflection on her past *"égarement,"* also referred to as her *"crime"* with her former lover, "j'espérai tirer de ma faute un moyen de la réparer" (III:XVIII, 323). To go back to the medieval love letters, we recall that Heloise never alluded to her illicit passion as a crime or sin. The misogynist conception of woman as sinner resembles the twelfth-century idea that women were branded the inferior sex, considered physically and psychologically weaker than men.[4] Scientific discourse in the Enlightenment perpetuated this stereotype, an ideology also maintained by Rousseau. To his way of thinking, women were naturally predisposed to physiological fragility. As Trouille postulates, biological theories targeted the uterus as the site of these domineering drives (43).[5] In

[4] To retrace the misogynist conception of women as sinners, see R. Howard Bloch's *Medieval Misogyny and the Invention of Western Romantic Love* (Chicago & London: Chicago UP, 1991): 40-91.

[5] To further buttress Trouille's theories, Paul Hoffmann considers women's natural predisposition for raising children and for performing the maternal role in *La Femme dans la pensée des lumières* (Paris: Edition Ophrys, 1977): 379.

harmony with this conception, Julie demonstrates weakness in confessing her illicit love to her father, who, in turn, persuades her to honor him by accepting his choice for her as a husband; she carries out her filial duty and acquiesces to the marriage. As the event approaches, she contemplates the dreaded moment with fear: "plus j'approchais du moment fatal, moins je pouvais déraciner de mon coeur mes premières affections" (III: XVIII, 332). Yet, she finds a way to preserve her true sentiments for her lover. The church provides the setting for a fascinating intertextual reading between the vows in the medieval text and Julie's marital ceremony: "Dans l'instant même ou j'étais prête à jurer à un autre une étérnelle fidélité, mon coeur vous jurait encore un amour éternel, et je fus menée au temple comme une victime impure" (332). Echoing the medieval Heloise, Julie's reflection points to a plurality of languages. She appears to accept Wolmar as her husband, but internally preserves her authentic feelings by simultaneously swearing her loyalty to her true lover. Although conjugal vows will transform her love, Julie carefully conceals her other love, the sensual desire belonging to the Julie of the past. It is this feminine manipulation of two discourses— the amorous and the conjugal—which constitutes Rousseau's complex invention of the "new Heloise." The subsequent middle section of the epistle concentrates on the pivotal moment when she takes her vows, a noteworthy scene in the transformation of Julie into a virtuous figure. The epistle abruptly changes tone when she describes hearing the voice of God, which anticipates a dramatic change within her:

> La pureté, la dignité, la sainteté du mariage, si vivement exposées dans les paroles de l'Ecriture, ses chastes et sublimes devoirs si importants au bonheur, à l'ordre, à la paix, à la durée du genre humain. (III: XVIII,333)

Hoffmann also explores the ides of feminine inferiority, adding dimension to Rousseau's position concerning sexual difference.

Gradually, she moves towards sacrificing her passion for conjugal union : "je crus sentir intérieurement une révolution subite" (333). She goes on to add that the disorder of her passion and her affection for her lover are suddenly abated at the moment she commits herself to the laws of duty and nature. Here, Rousseau revises the medieval Heloise's vow scene at the altar. The original Heloise never mentions hearing the voice of God upon receiving the veil. On the contrary, she never ceased to think about Abelard or relinquish her unforgettable desire for him. But this "new Heloise" ostensibly welcomes the conjugal state: "J'envisageai le saint noeud que j'allais former comme un nouvel état qui devait purifier mon âme et la rendre à tous ses devoirs" (333). The drama of the scene builds as Julie approaches spiritual purification. Once again, she vaguely recalls Heloise, but her holy devotion to her vows constitutes a noteworthy reversal of the medieval nun. As Heloise's letters affirm, her veiled sensuous body never betrayed her loyalty to Abelard. Moreover, she never acknowledged the presence of God or the acceptance of her newly designated vocation, whereas Julie's body language emphasizes her allegiance to the conjugal state. The position of her bent submissive body, prone on the ground with her hands extended towards the heavens, signifies her pledge to Wolmar: "je me prosternai contre terre, j'élevai vers le ciel mes mains suppliantes, j'invoquai l'Etre dont il est le trône, et qui soutient ou détruit quand il lui plaît. . ."(III: XVIII, 336). She begins to pray to God and describes experiencing a violent passion, a seminal moment, enabling her to ultimately convert her passion into virtue. This sacrifice and transfiguration of her passion reflects Rousseau's views on the transgressive nature of desire. Paul Hoffmann noted that Rousseau condemned passion because it isolated the couple from the community.[6] In his invention of this "new Heloise," Rous-

[6] Hoffmann offers a concise commentary of Rousseau's negative ideas on passion, which is described as an excessive emotion, culminating in isolation

seau takes the authorial liberty of curbing her illicit, subversive passion so that he can reintegrate her into the order of the society. According to his philosophy, domestic bliss was the key to finding harmony and happiness, illustrated by the birth of the "new Heloise," the "porte-parole" for the positive social attributes of marital union. She reaffirms his ideals by swearing fidelity and chastity to Wolmar. Loving and honoring her husband also signifies her submissive recognition of the patriarchal structure of society. As a wife, she will respect the role that nature has delegated to her. Rousseau's use of a religious vocabulary not only underscores Julie's spiritual metamorphosis, but also directly reflects the rhetoric associated with the laws of conjugal union.

Before looking at Julie and Wolmar's conjugal contract, it is useful to further investigate some of the general ideas of marriage. Emanuel Swedenborg's eighteenth-century doctrine on conjugal love is enlightening, since he provides a detailed set of rules for the marital state. Analogous to Rousseau, he considers conjugal love a pure saintly union, but he goes further in establishing a correspondence with the holy marriage between God and the Church:

> Cet amour, considéré d'après son origine et sa correspondance, est céleste, spirituel, saint, pur et net, plus que tout autre amour qui, par le Seigneur, est chez les anges du Ciel et chez les hommes de l'Eglise. (93)

In addition, conjugal love is defined as a chaste, Christian state between a man and one wife. Furthermore, marriage represents the hope of attaining ultimate fulfillment. Julie's vows seal her commitment to uphold these values. Since Julie's life has changed drastically, it is also relevant to look at her corporeal evolution from a modern perspective. Specifically, what happens to her body? As a revisionist of Heloise, does Rousseau

from the community. See p. 411.

proclaim this new "Heloise," a mutilated woman who has irrevocably suffered the loss of her sexuality? Once again, Swedenborg's text sheds light on this question; he initially provides background that can be applied to Rousseau's representation of the female body.

As noted in the passage cited above, Swedenborg posits that those who really fulfill the conditions of conjugal love receive this exalted state from God.[7] Couples who pronounce their vows also swear to recognize that the conjugal state is inherently celestial and spiritual. But, in entering into holy marriage, the couple also embarks on a symbolic transcendance into the divine; the heavenly territory where the angels respect the same laws in their union with God. According to Swedenborg's doctrine, it would then be plausible to suspect that sexual desire might very well conflict with the sacred qualities of this conception of love. As Swedenborg also posits, "l'amour conjugal est appelé céleste et spirituel, parce que'il est chez les anges des Cieux" (97). This notion also poses an interesting gender question, which is associated with the celestial image of angels. As a result of their spiritual configuration, angels resist gender identification. Therefore, they are liberated from sexual constraints, assigned to males and females who possess material bodies. Moreover, this redefinition of gender can be applied to the study of Julie's body transformation. In taking her vows, she, too, experiences symbolic purification; leaving her body behind, her soul is lifted towards the heavens. Like the angels, she transcends gender construction and now possesses a more ambiguous image. As we will see in her new life, she will be gradually recreated into a virtuous wife, which causes her desiring body to fade from the narrative. Thus, Rousseau effaces her femininity; Julie's body becomes decentered as he remolds

---

[7] Emmanuel Swedenborg provides a detailed study of conjugal love and sheds light on the spiritual state of this specific union. For more information, see *L'Amour vraiment conjugal* (Meudon: Cercle Swedenborg, 1974).

her into a shapeless, angelic form. Her metamorphosis from a passionate woman into a saintly wife inadvertently alters the gender constructs of the text. She appears less as a young, sensual woman struggling with her guilt and self-reproach in the aftermath of committing the illicit sin of loving the wrong man, and more as an anomalous, double-gendered androgyne. Curiously, this androgynous vision was not uncommon in eighteenth-century philosophy; it was considered a pre-romantic theme, which peaked as a popular image found in nineteenth-century romantic literature in France and abroad.

Although such critics as John Lechte, Jeannette Rosso and Paul Hoffmann also offer androgynous readings of Julie, they do not consider why Rousseau alters and obscures Julie's body in order to convince his readers of the virtues of companionate relationships.[8] For the reader, the fact that her body has become less visible in the conversion process creates a problem of gender blurring. As Fitz Poole observes, the delineation of clear gender markings can also be identified with androgyny:

> In androgynous imagery, maleness (masculinity) and femaleness (feminity) are disassembled, transmuted, and reinscribed in imaginative ways that interweave, outreach, undercut, and sometimes overturn their ordinary prescriptions of boundedness and distinctiveness, with various entailments and consequences for the cultural reimagination of gender and its reinfusion in varied social context and cultural experiences.[9]

The spiritual ascendence of her soul tends to widen the imaginative boundaries of the text, her being now reconfigured and rearticulated to freely embody both masculine and feminine

---

[8] In addition to Hoffmann cited above, see, for example, John Lechte's "The Woman and the Veil," *French Studies* 39.4 (1985) : 423-441 and Jeannette Rosso's article, "Montesquieu, Rousseau et la féminité : De la crainte à l'angélisme," *Studi Francesi* 25.75 (1981): 482-489.

[9] Fitz John Porter Poole provides an interdisciplinary reading of images of androgyny in Western cultures. He focuses on the study of gender constructions and sexuality in his interesting essay, "The Procreative and Ritual Constitution of Female, Male and Other," *Gender Reversals and Gender Cultures,* ed. Sabrin Petra Ramet, (London & New York: Routledge, 1996): 201.

traits. She can more readily appropriate both masculine and feminine attributes. In her future, as the mistress of Clarens, she will be recognized as the cultivator of virtue. Defying gender constraints, Julie takes on a temporary masculine role as the designer of the elaborate plans for her gardens, and therefore, to phrase it in Poole's terms, she is "culturally reimagined" as a man. Also borrowing a masculine gender construct, she demonstrates her extraordinary intelligence by her skillful, competent running of the household and staff. This masculine stance is, however, inherently dangerous because her management could potentially threaten the stability of the patriarchal hierarchy, and so Rousseau limits her power to a creative, intellectual role. Here again, Rousseau abruptly destabilizes the gender construct. He fluctuates from his imaginative revision of her as a double-gendered androgyne, who drifts unhindered between maleness and femaleness, to a more traditional identification. He abruptly regenders Julie to the feminine by reverting to stereotypic role constraints whereby woman must submit to man's power. Since Wolmar replaces Julie's father as the paternal figure of authority, Julie's role as a wife means she must inevitably swing back over to her feminine side, which she does for the section of the novel devoted to Clarens. As Wolmar's faithful wife, she sacrifices romantic passion for conjugal purity, emptied of desire. Julie and Wolmar even subscribe to sexual separation, since passion creates social disorder. Thus, sexual encounters are limited to a procreative function. In fulfilling her predetermined biological role expectations, she replaces sexual pleasure with her nutritive duties as a mother. This analysis of the pivotal conversion scene underlines the significance of her acceptance of conjugal union.

After this main part of the letter describing the marriage ceremony, Julie turns to preparing St. Preux for the changes in her new life. She writes that everything has changed between them; she is no longer his "former Julie," the lover. As a result of her vows, he must honor her redemption from vice to virtue. She goes on to try to convince St. Preux that they must renounce their desire in order to love each other eternally. In harmony with her purification, she hopes they can become platonic lovers and that he, too, can be educated away from passion in order to imitate her morality and hence incorporate virtue into his life. Julie concludes her remarks to him by stressing the importance of chastity. The movement from disorderly passion to virtue is marked by the binary opposition between the weakened state of affection and her present empowering moral stance, infused by her spiritual conversion. She describes her deliverance from the slavery of love. Finally, she assures him that he has not lost a tender lover, but gained a faithful friend. From the ashes of carnal desire, the "new Heloise"is born, but does Rousseau also advocate complete elimination of the female body in shifting the emphasis to the soul?

Marital Bliss and the Effacing Female Body

After receiving news of her marriage, St. Preux embarks on a global voyage from England and the novel's focus turns to Julie's uxorial life. With the passage of time at Clarens, Julie, Wolmar and their children settle into constructing a domestic utopia, based on the principles of virtue and goodness. Julie's acceptance of her maternal obligations and role as moral educator mirror Rousseau's ideals of the feminine role, as dictated by nature. Here, she favors her feminine side since her experience with male power tends to be restricted and transitory. As a model of the perfect wife and mother, she never transgresses Rousseau's belief in predetermined gendered space, which stipulates that women must live in a private environment. She remains enclosed within the pastoral grounds of Clarens, and thus fulfills her domestic role expectations by not venturing into public spaces. In fact, Trouille suggests that perhaps Rousseau had greater social aspirations for Julie's family, which extended beyond the restrictions of her country home:

> In his detailed and enthusiastic dscriptions of daily life at Clarens, Rousseau presents his readers with a veritable manual of domestic economy and an eloquent exposition of his ideal of domesticity based on the bourgeois values of simplicity, order, utility, thrift, and virtue[...] The secret of the Wolmars' prosperity lies above all in the successful division of labor and harmonious cooperation between the two spouses in their daily tasks. (28)

This utopian ideal of domestic bliss does, however, leave readers to wonder about her former lover and her curious pledge in the church not to forget him. Thus, it is of no surprise that St. Preux rejoins the narrative. After six years, he returns to Clarens, invited by Wolmar, Claire and Julie, but the circumstances have dramatically changed; his position is immediately altered upon entering their home. Although Wolmar knows about their past intimate relationship, he now wishes to play a paternal role with him by regarding St. Preux as his son. He welcomes him to Clarens, preaching the moral attributes of virtue to him. It is his hope that St. Preux will eventually profit from Julie's morality and thereby imitate her admirable purity. Wolmar even offers to cure him of his desire for the "other" Julie. The dual image of Julie resurfaces in Wolmar's epistle to Claire:

> Ce n'est pas de Julie de Wolmar qu'il est amoureux, c'est de Julie d'Etange; il ne me haît point comme le possesseur de la personne qu'il aime, mais comme le ravisseur de celle qu'il a aimée. La femme d'un autre n'est point sa maîtresse[...] Il l'aime dans le temps passé: voilà le vrai mot de l'énigme. Otez-lui la mémoire, il n'aura plus d'amour. (IV: XIV, 492)

Even if Wolmar suceeds in erasing St. Preux's love, he expresses doubt when it comes to reading Julie's elusive feelings; her heart remains enigmatic. Once again, the image of the veil resurfaces: "un voile de sagesse et d'honnêteté fait tant de replis autour de son coeur, qu'il n'est plus possible à l'oeil humain d'y pénétrer"(492). In this instance, the veil is associated with the theme of dissimulation, which is also highlighted by the words: "replis autour de son coeur;" her true feelings toward St. Preux are concealed by her domestic mask of fidelity and honesty. Although the female body has supposedly been purified and is no longer vulnerable to experiencing sensuality, Wolmar's uncertainty causes discerning readers to wonder if she has really succeeded in converting her passion to a more chaste state. In any case, Wolmar reaffirms his intention to emphasize to St. Preux that Julie is now the wife of an honest man. As the older, wiser authoritative figure, he believes he can obliterate the memory of the couple's past sins or at least disguise it with this newer version of the moral Julie.

This attempt at deletion of her sexual desire has greater textual significance in regards to Rousseau's revision of Heloise. In this fiction, he, too, like other male co-authors, effaces the amorous Julie, by taking the liberty of suppressing her body from the text. Consequently, the female body becomes increasingly less visible as it fades from the narrative. In this manner, Rousseau resembles Abelard who deliberately altered Heloise's love discourse. Yet, the complexity of the novel resides in Rousseau's problematic representation of the female desiring body. In some instances, the text reveals that he loses ground in his portrayal of this ideal embodiment of the chaste wife. The dynamics of the text's epistles show a constant, and, at times, contradictory movement between spiritual redemption and brief glimpses of possible corporeal recovery. In fact, Julie's pledge of virtue remains constantly endangered by the reawakening of her sexual passion, which might push her to reclaim her body, and thus abandon her androgynous or asexual image in favor of a more clearly defined gender construct in which she would not be confined to her biological function, but rather regain her sexual desire. The idyllic perfection of Clarens threatens to come undone by the subversive nature of passion. Indeed, the famous lake promenade in the fourth part clearly shows signs that Julie has not completely buried her sentiments for her former tutor. In this episode, Julie and St. Preux embark on a ride to the lake and a visit to other outdoor sites, which are especially meaningful to the sensitive St. Preux. Like Colardeau, Rousseau constructs a luxurious landscape to amplify the romantic tenor of this nostalgic path leading to the past, and in doing so stresses the importance of nature in pre-romantic discourse. After a turbulent storm, which perhaps functions as a resounding echo of the violence of their passion, the couple goes off on a walk for a brief interlude. The rocks, the sunny skies, the water and the abundant foliage all wrap the former lovers in a lush, timeless ambiance in which they can cherish this moment of solitude with nature. The harmony of the outdoor environment celebrates their love, based on the sentimental union of their two *"coeurs sensibles."* Interestingly, Rousseau depicts St. Preux as the character who is more closely aligned with the natural landscape. In this way, he embodies pre-romantic sensibility; his heart expands in harmony with the depths of the water, the abysses and the formidable Alps, as they stretch into the horizon. The welcome isolation of this pastoral retreat evokes past moments when he freely abandoned himself to secretly writing his love letters to Julie The jagged, rough terrain of the winding paths and rocks symbolizes the multiple obstacles the couple's love has been forced to endure over the years. Along the path, St. Preux shows Julie a rock upon which he had engraved her name; the vision of these letters reawakens his passionate feelings. He launches into a romantic speech describing his past feelings for her. Julie gazes at him longingly, takes his hand silently, but the erotically charged moment is suddenly broken by her unexpected remark, "Allons-nous-en, mon ami, me dit-elle d'une voix émue; l'air de ce lieu n'est pas bon pour moi" (IV: XVII, 502-3). For St. Preux, the romantic imagery slowly transforms the walk into to a darker, more melancholy reality. He realizes he has been momentarily reliving mere remnants of previous experiences. St. Preux's tears underline his difficulty in accepting Julie's virtuous existence, a life in which he has no place. The bleaker, more disparaging aspects of this walk adumbrate St. Preux's dark dreams of Julie.

Looking for Julie's Body: St. Preux's Ventures into the Unconscious

In letter nine of the fifth part, St. Preux writes to Claire to relate a frightening dream about Julie. The dream takes place in a hotel room where St. Preux had already stayed at the time he he was in love with Julie. Contemplating his former lover sets the tone for the ensuing hallucinatory sequence, the main part of this epistle. During the night, his sleep is agitated; he is disturbed by strange inexplicable images, resuscitating the haunting presence of the dead. At the beginning of the dream, he revisits the bed of Julie's dying mother whose final wish is that her daughter fulfill her role as wife and mother. The ghost of the mother soon fades, and to St. Preux's horror, he discovers she has transformed into Julie:

> Je voulus lever les yeux sur elle. . .je la reconnus, quoique son visage fût couvert d'un voile. Je fais un cri, je m'élance pour écarter le voile, je ne pus l'atteindre; j'étendais les bras, je me tourmentais et ne touchais rien. Ami, calme-toi, me dit-elle d'une voix faible: le voile redoutable me couvre, nulle main ne peut l'écarter. (IV:IX,603)

Once again, the veil resurfaces; but here it suggests a more abstract, murky space; leading towards the interior recesses of his consciousness. As Hoffmann observes, "l'amour est chimère, invention, rêve" (408). Moreover, woman is a creature born of man's imagination. This aspect applies to St. Preux's dreams; he articulates unconsciously the desire he cannot express in words in front of her. The barrier separating him from Julie, Wolmar, reappears in the dream, but this time his mysterious presence augments St. Preux's turmoil. Wolmar's presence is symbolically represented by the image of the veil, which conceals Julie's face from St. Preux's probing gaze, since she is the wife of another man. Her voice pierces the silence as she reminds him that no one's hand can move the veil aside. For St. Preux, her words also imply he can never regain that lost plenitude of being with her again; her body remains elusive. If the desire cannot be realistically expressed through the body, it can only be played out unconsciously through fantasy, engendered by his imaginative powers. Rousseau's use of dreams underscores the insurmountable distance between the lovers and, in this way, partially reflects one of the more salient characteristics of the missive. We recall that the love letter enables lovers to reduce the immense space between them in order to conjure up the presence of the object of one's desire. Here, the phantasmatic presence of Julie allows St. Preux to approach her, but this is an illusion, because the veil impedes him from touching her. Once again, an intertextual echo resonates, leading the reader back to the original love correspondence. As images of the medieval lovers resurface, St. Preux resembles his castrated ancestor, Abelard. The veil accentuates the fact he is powerless, a veritable impotent being who cannot overcome this opaque obstacle, hindering him from reaching his evasive object of desire. Exhausted by this troubling vision, St. Preux abruptly wakes up, falls back asleep only to dream again, "toujours ce spectacle lugubre, toujours ce même appareil de mort, toujours ce voile impénétrable échappe à mes mains, et dérobe à mes yeux l'objet expirant qu'il couvre" (V: IX, 604). The troublesome sight in his dream ominously announces the destiny of Julie, but also underlines the complexity of the veil imagery. To read this through a different lens, the veil is emblematic of Rousseau's revisionist strategy of Heloise as a spiritual philosopher. In other words, he suppresses Julie's desire consciously and unconsciously. In her spiritual conversion, he (re)invents her as the ideal representative of virtue whose ambiguous, blurred body image resists St. Preux's masculine penetrating gaze. In addition, another question arises from the dream episode. Is this impenetrable veil reversible? Can it be turned back to reveal the mysterious female body or has Rousseau, like other male rewriters who took the liberty of reworking Heloise's text, performed a textual amputation and severed Julie permanently from her discourse of desire?

Surviving the Ruins of Lost Passion: The Death of the Saintly Julie

Rousseau's final part focuses on several lengthy letters devoted to the description of Julie's fortuitous death. The circumstances preceding her demise underline her exemplary selfless nature. She becomes ill after saving one of her children from drowning, but fulfills her role as an exceptional wife and mother, representing the apotheosis of the dying martyr, who has sacrificed everything in the quest to preserve the life of her child. Confronted by death, she valiantly yields to her destiny and even assures her doctor, "c'est mon corps et non mon esprit qui souffre; et je n'ai pas peur de finir mes jours. ."(VI: XI, 692). In these final pages, Rousseau reinserts the body in the text, but it resurfaces in another way; he focuses on the representation of Julie's suffering body, and thus significantly augments the fragmentation of her body image. Previously, she was divided between the carnal Julie and the moral "new Heloise." Here, the passionate Julie is replaced by the suffering, sickly maternal figure, which enhances her saintly persona. The deteriorating body is strikingly contrasted to the devout Julie, whose will and love of God allow her to virtually rise above her pain. Her grace overcomes the physical discomfort of her weakened state. Her strength lies in her devotion to God; Julie's soul is at peace because she realizes she has fully honored her conjugal and family commitments in a loving way. Consequently, she does not fear the final judgment or the passage into eternal life. Even the activities around her described by Wolmar in his letter to St. Preux focus on her admirable courage. There are meals with the family during which she partakes in food and libations and spends time with her children, husband and Claire. But the symbolic consumption of wine can also be interpreted as a veiled celebration of death. As she moves closer to leaving her family, she will acquire the freedom to resurrect her love for St Preux. In preparation, she leaves a letter for Wolmar and encloses another within it. She informs him he can read it, but the epistle is intended for her former lover. Her husband is instructed to open her missive after her death.

As death seeps into the final missives to claim Julie, Claire prepares her body in an haunting ritual which is intratextually linked to St. Preux's dream. She shrouds Julie's face, disfigured by illness and death, in a veil that St. Preux had brought her from India:

> Je la vis rentrer un moment après, tenant un voile d'or brodé de perles que vous lui aviez apporté des Indes. puis, s'approchant du lit, elle baisa le voile, en couvrit en pleurant la face de son amie, et s'écria d'une voix éclantante: "Maudite soit l'indigne main qui jamais lèvera ce voile! maudit soit l'oeil impie qui verra ce visage défiguré!" (VI: XI, 725)

Like St. Preux's dream, the veil hides the coming of death, but it also signifies their ultimate separation, as she transcends towards the heavens and leaves St. Preux behind on earth to see to the education of her children and the friendship of her family. But in addition to obscuring the view of her face, the veil conceals another more elusive corporeal secret. While the ornate veil discloses the unspoken secret truth, its golden emboidery celebrates her celestial ascension into paradise. In death, she is legitimately liberated from the earthly constraints of respecting her marital vows. To put it another way, her inert body is also a veil, dissimulating the most scandalous enigma of all: she confesses that she still loves St. Preux, which is revealed in the beginning of her posthumous letter addressed to him: "Je me suis longtemps fait illusion. Cette illusion me fut salutaire; elle se détruit au moment que je n'en ai plus besoin. Vous m'avez cru guérie, et j'ai cru l'être" (VI: XII, 728). Although she does not consider this avowal a contradiction to her loyalty to Wolmar, she partially recovers her original desire, articulated not by body language, but through the replacement of the written word. Once again, Rousseau's Julie uses sentimental feelings as a persuasive strategy; she hopes that St. Preux will conserve their love in the material world through the substitution of her body double, Claire: "Songez qu'il vous reste une autre Julie, et n'oubliez pas ce que vous lui devez. Chacun de vous va perdre la moitié de sa vie, unisez-vous pour conservez l'autre" (VI: XII, 729). These words serve as a preface for Julie's last written speech. It is her wish that St. Preux console her family and remain intimately associated with the occupants of Clarens. Her final words are strongly grounded in the language of amorous desire:

> Adieu, adieu, mon doux ami. . Hélas! j'achève de vivre comme j'ai commencé. J'en dis trop peut-être en ce moment où le coeur ne déguise plus rien[...] Mais mon âme existerait-elle sans toi? sans toi quelle félicité goûterais-je? Non, je ne te quitte pas, je vais t'attendre. La vertu qui nous sépara sur la terre nous unira dans le séjour éternel. Je meurs dans cette douce attente; trop heureuse d'acheter au prix de ma vie le droit de t'aimer toujours sans crime, et de te le dire encore une fois! (VI: XII, 731)

Julie reaffims her previous faithful commitment of her conjugal role, but her body, as a veil, reveals the other story, one that curiously introduces a resounding intertextual echo of Pope's and Colardeau's versions. Rousseau interpolates the familiar Ovidian trope of the tormented woman in love. Her monologic "plainte" consists of several questions, which emphasize the turbulence and instability of her emotions; it as if her body rises from the dead to seize the manipulation of this final diatribe, drenched with the pathos of this final parting. Like Pope's and

Colardeau's pre-romantic revisions of Heloise, Julie finds solace in waiting to rejoin her beloved in eternity so that she can freely proclaim her love to him. Differing from the poetic imitators, Rousseau tempers the hysterical, and, at times, fantastic previous revisions of Heloise with another intertextual fragment. His Julie recalls the strength of the rational, medieval Heloise who valiantly confronted separation from her beloved until their reunion after death. Moreover, her letter emphasizes her inability to forget St. Preux, just as Heloise could never extinguish her passion for Abelard. Rousseau also mimics the medieval conclusion more than the contemporary versions; he does not perpetuate one of the most famous, romantic eighteenth-century fantasies of the legendary couple. In other words, his Julie does not hope to be buried with St. Preux in the same tomb; a popular sentimenal fantasy in other Heloise and Abelard imitations of the period. In this secret letter, Rousseau allows the reader to catch a glimpse of her desiring body that had faded from the narrative after her marriage. The reappearance of her dying body signifies a partial restoration of her original discourse of passion. But this posthumous letter has other authorial implications in Rousseau's (re)invention of this "new Heloise," which is directly related to the theme of death.

The Politics of Dying

The mysterious and fascinating posthumous letter ostensibly contradicts Rousseau's virtuous (re)invention of Julie. Although she embodies the ideal of fidelity and devotion to Wolmar until the very end, the last letter reverses her faith in spiritual love. Her exceptional moral qualities as a quintessential symbol of moral perfection appear undermined in this final confessional letter by the recovery of desire. Readers might be tempted to simply conclude that utopian spirituality, devoid of passion, ultimately fails because she cannot completely convert her love for St. Preux. Related to this question, Trouille maintains that

Rousseau does not advocate the effacement of sexuality or erotic pulsions.[10] In fact, Julie's final confession ostensibly shows that the suppression of desire is impossible. To interpret this on a textual level, Rousseau appears to destabilize her indomitable virtue, whereby Julie, albeit susceptible to temptation, managed to suppress her feelings for St. Preux, fortified by her love of God and devotion to Wolmar. The final letter affirms the unraveling of Rousseau's previous stance that desire can be eradicated by virtue, because Julie's body returns to invade the narrative, infusing it with the undeniable presence of erotic desire. So what is Rousseau really saying about desire and sexual politics? His ideology on this subject is at times contradictory and complex, but it is enlightening to look at some of the key ideas relevant to Julie. As Joel Schwartz puts it, Rousseau stresses the political nature of sexuality (6-9). According to Schwartz's reading of Rousseau, sexuality creates danger because it fosters dependence and thus is inevitably associated with power and domination. Essentially, sexual relationships are characterized by discontent and disillusion. The most effective strategy in avoiding the trap of dependence is to relegate sexual encounters to the confines of one's imagination. Another aspect of Rousseau's ideology on sexuality is that he believed man was better off as asexual because he could successfully eschew codependence and ultimate unhappiness (153). This is illuminating because it provides further insight into understanding Julie's conversion and embrace of her marriage, devoid of passion. As an ideal wife, she transforms her sexual pulsions into a purely biological function. Rousseau (re)invents Julie as an asexual heroine whose faith in God enables her to privilege her soul over her carnal desire, but her final confession, reinserting feminine amorous passion into the text, dismantles Rousseau's

[10] Trouille explores the topic of desire, femininity and the soul on page 52. According to her interpretation, Julie and St. Preux were victims of their own sexual pulsions.

image of this exceptional "womanly" paradigm of virtue. But let's look at this issue in the context of the novel. Is Rousseau suggesting through his fictional character that if one cannot ultimately succeed in leading an asexual existence or eliminating corporeal desire, perhaps the only escape from desire is death? It is precisely the fact that he proclaims her dead that merits further consideration.

As noted, Rousseau's ambiguous reconcilation of "disorderly" feminine passion raises many questions pertaining to the image of the female body in his work. Borrowing from other imitators of Heloise, Rousseau writes the novel from a feminocentric position: the majority of the letters are written from Julie's or Claire's perspective. Although the novel bears little resemblance to the medieval love story, Rousseau's authorial strategy in (re)touching the narrative shows a familiar strategy shared by other revisionists. As a philosopher, he can more readily propose a moral lesson intended for the "fairer sex," using Julie as a "porte-parole," especially since letter novels had particular appeal to the female public who relished sentimental stories. In essence, he participates in what other male rewriters of the medieval love letters practiced long before he wrote his fictional version. By writing an epistolary novel, generally told from a feminine perspective, he, too, is partially guilty of appropriating the feminine. He even deftly imitates a "woman's" emotions by creating a simulacrum of her writing style. Although he portrays Julie as a brilliant, well-educated woman, who often espouses philosophical ideas on moral virtue, Rousseau reverts to common stereotypical, stylistic conceptions of female epistolary writing. His Julie, too, pours her emotions and tears onto paper, writes some disorganized missives and composes confessional letters. Like the seventeenth-century editors, he locks this new Heloise into the enclosed space of the symbolic confessional and forces her to disclose her past sexual secrets. Her unexpected avowal of love points to

Rousseau's participation in the widespread oppression of women. Like his peers, he reaffirms his superior position as a male (re)writer of Heloise. But to place this within the context of the text, perhaps he executes his authorial power by issuing a warning to women through his fictional character's destiny: illicit desire is inherently subversive and conflicts with patriarchal authority, which is intolerable and can ultimately lead to death. As Miller observes:

> Death is the highest calling of the fictional woman; marriage and a glimpse of the "happily ever," the tepid alternative—a traveled but less captivating route. In both cases, however, the disruptive potential of female sexuality is neutralized, removed from general circulation (152).[11]

Rousseau intervenes in the text to push Julie's passionate discourse, articulated through the last breaths of her weakened body, out of the text. It is a plausible to assume that he subscribes to Miller's idea of "neutralization" by performing the last textual rites of her dying body. Julie's soul will live on, and thus elevate their love to virtue, but here Rousseau creates his own original contribution to the legend. The lovers will never be rejoined, while other Enlightenment versions include a sentimental, tearful reunion in the hereafter, a fictional aspect that was very well received by readers. In permanently squelching Julie's desire through the ceremony of death, Rousseau repairs the balance or the correct polarization of the gendered sex roles of his times. According to Miller, the grammar of the eighteenth century stipulated that woman was the object of desire and man the subject. The death of the female heroine eliminated the subversive danger of uncontrollable passion, a breach of her naturally inferior sex role, and killing her thus eradicates any possible threat to the hegemonic structure of the society. But a

[11] Nancy Miller looks at the destiny of the eighteenth-century heroine from a broad perspective concerning such questions as illicit sex, virtue and marriage. See " The Exquisite Cadavers," *French Dressing: Women, Men and Ancien Régime Fiction* (New York & London: Routledge, 1995): 147-159.

closer look at the conclusion of the novel raises yet another contradiction. The death of Julie unexpectedly turns against Rousseau's atttempt at taming her pulsions; his dream of the androgyne's asexual nature falls apart. His fictional heroine appears to subvert her inventor's utopian vision by recovering her own voice, which might allow her to construct a new space to tell her "real" love story. As noted previously, she looks forward to telling him in her own voice that she loves him. In heaven, she will carve out another space, located in the uncharted territory of the beyond. In this other imaginative dimension where Julie awaits the return of St. Preux, she raises her voice to chant the Ovidian "plainte"of separation and passion, which travels back through time to reweave her poetics of lamentation with the threads of the other Heloises, who stand united with their original medieval predecessor. Together, this "new Heloise" and the medieval nun stage a revolt against those who wish to eradicate their corporeal desire, as demonstrated by Abelard and Rousseau. Perhaps they will see to it that fragments of the original discourse of feminine desire are retrieved and reconstructed by another modern sister, who will be textually resurrected by other female (re)writers' pen to tell a more "real" story.

9.

Learned Heloise Regained

Louise de Keralio's Heloise

At the close of the eighteenth century, Louise de Keralio's version of Heloise's letters appeared. Like Grenaille, Keralio wrote an anthology of famous works, but her text was dedicated to her fellow, female compatriots who deserved to be recognized, and whose remarkable writing talent, according to her, had been overlooked as a result of the sexual difference stereotype that continues to discriminate against women authors even now. In 1786, Keralio published her *Collection des meilleurs ouvrages françois composés par des femmes,* which was intended to pay homage to women writers. This anthology included a translation of Heloise and Abelard's love correspondence, one that deviated from the preeminent suffering, weak, representation of Heloise. In striking contrast to other Enlightenment male re-writers of Heloise's story, Keralio's Heloise also regains her medieval erudite persona, and, in part, reflects some egalitarian ideals as she is portrayed as Abelard's intellectual equal. During the Enlightenment, writers like Laclos were early supporters of women, and thus, indirectly, contributed to the reversal of Pope's sentimental portrayal of Heloise as a delirious woman. In reaction to the general misconception of women as irrational beings, Laclos invited women to reclaim their power, and to stoically wage the battle of the sexes to destroy masculine enslavement once and for all. But to go back to Keralio, it is impossible to speculate on her philosophical position on women since very little is known about her. As Lynn Hunt has pointed out, Keralio was a militant participant in the French Revolution, and is said to have written subversive propaganda against Marie-Antoinette (as many did during this time of great turbulence and instability in France).[1] Like other women writers before her (and especially in the seventeenth century), Keralio had supposedly written other works that were later attributed to Louis-Marie Prudhomme, and so, once again, a female signature had become the legal property of a man. Interestingly, Keralio's anthology of women's works did bear her signature in and of her own right. A paradoxical, revolutionary spirit thus permeates her work as she reverses the imitative trend and, concerning the correspondence, looks back to the Middle Ages to construct her revision of Heloise. For the first time since the original narrative, a version is produced that restores the intellectual dimension of Heloise; in turn, this introduces a new direction in the legend that departs radically from Bayle's, Pope's and Colardeau's renditions: Heloise is no longer a hysterical woman, but a discerning thinker who welcomes the challenge to confront her husband openly as his intellectual equal.

Heloise Canonized

Keralio's text is set off by several paratexts that reiterate the anthologist's intention to recognize works that were usually passed over in an age that privileged textual productions by men. By choosing to include Heloise's letters, Keralio canonizes her and thus revises a literary history that tended to deal mainly with masculine literary productions. Keralio's *Collection* is

[1] Lynn Hunt explores Louise de Keralio's involvement with subversive writings on key political figures in her essay, "The Many Bodies of Marie Antoinette: Political Pornography and the Problem of the Feminine in the French Revolution," *Eroticism and the Body Politic*, ed. Lynn Hunt (Baltimore & London, John Hopkins UP, 1991) 115-130.

diverse and includes plays, poetry, letters, and prose selections. In the first preface, Keralio refers to Heloise as the most famous woman of her time, a point that is developed later in an abbreviated version of the lovers' story. The preface is followed by an abridged history of twelfth-century literature, and this, in turn, provides the organizational frame for Keralio's sub-version of the *Historia*, which, quite interestingly, she renames *La Vie d'Héloïse*. In creating this additional paratext, Keralio invents a new focus as other versions had historically only reworked Abelard's *Historia*. This is the most significant paratext that pertains to Heloise and Abelard specifically. The other introductory texts were most likely intended to provide the reader with a more general knowledge of French literature, but, in *La Vie d'Héloïse*, the reader's attention is immediately drawn to the fact that Heloise was not just a body; she was reputed not only for her beauty and, but most importantly, for her remarkable, rare intellect. As Keralio highlights the details of the tragic story (as previously seen in various revisions of Abelard's *Historia*), she inserts additional information that elaborates on the epitaph inscribed on the lovers' grave. She critiques the prevalent fable regarding Abelard supposedly reaching out to receive Heloise into their common grave. Interestingly, Keralio is following biographical data with an attack on Heloise's imitators that not only provides proof that Keralio was familiar with other versions of the text, but also shows her intent to judge these violators who had taken too much liberty in representing Heloise as a hysterical woman. Specifically, Keralio attacks Bayle's licentious account of the couple's lives, as well as an edition by Dom Gervaise that mocked the melodramatic, sentimental Heloise. Keralio also includes a few remarks pertaining to Astrolabe, Heloise and Abelard's child, who, up until that time, had never been mentioned in other versions (her point being to show that he lived and was well educated). Included in the *Vie d'Héloïse* is a fragment from a letter that Heloise may have written to Astrolabe that stressed the importance of his education and the formation of his mind as an independent thinker. Keralio then reconsiders the problematic portrayal of the lovers' legend that had been solely predicated on their tragedy. She suggests that a significant part of their story had become distorted. What has been forgotten, according to her, is that the couple was above all learned and that Heloise was a genius, worthy of recognition and fame in her own right. In other words, the truth had yet to be told in the editions that had enjoyed such considerable success in the earlier part of the Enlightenment. Keralio cites several prominent publications of the love correspondence. She attacks male revisions of Heloise, in particular, Dom Gervaise's edition for its "romanesque" quality, but praises Bussy's translation as the best one ever written. In fact, Keralio uses Bussy's translation as a primary source and the similarity is striking in her own "translation." One notices, for example, that polyphonic dialogue is reintegrated into the text, and, in sharp contrast to Pope's and Colardeau's versions, Abelard recovers his voice after a prolonged absence. The seventeenth-century imitators of Bussy were indeed the last ones to use epistolary exchange, which had been abandoned by the sentimental male rewriters in the early part of the eighteenth century. But Keralio does not simply reproduce Bussy's version, she clearly places Heloise at the center of the exchange as she regains her voice and becomes the leader of the dialogue. Her mind is therefore restored, showing her as an astute thinker, a point to which I will now turn.

Letter 1: Reviving the Rational Heloise

Keralio's Heloise begins her letter as Heloise regained in the medieval text. The reader quickly notices the restoration of the references to Seneca and other philosophers that the medieval Heloise had included in her first epistle to Abelard. Keralio combines the learned aspects of Heloise's brilliant mind with her "Ovidian" struggle with solitude and ongoing battle with passion. The famous argument against the conjugal state reappears in this version, and it is amplified to include a strong socio-political condemnation of the material aspects of wealth versus pure love, devoid of economic gain. Once again, Heloise reiterates several times that Abelard's debt is to write to her as her husband and spiritual director. Keralio develops and augments the original accusation that Heloise only followed Abelard's orders when she took her vows. Her Heloise goes even as far as saying that she buried herself alive in the cloister, and that, instead of receiving spiritual sustenance from God, she was only kept alive by her pain, tears and worries. The false piety of her charade as a nun is enriched and may indicate a strategy on her part to attract Abelard's attention so that he will answer her. Keralio's Heloise is boldly rebellious; she takes Abelard to task and reproaches herself openly for allowing herself to become the slave of a man, completely devoted to her husband's orders. Interestingly, there are also instances in which she becomes the spokesperson for her gender as a whole. For Keralio's Heloise, women become victims of men's inconstance, which ultimately leads to abandon, and it is women who should give lessons of fidelity to men. Although the letter remains close to the medieval epistle, Keralio appears to fill in the blanks, and thus enhance what Heloise had originally endeavored to articulate in writing, until her voice was silenced by her body's suffering. At the same time, her speech is empowered by a well-developed intellect that concisely organizes her Ovidian "plainte" in order to underline the point that Abelard was the sole cause of her religious confinement, and therefore responsible for her unhappiness. This point is transmitted in her private confession, and the fact that Keralio restores intimate avowal is also a strengthening device: Heloise now exercises more control over her own language, and more effectively challenges Abelard on his neglect of her and her nuns' welfare.

She reproaches her husband severely for all that he has done to subject her to turmoil and conflict. As Keralio concludes the first letter, certain Latin expressions resurface, and the reader can glimpse more of the passionate yet rational argumentation of the medieval prototype. Although, ironically, Heloise had previously stated that she was virtually buried alive in the Paraclete, she is in a way resurrected. Keralio's more truthful representation of her divided heart allows her to recover her voice as well as her pen. As Laclos might have said, she regains the strength to challenge the oppressive system of patriarchal hegemony. Keralio's Heloise seems to declare the call to arms for other women to reclaim power and speak in their own voice without masculine intervention.

Letter 2: Abelard as a "Woman in Love"

Keralio begins Abelard's response in a way that is very similar to the medieval text, but after several lines it becomes apparent that she also translates closer to Bussy's sentimental revision of Abelard than to the original, austere, religious portrayal reflected in the Latin narrative. Abelard openly admits that he adores Heloise, (je vous adore avec plus d'ardeur que je n'ai jamais fait, II, 389),[2] and declares that he wishes to confide in her. At this point, the departure from the medieval text is striking. As Miller has shown, it was not uncommon for the sentimental hero in Enlightenment novels to display tears and suffering as women had previously done in medieval and seventeenth-century romances. In fact, men who cried profusely were believed to be exhibiting "authentic" passion as well as emotional sincerity. This recasting of Abelard as a sensitive lover, which was most likely borrowed from Bussy's innovative (re)invention of Abelard's persona, is a means to reconstruct the polyphonic exchange, which is repaired by the fusion of

[2] All of the quotes are taken from Louise de Keralio, *Collection des meilleurs ouvrages françois composés par des femmes I* (Paris: Lagrange, 1786).

tears. After a long absence, the couple is reunited through the outpouring of tears which bridges the chasm between them. Unlike her medieval predecessor, Keralio's Heloise at least has proof that Abelard loved her from his genuine display of suffering. But other consequences of this (re)creation of Abelard cannot be overlooked. Like her male predecessors, Keralio could be judged guilty of tampering with the text as we are, once again, confronted with a fictional account. The medieval Abelard would never have admitted his love, since he attempted to persuade Heloise to accept her role as the Bride of Christ, thus severing the personal bond that they once shared as lovers. In sharp contrast, Keralio's Abelard pursues a personal confession to his wife and professes his weakness and spiritual turmoil. Here, Keralio is ostensibly practicing reverse ventriloquism, just like the male imitators before her when they inserted words into Heloise's discourse to serve their own purposes. Keralio alters Abelard's persona as he steps into drag to impersonate Heloise. Abelard engages in a performative form of mimetic discourse, borrowing Heloise's language to articulate his passion. Keralio subverts the gender roles in exploring Abelard's "effeminate" identity as a eunuch. She enters his mutilated virility. The fact that he was already partially "effeminate" as a result of the castration allows her to redefine the gender roles. As Judith Butler puts it, gender can be a performative, fluid act that is comparable to travesty. Like a transvestite on stage, Keralio creates the artifice of Abelard in drag; he takes on the stereotypical role of a tormented "woman" in love. As Butler posited, gender can be innovative and unstable, which allows the eunuch to play out other roles:

> Gender is not passively scripted on the body, and neither is it determined by nature, language, the symbolic, or the overwhelming his-

> tory of patriarchy. Gender is what is put on, invariably, under constraint, daily and incessantly, with anxiety and pleasure. (252)[3]

This "effeminate" representation of Abelard also reinforces the private exchange of confidence, which dominates the exchange between the lovers. The couple appears to speak the same language when they engage in amorous discourse, and are therefore recast as equal partners torn between their faith and passion. Abelard speaks in a spontaneous, uncensored style directly from the heart. Like Pope, Keralio grafts Heloise's words onto Abelard's language, which highlights the mimetic quality of the exchange. Here, Keralio turns the weapon of gender against Abelard. He is made to imitate Heloise and is thus rewritten in her image, which, in turn, subverts the traditional portrayal of his persona. It is Abelard who says that Heloise is the obstacle between him and God, and admits repeatedly that his love of God is weak, a point previously associated with Heloise's spiritual crisis in other eighteenth-century sentimental versions.

In closing this second letter, Keralio does, however, suddenly waver and reverts to the original portrayal of Abelard, as he abruptly asks Heloise to concentrate on their salvation, and begs her not to write to him anymore. And yet, concluding the letter with a personal critique, Keralio adds that Heloise's love was more "vrai" than that of Abelard, who had other great passions, and she points to ambition as a factor in his weakened love.

Letters 3 and 4: Looking Backwards

Keralio concludes her translation with the final two letters, and they are clearly based on the medieval story. She now relies more on the traditional representation of Heloise and differs

[3] Judith Butler, "Performative Acts and Gender Constitution: An Essay in Phenomenology and Feminist Theory," *Performing Feminisms*, ed. Ellen Case. (Baltimore & London: John Hopkins UP, 1990): 252.

markedly from the defiant (re)vision she had offered in the previous letters. Suddenly, Heloise is no longer depicted as Abelard's equal as she reverts to the traditional self-reproach for causing Abelard's amputation. Here, Heloise confides in him that she was not truly devoted to God's service, and that she feels like she is buried alive in this place of penitence. Keralio seems to follow Bussy's version as well, since Heloise insists on her inability to find "repos" at the Paraclete. She does not hope to receive the crown of glory in the kingdom of God, but she only hopes to escape danger. Again, this conclusion is also very similar to Bussy's Heloise who openly admitted that her divided heart was the obstacle that prevented her from entering heaven. Abelard's reply to her admission of eternal love is to order her not to write to him anymore, but he succumbs to weakness and answers her amorously by writing directly from his heart. The deviation from the medieval text is strikingly evident as the original Abelard would never have admitted such internal struggle. As pointed out earlier, Keralio's lovers are clearly speaking the same language, as Abelard admits that his heart is still troubled, thus echoing Heloise's emotional confession. Like a woman in love, he, too, is torn between attachment to her and his commitment to the Church. Once again, Keralio alters Abelard's stereotypical gender by having him steal Heloise's passionate expressions; he speaks in a voice that closely resembles his wife's. Mirroring Heloise, he admits to playing out a charade; while his monks think that he is tranquil in his faith, he, too, is only dissimulating the real object of his devotion. Interestingly, Keralio amplifies the use of narrative travesty by reworking a portion of Heloise's text that had been reversed in the "Precious" versions. This time it is Abelard who is moved by the writing on the page, the letters traced by Heloise's hand, whereas, in Bussy's version, it was the opposite. Here, the sensuality of Heloise's hand caressing the page is articulated to Abelard and causes him to reflect on his own suffering. But his confession is brief, and, once again, Keralio unexpectedly reverts to the more traditional image of Abelard, as the rest of the letter concerns their salvation. Abelard asks Heloise to replace the image of him as a lover with that of a penitent so that they can be reunited in their tears, but this time in a spiritual way that anticipates the glorious reunion in God's kingdom. In the end, Heloise follows his will. The two closing letters thus reveal a transformation in the text: oddly the two previous ones were more erudite and challenging in their tone; the last one returns to a more sentimental representation of Heloise.

Keralio had started out with reconstructing the image of Heloise as learned and strong willed, but in the end she loses ground: Heloise succumbs to Abelard's will, and agrees to forget him as her lover. Keralio succeeds nonetheless in dismantling the previous revision of Heloise as raving and irrational that Pope and Colardeau had created before her. But in many ways, she uses exactly the same method; only the object is different since, like these male authors, she now takes the liberty of radically modifying Abelard's persona. Interestingly, one notes that Keralio used a pseudonym in order to control the publication of her own works. During the Revolution, she allegedly was involved in a clandestine publishing company with the Parisian publisher Lagrange, a venture which was very lucrative for a long period of time. Later, Keralio changed her name to Keralio-Robert (the name of her husband) in order to control the legal rights of her texts, since a woman's husband was the one who had control over his wife's literary productions. As Carla Hesse pointed out, at that time, male signatures dominated women's access to all literary domains.[4] So women appropriated men's signatures to try to gain entry into areas

[4] Carla Hesse looks at Keralio's involvement with the publishing business in her article, "Louise-Félicité de Kéralio-Robert," *Writers of the French Enlightenment* 1.313 (2005): 262-6.

normally closed off to them. Hesse suggests that Keralio uses a pseudonym to create a multitude of identities. But in masking her presence as a woman writer, she also takes advantage of this empowering strategy to do what others had done before her. Masquerading as a man, she practices a dual form of pseudo-androcentrism, when this time, she alters Abelard's persona. In many ways, this woman writer who goes under cover with a masculine name evens the score: to the sentimental (re)vision of Heloise she opposes an equally sentimental (re)vision of Abelard as a suffering lover. Furthermore, she repairs Heloise for the first time since the medieval period. In her modest and sometimes paradoxical way, Keralio sets a precedent for another woman who also used a masculine signature: Marc de Montifaud.

Lifting off the Veils-Uncovering the Body

The next text I will consider here is Marc de Montifaud's prose work, a text entitled *L'Abbesse du paraclet: histoire galante d'Héloïse et d'Abailard* published around 1890. Before looking at this text, it is important to clarify that Montifaud did indeed also write a version of the love letters, but since her translation strongly resembles Bussy's, it is more revealing to study her more noteworthy contribution which appears in her prose work. Even though it is not written in epistolary form, it is worth exploring. Interestingly, the text reads not only as a historical and erotic novel, but also as an open critique, as Montifaud cites passages loosely based on the original story. Her critical intentions are made clear in the paratexts. Although little is known about her background, the first paratext provides the reader with details that lead up to her own condemnation and exile from her native Belgium as a result of controversial writings that were also supposedly pornographic and licentious. Montifaud was also highly critical of the church, and in this text one can clearly identify many instances of blatant anti-clericalism. She offers some sketchy details about her artistic plight in Belgium, and then turns to the question of writing, specifically, on the problems of character representation in novels. As a pre-modern author, Montifaud considered that the literary creation should be considered as a separate entity from the author. She compares the creation of characters to the task of an artist; they both paint the nature of their subjects, which should be an independent experience, freed from societal criticism. On this point, Montifaud establishes her position against censorship by moralists, one of the repressive forces that infringed on the creativity and freedom of the artist:

> La mission du peintre est de la peindre, non de la corriger. Il n'est pas chargé de la mettre sur les rangs pour le prix Montyon, mais de lui assigner sa vraie place, de marquer sa vraie ressemblance dans l'innombrable variété des types qui composent l'humanité.[5] (20-21, préface)

After affirming that authors should not succumb to what moralists or the Church wanted artists to convey, she offers a preface that deals more directly with Heloise and Abelard. Like Keralio who had criticized Bayle and Pope, Montifaud openly attacks Rousseau for not depicting the "vraie" nature of the lovers. His novel, she claims, had no carnal passion, which was "invraisemblable," totally implausible since "Eloys" was only devoted to her husband as a lover.

> L'Héloïse de Rousseau ne porte en elle aucun des traits de feu de la véritable Eloys; l'amour y est abdiqué dans la dévotion; chaque élan de son coeur envers Saint-Preux est traversé d'une aspiration vers le ciel. (3)

Here, Montifaud criticizes the devotional aspect of Rousseau's revision of Heloise, as, for her, there was never any question of a divided heart. Rousseau misread Heloise and, once again, fell into the trap of creating her as a heroine instead of analyzing

[5] All of the citations are from Marc de Montifaud, *L'Abbesse du Paraclet: Histoire galante d'Héloïse et d'Abailard* (Paris: 1888).

her historical reality. The paratext then turns to the question of restoring the characters as lovers. Interestingly, Montifaud develops what Keralio had initially begun doing a century before: Abelard is represented more as a lover than as a scholar and theologian. In fact, Montifaud repairs the erotic narrative, strongly analogue to the medieval, even if it is fictionally enhanced and no longer preserves the pact of private correspondence between the couple. The most astonishing aspect of this nineteenth-century version is the reversal of the theme of love and devotion. Both Heloise and Abelard speak the same amorous language, as seen in parts of Keralio's translation, but they also totally leave aside questions of faith. Most strikingly, their passion is placed at the nexus of the text. In so doing, Montifaud subverts the medieval portrayal of the couple: Heloise and Abelard no longer struggle to conceal their love; on the contrary, they overtly flaunt their carnal desire for each other and try in vain to remember that they are now sworn to the Church. The veils are lifted; Montifaud tells it as it might have been told if Heloise's letters had not suffered alteration in the hands of male authors, and she also creates a discourse of desire for Abelard himself, a story that he could have told in his letters, and that he did allude to as he evoked reading romantic poetry with Heloise—in medieval times—during their tutoring sessions. Montifaud does not therefore totally "invent" the role of Abelard as a lover. Like Keralio, she bases the language she makes him use on his documented love songs and renowned prowess as a composer of verse. She grounds her text on some partial truth and then offers words that could recreate what the medieval Abelard had originally expressed in song to his beloved. For the first time, however, the body surfaces quite visibly in this text and it tells a story of erotically charged passion. Montifaud does not concentrate on one body; bodies are equally recovered and covered. It is, however, important to note the fragmentation of the original text. Epistolary dialogue is written out, and Montifaud inserts excerpts that have been retouched to capture what she believed to be the "vraie" nature of the lovers. While this radical reconstruction of the text takes great liberties in altering the original narrative, it also offers a new perspective based on the harmonious equality of the two not only as intellectuals (as Keralio had done before her), but as willing participants in a reenactment of erotic play that, as this version illustrates, continued well after the two lovers' confinement and separation.

Although a significant part of this sensual narrative is based on fiction, grounded in the cult of the medieval lovers, some of the themes developed are based on actual documents revealing that Montifaud had conducted serious and elaborate research into the history and fictional texts, a research on Heloise and Abelard that spanned several centuries. She surpasses Keralio in that she is not only familiar with the medieval text, but she also mentions chronicles as well as numerous seventeenth- and eighteenth-century imitations published in France and abroad. The text is placed into a contemporary context with frequent and detailed references to Lenoir, the well-known curator. Montifaud was obviously acquainted with the controversy that raged over the lovers' remains, and she includes information on Alexandre Lenoir's unorthodox business practices with their bones. Montifaud even warns her readers that the remains are probably not to be found in the tomb erected at Père-Lachaise. But her real contribution is to be found in revision of the couple as lovers, and a reversal of the theme of dissimulation that privileges erotic desire and the body over monastic duty.

Rewriting the Love Confession

Montifaud's lengthy narrative contains many chapters with digressions that are both critical and scholarly. She furnishes the readers with details that go back to the Latin text, Jean de Meun's translation, chronicles written in the Renaissance as well as seventeenth- and eighteenth-century versions of the correspondence. The format is dramatically altered as the epistolary form of the narrative is not preserved. Montifaud begins by modifying Abelard's *Historia,* which is replaced by a two-chapter sequence devoted to events in Heloise's life, but she also places the emphasis on the seductive tenor of the two lovers' courtship and on their passion after their separation. The style is highly descriptive, and the reader is supplied with colorful descriptions of Fulbert's house that include an elaborate account of the room where the amorous encounters took place. Interestingly, Heloise is represented as a young, attractive woman with long hair, garbed in elegant attire, and, while Abailard is wearing monastic clothes, they appear to disguise his true essence :

> Près d'elle, un homme dans la force de l'âge laisse entrevoir sous la longue robe de clerc des membres vigoureux, une stature majestueuse. Il tient en ses mains la rote sur laquelle il promène un archet à fil de métal et dont il tire des sons qui accompagnent sa voix.(43)

Here, Montifaud sets the tone for her revision of Abelard; his lifted robes offer no veiling of his bold sensuality. This recasting of his persona as a lover is established from the very beginning, and, in contrast to other versions, it is respected throughout the text. Montifaud ostensibly demystifies the myth that Abelard lost his sexual allure after his mutilation. She even inserts episodes never seen before, in which the two lovers supposedly meet at the Paraclete, after their separation, in a remote building where, if only for a brief moment, they are reunited. This incident also reveals the extent of Montifaud's extensive research, as it was a known fact that the Paraclete's land did contain an area where a series of small buildings were constructed. In addition, Montifaud boldly establishes the plausibility of her representation in providing the reader with parallel examples and comparisons with other monastic figures: she shows that religious men other than the medieval lovers suffered temptation. In fact, she bases the internal structure of her version on a balanced system of equality; Abailard's lusty monks are comparable to Eloys's licentious nuns. Amplifying Alluis's prose narrative, Montifaud builds up the debauchery plot in a third chapter in which the sexual adventures of the nuns are described; passages are invented in which Eloys's sisters, prior to their relocation at the Paraclete, supposedly entertained men in confessionals, freely partaking in libations and festivities with male visitors disguised as priests. (Contrary to other versions, Montifaud fills in the details for the originally sketchy story of the sins of Eloys's sisters, aspects which only allude to scandalous behavior at the cloister). Once again, Montifaud amplifies what Alluis had invented in his prose account; she places amorous intrigue at the locus of monastic life, and thus, at the same time, she provokes the Church by shattering the stereotype of devote clerical figures. Her highly sexual clerics radically dismantle the expected non-sexual image of religious men and women, and once again the anti-clerical tenor of the text surfaces. The overt sexual revision of these religious nuns and monks illustrates the physical stress on the body. As in Alluis's fictional account, Montifaud also extrapolates on the anecdote about a nun who ran off with her lover and relinquished her vows, clearly privileging the body over spiritual life, and she suggests that Abailard and Eloys, during their careers as administrators, were constantly confronted with indecency and prurient behavior in their retreats.

Resurrecting Desire

While Montifaud invented reciprocal passion between the unhappy lovers, she maintained this theme in reworking some of the more famous aspects of Pope's and Colardeau's sentimental versions. But while Pope and Colardeau had favored a paradoxical form of "monologic" dialogue, Montifaud departs from their texts by restoring Abailard's textual presence. One of the most striking examples of this revision is the portrayal of Eloys's nocturnal vision of her reunion with Abailard. Montifaud first imitates Pope as her tortured Eloys lays waiting for her lover in her bed; her sheets are described as being on fire:

> En lisant les description des fameuses nuits du Paraclet, on dirait que ses draps se collèrent à ses flancs comme une tunique de feu, comme une robe de Déjamire qui l'enfiévrait. (99)

Not only is the bed blazing with desire, but Eloys's prayers are drenched in tears of unfulfilled desire: "je me retrouve noyée dans une mer de passions ardentes" (151). After giving several examples of Eloys's relentless passion, Montifaud criticizes Pope's and Colardeau's depiction of Heloise as a penitent, and she openly challenges them to recognize that Eloys was not a devoted abbess, but frenetically "ivre de passion" until her death. Pope's and Colardeau's representation of Heloise is questioned by the intentional use of "langueurs monastiques," an expression borrowed from Colardeau's poem. But Montifaud goes even further. Not only does she intervene in the text to remind the readers that monks and nuns were reputed to have more desire than lay people, but as she embellishes the theme of imagination as seen in Colardeau's and Pope's texts, she subverts their stereotypic representation predicated on sexual difference. In so doing, she adds a new dimension to the conception of imagination, one that deviates from previous male authors. Her Eloys is not hysterical, but, as noted in the paratext, she is depicted as a voluptuous thinker; therefore her sexual imagination is positive and can be read as a strong revalorisation of women in general. Montifaud stresses the imaginative power of a woman in love, but without any hint of irrational, unstable behavior previously observed in the eighteenth-century sentimental versions:

> Sous la force du désir la femme saura concevoir le simulacre de tous les actes charnels de l'amour, sa couche ne sera plus solitaire, ses

> membres palpitants trouveront qui étreindre, et la nuit l'enveloppera d'un réseau voluptueux. (101)

It is during the solitude of the night that Montifaud's Eloys finds sanctuary and can at last play out her sexual fantasy, liberated from the diurnal masquerade as a devout nun. As was also shown in Bussy's version, it is in her dreams that Eloys loses herself in the "other" amorous scene where she imagines seeing Abailard and talking to him. Montifaud rewrites her as a seducer who, in an invented episode, succeeds in luring Abailard to visit her at the Paraclete. But here the similarity with Bussy's text ends abruptly, or rather takes on new dimensions. As Montifaud amplifies Heloise's power of imagination as well as the bond that linked the couple together, she reverses the image of Abelard as an impotent eunuch, a recurrent feature since the Middle Ages. In this version, Abailard has not lost his sexual allure as a lover; on the contrary he is credited with creativity and great inventive acumen; "il est un fait que l'on doit se rappeler, c'est que'Abailard avait été très fertile en inventions amoureuses" (106). Here, Montifaud plays on the myth that eunuchs were completely powerless, which also may point to the extent of her research. In fact, many eunuchs were able to perform quite well and above all were especially attractive to women, as they were reputed to be able to provide them with great physical pleasure even if amorous play deviated from the more traditional positioning of the body during intimate encounters. But to go back to the lines cited above, while Montifaud bases this rewriting on some fact (Abelard was renowned as a brilliant composer of love songs), she further embellishes the story:

> On a fait d'Abailard un infortuné qui ne possédait plus rien pour aimer; mais quoi, se trouvait-il paralytique, sourd, aveugle ou muet? Lui était-il impossible de jouir d'Eloys avec les autres sens qui lui restaient? Il pouvait du moins caresser ces formes charmantes; blanche charnure des membres, gorge ferme "comme des pommes de coings. » (103)

Montifaud amplifies the erotic narrative as she also suggests that with Eloys he abandoned himself to passionate kisses and ardent caresses. The sensuality of the mouth and the hands is privileged as an additional technique for recovering the body. In showing that Abailard can attain "jouissance," Montifaud inserts here what no other rewriter of the correspondence had invented before her. Not only does she restore Abelard's libido, she shows that castration, or the power of the Church, did not succeed in crushing him in the flesh. Moreover, as an equal partner in love, he mirrors the sensuality of Eloys's erotic reverie as he, too, endures the torture of not being able to forget the body of his beloved. Montifaud goes even further and carries this alteration into the restructuring of his mind. As shown above, she reworked Bussy's dream sequence, and even expanded it. In addition, she revises Pope's rendition of erotic reverie, which was borrowed from Bussy's. Montifaud dismantled Pope's seminal image of the Gothic prison that eventually contributed to Heloise's descent into hallucination. From a distance, Montifaud's Abailard hears Eloys's plea against abandon and unrequited desire, and he mirrors her sentiments through the reciprocal avowal of similar feelings. In this way, Eloys retains hope and reason; she reaches her lover and at least she has the consolation that both of them are equally tormented in their remote retreats. Furthermore, the traditional depiction of Abelard as a religious man is reversed. The spiritual, moral language of the medieval Abelard is replaced with a passionate confession reminiscent of the scene where Eloys takes the veil, only to be plagued by memories of Abailard. This time, however, it is Abailard who cannot hide his true object of devotion:

> Si, dans le temple, je fais ma prière à la Vierge dont j'implore le secours en contemplant la mère de mon Dieu, je crois voir en ses traits divins ceux de ma chère Eloys, je lui jure un amour éternel. (100)

And this reversal is not an isolated occurrence, since, later in the text, Abailard has a vision analogue to Eloys's nocturnal reverie. In the silence of the halls of St. Gildas, he imagines that he sees her walking and calling out to him. A parallel is established with another famous monastic figure, one Abbot of Rancé, who was also in love with a woman he could not forget, and consequently he was haunted until the end of his days by her absence. Interestingly, Montifaud grafts Pope's Gothic description of Heloise at the Paraclete onto the physical surroundings of St. Gildas. Abailard is tortured by these recurring visions of Eloys wandering aimlessly, which is intensified in the text by the rocky, unstable landscape that lies beyond the walls of the cloister. More than Pope's Gothic ambiance, however, Montifaud's revision of the Gothic transforms into a romantic communion with nature. Abailard's torment is in harmony with nature's turbulence and, once again, balanced to mirror Eloys's acute suffering. The night brings no solace to him either.

From Grave to Engravings

Montifaud develops many aspects of the text already considered in previous translations, but one of the most striking variations in this prose rendition is the spiritual revival of the couple from the grave. As mentioned above, Montifaud was very critical of Lenoir's commercial venture and his capitalizing on the lovers' remains; and she was skeptical of what was really laid to rest in the tomb erected during the nineteenth century at Père-Lachaise. The final chapter of her narrative is devoted to the theme of death, and, here again, she reverses the eighteenth-century sentimental depiction of the lovers' demise. She begins by providing the readers with elaborate details concerning the physical fragmentation of their body parts, and this, we know, was based on truth: as Charrier also affirmed, it is a fact that Lenoir sold off parts of the lovers' remains to affluent people.[6] Thereby, Lenoir capitalized on an interest for the couple that, by the nineteenth century, had turned into a cult.

To look at this from another perspective, since Montifaud is actually introducing extraneous elements in this concluding chapter, by this time the original narrative has also suffered a fragmentation which, ironically, recalls the physical diffusion of the lovers' bodies. Here, there is a parallel between the circulation of the body parts, as noted above, and the dissemination of the legend. The popular, tragic story of the couple's misfortunes had become so distorted through revision and reinvention that Montifaud proposed re-reading the original letters for a more accurate account of the events that had touched the lovers' lives. Interestingly, she criticizes Lenoir's desecration of their remains, but suggests that one can repair the fragmentation by reverting to the correspondence:

> C'est dans ses lettres qu'il faut voir et connaître Eloys, c'est là qu'elle passe, le front couronné de myrthe, ainsi que les amoureuses qui assistèrent aux banquets philosophiques de la Grèce [...] On voit qu'elle enchaîne les mots, non pas à la façon des rhéteurs, mais qu'elle trouve un secret enivrement à leur donner une solide armure, à ren-fermer en eux un sentiment aussi voluptueux qu'elle en éprouverait à faire ce qu'ils expriment. (172)

Montifaud posits that the letters hold the key to unlock the true story. She creates a break in the fable that the two lovers were ever reunited in the tomb. She challenges other writers before her and reaffirms that it was impossible for Eloys to live out the rest of her life devoted to the Church. She uses Sappho as an other example of a woman empowered by the gift of eloquently expressing her desire, and this, in turn, is used in conjunction with Eloys as a bold, defiant muse. The parallel to Sappho represents Eloys as a spirited, resistant writer who courageously welcomes the challenge of writing a discourse charged with passion as her pen tears through the heavy veil of simulated

[6] Charrier provides details about Lenoir's involvement with marketing the couple's body parts on pp. 332-363.

religious devotion. As Montifaud puts it, "Eloys écrit sous l'influence de son démon. Elle se sert de sa rhétorique comme Sappho se servait de sa lyre" (173). Montifaud intervenes in the text to insist that the blazing love letters themselves hold the key to Eloys's authentic personality, as she wants her to be considered as a living presence and not a romanesque heroine in a dead story. Paradoxically, she uses a fictional device, the invention of an eighteenth-century visitor who allegedly visited the Paraclete: there, he discovered that banquets were held to honor Eloys and Abailard, and that all the nuns had portraits of them in their cells so as to never forget them. The lovers' story is therefore inscribed or "affiché" on the very walls that Abailard had himself erected with his own hand, and these portraits openly display an immortal passion which is not hidden but rather celebrated in a sacred place:

> Le Paraclet, est, je crois, dans le monde, l'unique couvent où les plaisirs et les malheurs de deux amants soient un sujet continuel de réflexions et de discours. (181)

The two lovers are thus revived and immortalized on the walls of the Paraclete to give others strength and guidance. The pictorial motif is yet another subversive element in Montifaud's rewriting of the couple as defiant and rebellious instead of victims of tragic circumstances. The fact that the visitor finds their portraits after many generations have passed indicates that their passion has entered into the universal to touch the human heart. In the lovers' time, their story was private, as illustrated in the intimate form of the missive, but centuries later, it entered the universal to suggest that human love is empowering and can triumph over the obstacle of physical separation, to live on. In sharp contrast to Pope's and Colardeau's texts, the lovers' are not buried and thus do not fade out of the field of vision. They are kept alive, suspended in the picture frame, and this time, there is no mention of the symbolic (re)union that supposedly took place below ground, in the tenebrous intimacy of the tomb. Montifaud preserves their memory above ground. In addition, the portraits are also strategically placed on the nuns' bedside tables, which eternalizes the lovers' in a visually enhanced, more lively form, and other nuns even learned to write amatory discourse because of the couple's gift for this particular genre. And Montifaud concludes her text by establishing, once again, a bond of reciprocity between the couple. For her, if Eloys was a prisoner of the cloister, Abailard, too, was enslaved by the Church, and his story may have been quite different if religious conventions had not repressed his "other," more erotic, dialogue with his wife.

Although a significant part of this last chapter is fictional, Montifaud subverts other versions to produce a text that is defiant, resistant as well as overtly anti-clerical. The two lovers are depicted as a rebellious couple, united in their desire to rekindle their love instead of pursuing religious devotion. As Montifaud recovers the bodies of the lovers and privileges desire over monastic constraints, she lifts off the veils and pushes aside the age-old controversy over Heloise's faith. In her text, there is no doubt that Eloys was completely devoted to her lover. But as Montifaud attempts to repair the fragmentation suffered by the lovers' discourse as it fell into the hands of numerous male writers before her, she, too, produces another form of fragmentation. At the same time, she also takes great liberty with the text in grafting numerous fictional episodes onto the original narrative. In her attempt to restore the original amatory discourse and write one for Abailard, she returns to the most outstanding aspects of the authentic story in order to build up the erotic, controversial narrative in which her most notable contribution is the reconstruction of Heloise's persona. She begins by weaving in fragments from other, male writers before her. For instance, Bussy's nocturnal reverie and (re)invention of Abelard as a sensitive lover are significantly developed. The Gothic references to Pope and Colardeau are easily recognizable, as are the intertextual passages that reveal that Montifaud, too, was well versed in the medieval story. She openly practices selective borrowing from these men as blatantly as they had done prior to her version. But she does not hide, as is reflected also by the use of the male pseudonym, Marc (everyone knew that she was a woman). Indeed, she is openly in drag and flaunts it, mimicking a man and destroying the very notion of gender. In Abelard's and Heloise's case, Montifaud goes beyond gender as both characters are remolded to efface their sexual difference and thus are reconstructed as equals, the quintessential embodiment of the androgynous couple. As Montifaud borrows from other male writers, she reverses their position and deconstructs their discourse on Heloise. In contrast to Bussy's work, her Eloys does not simply settle for nocturnal reverie; she arranges a "supposed" clandestine meeting with Abelard on the grounds of the Paraclete. In striking deviation to Pope's and Colardeau's depiction of a reverie that borders on madness, Montifaud's Eloys never experiences feelings of guilt or shame that could possibly push her towards God. Reversing the moral fiber that runs through the Gothic versions, Eloys describes passion as her sheets blaze with desire. The focus is directed on sexual attraction; it is built up through the insertion of invented fictional episodes, which, in turn, enhances this more sensuous version. Yet, Montifaud also has a personal intention. Not only does she want to strengthen women's voices, but she also uses Heloise's story to be critical of the Church. She attacks the intrusion of Christian dogma in people's private lives and takes a stand against censorship. As stated in the paratext, Montifaud believed in the human heart, which she illustrates as her Eloys and Abailard defy the constraints of monastic life. Indeed, Montifaud seems to both feminist and anti-clerical, two stances that are not unrelated. She not only restores the medieval voice of the "uncensored" Heloise that fractures the silence of centuries of repression; her Eloys reclaims the right to articulate amorous speech to her lover within the privacy of the couple. This time her human love is accepted and even glorified instead of seen as inherently scandalous, as in the medieval text. In her version, Montifaud reverses the original depiction of the couple as tragic victims of temptation and carnal sin. If they are victims in this more modern text, it is because others have intruded in their lives. Interestingly, the lovers are vindicated in a romantic way as martyrs. The couple represents a defiance, the individual's struggle against an intolerant, repressive society, and in the end they do not retreat into the societal constraints that had (in previous renditions) traditionally privileged religion over desire. Montifaud achieves what no other writer before her had even attempted to explore. She does not bury the lovers; she preserves them in the permanent image of the portrait so that they might inspire others to love freely and privately without fear of public scorn. Abailard and Eloys continue to wander among the living as they are constantly renewed, and thus they do not rest in the cemetery of inert, age-old literary characters who have finally been laid to rest as relics of the times in which they lived.

EPILOGUE

The Revival of Heloise in Popular Culture

Before examining the contemporary dissemination of the legend, it is important to briefly document what happened to the medieval lovers' remains during the nineteenth century before they were moved to their permanent tomb at Père-Lachaise. Once again, one should consider Lenoir's role in the construction of the couple's burial site. In addition to being a successful artist, he was also the director of the Musée des monuments français, and was credited with building an ornamental grave for Heloise and Abelard in his Jardin Elysée, an English-style garden. Charrier provides details about Lenoir's elaborate memorial, and more recently Mary Shepard has studied the history of Lenoir's tomb for Heloise and Abelard.[1] The facts surrounding Lenoir's involvement are relevant because the bodies were moved after the French Revolution from the Paraclete to their resting place at Nogent-sur-Seine. During the turbulence of the Revolution, the grave containing the couple's remains was vandalized by thieves, who clamored for authentic remnants of the famous couple. By the nineteenth century, Abelard and Heloise had become legendary figures of romantic love.

[1] See Mary Shephard's article, "A Tomb for Abelard and Heloise," *Romance Studies* 25.1 (2007): 29-42. In this discussion, Shephard provides details pertaining to Lenoir and his capitalization of the widespread popularity of the couple's legend.

Lenoir had permission to not only oversee the transport of their remains, but to verify that the bones were actually those of the medieval lovers. For his tomb, Lenoir envisioned a Gothic grave that would promote the familiar weeping image of loss, which had become so famous in Pope's and Colardeau's revisions of Heloise. As Shepard maintains, Lenoir believed that the Gothic style would best evoke the feeling and spirit of the medieval period in which they lived. Shepard also adds that Lenoir wanted other lovers to visit the grave to partake of the tears associated with the lovers' tragic story.[2] It is difficult to mention Lenoir without including a very strange detail surrounding his participation in the commemoration project. He was known to offer gifts of the lovers' remains to influential people he knew.[3] Interestingly, this fragmentation of the lovers' bodies from the early nineteenth century on prefigures the textual transmutation of their story in the twentieth century. From the ashes of their tomb, modern authors resurrected parts of their medieval personas to rekindle their story, shifting it into a variety of genres that would assure that their story and bodies lived on at the dawn of the postmodern era.

The enthusiasm infusing the legend of Heloise and Abelard began to wane by the close of the nineteenth century, but nonetheless continued to attract attention in the early part of the twentieth century. It is relevant to look at the evolution in the transformation of the medieval lovers with emphasis on Heloise's persona, especially in some of the more original, recent imitations that have appeared in the cinema and in Francophone literature.[4] For this reason, the core of this concluding part of the discussion will explore the works of two seminal

[2] Shepard 31-33.
[3] Shepard 38.
[4] For instance, Marie Laberge's play *Pierre ou la consolation* and the British film, *Stealing Heaven*, a version which is mainly based on the medieval story of the couple's tragedy. Also, Anne Hébert's *Héloïse*, a surrealistic novel published in 1980.

Francophone women authors: Marie Laberge and Anne Hébert. But before the publication of these two francophone works, relatively unknown for Heloise and Abelard scholars, there were numerous minor novels that appeared in the early part of the twentieth century. For instance, authors such as Marcelle Vioux, Pierre Lasserre, Jules Perrin, Maurice de Waleffe, and Madame Jean Bertheroy all published imaginary versions of the famous couple's misfortunes.[5] One of the rarer texts, *Héloïse et Abélard,* was written in 1925 by Antonin Artaud and is a part of his famous *Ombilic des Limbes*. Hélène Casanova characterizes this surrealist work as a collage composed in a fragmentary style, containing a myriad of genres that are partly critical, scientific and lyrical.[6] In 1933, Helen Waddell published her prose novel, *Peter Abelard,* which was more successful than the others mentioned above and has even attracted some scholarly attention. As the title suggests, Waddell's intention was to shift the focal point back to Abelard's story, but the plot is immediately altered with the invention of a character named Gilles de Vannes. As Glorianna Locklear reads it, Gilles is intended to espouse modern attitudes within the context of the twelfth century. She describes Gilles de Vannes as the fictional character playing the role of a spiritual mentor to the couple.[7] For the reader, it is of no surprise to rediscover the conflict between love and philosophy. Above all, the author, a medievalist, set the precedent for other fictional imitators to follow by attempting to restore the medieval context, but deviated from the philosophy of the times by interpolating more modern perspectives into the plot. Robertson also describes Waddel's novel as a

---

[5] Charrier mentions these authors on pp. 550-556.

[6] Hélène Casanova characterizes Artaud's version as a cubist collage. See "Autofiction et création dans Héloïse et Abélard d'Antonin Artaud, " *Romance Studies* 37.2 (1997) : 139-145.

[7] See Glorianna Locklear's article, "Delicious Poison: Heloise and Abelard out of Time," *Popular Culture Review* 4.1 (1993): 39-43.

work of "sentimental humanitarism" to emphasize the highly emotional, yet sensitive portrayal of the couple.[8]

The next wave of fictional accounts that will be considered here supports the spread of the popularity of Heloise's persona in French-Canadian literature, notably Anne Hébert's novel, *Héloïse,* which was published in 1980. Hébert's novel is very loosely associated with Heloise. In fact, the textual structure resembles a cinematographic novel, especially since the medieval nun is radically reinvented as a vampire. Curiously, Abelard is deleted from the novel, and there is no reference to him at all in the narrative. To embed the visual into the plot structure, Hébert focuses on the city streets of Paris, the métro and many other famous tourist spots in Paris. Hébert scholars often consider this novel as one of her black comedies, and it is also characterized as surrealistic, mainly because the text contains many odd, fortuitous encounters in the streets of Paris. From the opening scene, the protagonist, Bernard, is intrigued by the strange sound of a siren's voice that echoes in the train. For the vampire, Héloïse, the search to target a willing mortal begins by captivating the victim so that he eventually succumbs to her embrace, which constitutes the quintessential pleasure experience. In fact, the seduction is initiated from the very first moment that Bernard sees her in the métro. Bernard notices the odd, darkly clad woman at the back of the train and is immediately fascinated by her haunting presence. Héloïse's body image is skeletal; her face is pale and glacial, the cheekbones are sharply defined, but Bernard finds himself attracted to her. He is already experiencing the preliminary stages of his attraction to death. From this initial contact, Bernard begins his retreat from life, symbolized by his fianceé's vital body image. One of the key surrealistic aspects of the novel is Hébert's use of reverie as a seductive device. Like the surrealists' fascination for the

[8] See D. W. Robertson's book, *Abelard and Heloise* (New York: Dial Press, 1972): 221.

liberation of the consciousness through dreams, Bernard also frees himself from earthly life with his fiancée, Christine, by contemplating the intriguing temptress. Gradually, with each encounter with the exotic vampire, Bernard succumbs to her trap, rejecting his human lover. Although the story is far removed from any real resemblance to the medieval Heloise's, the author ostensibly creates her contemporary Héloïse based on the nineteenth-century gothic Heloise. However, she is not an overly sentimental woman but a resourceful, voracious vamp, searching perpetually for fresh blood to be found from innocent prey like Bernard. The closest parallel to the medieval Heloise is the portrayal of her as a seductive temptress. To the reader, her medieval vestiges are visible in her timeless body, her retro clothing and earthy, musty fragrance, thus suggesting that she might indeed be very old, perhaps dating back to medieval times and having been buried. It is as if Hébert amplifies the medieval Heloise's formidable intelligence, for her vamp is a keen thinker who overcomes all barriers separating the space of the undead from the living. Hébert's Héloïse is not content to stay below ground in the dark métro, the territory of her fellow brethren. She wanders above ground and disguises herself amongst the living to better seek out her victims. She delights in the pleasure of a complex hunt and in doing so utilizes the power of her sharp mind to obtain the coveted prize of young, succulent blood. This postmodern Héloïse appears to retain the most positive aspects of her medieval sister: she is clever, sexy and always lures her man into her seductive lair. Above all, the vampire Héloïse reverses the gender roles as a preternatural being. While she is cast in the active role, the males around her play a weaker part and are inevitably rendered impotent by the haunting power of her sensual allure. In this way, Hébert's Héloïse can be compared to the highly intelligent medieval Heloise, and the learned, independent Heloise seen in Keralio's version. The author simply shifts the focus to a supernatural fantasy, but retains some vague, recognizable remnants of the twelfth-century Heloise

The cinematographic quality of Hébert's novel fortuitously anticipates the emergence of a film in the 80s about the life of the famous couple. In 1988, Clive Donner directed the film, *Stealing Heaven,* a film adaptation from a popular novel by the same name. In sharp contrast to Hébert's novel, the medieval context is again restored as Donner attempts to provide his audience with the biographical highlights of the couple's tragic love story, which unfolds from a retrospective point of view. In the opening scenes of the film, Heloise is on her deathbed surrounded by her devoted nuns. She is cast in her famous role as the spiritual director of the Paraclete. Suddenly, she throws her crucifix against the wall. The audience can immediately surmise that religion was not her true calling, and so her story unwinds on screen. Although Donner situates the story in medieval times, he, at times, modifies the scenario, privileging the romantic over the historical facts that readers recognize from Abelard's *Historia.* As the plot progresses, Heloise is depicted as an intelligent, attractive teenager around seventeen, and Abelard is cast as a sexy, charismatic theologian and teacher. He appears to be no older than in his late 30s in this version. Donner places much emphasis on Abelard as a respected teacher, who attracted throngs of students to his seminars on philosophy, performing brillantly as a teacher of philosophy and theology by engaging in open, socratic dialogues with his young pupils. His energy and dynamic teaching style are highlighted in the film in numerous scenes; thus it is not surprising that the young Heloise not only hears of his reputation, but is intrigued by his formidable persona. For the viewer, the fictional encounter in the streets of Paris is almost plausible, as the scene reveals a powerful mutual attraction from the moment they first see one another. Although Donner's version amplifies the romantic sensuality between the lovers, the earlier details of their relationship appear more or less faithful to the medieval text. Donner even alludes to Abelard's political enemies within the Church, and the viewer cannot help but wonder if a lot of his problems were not fueled by jealousy, especially due to the popularity of his relationship with his students. The director devotes numerous scenes to the social and intellectual interaction between Abelard and his male students. The film flows into the natural aspect of Abelard's eventual academic connection with the young Heloise. After Heloise comes to live with her uncle, Fulbert, she is eventually tutored by Abelard, which sets the rest of their sensual story in motion.

As noted above in Waddell's novel, Donner's representation of Heloise reveals an invented, modern portrayal of her, which tends to clash with the cultural context of medieval times. From the early scenes of the film when Fulbert is preparing to remove Heloise from the convent (in his discussions about marriage with her), he refers to his young niece as "chattel." "Chattel" smacks of a contemporary discourse of the idea of woman as object in the marriage market.[9] To place this is in a feminist context, woman was historically seen as the object exchanged between two males, her father and her future husband. In other words, Heloise has no choice; she must acquiesce to her uncle's wish to marry her off to the chosen suitor. The reference to this term seems out of place for the medieval context of the film. But Donner's Heloise is no demure young girl, for she rejects some of Fulbert's choices for husbands to hold out for someone of a more refined, intelligent nature. The director remains faithful to the medieval story; his Heloise opposes Abelard's plan to marry her out of respect for his profession as a philosopher, but nonetheless she secretly marries him after becoming pregnant. Here, the plot closely follows the biographical facts found in the *Historia*. To avoid reiterating familiar

[9] Locklear comments on the use of the word "chattel" on page 44.

historical facts about the medieval couple, it is more useful to look at some of the original aspects in the main part of the film.

One of the most memorable aspects of the film is how the castration scene is depicted and its repercussions on the young lovers. Once again, the director takes great liberty with the interpretation of this pivotal event. Heloise leaves the convent where Abelard had placed her to flee to his bedside. Her immediate reaction is that there is no God, a response that remains faithful to her resistance to a monastic career, whereas Abelard is portrayed as a penitent figure. He says he deserves this punishment for committing the sin of fornication. Donner seems to expand on the repercussions of the castration, as the event effects the lives of all of the main characters. Fulbert is cursed and boldly condemned by Heloise and is eventually banished from the Church in Paris. This modern Heloise is outspoken, vowing to remain at her husband's side in spite of his mutilation. But Abelard succumbs to constant suffering and self-loathing because he cannot love her anymore. It is this incident that points to the most altered aspect of the film. As Locklear reads it, Abelard is portrayed as weak and overly romantic.[10] Above all, Abelard openly acknowledges his love for his wife, which deviates dramatically from his autobiographical account told in the *Historia.*

The remainder of the plot is familiar to those who know their story. The two are separated, and Heloise is forced to lead a monastic life. In Donner's scenario, she does see Abelard from time to time, and they develop a religious friendship based on mutual respect. There are several encounters between them, ostensibly for spiritual reasons pertaining to the direction of the Paraclete. One of the most original fictional scenes is the meeting between Heloise, Abelard and their son, Astrolabe. He is

[10] Here, Locklear also studies Donner's portrayal of the castration. Interestingly, the film reveals an image of Abelard as a lover who never relinquished romance. See page 44.

brought to her convent by a loyal friend, an invented character named Jordaine. It is possible that Donner may have created Jordaine to construct a love triangle, as he, too, is cast early on in the film as clearly in love with Heloise. He even offers Heloise a marriage proposal to give her son a proper home after Abelard's scandalous mutilation. Their son, Astrolabe, ends up in the service of Jordaine, who assumes the role of surrogate father for the absent Abelard. As we recall, Abelard had chosen religious retreat after his misfortune. The film concludes with a fictional scene, building on Abelard's original wish to be buried at the Paraclete. In Donner's version, Abelard expresses his sincere desire to be interred with Heloise, so that they can share a bed in eternity. Donner' s Abelard says to Heloise, "in God's good time, you will share my bed" (44-5). For the most part, Donner attempts to revive the legendary aspects of the couple's undying love, but insists far too much on an overly romanticized Abelard, focusing on his powerless role after his castration. Although the male director represents Heloise as very bright, he diminishes her celebrated intellectual identity by aligning her character toward the romantic discourse and removing the original religious rhetoric, an integral part of her erudite persona.

It is curious that the next version to be considered restores the religious aspect of Heloise's life. In 1992, a French-Canadian play was written by Marie Laberge. Although she situates her play in the twelfth century, Laberge states in the preface that she takes great liberty with her production, and her intention is not to remain faithful to the historical facts surrounding the couple's lives. However, the context is based on an actual event. The playwright chooses the night Heloise's friend, Pierre le Vénérable, delivered Abelard's body for burial. Laberge is interested in exploring what Heloise might have gone through the night she received her husband's body at her convent. To stage the setting, Abelard's body occupies the center of the stage, and their mutual friend, Pierre, is the one who accompanies the body to the Paraclete, a detail based on true events. On a symbolic level, Abelard's remains point to a textual resurrection of the seminal conflict between vivid memories of undying passion and Heloise's ongoing struggle to come to terms with her vocation as a nun and spiritual leader of the Paraclete. During this dramatic encounter, the arrival of Abelard's body immediately unleashes the flow of Heloise's past memories, which collide with the present, her monastic life. Heloise's painful past is captured in a poignant, poetic interpretation. She is particularly intrigued by the conflict between devotion to God and carnal desire, especially the way that the Church deals with irreconcilable desire. As Laberge explains, "Héloïse dévouée à Dieu, abbesse mais toujours brûlante de désir charnel inassouvi et incapable d'en effacer le souvenir-quand le corps a dansé, il est bien difficile de lui faire oublier la musique."[11] The author describes her play as a fictional interpretation, as is evident in the division into three sections. These sections are related to the daily ritual of the nuns' prayers, and the author even inserts an invented fictional nun named Guillemette. It is possible that this young novice is cast in moral contrast to Heloise, for she is solely devoted to God and has no experience with love or physical temptation. On the contrary, Laberge casts Pierre le Vénérable and Heloise as two tortured souls who share the perpetual struggle with spiritual devotion and physical desire. Pierre's character is even described as a handsome man; he comes to life to speak of his tormented soul with Heloise, as the two engage in reciprocal confession about physical passion. Laberge considers her play to be a lyrical representation of a very human dilemma situated within the sequestered space of the Church.

---

[11] See Marie Laberge's play, *Pierre ou la consolation.* (Montréal: Boréal, 1992). Laberge includes her own critical reading of the couple's story in a section following the play.

To reinforce her vision, the dramatist creates her own rendition by inventing new words and combining them with old French spellings to recreate language that could possibly date back to the medieval period. Anne Berthelot reads Laberge's play as a poetic imitation which only partially reproduces medieval language.[12] Some of the more striking examples of Laberge's invented expressions are: "désirance," "doliance," "verté, and "souvenance." Her goal seems to be to create an internal sonority of the language, so as to rekindle the atmosphere of the twelfth century. Berthelot also considers the play to be a plaintive reflection on pain, thus recalling not only the Ovidian tradition of the heroine's "plainte," but also the visceral suffering of the famous seventeenth-century Portuguese nun, Marianne. At the core of Laberge's play is the theme of loss.

The thematic of unbearable loss is expanded to dialogues on castration, abandonment, absence, silence and death. One of the most original aspects of Heloise's discussion with Peter addresses her struggle with "désirance." Heloise speaks of her spiritual battle with desire, and Pierre admits that he, too, shared a similar struggle between physical temptation and faith. On stage, the two characters seem to create a private confessional, a space where they can freely speak of their mutual sins of lust and carnal desire. Like her medieval ancestor, this contemporary Heloise's veil disguises the truth of her dilemma: her undying passion for her beloved Abelard. Like Heloise's veil, Pierre's desire is concealed by his monastic hood. Here, Laberge expands the symbolism of veiling, showing that males in the Church can also dissimulate a similar desire, which threatens to undo their spiritual vows and devotion to God. In creating this fictional encounter between the two friends, Laberge's most original creation to the contemporary dissemina-

[12] Anne Berthelot analyzes Laberge's play by situating the portrayal of the lovers between medieval and contemporary literature. See the introduction to her article, " La Renaissance du moyen âge : *Pierre ou la consolation de Marie Laberge.* " *Etudes Francophones* 12.1 (1997): 37.

tion of the legend may very well be a humanistic reflection on painful loss and irrepressible desire, which reaches across the gender divide within the Church to resonate with both nuns and clerics. These servants of God are portrayed as vulnerable beings who yearn for the meaningful comfort of reciprocal passion in their solitary lives The locus of this difficult dilemma still exists in the Catholic Church today; thus Laberge skillfully interweaves a medieval setting with a postmodern observation on the ongoing battle between corporeal sin and spiritual devotion.

The transmutation of the famous couple's love story did not abruptly cease at the end of the twentieth century. Currently, there are versions that continue to appear on bookstore shelves. Since these are only marginally related to our discussion, a few of these recent works will be briefly considered. The first novel is Antoine Audouard's *Adieu mon unique* which came out in 2000. The author restores the medieval story, but the main modification is the invention of a character named Guillaume d'Oxford. The narrative is told from his perspective and spans twenty years from his early days of a student of Abelard's, to the celebrity of Abelard as a theologian and philosopher, and on through the unfolding of the familiar tragic events of his life with Heloise. It is through the invention of the fictional Guillaume that Audouard creates a secret unrequited love on the part of Guillaume, which is not reciprocated by Heloise. Other noteworthy fictional details are the double castration. Here, Abelard is not the only victim of Fulbert's henchmen, but Guillaume, too shares this horrific mutilation with his friend. Although Audouard ostensibly follows the most significant facts surrounding the couple's lives, he invents a new fictional element by creating a love triangle among Guillaume, Abelard and Heloise. In fact, Guillaume is often cast as a voyeur who secretly listens and watches the couple either praying or talking in Abelard's private quarters. For the reader, Guillaume's affinity for the couple seems to suggest that he is writing his own story upon their own, thus fusing the two intersecting accounts of their enduring friendship. As Audouard's Guillaume puts it, "nous étions trois et un à la fois, affreusement murés dans nos solitudes, secrètement unis en amour " (310) . One of the most surprising and original aspects of the novel is situated at the close. After Heloise and Abelard have died, Guillaume devotes himself to the project of writing their letters by imagining how Abelard would have penned the *Historia* and how Heloise would of tearfully received his autobiographical account of his life. As an intimate friend and witness to the events of their lives, Guillaume records his memories, while drawing on the power of his own imagination to envision how the couple would of composed their story. Once again, a blurring of his own story and theirs takes place on paper. As Audouard's Guillaume describes it, "Les mots qui passaient par ma plume n'étaient plus miens, mais leurs, et j'accomplissais en retenant mes larmes (car il ne faut jamais pleurer comme on écrit) un vœu beaucoup plus grand que moi " (378). To transmit their story to the public, Guillaume's inner wish is that the letters find their way to the Paraclete where people can find them, read the missives and copy them to assure that their love is never forgotten, but eternally alive for centuries to come. Interestingly, the closing words of the novel prefigure the task of translators, imitators and other revisionists for future work on the couple's correspondence.

The next text to be considered appeared shortly after Audouard's novel and is also situated in the medieval context. In 2001, Suzanne Bernard published a novel entitled, *Le Roman d'Héloïse et Abélard.* This work consists of two prose pieces in one volume. The first one is *Plus jamais Héloïse,* written in 1988, and the other is *La Fin d'Abélard,* published in 1991. The first novel cited above was actually based on Abelard's *Historia;* thus the focus is on his series of misfortunes and does not offer much originality. But one of the more noteworthy characteristics of this text is the combination of introspective reflection with personal recollections. In sharp contrast to Laberge's play, Bernard restores Abelard to the text and positions him as the focus of her revision. Moreover, she revises him to create a meditative, dreamy character. Like Laberge, Bernard restores the medieval context and even mirrors Laberge in that she insists on the carnal aspect of their relationship, but in a more provocative way. There is also further evidence of textual fragmentation, as Bernard embeds selected quotes taken from the couple's love correspondence, thus creating a hybrid text in its contemporary construction. One of the most striking aspects of Bernard's novel is her insistence on the more famous elements of the couple's story. For instance, the seduction scenes appear more frequently and are embellished, especially during the tutoring session in Fulbert's house. In particular, the author highlights the fact that this fictional Heloise took great pleasure in Abelard's supposed beatings of her. Bernard even adds scenes in which Heloise willingly removes her clothes, so he can hurt her. To further capture the reader's attention, the castration event is described as monstrous; it is depicted in a highly graphic style, highlighting Abelard's shame after the castration, an aspect reminiscent of Donner's portrayal of Abelard's regret that he can no longer love his wife. In addition, Bernard grafts Heloise's resistance to her vows onto her depiction of Abelard, underscoring the radical deviation from Abelard's account of his life in the *Historia.* By shifting the focus to his prolonged meditations on philosophy and teaching, Bernard suggests that Abelard was not guided by his monastic vocation at all.

The tone of the second book, *La Fin d'Abélard,* is much more subdued and mainly uneventful. The text contains a reconfigured structure, one which vaguely resembles a tragedy. In particular, it contains a prologue, and the first part focuses on Abelard's condemnation by the Church for his controversial book deemed as heresy. As we recall, his fate was decided by the Council of Sens. Here, Bernard interweaves the historical facts with fiction, as Abelard is welcomed to the abby at Cluny in 1140 by his dear friend, Peter the Venerable. This religious retreat is portrayed as his last refuge, especially since Bernard alludes to many of Abelard's political problems within the Church, including his infamous disagreements with his enemy, Bernard Le Clairvaux. After this lengthy section of Abelard's painful retreat, Bernard inserts an interlude, and invents a second part called the transfiguration, focusing on an aging and sickly Abelard in the waning days of his life. The concluding part is known as the agony, which is followed by a brief epilogue. The theme of the agony and the epilogue emphasize Abelard's slow death, as he is fictionally depicted walking through a desert, tracing a path to his final resting place. In this arduous walk through this hallucinatory desert, he is accompanied by St. Jerome, another famous eunuch discussed earlier in the medieval chapters. The insertion of St. Jerome seems to offer spiritual consolation and fellowship to this suffering Abelard, as he also appears to be carving out a path that gives Abelard a final glimpse, albeit a hallucinatory encounter, with his beloved wife, Heloise. The epilogue shows that he has finally reached home, as his body reaches Heloise's Paraclete. It is possible that these textual divisions are created for dramatic effect to chart the development of their love and their eventual separation, mainly rescripted in a parallel way as the two adjust to their own cloistered life. Perhaps the most fictional aspect of the novel is Bernard's insertion of a dream, which takes place in the concluding scenes of the novel. Within this invented space, Abelard sees Heloise. Interestingly, he has a vision of a tearful Heloise waiting to see him again. It would seem that Bernard's Heloise is a revamped sentimental Heloise, evoking both Pope's and Colardeau's representations. Once again, the idea of reuniting with one another in death reverts not only to most of the other eighteenth-century romanticized versions, but also to the fictional park erected by Lenoir in the nineteenth century. Interestingly, Bernard seems to echo Laberge, as the concluding scenes of the epilogue focus on the transport of Abelard's remains to Heloise's convent at the Paraclete, the main scene of Laberge's play. But Bernard's originality is explained by the fact that she selectively borrows authentic elements, and then creates a fiction around the events of Abelard's death. For instance, there is a fictional monk who narrates the scene in which Peter the Venerable accompanies the body to the Paraclete. Abelard's death is described as an ultimate deliverance from the series of adversities he lived through. The idea of the classical chorus lamenting the death of Peter Abelard is represented by the nuns and monks, Heloise and Peter the Venerable who come together to collectively mourn the death of a brilliant theologian and philosopher.

Conclusion

Through the course of this analysis, a close look at a variety of versions of Heloise and Abelard's love correspondence facilitated the study of the fragmentation process as a woman's text fell into the hands of male rewriters. In the medieval narrative, it is has been shown that Heloise's love letters many have already been altered by Abelard's intervention in her erotically charged discourse as a means of steering her on the road that led to holy devotion as the Bride of Christ. As Charrier and other noteworthy medieval scholars read it, Abelard may have indeed have taken considerable liberty with Heloise's epistles in order to repress her expression of carnal desire so as to see to her spiritual conversion. Since Abelard's goal was to convert her, Heloise's discourse was then repeatedly forced to submit to the editing of his pen.

In the seventeenth-century versions, Grenaille's rendition that came out in 1642 marked the first partial translation of the couple's love letters. Like Abelard, Grenaille also intervened in Heloise's discourse to reinvent her "La Magdalene Française," a penitent, self-sacrificing role model for other women to emulate. But Grenaille took more liberty than Abelard as he locked Heloise into the confessional and forced her to admit her sins before the world. Furthermore, as he invented two fictional letters, mimicking Heloise's style and even signing them in her name, he also committed a travesty of signature. This penitent revision of Heloise was followed by Alluis'1675 prose version, a text which recreated an adventurous heroine and, for the first time, showed signes of inventing a more libertine portrayal of Heloise and Abelard as lovers. But the most successful version was yet to be be composed. In 1687, Bussy's precious edition came out and enjoyed great popularity, as he not only restored the original epistolary form, but reinvented the couple as courtly, gallant suitors who were placed in a more public, secular space that evoked the luxurious interiors of the salons. In this public space, Bussy reinvented the lovers and wrote for them an amorous, seductive dialogue that allowed them to focus solely on their love instead of the more austere, religious discussions to which their medieval counterparts always reverted in their missives. Although Bussy did restore the structure of the original text, he was, however, also guilty of tampering with Heloise's text. She was recast as a precious, less learned woman, and, in the closing epistle, Heloise succumbed to illness from her unfilled desire, a motif which is significantly developed in the eighteenth-century versions. Other more recent eighteenth-century translations have made it possible to study the trope of the suffering Heloise. For instance, Bayle wrote several articles devoted to the couple in his *Dictionnaire historique et critique,* which was published in 1697. Bayle's articles are of particular interest because he was fascinated by Abelard's castration, another aspect augmenting the tragic portrayal of the couple. Like Bayle, Dom Gervaise wanted to restore a more faithful account of the lovers by revisiting the facts associated with the twelfth century. Moreover Gervaise's 1723 translation of the correspondence is important because he, too, deals with Enlightenment perceptions of ideas pertaining to the subject of eunuchs and castration. Gervaise, too, contributed to the widespread growth of the legend of the couple's misfortunes.

Pope's and Colardeau's sentimental, Gothic versions continued to reveal fragmentation of Heloise's persona as her love letters were significantly altered by male rewriters with strong pseudo-feminocentric tendencies. Pope's poetic narrative plagiarized many aspects of Bussy's text as he enhanced Eloisa's nocturnal reverie. However, the most striking image is his transformation of Eloisa into a hysterical, overly imaginative "woman." Colardeau's version closely imitated Pope's, but he toned down (albeit slightly) the depiction of her madness to insert her in a pastoral, sensual setting. Both Pope and Colardeau fragmented Heloise by de-emphasizing her reputation as a brilliant, rational thinker, depicting her as victim of tragic circumstances that resulted in an eternal (textual) confinement to her monastic cell. By 1761, prose versions of the couple's story would resurface in bookstores. For instance, Rousseau had great success with his bestseller, *Julie ou la Nouvelle Héloïse*, a novel loosely based on the medieval couple. Here, Rousseau took great liberty in his revision of Heloise by recasting her as a model of virtue and maternal perfection, as he veils her desire for St. Preux in favor of a companionate marriage.

Heloise would not regain many faces of her original persona until Keralio's translation near the end of the eighteenth-century. Keralio made the first attempt to squelch centuries of pseudo-feminocentrism by giving Heloise her pen and voice back. But as her text contained numerous contradictions, she was only partially successful in her attempt to restore the intellectual, reasonable Heloise. Clearly, the most aggressive production was Marc de Montifaud's nineteenth-century version, the first text to take a strong position against the Church and society. Montifaud recasts the lovers as a defiant couple who resisted textual burial. Not only were they preserved in an engraving at the Paraclete, but they became a source of inspiration for the nun's discussions on love. With Montifaud, Heloise and Abelard represent proof that human love can triumph and remain undefeated by the Church. This vindication is open toward the future; Montifaud's lovers look forward instead of backward, as in previous versions. Seventeenth-and eighteenth-century male authors stressed Heloise's weakness and even irrationality, but it would take these two women to give Heloise a different voice and recreate the couple as equals. The couple's voices are no longer repressed; they are no longer buried in a tomb. Immortalized and empowered, as demonstrated by the Donner film and more recent twentieth-century novels, Abelard and Heloise come together defiantly in a more postmodern space, one in which they are free to live as equals and were passion is not repressed, but eternally celebrated.

BIBLIOGRAPHY

Primary Sources

Abelard and Heloise. *The Letters and Other Writings.* Trans. William Levitan. Indianapolis and Cambridge: Hackett, 2007.

Abelard, Peter. *Abélard-Héloïse correspondance: Lettres I-VI.* Ed. Roland Oberson. Paris: Hermann, 2008.

Abélard, Pierre et Héloïse. *Correspondance.* Texte traduit par Paul Zumthor. Paris: 10/18, 1979.

———. *Lamentations, suivies de histoire de mes malheurs, et de la Correspondance avec Héloïse.* Paris: Babel, 1992.

Alluis, Jacques. *Les Amours d'Héloïse et d'Abélard.* Amsterdam: Chayer, 1695.

Ancillon, Charles. *Traité sur les eunuques.* Paris: Ramsay, 1978.

Audouard, Antoine. *Adieu, mon unique.* Paris: Gallimard, 2000.

Bayle, Pierre. *Dictionnaire historique et critique.* Tome 7. Paris: DeSoer, 1820.

———. *Personnages de l'affaire Abélard.* Lausanne: L'Age d'Homme, 2002

———. *The Dictionary Historical and Critical of Mr. Peter Bayle.* New York: Garland, 1984.

Bussy, Roger de Rabutin, comte de. *Lettres d'Héloïse et d'Abélard.* Paris: Lacrampe Fils et Comp, 1847.

———. *Lettres de messire Roger de Rabutin, comte de Bussy.* Paris: Florentin et Pierre Delaulne, XV,tome I, 1697.

Colardeau, Pierre. *Oeuvres de Colardeau de l'académie françoise.* Tome second. Paris: Ballard, LeJay, 1779.

Crenne, Hélisenne de. *Epîstres familières et invectives.* Paris: Champion, 1966.

Gervaise, Dom François-Armand. *Lettres d'Héloïse et d'Abailard avec vie d'Abailard par M. De l'Aulnaye.* Lausanne: l'Age d'Homme, 2002.

Gréard, M. ed. *Lettres complètes d'Abélard et d'Héloïse*. Traduction nouvelle. Paris: Garnier, 1869.

Grenaille, François de. *Nouveau recueil de lettres de dames tant anciennes que modernes*. Paris: Quinet, 1642.

Guilleragues. *Lettres portugaises*. Paris: Garnier Frères, 1962.

Hébert, Anne. *Héloïse*. Paris: Seuil, 1980.

Keralio, Louise. *Collection des meilleurs ouvrages composés par des femmes*. Tome premier. Paris: Lagrange, 1786.

Lettres des deux amants. Attribuées à Héloïse et Abélard. Paris: Gallimard, 2005.

Laberge, Marie. " Pierre ou la consolation." Québec: Boréal, 1992.

Montifaud, Marc de. *L'Abbesse du Paraclet: Histoire galante d'Héloïse et d'Abailard*. Paris: 1888.

———. *Histoire d'Héloïse et d'Abailard, suivie des Lettres les plus mémorables des deux immortels amants*. Paris: 1890.

———. *Marc de Montifaud devant l'opinion publique; sa justification; lettre à M. Félix Delhasse*. Londres: 1882.

Ovid. *Heroides*. Trans. Harold Isbell. London: Penguin Books, 1990.

Pope, Alexander. *Eloisa to Abelard*. Miami: University of Miami Critical Studies, 1965.

Rousseau, Jean-Jacques. *Julie ou La Nouvelle Héloïse*. Paris: Garnier, 1988.

The Letters of Heloise and Abelard: A Translation of their Collected Correspondence and Related Writings. Trans. Mary Martin McLaughlin with Bonnie Wheeler. New York: Palgrave Macmillan, 2009.

Urfé, Honoré d'. *L'Astrée*. Paris: Gallimard, 1984.

Verger, Jacques. *L'Amour castré: L'histoire d'Héloïse et Abélard*. Paris: Hermann, 1996.

Secondary Sources

Ackerman, Stephen. "The Vocation of Pope's Eloisa." *Studies in English Literature* 19.3 (1979): 445-457.

Ackroyd, Peter. *Dressing Up: Transvestism and Drag: The History of an Obsession*. New York: Simon & Schuster, 1979.

Adams, Parveen. "Hysteria, Writing, Literature: Symptoms and Hysteria." *Oxford Literary Review* 8.1-2 (1986): 178-183.

Agger, Ben. *Gender, Culture, and Power: Toward a Feminist Post-modern Critical Theory*. Westport & London: Praeger, 1993.

Alberoni, Francesco. *L'Erotisme*. Paris: Ramsay, 1990.

———. *Le Choc amoureux*. Paris: Ramsay, 1979.

Alkalay-Gut, Karen. "Woman in a Trap: Pope and Ovid in "Eloisa to Abelard." *College Literature* 15.3 (1988): 249-261.

Altman, Janet Gurkin. *Epistolarity: Approaches to a Form*. Columbus: Ohio State UP, 1982.

———. "Portuguese Writing and Women's Consciousness: the Loneliness of the Long-Distance Lover." *Degré Second* 7 (1983): 163-175.

———. "The Letter Book as a Literary Institution 1539-1789: Toward a Cultural History of Published Correspondances in France." *Yale French Studies* 71 (1986): 17-62.

———. "The Triple Register": Introduction to Temporal Complexity in the Letter Novel." *Esprit Créateur* 17.4 (1977): 302-310.

Amsler, Mark. "Genre and Code in Abelard's *Historia* Calamitatum." Essays: *Critical Approaches to Medieval & Renaissance Texts*. 1 (1981): 35-50.

Anderson, David. "Abélard and Héloïse: Eighteenth-Century Motif." *Studies on Voltaire & the 18th Century* 84 (1972): 7-51.

André, Pessel. "De la conversation chez les précieuses." *Communications* 30 (1979): 14-30.

Anson, John. "The Female Transvestite in Early Monasticism: The Origin and Development of a Motif." *Viator* 5 (1974): 1-32.

Archambault, Paul. "The Silencing of Cornelia: Heloise, Abelard, and their Classics." *Papers on Language and Literature* 6.1 (1970): 3-17.

Armstrong, Nancy. *Desire and Domestic Fiction: A Political History of the Novel*. Oxford & New York: Oxford UP, 1987.

Aronson, Nicole. *Madame de Rambouillet ou la magicienne de la chambre bleue*. Paris: Fayard, 1988.

Arrou-Vignod, Jean-Philippe. *Le Discours des absents*. Paris: Gallimard, 1993.

Asse, Eugène. *Lettres Portugaises, avec les réponses*. Lettres de Mlle Aissé, suivies de celles de Montesquieu et de Madame du Deffand au chevalier d'Aydie, etc. Paris: Charpentier, 1873.

Avigdor, Eva, ed. *Coquettes et Précieuses*. Paris: Nizet, 1982.

Backer, Dorothy. *Precious Women*. New York: Basic Books, 1974.

Badinter, Elisabeth. *L'Un est L'autre*. Paris: Odile Jacob, 1986.

———. *XY De l'identité masculine*. Paris: Odile Jacob, 1992.

Bakhtin, M. M. *The Dialogic Imagination*. Trans. Caryl Emerson & Michael Holquist. Austin: U of Texas Press, 1981.

———. *Problems of Dostoevsky's Poetics*. Trans. and ed. Caryl Emerson. Minneapolis and London: U of Minnesota Press, 1984.

Ballaster, Ros. *Seductive Forms: Women's Amatory Fiction from 1684 to 1740*. Oxford: Clarendon Press, 1990.

Barnett, Richard. "The Castrated Text: Discursive Annihilation in "Les Lettres Portugaises." *The Language Quarterly* 24.3-4 (1986): 23-30.

Barthes, Roland. *A Lover's Discourse: Fragments*. New York: Hill & Wang, 1978.

———. *Fragments d'un discours amoureux*. Paris: Seuil, 1977.

———. "Language et vêtement." *Critique* 142 (1959): 242-252.

Baudrillard, Jean. *Seduction*. Trans. Brian Singer. New York: St. Martin's Press, 1979.

Baumann, Emile. *Héloïse: L'amante et l'abbesse*. Paris: Albin Michel, 1934.

Bazin, Nancy Topping & Freeman, Alma. "The Androgynous Vision." *Women's Studies* 2 (1974): 185-227.

Beasley, Faith. *Revising Memory*. New Brunswick & London: Rutger UP, 1990.

Beaulieu, Jean-Philippe. "Le Statut des lettres portugaises dans les formes épistolaires du XVIIe siècle." *Orbis Litterarum* 45 (1990): 330-340.

Beer, Gillian. "Our Unnatural No-voice": "The Heroic Epistle, Pope, and Woman's Gothic." *Yearbook of English Studies* 12 (1982): 125-151.

Beizer, Janet. *Narratives of Hysteria in Nineteenth-Century France*. Ithaca & London: Cornell UP, 1993.

Bell, Thomas. *Peter Abelard after Marriage: The Spiritual Direction of Heloise and her Nuns through Liturgical Song*. Kalamazoo: Cistercian Publications, 2007.

Benjamin, Jessica. "A Desire of One's Own: Psychoanalytic Feminism and Intersubjective Space." *Feminist Studies. Critical Studies*. Ed. Teresa de Lauretis. Bloomington: Indiana UP, 1986.

Benstock, Shari. "From Lettres to Literature: *La Carte Postale* in the Epistolary Genre." *Genre* 28.3 (1985): 257-289.

———. *Textualizing the Feminine: On the limits of Genre*. Norman and London: U of Oklahoma Press, 1991.

Benton, John F. and Ercoli, Fiorella Prosperetti. "The Style of the "*Historia* Calamitatum": A Preliminary Test of the Authenticity of the Correspondence Attributed to Abelard and Heloise." *Viator* 6 (1975): 59-77.

Berg, Elizabeth. "The Third Woman." *Diacritics* 12 (1982): 11-20.

Berthelot, Anne. "La Renaissance du moyen âge: *Pierre ou la consolation* de Marie Laberge." *Etudes Francophones* 12.1 (1997): 37-45.

Beugnot, Bernard. "Style ou styles épistolaires?" *Revue d'Histoire Littéraire de la France* 6 (1978): 939-949.

Bloch, Howard. *Medieval Misogyny and the Invention of Western Romantic Love*. Chicago and London: U of Chicago Press, 1991.

Bloom, Harold, ed. *Deconstruction and Criticism*. New York: Seabury Press, 1979.

Bornstein, Kate. *Gender Outlaw: On Men, Women and the Rest of us*. New York and London: Routledge, 1994.

Bossis, Mireille, ed. *L'Epistolarité à travers les siècles*. Stuttgart; Verlag, Gunter Narr, 1990.

———. *La Lettre à la croisée de l'individuel et du social*. Paris: Kimé, 1994.

Boulogne, Jean-Claude. *L'Histoire de la pudeur*. Paris: Orban, 1986.

Bourgain, Pascale. "Héloïse." *Abélard en son temps*. Actes du Colloque International organisé à l'occasion du 9e centenaire de la naissance de Pierre Abélard (14-19 mai 1979). Paris: Les Belles Lettres, 1981.

Bowie, Malcolm. *Lacan*. Cambridge: Harvard UP, 1991.

Bozzolo, Carla. "L'Humaniste Gontier Col et la traduction française des Lettres d'Abélard et Héloïse." *Romania* 95 (1974): 199-215.

Bray, Bernard. *L'Art de la lettre amoureuse. Des Manuels aux romans*. (1500-1700). Paris: Mouton, 1967.

———. "L'Epistolier et son public en France au XVIIe siècle." *Trauvaux de Linguistique et de Littérature* 11.2 (1973): 7-17.

———. "Héloïse et Abélard au XVIIIe siècle en France: une imagerie épistolaire." *Studies on Voltaire and the 18th Century* 151 (1976): 385-404.

———. "La Signification des structures adversatives dans la IVe Lettre Portugaise." *Actes de New Orleans* Paris: Papers on French 17th Century Literature, 1968.

Bray, René. *La Préciosité et les précieux*. Paris: Albin Michel, 1948.

Brengues, Jacques. "La Correspondance amoureuse et le sacré." *Ecrire, publier, lire les correspondances*. Eds. Jean-Louis Bonnat and Mireille Bossis. Nantes: Publication de l'Université de Nantes, 1983.

Brenkman, John. "The Other and the One: Psychoanalysis, Reading, the Symposium." *Yale French Studies* 55.56 (1977): 396-456.

Brittan, Arthur. *Masculinity and Power.* Oxford: Basil Blackwell, 1989.

Brivic, Sheldon. *The Veil of Signs: Joyce, Lacan and Perception.* Urbana and Chicago: U of Illinois Press, 1991.

Brook, Leslie. "Reiterated Quotations and Statements in Jean de Meun's Translation of the Abelard-Heloise Correspondence." *Zeitschrift fur Romanische Philologie* 105.1-2. (1989): 81-91.

Brooks, Peter. *Body Work: Objects of Desire in Modern Narrative.* Cambridge: Harvard UP, 1993.

———. *Reading for the Plot*. New York: Knopf, 1984.

Broome, Judith. *Fictive Domains: Body, Landscape, and Nostalgia, 1717-1770.* Lewisburg: Bucknell UP, 2007.

Brown, Peter. *The Body and Society: Men, Women and Sexual Renunciation in Early Christianity*. New York: Columbia UP, 1988.

Brückman, Patricia. "Religious Hope and Resignation": The Process of "Eloisa to Abelard." *English Studies in Canada* 3 (1977): 153-63.

Buffault, Anne Vincent. *The History of Tears: Sensibility and Sentimentality in France*. Marseille: Macmillan Press, 1991.

Burns, Jane. "The Man behind the Lady in Troubadour Lyric." *Romance Notes* 25.3 (1985): 254-270.

Burge, James. *Heloise and Abelard: A New Biography*. San Francisco: HarperCollins, 2003.

Butler, Judith. *Gender Trouble: Feminism and the Subversion of Identity*. New York and London: Routledge, 1990.

———. "Performative Acts and Gender Constitution: An Essay in Phenomenology and Feminist Theory." *Performing Feminisms*. Ed. Ellen Case. Baltimore & London: John Hopkins UP, 1990.

Bygrave, Stephen. "Missing parts: Voice and Spectacle in Eloisa to Abelard." *Pope. New Contexts*. Ed. David Fairer. New York & London: Harvester Press, 1990.

Bynum, Caroline Walker. *Fragmentation and Redemption: Essays on Gender and the Human Body in Medieval Religion*. New York: Zone Books, 1991.

———. *Gender and Religion: On the Complexity of Symbols*. Eds. Caroline Walker Bynum, Stevan Harrell and Paula Richman. Boston: Beacon Press, 1986.

———. *Jesus as Mother: Studies in the Spirituality of the High Middle Ages*. Berkeley & Los Angeles, U of California Press, 1982.

Byrd, Max. "The Madness, The Whorehouse, and the Convent." *Partisan Review* 47.2 (1977): 268-78.

Cadden, Joan. *Meanings of Sex Difference in the Middle Ages: Medicine, Science and Culture*. Cambridge: Cambridge UP, 1993.

Caillois, Roger. *Les Jeux et les hommes*. Paris: Gallimard, 1967.

Calabrese, Michael. "Ovid and the Female Voice in the *De Amore* and the *Letters* of Abelard and Heloise." *Modern Philology* 95.1 (1997): 1-26.

Caplan, Pat, ed. *The Cultural Construction of Sexuality*. London & New York: Tavistock, 1987.

Carlo, François. *Précieuses et autres indociles*. Birmingham: Summa, 1987.

Carrell, Susan Lee. "From Dialogue to Monologue: Mariane's Fourth Letter." *Actes de New Orleans*. Biblio 17. Paris: Papers on French 17th Century Literature, Colloquium on *Les Lettres portugaises*, 1968.

———. *Le Soliloque de la passion féminine ou le dialogue illusoire*. Paris: Gunter Narr Verlag, 1982.

Casanova. Hélène. "Autofiction et création dans Héloïse et Abélard d'Antonin Artaud. " *Romance Notes* 37.2 (1997): 139-145.

Castle, Terry. *Masquerade and Civilization: The Carnavelesque in Eighteenth-Century English Culture and Fiction*. Stanford, CA: Stanford UP, 1986.

Charrier, Charlotte. *Héloïse dans l'histoire et dans la légende*. Genève: Slatkine Reprints, 1977.

Cheney, Victor. *A Brief History of Castration*. Bloomington: AuthorHouse, 2006.

Chupeau, J. "Remarques sur la genèse des 'Lettres Portugaises.'" *Revue d'Histoire Littéraire de la France* 3-4 (1969): 506-524.

Cixous, Hélène. *La Venue à l'écriture*. Paris: 10/18, 1977.

Cizewski, Wanda. "From *Historia* calamitatum to Amours et infortunes: The Legend of Abelard and Heloise in Seventeenth-Century France." *Studies in Medievalism* 3.1 (1987): 71-82.

Clanchy, M. T. *Abelard: A Medieval Life*. Oxford: Blackwell Publishers, 1997.

Clark, S.H. *Sordid Images: The Poetry of Masculine Desire*. London & New York: Routledge, 1994.

Clark, Timothy. *Derrida, Heidegger, Blanchot: Sources of Derrida's Notion and Practice of Literature*. Cambridge: Cambridge UP, 1992.

Costello, Jeanne. "Taking the "Woman" Out of Women's Autobiography: The Perils and Potentials of Theorizing Female Subjectivities." *Diacritics* 21 (1991): 123-134.

Cronk, Nicolas. " Picturing the Text : Authorial Direction of Illustration in Eighteenth-Century French Fiction. " *Eighteenth-Century Fiction* 14.3.4 (2002): 393-414.

Cryle, Peter. *Geometry in the Boudoir*. Ithaca & London: Cornell UP, 1994.

Culler, Jonathan. *On Deconstruction: Theory and Criticism after Structuralism*. Ithaca, New York: Cornell UP, 1982.

Cummings, Katherine. "A Spurious Set (Up): "Fetching Females" and "Seductive" Theories in Phaedrus, Plato's Pharmacy", and Spurs." *Genders* 8 (1990): 38-61.

———. *Telling Tales: the Hysteric's Seduction in Fiction and Theory*. Stanford: Stanford UP, 1991.

Danahy, Michael. "Social, Sexual and Human Spaces in *La Princesse de Clèves. French Forum*. 63 (1981): 212-223.

Dardigna, Anne-Marie. *Les Châteaux d'Eros ou l'infortune du sexe des femmes*. Paris: Maspero, 1980.

DeJean, Joan. *Fictions of Sappho*. Chicago: U of Chicago Press, 1989.

———. *Libertine Strategies: Freedom and the Novel in Seventeenth-Century France*. Columbus: Ohio State UP, 1981.

———. *Literary Fortifications: Rousseau, Laclos, Sade*. Princeton: Princeton UP, 1984.

———. *Tender Geographies: Women and the Origins of the Novel in France*. New York: Columbia UP, 1991.

Delcourt, Marie. *Hermaphrodite: Myths and Rites of Bisexual Figure in Classical Antiquity*. London: Studio Books, 1961.

DeLey, Herbert. "Dans les Regles du plaisir": Transformation of Sexual Knowledge in Seventeenth-Century France." *French Literature Series*. 10 (1983): 10-19.

Deloffre,M. "Les "Lettres Portugaises" miracle d'amour ou miracle de culture." *CAIEF* 20 (1968): 19-37.

Démoris, R. "Esthétique et libertinage: Amour de l'art et art d'aimer." *Eros philosophe. Discours libertin des Lumières.*

Eds. Fr. Moreau et A.M. Rieu. Paris: H. Champion, 1984, pp. 149-161.

Denby, David. *Sentimental Narrative and the Social Order in France, 1760-1820.* Cambridge: Cambridge UP, 1994.

Denis, Delphine. "Conversations et enjoûment au XVII siècle." *Du Goût, de la conversation & des femmes*. Etudes rassemblées par Alain Montandon. Clermont Ferrand: Littératures, Association des publications de la Faculté des Lettres et Sciences Humaines de Clermont-Ferrand, 1994.

Dens, Jean-Pierre. "L'Art de la conversation au dix-septième siècle." *Lettres Romanes* 27 (1973): 215-224.

Derrida, Jacques. *La Carte postale de Socrate à Freud et au-delà.* Paris: Flammarion, 1980.

———. *Dissemination*. Trans. Barbara Johnson. Chicago: U of Chicago Press, 1981.

———. "Fors." *Georgia Review*. Trans. Nicolas Abraham and Maria Torok. 31.1 (1977): 64-116.

———. *Limited Inc.* Trans. Samuel Weber. Evanston: Northwestern UP, 1988.

———. "Living On: Border Lines." Trans. James Hulbert. *Deconstruction and Criticism*. Eds. Harold Bloom, Paul de Man, Jacques Derrida, Geofrrey H. Hartman, and J. Hillis Miller. New York: Seabury Press, 1983.

———. *Spurs: Nietzche's Styles*. Trans. Barbara Harlow. Chicago & London: U of Chicago Press, 1979.

———. *The Ear of the Other*. Trans. Peggy Kamuf. Lincoln and London: U of Nebraska Press, 1985.

DesCamps, Marc-Alain. *Le Nu et le vêtement*. Paris: Editions Universitaires, 1972.

Desjardins, Marie-Catherine. *Lettres et billets galants*. Ed. Micheline Cuénin. Publications de la Société d'Etude du XVIIe siècle, 1975.

Didier, Béatrice. *L'Ecriture femme*. Paris: PUF, 1981.

Doane, Mary Ann. "Veiling over Desire: Close-Ups of the Woman." *Feminism and Psychoanalysis*. Eds. Richard Feldstein and Judith Roof. Ithaca & London: Cornell UP, 1989.

Doody, Margaret Anne. "Deserts, Ruins and Troubled Waters: Female Dreams in Fiction and the Development of the Gothic Novel." *Genre* 10.4 (1977): 529-573.

Dronke, Peter. *Abelard and Heloise in Medieval Testimonies*. Glasgow: Glasgow UP, 1976.

———. "Héloïse and Mariane." Some Reconsiderations." *Romanische Forschungen* 72 3-4 (1960): 223-256.

———. *Women Writers of the Middle Ages: A Critical Study of Texts from Perpetua (+203) to Marguerite Porete (+1310)*. Cambridge: Cambridge UP, 1984.

Dubois, Page. *Sowing the Body: Psychoanalysis and Ancient Representations of Women*. Chicago & London: U of Chicago Press, 1988.

Duchêne, Jacqueline. *Bussy-Rabutin*. Paris: Fayard, 1992.

Duchêne, Roger. "Lettre et portrait au XVII siècle." *Le Portrait littéraire*. Directed by K. Kupisz, G.A. Pérouse and J.Y. Debreuille. Lyon: PUL, 1988.

———. "Les Métamorphoses d'une correspondance privée." *RHLF* 1 (1976): 29-46.

———. "Réalité vécue et réussite littéraire: le statut particulier de la lettre." *Revue d'Histoire littéraire de la France* 2 (1971): 177-194.

Dulong, Claude. *L'Amour au XVII siècle*. Paris: Hachette, 1969.

Dumonceaux, Pierre. *Langue et sensibilité au XVII siècle*. Genève: Droz, 1975.

Eagleton, Terry. *The Ideology of the Aesthetic*. Oxford: Basil Blackwell, 1990.

Earnshaw, Doris. *The Female Voice in Medieval Romance Lyric*. New York: Peter Lang, 1988.

Eliade, Mircea. *Mephistopheles and the Androgyne*. Trans. J.M. Cohen. New York: Sheed and Ward, 1965.

Fairer, David. "Milton's Lady and Pope's Eloisa." *Southern Review* 12.3 (1979): 209-226.

Faret, N. *L'Honnête homme ou l'art de plaire à la cour*. Paris: Besoigne, 1681.

Favret, Mary. *Romantic Correspondence: Women, Politics and the Fiction of Letters*. Cambridge: Cambridge UP, 1993.

Feilla, Cecilia. "From "Sainted Maid" to "Wife in all her Grandeur": Translations of Heloise, 1687-1817." *Eighteenth-Century Life* 28.2 (2004): 1-16.

———. "Translating Communities: The Institutional Epilogue to the Letters of Abelard and Heloise." *The Yale Journal of Criticism* 16.2 (2003): 363-379.

Felman, Shoshana. *What Does a Woman Want? Reading and Sexual Difference*. Baltimore & London: John Hopkins UP, 1993.

Ferguson, Chris. "Autobiography as Therapy: Guibert de Nogent, Peter Abelard, and the Making of Medieval Autobiography." *Journal of Medieval and Renaissance Studies* 13.2 (1983): 187-212.

Ferguson, Rebecca. *The Unbalanced Mind: Pope and the Rule of Passion*. Sussex: Harvester Press, 1986

Fisher, Sheila and Halley Janet, eds. *Seeking the Woman in Late Medieval and Renaissance Writings*. Knoxville: U of Tennessee Press, 1989.

Foster, Dennis. *Confession & Complicity in Narrative*. Cambridge: Cambridge UP, 1987.

Foster, Edward. "Rhetorical Control in Pope's *Eloisa to Abelard.*" *Tennessee Studies in Literature* 13 (1968): 63-73.

Foucault, Michel. *Madness and Civilization: A History of Insanity in the Age of Reason*. Trans. Richard Howard. New York: Vintage Books, 1965.

———. *Power/Knowledge: Selected Interviews & Other Writings 1972-1977*. Trans. Colin Gordon, Leo Marshall, John Mepham & Kate Soper. New York: Pantheon Books, 1980.

———. *The History of Sexuality: Volume 1: An Introduction*. Trans. Robert Hurley. New York: Pantheon Books, 1978.

———. *The Order of Things: An Archaeology of the Human Sciences*. New York: Vintage Books, 1994.

Fraioli, Deborah. "Pierre Bayle's Reflections on a Much Discussed Woman: the Heloise Article in the *Dictionnaire historique et critique*." *Listening to Heloise: The Voice of a Twelfth-Century Woman*. Ed. Bonnie Wheeler. New York: St. Martin's Press, 2000. 341-360.

Francus, Marilyn. "An Augustan's Metaphysical Poem: Pope's *Eloisa to Abelard*." *Studies in Philology* 87 (1990): 476-491.

Frank, Donald. "Abelard as Imitator of Christ." *Viator* 1 (1970): 107-113.

Frappier-Mazur, Lucienne. "Marginal Canons: Rewriting the Erotic." *Yale French Studies* 74 (1988): 112-128.

Freydberg, Bernard. "Nietzche in Derrida's *Spurs*: Deconstruction as Deracination. " *History of European Ideas* 11 (1989): 685-693.

Garaud, Christian. "Qu'est-ce que le Rabutinage." *Dix-Septième Siècle* 93 (1971): 27-53.

Garber, Marjorie. *Vested Interests: Cross-Dressing and Cultural Anxiety*. New York: Harper, 1992.

Gelpi, Barbara Charlesworth. "The Politics of Androgyny." *Women's Studies* 2 (1974): 151-160.

Genette, Gérard. *Narrative Discourse: An Essay in Method*. Trans. Jane E. Lewin. New York: Cornell UP, 1993.

———. "Vraisemblance et motivation." *Communications* 11 (1968): 5-21.

Georgianna, Linda. "Any Corner of Heaven: Heloise's Critique of Monasticism." *Mediaeval Studies* 49 (1987): 221-53.

Gérard, Mireille. "Art epistolaire et art de la conversation: Les Vertus de la familiarité." *Revue d'Histoire Littéraire de la France* 6 (1978): 958-974.

Gilson, Etienne. *Heloise & Abelard*. Ann Arbor: U of Michigan Press, 1960.

Goldsmith, Elizabeth. *Exclusive Conversations: The Art of Interaction in Seventeenth-Century France*. Philadelphia: U of Pennsylvania Press, 1988.

———. "The Politics of Sociability and Sincerity in the Letters of Bussy-Rabutin." *French Forum* 3.8 (1983): 232-242.

———. *Writing the Female Voice*. Boston: Northeastern UP, 1989.

Goodwin, Sarah Webster, & Elisabeth Bronfen, eds. *Death and Representation*. Baltimore & London: John Hopkins UP, 1993.

Gordon, I .R. F. *A Preface to Pope*. London & New York: Longman, 1976.

Grosz, Elizabeth. *Volatile Bodies: Toward a Corporeal Feminism*. Bloomington & Indianapolis: Indiana UP, 1994.

Guénoun, Solange. "Séparation, séduction, épistolarité: le geste épistolaire." *Les Visages de l'amour au XVII siècle*. Toulouse: Service des Publications l'Université de Toulouse, 1984.

Guggenheim, Michel, ed. *Women in French Literature*. Saratoga: Anma Libri, 1988.

Guillerm, Alain. " Le Système de l'iconographie galante. " *Dix-huitième siècle* (1980): 177-194.

Hagstrum, Jean. *Sex and Sensibility: Ideal and Erotic Love from Milton to Mozart*. Chicago: U of Chicago Press, 1980.

Hamilton, Elizabeth. *Heloise*. New York: Doubleday & Company, 1967.

Hans, Marie-Françoise. *Les Femmes, la pornographie, l'érotisme*. Paris: Seuil, 1978.

Harris, Daniel. "Androgyny: "The Sexist Myth in Disguise." *Women's Studies* 2 (1974): 171-184.

Harth, Erica. *Cartesian Women: Versions and Subversions of Rational Discourse in the Old Regime*. Ithaca & London: Cornell UP, 1992.

Harvey, Elizabeth. *Ventriloquized Voices: Feminist Theory and English Renaissance Texts.* London: Routledge, 1992.

———. "Ventriloquizing Sappho: Ovid, Donne and the Erotics of the Feminine Voice." *Criticism: A Quarterly for Literature and the Arts* 31.2 (1989): 115-138.

Haskins, Susan. *Mary Magdalen : Myth and Metaphor.* New York & London: Harcourt Brace, 1993.

Heath, Stephen. "Difference." *Screen* 19.3 (1978): 51-112.

Heilbrun, Carolyn. *Toward a Recognition of Androgyny*. New York: Knopf, 1973.

Hepworth, Mike and Turner, Bryan. *Confession: Studies in Deviance and Religion*. London: Rouledge and Kegan Paul, 1982.

Herman, Jan. *Le Mensonge romanesque*. Amsterdam: Leuven UP, 1989.

Hesse, Carla. "Enlightenment Epistemology and the Laws of Authorship in Revolutionary France, 1777-1793." *Representations* 30 (1990): 109-131.

———. "Louise-Félicité de Kéralio-Robert" *Writers of the French Enlightenment.* 1.131 (2005): 262-6.

———. *Publishing and Cultural Politics in Revolutionary Paris, 1789-1810*. Berkeley: U of California Press, 1991.

Hipp, Marie-Thérèse. *Mythes et Réalités: Enquête sur le roman et les mémoires* (1660-1700). Paris: Klincksieck, 1976.

Hodgson, Richard. "Le Roman paradoxal: Une Analyse des polarités dans *Les Lettres Portugaises*." *Actes de New Orleans*. Biblio 17. Paris: Papers on French 17th Century Literature, Colloquium on *Les Lettres Portugaises*, 1968.

Hodnett, Edward. *Image and Text : Studies in the Illustration of English Literature.* London: Scolar Press, 1982.

Hoffmann, Paul. *La Femme dans la pensée des lumières.* Paris : Editions, Ophrys, 1977.

Holloway, Julia Bolton, Wright, Constance, and Bechtold, Joan, eds. *Equally in God's Image: Women in the Middle Ages*. New York: Peter Lang, 1990.

Houillon, H. "La Femme en France aux XVIIè et XVIIIè siècles." *Histoire mondiale de la femme*. Ed. P. Grimal. vol.4. Paris: Nouvelle Librairie de France, 1966. 1-98.

Howard, Jacqueline. *Reading Gothic Fiction: A Bakhtinian Approach*. Oxford: Larendon Press, 1994.

Howells, Coral Ann. *Love, Mystery & Misery: Feeling in Gothic Fiction*. London: University of London, Athlone Press, 1978.

Huchet, Jean-Charles. "La Voix d'Héloïse." *Romance Notes* 25.3 (1985): 271-287.

Hume, Robert. "Exuberant Gloom, Existential Agony, and Heroic Despair: Three Varieties of Negative Romanticism." *The Gothic Imagination: Essays in Dark Romanticism*. Ed. G.R. Thompson. Pullman: Washington State UP, 1974.

———. "Gothic Versus Romantic: A Revaluation of the Gothic Novel." *PMLA* 84.2 (1969): 282-290.

Hunt, Lynn, ed. *Eroticism and the Body Politic*. Baltimore & London: John Hopkins UP, 1994.

Ihde, Don and Hugh J. Silverman, eds. *Descriptions*. New York: State U of New York Press, 1985.

Irigaray, Luce. *Sexes and Genealogies*. Trans. Gillian C. Gill. New York: Columbia UP, 1993.

———. *This Sex which is not One*. Trans. Catherine Porter. New York: Cornell UP, 1985.

Jack, R.D.S. "Pope's Mediaeval Heroine: *Eloisa to Abelard*." *Alexander Pope: Essays for the Tercentary*. Ed. Colin Nicholson Aberdeen: Aberdeen UP, 1988.

Jackson, Wallace. *Vision and Re-Vision in Alexander Pope*. Detroit: Wayne State UP, 1983.

Jaeger. C.S. "The Prologue to the *Historia* Calamitatum and the "Authenticity Question." *Euphorion* 74 (1980): 1-15.

Jaeger, Stephen. " Epistolae duorum amantium & the Ascription to Heloise & Abelard. " *Voices in Dialogue: Reading Women in the Middle Ages*. Eds. Linda Olson & Kathryn Kerby-Fulton. Notre Dame: Notre Dame UP, 2005. 125-66.

Jankelevitch, V. *L'Irréversible et la nostalgie*. Paris: Flammarion, 1974.

Jansen, Katherine Ludwig. *The Making of the Magdalen: Preaching and Popular Devotion in the Later Middle Ages*. Princeton: Princeton, UP, 2000

Jensen, Katherine. "Rewriting for Vraisemblance: Grenaille's Versions of Héloïse." *Cahiers du dix-septième* 3.1 (1989): 155-167.

———. *Writing Love: Letters, Women, and the Novel in France, 1605-1776*. Carbondale & Edwardsville: Southern Illinois UP, 1995.

Jones, John. *Pope's Couplet Art*. Ohio: Ohio UP, 1969.

Jost, François. "Le Roman épistolaire et la technique narrative au XVIIIe siècle." *Comparative Literature Studies* 3.4 (1966): 397-421.

Jouhandeau, Marcel. Introduction. "Deux religieuses et l'amour." *Lettres d'Héloïse et d'Abélard et lettres de la religieuse portugaise*. Paris: Armand Colin, 1959.

Juvenal, Felix. *Le Portrait de la coquette*. Paris: Charles de Sercy, 1659.

Kahn, Madeleine. *Narrative Transvestism: Rhetoric and Gender in the Eighteenth-Century English Novel*. Ithaca & London: Cornell UP, 1991.

Kalmey, Robert. "Pope's Eloisa to Abelard and "Those Celebrated Letters." *Philological Quarterly* 47. 2 (1968): 164-178.

———. "Pope's Eloisa to Abelard and some 'pretty conceptions' from Crashaw." *Studies in Voltaire and the Eighteenth Century* 241 (1986): 29-40.

Kamuf, Peggy. *Fictions of Feminine Desire*. Lincoln: U of Nebraska Press , 1982.

———. *Signature Pieces: On the Institution of Authorship*. Ithaca & London: Cornell UP, 1988.

———. "Writing like a Woman." *Women and Language in Literature and Society*. Eds. Sally McConnell-Ginet, Ruth Borker and Nelly Furman. New York: Praeger, 1980.

Kany, Charles. *The Beginnings of th Epistolary Novel in France, Italy and Spain*. Berkeley: Berkeley UP, 1937.

Kauffman, Linda. *Discourses of Desire: Gender, Genre and Epistolary Fictions*. Ithaca, New York: Cornell UP, 1986.

———. *Special Delivery: Epistolary Modes in Modern Fiction*. Chicago: Uof Chicago Press, 1992.

Kaufman, Vincent. *L'Equivoque épistolaire*. Paris: Minuit, 1990.

Kearney, Eileen. "Heloise: Inquiry and the *Sacra Pagina*." *Ambiguous Realities: Women in the Middle Ages and Renaissance*. Eds. Carole Levin and Jeanie Watson. Detroit: Wayne State UP, 1987.

Kelly, Veronica and Dorothea Von Mücke, eds. *Body & Text in the Eighteenth Century*. Stanford: Stanford UP, 1994.

Kenan-Rimmon, Shlomith. *Poetics Today* 1.4 (1980): 151-159.

Kestner, Joseph. *The Spatiality of the Novel*. Detroit: Wayne State UP, 1978.

Koepke, Wulf. "Epistolary Fiction and its Impact on Readers: Reality and Illusion." in *Aesthetic Illusion: Theoretical & Historical Aproaches*. Berlin & New York: Gruter, 1990.

Krieger, Murray. "Eloisa to Abelard": The Escape from Body or the Embrace of Body." *Eighteenth Century Studies* 3.1 (1969): 28-47.

Kristeva, Julia. *Soleil noir: Dépression et mélancolie*. Paris: Gallimard, 1987.

———. *Tales of Love*. Trans. Leon S. Roudiez. New York: Columbia UP, 1987.

———. *Le Texte du roman: Approche sémiologique d'une structure discursive transformationnelle*. Paris: Mouton, 1970.

Kuefler, Matthew. "Castration and Eunuchism in the Middle Ages. " *Handbook of Medieval Sexuality*. Eds. Vern L. Bullough & James A. Brundage. New York & London: Garland, 1996. 279-306.

Kuhn, Annette; *The Power of the Image: Essays on Representation and Sexuality*. London: Routledge, 1985.

Lacan, Jacques. *Feminine Sexuality: Jacques Lacan and the école freudienne*. Eds. Juliet Mitchell and Jacqueline Rose, Trans. Jacqueline Rose. New York: Pantheon Books & W.W. Norton, 1985.

Lamarche-Vadel, Gaëtane. *De la Duplicité: Les figures du secret au XVIIe siècle*. Paris: La Différence, 1994.

LaPlanche, Jean et Pontalis, J. B. *Vocabulaire de la psychanalyse* Paris: Presses Universitaires de France, 1967.

Lathuillère, Roger. "La Langue des précieux." *Travaux de Linguistique et de Littérature* 26.1 (1987): 243-269.

Laufer, Roger. *Style Rococo, style des "lumières*. Paris: José Corti, 1963.

Lebeque, Raymond. *La Préciosité: étude historique et linguistique*, tome 1. Genève: Droz, 1966.

———. "La Sensibilité dans les lettres d'amour au XVII siècle." *CAIEF* 11(1959): 77-85.

LeBrun, Jacques. "L'Institution et le corps lieux de la mémoire." *Corps ecrit* 3 (1984): 111-121.

Lechte, John. "Woman and the Veil-or Rousseau's Fictive Body. " *French Studies* 39.4 (1985): 423-441.

LeClerq, Jean. "Modern Psychology and the Interpretation of Medieval Texts." *Speculum* 28.3 (1973): 476-490.

Leibacher-Ouvrard, Lise. «L'Eunuque anathema et prétexte : economie libidinale et construction de l'hétérosexualité, " *Sexualité, marriage et famille au XVIII*[e] *siècle*. Laval : Laval UP,

Lemaire, Anika. *Jacques Lacan*. London: Routledge & Kegan Paul, 1977.

Lemoine-Luccioni, Eugénie. *La Robe: Essai psychanalytique sur le vêtement*. Paris: Seuil, 1983.

Lennon, Thomas. *Reading Bayle.* Toronto : U of Toronto Press, 1999.

Lévêque, André. "L'Honnête homme" et "L'Homme de bien" au XVII siècle." *PMLA* 4.1 (1957): 620-632.

Libis, Jean. *Le Mythe de l'androgyne*. Paris: Berg, 1980.

Lipking, Lawrence. *Abandoned Women & Poetic Tradition*. Chicago & London: U of Chicago Press, 1988.

Lipton, Eunice. "Women Pleasure and Painting." *Genders* 7 (1990): 69-85.

Locklear, Glorianna. "Delicious Poison; Heloise and Abelard out of Time." *Popular Culture Review*. 4.1 (1993): 39-47.

Lougee, Carolyn. *Le Paradis des femmes: Women, Salons, and Social Stratification in Seventeenth-Century France*. Princeton: Princeton UP, 1976.

Lyons, John & Nichols, Stephen, eds. *Mimesis: from Mirror to Method*. Hanover & London: University Press of New England, 1982.

MacArthur, Elizabeth. *Extravagant Narratives: Closure and Dynamics in the Epistolary Form*. Princeton, New Jersey: Princeton UP, 1990.

MacLean, Ian. *Woman Triumphant: Feminism in French Literature 1610-1652*. Oxford: Clarendon Press; 1977.

Magendie, Maurice. *La Politesse mondaine et les théories de l'honnêteté en France, au XVII siècle de 1660-1660*. Paris: Felix Alcan, 1926.

Marmon, Shaun. *Eunuchs and Sacred Boundaries in Islamic Society*. NY & Oxford: Oxford UP, 1995.

Marshall, Donald, ed. *Literature as Philosophy. Philosophy as Literature*. Iowa City: U of Iowa Press, 1987.

Martin, Chris. *Dangereux suppléments: l'illustration du roman en France au dix-huitième siècle.* Louvain & Paris: Peeters, 2005.

Matlock, Jann. *Scenes of Seduction: Prostitution, Hysteria, and Reading Difference in Nineteenth-Century France*. New York: Columbia UP, 1994.

Mauzi, Robert. *L'Idée du bonheur dans la littérature et la pensée française au XVIIIe siècle.* Paris: Albin Michel, 1994.

Mayo, Janet. *A History of Ecclesiastical Dress*. New York: Holmes and Meier, 1984.

McLaughlin, Mary. "Abelard as Autobiographer: The Motives and Meaning of his "Story of Calamities." *Speculum* XLII.3 (1967): 463-488.

McLeod, Enid. *Héloïse*. London: Chatto & Windus, 1971.

McLeod, Glenda. "Wholly Guilty, Wholly Innocent": Héloïse to Abélard in *Dear Sister: Medieval Women and the Epistolary Genre*. Eds. Karen Cherewatuk and Ulrike Wiethaus. Philadelphia: U of Pennsylvania Press, 1993.

McNamer, Elizabeth Mary. *The Education of Heloise: Methods, Content and Purpose of Learning in the Twelfth-Century*. Lewiston, Queenston, Lampeter: Edwin Mellen Press, 1991.

Mews, Constant. *Abelard and Heloise.* Oxford: Oxford UP, 2005.

———. "Heloise, the Paraclete Liturgy and Mary Magdalen." *The Poetic and Musical Legacy of Heloise and Abelard: An Anthology of Essays by Various Authors.* Ed. Marc Stewart and David Wulstan. Ottawa: The Institute of Medieval Music, 2003. 100-112.

———. "Philosophical Themes in the *Epistolae duorum amantium:* The First Letters of Heloise and Abelard." *Listening to Heloise: The Voice of a Twelfth-Century Woman.* Ed. Bonnie Wheeler. New York: St. Martins Press, 2000. 36-52.

———. *La Voix d'Héloïse: un dialogue de deux amants.* Trans. Emilie Champs. Fribourg: Cerf, 2005.

———. *The Lost Love Letters of Heloise and Abelard : Perceptions of Dialogue in Twelfth-Century France.* New York : Palgrave, 2001.

Miles, Margaret. *Carnal Knowing: Female Nakedness & Religious Meaning in the Christian West*. Boston: Beacon Press, 1989.

Miller, Nancy. "Changing the Subject: Authorship, Writing, and the Reader." *Feminist Studies Critical Studies*. Ed. Teresa de Lauretis. Bloomington: Indiana UP, 1986.

———. *French Dressing: Women, Men and Ancien Regime Fiction*. New York & London: Routledge, 1995.

———. "I's in Drag": The Sex of Recollection. *The Eighteenth Century* 22 (1981): 48-53.

———. "Men's Reading, Women's Writing: Gender and the Rise of the Novel." *Yale French Studies* 75 (1988): 40-55.

———. "The Text's Heroine: A Feminist Critic and her Fictions." *Diacritics* (1982): 48-53.

Moi, Toril. "Patriarchal Thought and the Drive for Knowledge." *Between Feminism and Psychoanalysis*. Ed. Teresa Brennan. London & New York: Routledge, 1989.

Monick, Eugene. *Castration and Male Rage: The Phallic Wound*. Toronto: Inner City Books, 1991.

Monglond, André. *Le Préromantisme français*. Grenoble: Arthaud, 1924.

Montandon, Alain, ed. *Etiquette et politesse*. Clermont-Ferrand: Association des Publications de la Faculté des Lettres et Sciences Humaines, 1992.

Moore, Henrietta. *A Passion for Difference: Essays in Anthropology and Gender*. Bloomington & Indianapolis: Indiana UP, 1994.

Morabito, Raffaele. "Pratiques épistolières et épistolarité restreinte." *Orbis Litterarum* 44 (1989): 191-203.

Morgan, Thaïs, ed. *Men Writing the Feminine: Literature, Theory, and the Question of Genders*. Albany: State U of New York Press, 1994.

Morris, David. "The Visionary Maid": Tragic Passion and Redemptive Sympathy in "Eloisa to Abelard." *Alexander*

Pope. Ed. Harold Bloom. New York, New Haven & Philadelphia: Chelsea House Publishers, 1986.

Mortier, Roland. *Clartés et ombres du siècles des lumières*. Genève: Droz, 1969.

Muckle, J.T. "The Personal Letters Between Abelard and Heloise." *Mediaeval Studies* 15 (1953): 47-94.

Nelson, Lowry Jr. "Night Thoughts on the Gothic novel." *Yale Review* 52.2 (1962): 236-257.

Newman, Barbara. "Authority, Authenticity and the Repression of Heloise." *Journal of Medieval and Renaissance Studies* 22.3 (1992): 121-141.

Niderst, A. "Madeleine de Scudéry, construction et dépassement du portrait romanesque." in *Le Portrait littéraire*. Directed by K. Kupisz, G.A. Pérouse, J.Y. Debreuille. Lyon: PUL, 1988.

Nies, Fritz. "Un Genre féminin?" *RHLF* 6 (1978): 994-1003.

Nietzsche, Friedrich. *The Gay Science*. Trans. Walter Kaufmann. New York: Random House, 1974.

Nouvet, Claire. *Abélard et Héloïse : La Passion de la maîtrise*. Villeneuve d'Ascq : Presses Univsersitaires du Septentrion, 2009.

———. "La Castration d'Abélard: impasse et substitution." *Poétique* 83 (1990): 259-279.

———. "The Discourse of the "Whore": An Economy of Sacrifice." *MLN* 105.4 (1990): 750-773.

Nye, Andrea. "A Woman's Thought or a Man's Discipline? The Letters of Heloise and Abelard." *Hypatia* 7.3 (1992): 1-22.

Oberson, Roland. *Héloïse et Abélard: a singulière esclave, maître spécial*. Paris: Hermann, 2010.

O'Dea, Michael. "The Dialogics of Desire in *La Nouvelle Héloïse*." *Eighteenth-Century Fiction*. 7.1 (1994) : 37-50.

O'Flaherty,Wendy Doniger. *Women, Androgynes, and Other Mythical Beasts*. Chicago & London: U of Chicago Press, 1980.

O'Hehir, Brendan. "Virtue and Passion: The Dialectic of *Eloisa to Abelard.*" *Texas Studies in Literature and Language*. 2.1 (1960): 219-232.

Oliver, Kelly. *Womanizing Nietzsche*. New York & London: Routledge, 1995.

Ouellet, Réal. "La Théorie du roman épistolaire en France au XVIIIe siècle." *Studies on Voltaire and the 18th Century* 89 (1972): 1209-1227.

Ouvrard-Liebacher, Lise. "L'Eunuque anathema et prétexte: économie libidinale et construction de l'hétérosexualité." *Sexualité, mariage, et famille au XVIIIe siècle.* Eds. Olga B. Cragg and Rosena Davison. Quebec: Laval UP, 1998. 11-25.

Partner, Nancy. "No Sex, No Gender." *Speculum: A Journal of Medieval Studies* 68.2 (1993): 419-443.

Pelous, Jean-Michel. *Amour Précieux, Amour Galant*. Paris: Klincksieck, 1980.

Pernoud, Régine. *Heloise and Abelard*. New York: Stein and Day, 1973.

Perry, Ruth. *Women, Letters and the Novel*. New York: AMS Press, 1980.

Plaisant, Michèle. "Eloisa et Belinda: Les Désordres de l'âme et du corps." *Bulletin de la Société et d'études anglo-américaines des XVIIe et XVIIIe siècles*. (1985): 75-88.

Pollak, Ellen. *The Poetics of Sexual Myth: Gender & Ideology in the Verse of Swift & Pope*. Chicago & London: U of Chicago Press, 1985.

Ponton, Jeanne. *La Religieuse dans la littérature française*. Québec: Les Presses de l'Université Laval, 1969.

Poole, Fitz John Porter. "The Procreative and Ritual Constitution of Female, Male and Other." *Gender Reversals and Gender Cultures.* Ed. Sabrina Petra Ramet. London & New York: Routledge, 1996. 197-218.

Prévot, Jacques. "Le Portrait chez Bussy-Rabutin." *RHLF* 1 (1969): 1-12.

Prince, Gerald. "Introduction à l'étude du narrataire." *Poétique* 14 (1973): 178-196.

Rand, Erica. "Agency, the French Revolution, and the Art of Boucher and David." *Genders* 7 (1990): 47-65.

Restif de la Bretonne. *Le Nouvel Abélard ou lettres de deux amants qui ne se sont jamais vus*. Tome 1. Neuchâtel: Slatkine, 1987.

Richmond, Ian. *Héroisme et galanterie: l'abbé de Pure témoin d'une crise 1653-1665*. Québec: Sherbrooke, Naaman, 1977.

Ridon, Jean-Xavier. "La Carte postale ou l'impossible discours amoureux." *Dalhousie French Studies* 22 (1992): 111-118.

Robertson, D.W. *Abelard and Heloise*. New York: The Dial Press, 1972.

Roger, Alain. "La Lettre d'amour et l'effemination épistolaire." *Ecrire, publier, lire les correspondances*. Eds. J.L. Bonnat, and M. Bossis. Nantes: Publication de l'Université de Nantes, 1983.

Rogers, Katherine. *The Troublesome Helpmate: A History of Misogyny in Literature*. Seattle and London: U of Washington Press, 1966.

Rolt-Wheeler, Ethel. *Women of the Cell and Cloister*. London: Methuen & Co, 1913.

Rosbottom, Ronald. "Motifs in Epistolary Fiction: Analysis of a Narrative Sub-genre." *Esprit Créateur* 17.4 (1977): 279-301.

Rouben, C. *Bussy-Rabutin, Epistolier*. Paris: Nizet, 1974.

Rossard, Janine. *Une Clef du romantisme, la pudeur*. Paris : Nizet, 1974.

Rosso, Jeannette. "Montesquieu, Rousseau et la féminité : De la crainte à l'angélisme. " *Studi Francesi* 25.75 (1981) : 482-489.

Rousset, Jean. *Forme et Signification: Essais sur les structures littéraires de Corneille à Claudel*. Paris: José Corti, 1962.

Rubin, Gayle. "The Traffic in Women: Notes on "the Political Economy" of Sex." *Toward an Anthropology of Women*. Ed. Raynow Reiter. New York & London: Monthly Review Press, 1975.

Sarde, Michèle. *Regard sur les françaises*. Paris: Stock, 1983.

Schaberg, Jane. *The Resurrection of Mary Magdalene: Legends, Apocrypha, and the Christian Testament*. New York & London: Continuum, 2002.

Scholz, Piotro. *Eunuchs and Castrati: A Cultural History*. Princeton: Markus Wiener, 2001.

Schwartz, Joel. *The Sexual Politics of Jean-Jacques Rousseau*. Chicago & London: U of Chicago Press, 1984.

Scudéry, Madeleine. *Nouvelles conversations sur divers sujets par Mlle de Scudéry. Nouvelle Edition*. Tome 1. La Haye: Guillaume de Vays, 1710.

Secor, Cynthia. "Androgyny: An early reappraisal." *Women's Studies* 2 (1974): 161-169.

Sedgwick Kosofsky, Eve. *Between Men: English Literature and Male Homosocial Desire*. New York: Columbia UP, 1985.

———. "The Character in the Veil: Imagery of the Surface in the Gothic Novel." *PMLA* 96.2 (1981): 255-270.

———. *The Coherence of Gothic Conventions*. New York: Arno Press, 1980.

Seidler, Victor. *Rediscovering Masculinity: Reason, Language, and Sexuality*. London and New York: Routledge, 1989.

Sgard, Jean. "La Notion d'égarement chez Crébillon." *Dix-Huitième siècle* 1 (1969): 241-247.

Shepard, Mary. "A Tomb for Abelard and Heloise." *Romance Studies* 25.1 (2007): 29-42.

Showalter, Elaine. "Critical Cross-Dressing: Male Feminists and the Woman of the Year." *Raritan* (1983): 130-150.

Showalter, English. *The Evolution of the French Novel*. Princeton, New Jersey: Princeton UP, 1972.

Singer, June. *Androgyny: Toward a New Theory of Sexuality*. New York: Doubleday, 1976.

Sojcher, Jacques. "Du Mensonge à la politesse." *La Séduction*. Colloque de Bruxelles. Eds. Maurice Olender and Jacques Sojcher. Paris: Aubier, 1980.

Solé, Jacques. *L'Amour en occident à l'époque moderne*. Paris: Editions Complexe, 1976.

Sorel, Charles. "Les Lois de la galanterie." *Recueil de pièces en prose les plus agréables de ce temps composées par divers auteurs*. Paris: Charles de Sercy, 1660.

Southern, R.W. *Medieval Humanism and Other Studies*. Oxford: Basil Blackwell, 1970.

Spivak, Gayatri Chakravorty. "Feminism and Deconstruction, again: Negotiating with unacknowledged Masculinism." *Between Feminism and Psychoanalysis*. Ed. Teresa Brennan. London & New York: Routledge, 1989.

———. "Love me, Love my ombre, Elle." *Diacritics* (1984): 19-36.

Stamelman, Richard. *Lost Beyond Telling: Representations of Death and Absence in Modern French Poetry*. Ithaca & London: Cornell UP, 1990.

Stanton, Domna. *The Aristocrat as Art*. New York: Columbia UP, 1980.

———. "The Fiction of Préciosité and the Fear of Women." *Yale French Studies* 62 (1981): 107-134.

Starobinski, Jean. "Sur la flatterie." *Nouvelle Revue de Psychanalyse* 4 (1971): 131-151.

Staten, Henry. *Eros in Mourning: Homer to Lacan*. Baltimore & London: John Hopkins UP, 1995.

Stewart, Philip. *Engraven Desire: Eros, Image & Text in the French Eighteenth Century*. Durham & London: Duke UP, 1992.

———. *Le Masque et la parole: le langage de l'amour au XVIII siècle*. Paris: José Corti, 1973.

———. " L'Illustration du roman au dix-huitième siècle. " *The Eighteenth-century Now : Boundaries and Perspectives.* (2005): 226-235.

———. "On the 'Iconology' of Literary Illustration. " *Dilemmes du roman ; Essays in Honor of Georges May.* Ed. Catherine Lafarge. Saratoga: Anma Libri, 1989. 251-267.

Stewart, Susan. *On Longing*. Durham & London: Duke UP, 1993.

Stoller, Robert. *Presentations of Gender*. New Haven: Yale, UP, 1985.

Swedenborg, Emanuel. *L'Amour vraiment conjugal*. Meudon: Cercle Swedenborg, 1974.

Sweetser, Marie-Odile. "Images de la femme abandonnée: traditions, contaminations, créations." *Onze Etudes sur l'image de la femme dans la littérature française du 17ième siècle*. Ed. W. Leiner. Paris: J.M. Place, 1984.

Tambling, Jeremy. *Confession: Sexuality, Sin the subject*. Manchester & New York: Manchester UP 1990.

Taylor, Anne Robinson. *Male Novelists and their Female Voices: Literary Masquerades* New York: Whitson, 1981.

Taylor, Gary. *Castration: An Abbreviated Histoty of Western Manhood*. New York: Routledge, 2000.

Thomas, R. *Dreams of Authority: Freud and the Fictions of the Unconsciousness*. Ithaca & London: Cornell UP, 1990.

Todorov, Tzvetan. *Littérature et Signification. Langue et langage*. Paris: Larousse, 1967.

Trask, Haunoni-Kay. *Eros & Power: The Promise of Feminist Theory*. Philadelphia: U of Pennsylvania Press, 1986.

Trouille, Mary Seidman. *Sexual Politics in the Enlightenment: Women Writers read Rousseau.* Albany: State UP of New York, 1997.

Trowbridge, Hoyt. "Pope's Eloisa and the Heroides of Ovid." *Studies in the Eighteenth- Century Culture: vol 3, Racism in the Eighteenth Century*. Cleveland & London: Case Western UP, 1973.

Van baal, Jan. *Reciprocity & the Position of women*. Amsterdam: Van Gorcum, 1975.

Van Den Eynde, P. "Details biographiques sur Pierre Abélard." *Antonianum* 38 (1963): 220-223.

Verdier, Gabrielle. "Gender and Rhetoric in Some 17th Century Love Letters." *Esprit Créateur* 23.2 (1983): 45-57.

Versini, Laurent. *Le Roman épistolaire*. Paris: PUF, 1979.

Viala, Alain. "La Genèse des formes épistolaires en français: et leurs sources latines et européennes." *Revue de Littérature Comparée* 55.2 (1981): 168-183.

Vitz, Evelyn Birge. "Type et individu dans "l'autobiographie" médiévale: étude d'*Historia* Calamitatum." *Poétique* 24 (1975): 426-445.

Walter, Eric. "Le Complexe d'Abélard ou le célibat des gens de lettres." *Dix-Huitième Siècle* 12 (1980): 127-152.

Walton, Kendall. *Mimesis as Make Believe: On the Foundations of the Representational Arts*. Cambridge: Harvard UP, 1990.

Ward, John and Neville Chiavaroli. « The Young Heloise and Latin Rhetoric : Some Preliminary Comments on the 'Lost Love Letters of and Their Significance. » *Listening to Heloise: The Voice of a Twelfth-Century Woman*. Ed. Bonnie Wheeler. New York : St. Martins Press, 2000. 53-119.

Weil, Kari. *Androgyny and the Denial of Difference*. Charlottesville and London: UP of Virginia, 1992.

Winn, James. "Pope Plays the Rake: His Letters to Ladies and the Making of the Eloisa." *The Art of Alexander Pope*. Eds. Howard Erskine-Hill and Anne Smith. New York: Barnes and Noble Books, 1979.

Wood, Diane. "The Evolution of Hélisenne's Persona." *Symposium* 45.2 (1991): 140-151.

Wright, Lawrence. "Eighteenth-Century Replies to Pope's Eloisa." *Studies in Philology* 31 (1934): 519-533.

Wulstan, David. "Heloise at Argenteuil and the Paraclete. " *The Poetic and Musical Legacy of Heloise and Abelard: An Anthol-*

ogy of Essays by Variosu Authors. Eds. Marc Stewart and David Wulstan. Ottawa: The Institute of Medieval Music, 2003. 67-90.

Zimmerman, Elizabeth. "It is not the Deed but the intention of the Doer;" The Ethics of Intention and Consent in the First Two letters of Heloise." *Forum for Modern Language Studies* 42.3 (2006): 249-267.

Zumthor, Paul. "Héloise et Abelard." *Revue des Sciences Humaines* (1958): 313-332.

INDEX

A

abandoned woman motif, 16–18, 63, 76, 79, 83, 121, 146, 311

Abandoned Women and Poetic Tradition (Lipking), 231

Abelard: background information, 31; Bayle's portrayal, 189–99, 349–50; black bride metaphor, 88–90; book-burning incident, 46; burial site, 333–34; Bussy-Rabutin's revisions, 161–67, 173–75, 349; castration, 35–39, 41–45, 49–50, 73, 91–95, 109, 183–84, 188–89, 191–99, 210–12, 324–25, 346; Colardeau's portrayal, 256–69, 322–23, 350; eighteenth-century versions, 223–69, 349; feminization/emasculation, 37–39, 42, 43–45, 49, 70, 73–76, 79–80, 84–85, 91, 95–96, 166, 313–14; fictional transformations, 183–84; Gervaise's translation and revisions, 205–22, 350; Grenaille's translations and revisions, 102–34, 349; *Historia Calamitatum*, 18, 28–51; illustrated text, 215–22; Keralio's portrayal, 307–17, 350–51; love songs, 68–70, 158, 190, 319; marriage to Heloise, 34–37, 62–66, 110–11; Montifaud's portrayal and revisions, 317–31, 351; nuns' prayers, 72–76; Pope's translation and revisions, 223–56, 322–23, 350; popular translations and revisions, 256–69; religious retreat, 46–47; Rousseau's portrayal, 271–306, 350; seduction of and affair with Heloise, 32–34; self-serving motivations, 53–54, 66–67, 72–73; textual revisions and manipulations, 66–67, 72, 77–79, 88–92, 97–98; twentieth-century versions, 334–45; twenty first-century versions, 345–48; victimization stories, 28–30, 38, 41, 44–48, 76

absent lover motif, 16, 63, 155

Adieu mon unique (Audouard), 344–45

Alberic, 46, 139–40, 142, 144

Alluis, Jacques, 20, 135–45, 322, 349

A Lover's Discourse: Fragments (Barthes), 74

Altman, Janet, 54, 55, 57, 149, 151

amorous correspondence. *See* love letters

Amour précieux amour galant (Pelous), 157

Amsler, Mark, 37, 38, 43, 46

anamnesis, 165

Ancillon, Charles, 186–87, 188

Anderson, David, 256, 257–58

Andréini, Isabella, 15, 16, 19, 102

androgyny, 36–37, 39–41, 44, 73–75, 96–97, 196, 291–92

angel motif, 74–75, 97, 290–91

Anselm of Laon, 31

antifeminist discourse, 43–44

anti-marriage arguments, 105–8, 141–42, 157, 200, 260, 311

Argenteuil, 35, 36, 42

Aristocrat as Art, The (Stanton), 166

Aristophanes, 36–37, 39, 41, 97

Artaud, Antonin, 335

Asella, 49

asexuality, 303–6

Astrolabe, 33, 309–10, 340–41

Audouard, Antoine, 344–45
authorial moralizing, 107–8, 114–19, 132
autobiographical genre, 28–30, 50

B

Bakhtin, M. M., 59, 70, 79, 82, 279
Ballade des dames du temps jadis (Villon), 100
Ballaster, Ros, 110
Barthes, Roland, 74, 133, 166, 181
Bayer-Barenbaum, Linda, 227, 228, 240
Bayle, Pierre, 21, 180, 183–84, 189–203, 206, 309, 349–50
Beauchamp, François Godard de, 256
Beer, Gillian, 228, 233
Beizer, Janet, 248
Benton, John, 54
Bernard, Suzanne, 345–48
Berthelot, Anne, 343
Bertheroy, Madame Jean, 335
bienséance, 102, 107, 109, 110, 114, 136, 145
billets, 141, 142, 159
black bride metaphor, 88–90, 213, 245
Black Melancholy, 241, 262
Bloch, Howard, 43
book-burning incident, 46
borrowing a woman's voice, 43–44, 69–70
Boucher, François, 262, 263
Boursault, Edme, 17
Bray, Bernard, 11, 15, 101–2, 259
Brooks, Leslie, 99
Brooks, Peter, 110
Brown, Peter, 94
Burns, Jane, 69
Bussy-Rabutin, R. de, 15, 17, 20–21, 146–82, 200, 310, 349
Butler, Judith, 313
Bynum, Caroline Walker, 38, 73, 79
Byzantine Empire, 185

C

Cabinet, 116, 119, 130
Casanova, Hélène, 335
castration: Abelard, 35–39, 41–45, 49–50, 73, 91–95, 109, 183–84, 188–89, 191–99, 210–12, 324–25, 346; castrati practice, 185–86; Catholic doctrine, 41–42, 76; Colardeau's portrayal, 260; double castration, 42–44, 63, 77, 82, 111, 242; eunuchism, 37, 41, 45–46, 73, 184–89, 191–99, 324; Gervaise's perspective, 210–13, 350; historical perspective, 184–89; illustrated text, 218–19; philosophical perspectives, 194–99; spiritual castration, 46; story of Combabus, 192–94; surgical methods, 187–88
Champeaux, William of, 31, 189
Charrier, Charlotte, 15, 20, 42, 53–54, 64, 77, 92, 99–100, 134, 146, 153, 179, 181, 206, 215, 217–18, 256, 262, 326–27, 333, 348
chastity, 212, 293–95
Cheney, Victor, 188, 191
Christian antifeminist discourse, 43–44
Claire, 272, 275–77, 294, 297
Clairvaux, Bernard de, 79
clandestine meetings, 143–45, 156
Clark, S. H., 230, 255
Classical Age, 13–14
closed space motif, 56–58, 61–62, 71–72
coded messages, 110
code of gallantry, 148–51, 155, 158, 166, 172
Colardeau, Pierre, 22–23, 203, 256–69, 322–23, 350

Collection des meilleurs ouvrages françois composés par des femmes (Keralio), 23–24, 307
Combabus, 192–94
companionate marriage, 284, 287–92
concealed flesh, 83–84
confessional letters, 108–26, 243–45, 304–5, 312–16
Confessions (Rousseau), 23
conjugal debt, 109–11
conjugal love, 284, 287–92
consolation writings, 28–30, 58–61, 71, 199
conversation guidelines, 149–51, 155–56, 159
courtly love, 12
cowls, 83–84, 86
Crébillon, Claude-Prosper Jolyot de, 266
Crenne, Hélisenne de, 12–13
cross-dressing motif, 79, 87
Cryle, Peter, 264
crypt motif, 57, 71–72, 252–56, 262

D

d'Amboise, François, 257
debauchery, 77
debt motif, 61–62
DeJean, Joan, 18, 24–25, 116, 119, 126–28
de la Serre, Puget, 13–14
Derrida, Jacques, 57, 71, 85–86, 115, 165, 178, 254–56, 269
Des Cours, Remond, 181
d'Etrange, Julie. *See Julie ou la Nouvelle Héloïse* (Rousseau)
Deutsch, S. M., 53
Dictionnaire historique et critique (Bayle), 21, 183, 349–50
discourse of desire, 57–64, 67, 71, 76–88, 108–18, 121–24, 131, 152–53, 165–69, 258, 268–69, 275, 319
discourse of pathos, 80–83, 121–22, 146, 155, 301–2
Dissemination (Derrida), 165
dissimulation, 60, 83–86, 93, 125, 276, 295, 343
distance, 277
Doane, Mary Ann, 83
domestic bliss, 293–94
domestic responsibilities, 285
Donner, Clive, 338–41
Doody, Margaret, 228, 245, 249
double castration, 42–43, 63, 77, 82, 111, 242
double-gendered androgyne, 291–92
double-voiced discourse, 59, 70, 77, 79, 81–83, 87–88, 94, 279
drawings, 215–22
dream sequences, 151, 169–71, 174, 178, 228, 245–52, 264–65, 297–99, 324–26, 347–48
Dronke, Peter, 42, 54, 92
Dubois, Page, 181–82
Durand, Béatrice, 268
Du Tronchet, Etienne, 12

E

Earnshaw, Doris, 44, 69, 70
Ear of the Other, The (Derrida), 115
eighteenth-century versions: Colardeau's portrayal, 256–69, 350; Pope's translation and revisions, 223–56, 322–23, 350; Rousseau's portrayal, 271–306, 350
"Eloisa to Abelard" (Pope), 22, 223–56
Eloize, 103–34
engravings, 215–22
Enlightenment era, 185, 256, 271–77, 312
epistolary genre: Alluis's translations and revisions, 135–45, 349; Bussy-Rabutin's translations and revi-

sions, 146–82, 200, 349; Colardeau's portrayal, 256–69, 322–23, 350; eighteenth-century versions, 223–69, 349; Gervaise's translation and revisions, 205–22, 350; Gothic influences, 227–56; Grenaille's translations and revisions, 102–34, 349; *Historia Calamitatum*, 28–51; historical perspective, 11–18, 101–2; illustrated text, 215–22; Keralio's portrayal, 307–17, 350–51; love letters, 54–64; Meun translation, 99–100, 200; Montifaud's portrayal and revisions, 317–31, 351; poetic format, 224–56; polyphonic format, 272; Pope's translation and revisions, 223–56, 322–23, 350; Rousseau's portrayal, 271–306, 350; sexual oppression, 125–28; twentieth-century versions, 334–45; twenty first-century versions, 345–48
Epîstres familières et invectives (de Crenne), 12–13
erotic dreams, 151, 169–71, 174, 178, 228, 245–52, 264–65, 297–99, 324–26
Ethiopian bride metaphor, 88–90, 213, 245
eunuchs/eunuchism, 37, 41, 45–46, 73, 76, 87, 95–96, 184–89, 191–99, 324

F

female body, 273, 276, 280–84, 288
female hysteria, 228–29, 245–51, 254
female impersonation, 19, 68–70, 79–80, 84–85, 91, 95–96, 128–29, 268–69, 280, 313–14
Ferguson, Chris, 28
Ferrand, Madame, 17
fictional letters, 103, 108, 133–34, 136–45, 167–72, 175–82, 256–57
fictional transformations, 183–84
Fictions of Sappho 1546-1937 (DeJean), 18
forgetfulness motif, 275
fornication, 77, 91–92
"Fors" (Derrida), 57, 71, 254–56
Foster, Edward, 224, 226
Foucault, Michel, 109, 113, 247–48
Foulques, 194–99
fragmented discourse, 18–19, 67, 70, 97–98, 119, 129–34, 326–31
Fraioli, Deborah, 200
Francus, Marilyn, 250
Fulbert, 32–34, 35, 41, 108, 137–42, 145, 236, 339

G

Garber, Marjorie, 75, 79, 83–84, 86, 87
gender constructs, 73–75, 79–80, 86–87, 95–97, 125–28, 164–66, 268–69, 290–96, 313–14, 330
Genette, Gérard, 107
geographical separation, 277
Gérard-Gailly, E., 147
Gervaise, Dom, 21, 205–22, 309, 310, 350
Gilson, E., 54, 92
Godard de Beauchamp, François, 256
Goldsmith, Elizabeth, 149, 150
Gothic Revival literature, 227–56, 258, 260–62
Greek writers, 11
Grenaille, François de, 15, 19–20, 102–34, 149, 176, 244, 254, 349
Guillaume d'Oxford, 344–45

H

Halbon, L. M., 220
Harth, Erica, 150, 153
Harvey, Elizabeth, 44

Haskins, Susan, 214
Hébert, Anne, 335, 336–38
Héloïm, 95
Heloise: affair with Abelard, 32–34; Alluis's translations and revisions, 135–45, 349; Bayle's portrayal, 199–203, 349–50; as bride of Christ, 88–89, 91, 95, 131–32, 213–14, 220, 243–45, 264, 313, 348; burial site, 333–34; Bussy-Rabutin's translations and revisions, 146–82, 200, 349; Colardeau's portrayal, 256–69, 322–23, 350; debt motif, 61–62; eighteenth-century versions, 223–69, 349; fictional transformations, 183–84; Gervaise's translation and revisions, 205–22, 350; Grenaille's translations and revisions, 102–34, 349; *Historia Calamitatum*, 28–51; illustrated text, 215–22; invented letters, 175–82; Keralio's portrayal, 307–17, 350–51; love letter composition and structure, 55–64, 75–78; love letter restructuring, 66–67, 72, 77–79, 88–92, 97–98, 102–22; marriage refusal, 64–66; marriage to Abelard, 34–37, 62–66, 110–11, 200; Meun translation, 99–100, 200; Montifaud's portrayal and revisions, 317–31, 351; moral representation, 264–66; move to the Paraclete, 47–48; Pope's translation and revisions, 223–56, 322–23, 350; popular translations and revisions, 256–69; pregnancy, 62, 107–8, 141–42; Rousseau's portrayal, 271–306, 350; sexual loss, 42–43, 60–64, 71–72, 76, 80–83, 108–11; twentieth-century versions, 334–45; twenty first-century versions, 345–48
Héloïse et Abélard (Artaud), 335
Héloïse (Hébert), 336–38
Hepworth, Mike, 116, 119
Heroides (Ovid), 11, 15, 101
Hesse, Carla, 316–17
Histoire d'Eloïse et d'Abélard (Des Cours), 181
Histoire des amours et infortunes d'Abélard et d'Eloïse (Dubois), 181–82
Historia Calamitatum (Abelard), 18, 28–51
History of Sexuality (Foucault), 113
Hodnett, Edward, 216
Hoffmann, Paul, 288–89, 291, 297
honnêteté code, 148–51, 155, 158, 166, 172
Huchet, Jean-Charles, 43, 63, 64
Hughes, John, 223–24, 254
humanist writers, 12
Hunt, Lynn, 308
hypocrite theme, 124–25
hysteria, female, 228–29, 245–51, 254

I

illegitimacy, 77
illegitimate pregnancy, 286
illustrated text, 215–22
imaginary death scene, 252–54
Imaginary Order, 39, 40
impotence motif, 261–62; . *See also* castration
innocence motif, 214
invented letters, 103, 108, 133–34, 136–45, 167–72, 175–82, 256–57
Irigaray, Luce, 126
Italian castrati, 185–86
"I"/"you" dialectic, 55, 72, 76

J

Jackson, Wallace, 232–33, 234
Jansen, Katherine, 208–9, 212

Jensen, Katherine, 107, 119–20, 128–29
Julie ou la Nouvelle Héloïse (Rousseau), 23, 199, 221, 271–306, 350

K

Kahn, Madeline, 96
Kamuf, Peggy, 56, 59, 81, 89–90, 93, 95, 120, 133
Kany, Charles, 11, 15
Kauffman, Linda, 58–59, 60, 62, 152
Keralio, Louise de, 23–24, 307–17, 350–51
Krieger, Murray, 238, 250, 251
Kristeva, Julia, 242
Kuefler, Matthew, 187

L

L'Abbesse du paraclet: histoire galante d'Héloïse et d'Abailard (Montifaud), 24, 317–31
Laberge, Marie, 335, 341–44
Lacanian theory, 39–40, 42–43, 60, 64, 77, 86–87, 230, 232
Lacan, Jacques, 39
Laclos, Choderlos de, 271, 307, 312
La Fin d'Abélard (Bernard), 346–47
Lalanne, Ludovic, 53
La Magdalene Française. *See* Eloize
Laon, Anselm of, 31
Lasserre, Pierre, 335
L'Astrée (d'Urfé), 14
Lathuillère, Roger, 159, 167
La Vie d'Héloïse (Keralio), 309–10
Lechte, John, 291
Le Grand Cyrus (Scudéry), 14
Lennon, Thomas, 197
Lenoir, Alexandre, 320, 326–27, 333–34
Le Philosophe amoureux (Dubois), 182
Le Roman de la rose (Meun), 99
Le Roman d'Héloïse et Abélard (Bernard), 345–48
Les Amours d'Abailard et d'Héloïse (Alluis), 20, 136
Le Secrétaire de la cour, ou la manière d'écrire selon le temps (de la Serre), 13–14
Letter 1: Bussy-Rabutin's translations and revisions, 152–61; debt and loss, 61–64, 71–72; Grenaille's translation, 104–8; Keralio's portrayal, 310–12
Letter 2: Bussy-Rabutin's translations and revisions, 161–67; Grenaille's translation, 108–21; Keralio's portrayal, 312–14; spiritual focus, 72–75
Letter 3: Bussy-Rabutin's translations and revisions, 167–72; discourse of desire, 75–80; Grenaille's translation, 121–29; Keralio's portrayal, 314–17
Letter 4: black bride metaphor, 88–90; Bussy-Rabutin's translations and revisions, 173–75; Grenaille's translation, 129–34; Keralio's portrayal, 314–17; spiritual focus, 88–97
Letter 5, 175–81
letter manuals, 12–15, 101–2, 119, 149–51, 155–56, 159
letter novel, 15
"Lettre d'Héloïse" (Colardeau), 22–23
lettres chrétiennes, 103
Lettres de Babet (Boursault), 17
Lettres de Cléante et Bélise (Ferrand), 17
Lettres portugaises (Guilleragues), 16, 17, 146–47, 154, 202
Lettres très portugaises, 16–17
Levi-Strauss, Claude, 126
Libis, Jean, 75, 96–97

Lipking, Lawrence, 231
Locklear, Glorianna, 335, 340
Lost Beyond Telling (Stamelman), 233
Lotulphe, 46
Lougee, Caroline, 106
love letters: Alluis's translations and revisions, 135–45, 349; authenticity, 53–54; Bussy-Rabutin's translations and revisions, 146–51, 200, 349; characteristics and functional role, 54–61; Colardeau's portrayal, 256–69, 322–23, 350; conversation guidelines, 149–51, 155–56, 159; eighteenth-century versions, 223–69, 349; Gervaise's translation and revisions, 205–22, 350; Gothic influences, 227–56; Grenaille's translations and revisions, 102–34, 349; historical perspective, 11–18, 101–2; illustrated text, 215–22; Keralio's portrayal, 307–17, 350–51; medieval love correspondence, 286; Meun translation, 99–100, 200; Montifaud's portrayal and revisions, 317–31, 351; origins, 53–54; poetic format, 224–56; Pope's translation and revisions, 223–56, 322–23, 350; popular translations and revisions, 256–69; pseudo-feminocentrism, 19, 54, 66, 74, 97–98, 128–29, 254–55; Rousseau's portrayal, 271–306, 350; salutation modifications, 75–76, 88; twentieth-century versions, 334–45; twenty first-century versions, 345–48; veil motif, 83–88
A Lover's Discourse: Fragments (Barthes), 74
love–sexual difference connection, 36–37, 39–40, 86–87
Luce, 142–43
Lyon, John, 154, 175
lyre motif, 68–69

M

MacArthur, Elizabeth, 57, 67, 131
marital bliss, 293–94
Mars, 38
Martin, Christophe, 217
Mary Magdalene, 208–9, 212, 214
mask switching, 86, 96
McLaughlin, Mary, 29
medieval love correspondence, 286
medieval misogyny, 38, 43–44, 62, 69, 78, 92–94, 105, 194–95, 262, 286–87
metonymy, 57–58, 63, 67, 110
Meun, Jean de, 19, 99–100, 200
Middle Ages, 12, 23–24, 28, 44, 62, 69, 73, 78–79, 100, 308
military motif, 77, 172, 173
Miller, Nancy, 18, 19, 66, 74, 120, 128, 129, 254, 305, 312
miming narratives, 165
miscarriage, 286
modesty motif, 282–84
monastic garments, 44–45, 73, 75, 79–80, 83–84, 86, 343
Montesquieu, Charles de Secondat, 185
Montifaud, Marc de, 23, 24, 317–31, 351
moral behaviors, 107–8, 114–19, 132, 264–66, 276–95
Muckle, J. T., 42, 53, 54, 92

N

narcissism, 40–41, 67, 96
Newman, Barbara, 23, 54
Nietzsche, Friedrich, 85–86
nocturnal adventures, 143–45, 156
Nouveau recueil de lettres de dames tant anciennes que modernes (Grenaille), 15–16, 19–20, 102

Nouvelles conversations sur divers sujets (Scudéry), 150, 159
Nouvet, C., 43, 54, 65–66, 84–85, 95, 96, 97

O

Oberson, Roland, 207, 208
O'Dea, Michael, 275
Ombilic des Limbes (Artaud), 335
On the Unity and Trinity of God (Abelard), 46
operati castrati, 185–86
oppressive space, 33
Orelli, J. G., 53
Origen, 45–46, 49, 94
Ottoman Empire, 185
Ouvrard-Leibacher, Lise, 187
Ovid, 11, 15, 58, 76, 101, 146, 224
Ovidian plainte: abandoned woman motif, 76, 121; Bussy-Rabutin's translations and revisions, 146, 152, 155, 163–64, 166, 168–69, 173, 179; Colardeau's portrayal, 257, 259; Keralio's portrayal, 311; Laberge's portrayal, 343; Pope's translation and revisions, 224, 232, 243, 252; Rousseau's portrayal, 273, 301–2, 306

P

Pacteau, Francette, 40, 41
Paraclete, 47–48, 56, 229, 231, 239–40, 258, 262–63, 321
paratexts, 103, 109, 257, 308–9, 317–19
Pasquier, Etienne, 12
Paula, 49
Pelous, Jean-Michel, 157, 159
penitential rituals, 208–10, 214
Père-Lachaise cemetery, 326, 333
Perrin, Jules, 335
Peter Abelard (Waddell), 335
Peter the Venerable, 99, 220, 341–42, 343, 347–48
phallocentric symbols, 39–40, 49–50, 66, 86–87, 189
Pharsalia (Lucan), 76
pictorial images, 154–55
plainte amoureuse, 68–69, 145; . *See also* Ovidian plainte
Plaisant, Michèle, 245
plantation/seed/germination motif, 62–63, 110–11
Plato, 36, 39, 96
Plus jamais Héloïse (Bernard), 345–46
poetic revisions, 224–56
Poetics of Sexual Myth, The (Pollak), 230
Pollak, Ellen, 230
polyphonic epistolary form, 272, 310, 312
Poole, Fitz John Porter, 292
Pope, Alexander, 22, 203, 223–56, 322–23, 350
portraiture, 154–55, 175, 257–58, 280–84, 328
portugaise genre, 16–17, 146–47, 154, 202
posthumous letters, 302–3
precious rhetoric, 104–7, 139, 156–61, 169, 315–16
pre-Romantic themes, 262–63, 282, 291
private correspondence, 14–15
Problems of Dostoevsky's Poetics (Bakhtin), 59
Prudhomme, Louis-Marie, 308
pseudo-androcentrism, 317
pseudo-consummation, 238, 252
pseudo-feminocentrism, 19, 54, 66, 74, 97–98, 128–29, 254–55
purity motif, 277–78

R

Rambouillet, Madame de, 101
Rand, Erica, 263
reciprocal love, 157–58
Rémusat, Charles de, 183
Renaissance, 12–13, 44, 100, 126, 320–21
Richardson, Samuel, 271
Robertson, D. W., 147, 152, 335–36
Roger, Alain, 164
Roman Empire, 185
Romanet, A., 221
Roman writers, 11
Rossard, Janine, 282, 283
Rosso, Jeannette, 291
Rouben, C., 146–47, 179
Rousseau, Jean-Jacques, 23, 30, 199, 221, 271–306, 318, 350
Rubin, Gayle, 126, 127
Rudolphe, 46

S

sacred love, 123–24, 131
Sade, Marquis de, 266
salons, 13–15, 105–6
salutation modifications, 75–76, 88
Sappho, 18, 327–28
Schaberg, Janet, 212
Schmeidler, Bernhard, 53
Scholz, Piotr O., 184, 188
Schwartz, Joel, 303
Scudéry, Madeleine de, 14, 101, 106, 119, 127, 150, 155–56, 159
Le Secrétaire de la cour, ou la manière d'écrire selon le temps (de la Serre), 13–14
Sedgwick, Eve, 84, 128
self-consolation, 28–30
self-flagellation, 208–10
self-representation, 13
Semiramis, 184
Seneca, 28
separation–distance discourse, 55, 72, 76–77, 277
Sévigné, Madame de, 14–15, 17, 146
sexual difference, 36–37, 39–40, 86–87
sexual oppression, 125–28, 130, 139–40, 202, 228–30, 275–76, 284–87, 310–12
Shepard, Mary, 333, 334
signatures, 132–33, 160, 164, 316–17
sign system, 110
Simonet, J. B., 220
socialization, 13–15
Soissons, 46
Soleil Noir: Dépression et mélancolie (Kristeva), 242
Solé, Jacques, 123
Song of Songs, 88, 213
sonnets, 12
Sordid Images: The Poetry of Masculine Desire (Clark), 230
souillure, 92
spiritual castration, 46
Spurs (Derrida), 86
Stamelman, Richard, 233
Stanton, Domna, 150, 166, 172
Starobinski, Jean, 150
St. Denis abbey, 36, 45
Stealing Heaven (film), 338–41
Stewart, Phillip, 215–16, 217, 218, 219
Stewart, Susan, 154–55, 231–32
St. Gildas de Rhuys monastery, 28, 47, 50, 326
St. Jerome, 45, 48–49, 347
Stoller, Robert, 164
St. Preux, 272, 273–84, 286, 293–303
Swedenborg, Emanuel, 289, 290
Symbolic Order, 39, 40

T

Tambling, Jeremy, 114–15
Taylor, Gary, 191

tears, use of, 152–53, 197, 213, 234–35, 259, 312–13
Tender Geographies (DeJean), 24–25, 116
theory of desire, 39–40, 42–43, 57–64, 67, 71, 76–83
Traité des eunuques (Ancillon), 186
transvestism theory, 96
Treize lettres amoureuses d'une dame à un chevalier (Boursault), 17
triangular desire, 139–40
troubadours, 69–70
Trouille, Mary, 285, 286–87, 294, 303
Troyes, 46
Turner, Bryan, 116, 119
twentieth-century versions, 334–45
twenty first-century versions, 345–48

U

Unattainable Other, 40, 42, 64, 77, 85
Urfé, Honoré de, 14
use of tears, 152–53, 197, 213, 234–35, 259, 312–13

V

veil motif: Alluis's translations and revisions, 143; Bussy-Rabutin's translations and revisions, 171; Colardeau's portrayal, 261; erotic implications, 83–89, 112, 171; female voice, 70; Grenaille's revisions, 120; inner secrets, 60, 71, 117; Laberge's portrayal, 343; monastic garments, 45; Montifaud's portrayal, 24, 319, 321, 325, 328, 329; Pope's translation and revisions, 237, 240; pseudo-feminocentrism, 54; Rousseau's portrayal, 23, 273, 278–84, 288, 295, 297–301; sexual loss, 42–43
Versini, Laurent, 11
vestimentary transvestism, 193
Vie d'Abailard (Gervaise), 206
Villedieu, Madame de, 127
Villon, François, 100
Vioux, Marcelle, 335
Virgin Mary, 212
Vision and Re-Vision of Alexander Pope (Jackson), 233
Vitz, Evelyn, 30, 54

W

Waddell, Helen, 335
Waleffe, Maurice de, 335
Walter, Eric, 189, 200
Watteau, Antoine, 262–63
Weil, Kari, 36–37
whore versus mistress, 64–66
William of Champeaux, 31
Wolmar, Baron de, 272, 284, 286–89, 292, 293–95, 298
women: Bayle's portrayal, 199–203; as chattel, 339; epistolary manuals, 12–15, 101–2, 119, 149–51, 155–56, 159; Gervaise's portrayal, 207–8; sexual oppression, 125–28, 130, 139–40, 202, 228–30, 275–76, 284–87, 310–12

Z

Zumthor, Paul, 68, 78, 109, 120

www.ingramcontent.com/pod-product-compliance
Lightning Source LLC
LaVergne TN
LVHW102226300926
849160LV00005B/33
* 9 7 8 9 0 4 2 0 3 9 0 5 6 *